Boundaries, Territory
and Postmodernity

Books of Related Interest

Land-Locked States of Africa and Asia
Dick Hodder, Sarah J. Lloyd and Keith McLachlan (eds.)

Geoproperty
Foreign Affairs, National Security and Property Rights
Geoff Demarest

The State in Western Europe
Retreat or Redefinition
Wolfgang Müller and Vincent Wright (eds.)

Geopolitics and Strategy
Colin S. Gray and Geoffrey Sloan (eds.)

Boundaries, Territory and Postmodernity

Edited by
DAVID NEWMAN

FRANK CASS
LONDON • PORTLAND, OR

First publised in 1999 in Great Britain by
FRANK CASS PUBLISHERS
Newbury House, 900 Eastern Avenue,
London, IG2 7HH, England

and in the United States of America by
FRANK CASS PUBLISHERS
c/o ISBS
5804 N.E. Hassalo Street
Portland, Oregon 97213-3644

Website: www.frankcass.com

Copyright © 1999 Frank Cass & Co. Ltd.

British Library Cataloguing in Publication Data

Boundaries, territory and postmodernity. – (Cass studies in geopolitics; no.1)
1. Geopolitics 2. Boundaries 3. Territory, National
4. State, The
I. Newman, David
320.1'2

ISBN 0 7146 4973 2 (cloth)
ISBN 0 7146 8033 8 (paper)

Library of Congress Cataloging in Publication Data

Boundaries, territory and postmodernity / edited by David Newman.
   p. cm. – (Cass studies in geopolitics)
Includes bibliographical references and index.
   ISBN 0-7146-4973-2 (hbk. : alk. paper) – ISBN 0-7146-8033-8 (pbk. : alk. paper)
   1. Geopolitics. 2. Postmodernism–Political aspects. I. Newman, David, 1956–   . II. Series.
JC319.B68   1999
320.1'2–dc21   99-22414
                                                                  CIP

This group of studies first appeared in a Special Issue on 'Boundaries, Territory and Postmodernity' of *Geopolitics* 3/1 (Summer 1998) (ISSN 1465-0045) published by Frank Cass.

All rights reserved. No part of this publication may be reproduced, stored in a retrieval system or transmitted in any form, or by any means, electronic, mechanical, photocopying, recording or otherwise, without the prior permission of Frank Cass and Company Limited.

Printed in Great Britain by Antony Rowe Ltd, Chippenham, Wiltshire

Contents

Geopolitics Renaissant: Territory, Sovereignty and the World Political Map	**David Newman**	1
De-Territorialised Threats and Global Dangers: Geopolitics and Risk Society	**Gearóid Ó Tuathail (Gerard Toal)**	17
International Boundaries, Geopolitics and the (Post)Modern Territorial Discourse: The Functional Fiction	**Fabrizio Eva**	32
On Boundaries, Territory and Postmodernity: An International Relations Perspective	**Mathias Albert**	53
Boundaries as Social Processes: Territoriality in the World of Flows	**Anssi Paasi**	69
Beyond the Borders: Globalisation, Sovereignty and Extra-Territoriality	**Alan Hudson**	89
A Treaty of Silicon for the Treaty of Westphalia? New Territorial Dimensions of Modern Statehood	**Stanley D. Brunn**	106
Globalisation or Global Apartheid? Boundaries and Knowledge in Postmodern Times	**Simon Dalby**	132
Pseudo-States as Harbingers of a New Geopolitics: The Example of the Trans-Dniester Moldovan Republic (TMR)	**Vladimir Kolossov and John O'Loughlin**	151
Regional Identity and the Sovereignty Principle: Explaining Israeli–Palestinian Peacemaking	**Mira Sucharov**	177
Abstracts of Articles		197
Notes on Contributors		202
Index		205

Geopolitics Renaissant: Territory, Sovereignty and the World Political Map

DAVID NEWMAN

This special issue of the renamed journal, *Geopolitics*, attempts to place the renaissant discipline of geopolitics within the context of the post-modern debate concerning territory, boundaries and sovereignty, and the role of the State in a world which has been impacted by globalisation on the one hand, and the resurgence of ethnic and national identities on the other. Geopolitics, as a discipline, has undergone a major renaissance during the past decade, from being blackballed and excluded from much of the academic discourse during the three to four decades following the end of the Second World War, to having, once again, become a legitimate area of study.[1] Its past associations with the German school of geopolitics of the 1930s and 1940s, not to be ignored, is being reassessed and located within a longer tradition of the study of geopolitics, broadly defined as the study of the changing world political map and an understanding of the 'geo' dimension of global, regional and state politics,[2] or simply, the 'political geography of international relations'.[3]

Like its academic sister, political geography, the comeback has been gradual, often disguised in alternative terms, such as 'new geopolitics',[4] 'critical geopolitics'[5] or the 'changing world political map'.[6] The return of political geography was itself a tortuous experience, commencing with quantitative studies of electoral geography in the 1960s, a critical geographical focus on the local state and urban politics in the 1970s, before feeling confident enough to discuss global affairs and, by association, geopolitics in the 1980s. It is interesting 17 years on, to note that in the first editorial of the, then, new journal, *Political Geography Quarterly*, the editors saw the research agenda of the journal as focusing on such issues as the spatial organisation of the State, internal state politics and the study of locational conflict.[7] The nearest they came to raising issues which could be defined as falling within the broader realm of geopolitics, was the revival of geostrategic studies and the concept of the nation state. Since that point in time, the research agenda of political geography has undergone major changes and probably sees geopolitics as being no more than one sub-constituent of the wider study of the relationship between politics and space. More recently, the collapse of the Soviet Union and the territorial reordering of Central and Eastern Europe, together with the impact of globalisation and supra-national processes on what is traditionally seen as the Westphalian territorial compartmentalisation of the world into sovereign states, has raised a host of new questions concerning the nature of the world political map.[8] The study of these topics has assisted in the re-legitimisation of Geopolitics as an academic sub-discipline, and has been illustrated in the reports reflecting the development of Political Geography during the past two decades, with the introduction of such concepts as the new world order in 1991,[9] critical geopolitics in 1992,[10] and theorising the nature of the contemporary world disorder in 1995.[11]

The final nails in the coffin of geopolitical excommunication were to be seen in two recent international conferences, the one focusing on a reassessment of past geopolitical writings, the other highlighting the contemporary geopolitical research agenda. A meeting held around the theme of Europe Between Political Geography and Geopolitics, in Trieste in December 1997,[12] was convened to mark 100 years since the publication of Ratzel's Politische Geografie.[13] This rehabilitation of Ratzel,[14] for so long seen as the theoretical *bete noir* of geopolitics, is leading to a reexamination of many classic geopolitical texts, as well as the formulation of new geopolitical concepts and ideas which are relevant to the contemporary period of global change.

A subsequent meeting in Israel in January 1998 dealt with the theme of Geopolitics and Globalisation in a Postmodern World, with presentations focusing on the changing territorial patterns of world order and raising questions associated with the so-called postmodern discourse of state deterritorialisation, the disappearance of boundaries, and the impact of globalisation and cyberspace in undermining the Westphalian State system.[15] New texts, emphasising both classic and contemporary approaches to the study and definition of geopolitics,[16] and the launching of a journal under the sole name of 'Geopolitics'[17] are clear indications of the geopolitical renaissance.

The changing territorial dimensions of the world order of the past decade have played a major role in this process of relegitimation. The collapse of the bi-polar world which dominated our perceptions of global politics since the end of the Second World War necessitated a rethinking of the dynamics of state formation, the relationship between states at both global and regional levels, as well as the changing nature of war, peace, shatterbelts, rimlands, superpower domination, and a host of other concepts which had been normative for most western thinkers on the topic during this period. Gone are the days when the study of geopolitics could be neatly divided into two neat parallel compartments: the organic state (the Ratzel and Kjellen tradition) and geostrategy (the Mahon, Mackinder and Spykman tradition), respectively.[18] For some, the setting of an agenda for the contemporary study of geopolitics requires the reclamation of the geopolitical tradition from its domination by the strategic community and, altruistically, converting it from a 'discipline for war to a discipline for peace'.[19]

By its very nature Geopolitics is multi disciplinary. Although closely related to political geography, it does not deal solely with the spatial dimensions of the political process at all levels of analysis. Rather, it focuses on the changing role of the State and the dynamic nature of the relationships between States at both global and regional levels. It is, for some, no more than an alternative way of looking at International Relations, with a stronger emphasis on the 'geo' than is apparent in many of the traditional political and IR analyses, from which the territorial and spatial dimensions are frequently lacking.[20] It is also of interest to specialists in international law and must, by its very definition, be of concern to national, regional and global policymakers. The *Geopolitics* journal is designed to reflect this multi-disciplinary interest, drawing on diverse, but complementary, analyses of the changing dynamics of the evolving world political map. This includes both the empirical analyses of case studies on the ground, of redrawn boundaries and changing territorial and national identities, as it does the reconceptualisation of the relationship between territory, sovereignty, identity and global hegemonies.

The identification of key themes in the contemporary study of geopolitics would include the following:

1. Globalisation and the changing function of state sovereignty. The impact of globalisation has raised major questions concerning our state-centered approaches to understanding the world political map.[21] For some, this has developed into the 'end of the nation state' thesis as the world is seen (particularly by economists) as a single corporate conglomerate. This largely ignores the process of territorial reordering which is taking place as groups seek their own alternative identities, at both regional and global levels, the dual dimensions of 'glocalisation'.[22]

2. The deterritorialisation of the state and the associated changing roles and functions of international boundaries. Notions of state deterritorialisation largely follow on the 'end of the nation state' thesis, and assume that the era of 'territorial absolutism' is ended.[23] By association, boundaries, the demarcators of territorial compartmentalisation, have also disappeared. While the functions and roles of boundaries have, indeed, changed as they become more permeable to trans-boundary movements and flows, they continue to display a powerful impact on the world map, with more boundaries of territorial

separation being erected between ethnic and national groups seeking their own respective self-government and independence.[24] These two themes, the impact of globalisation on state sovereignty, and the de-territorialisation of the state thesis,[25] form the core of what has been called the postmodern debate in geopolitics and form the theme around the contents of this volume.

3. The study of geopolitical texts, narratives and traditions.[26] The texts and narratives of geopolitical discourse are varied. They range from the memoirs of policy makers and statesmen, past and present, to the analysis and deconstruction of that most basic of geo-texts, the map. The villains of the geopolitical story, such as Mackinder and Haushoffer, are now legitimate subjects for study, not simply for the ideas they propagated, but also in terms of textual deconstruction concerning their own positioning with respect to the academic and national communities within which they worked; academics in service of their states, feeding on and, in turn, promoting notions of imperialism, geostrategic power, and attempts at global dominance. The politics of map-making is another area that is beginning to attract significant interest, as the power of maps in the formation of foreign policy is reflected in the scale used, the semantics and naming of places and the extent to which they are used as part of a wider process of cartographic propaganda and territorial socialisation.[27] The geopolitical texts and narratives of the non-English speaking world are also of great importance in any attempt at understanding how the complex system of states undergoes constant positioning and re-positioning in the re-ordering of the world political map.[28]

4. The geopolitical imagination. The relative location of a state in the global system is a function of the position accorded it by other states within the system, as well as the imagined preferences of its own citizens. The geopolitical imagination follows on from such notions as 'imagined communities'[29] and 'banal nationalism'[30] which relate to the national imaginations held by citizens of the state, at both the individual and collective level, and which reflect, in turn, the preferred geopolitical location of these groups within the global system. The fact that the position accorded the state does not necessarily coincide with the preferred location of the state, as reflected in its geopolitical imagination(s), may often be the cause for conflict and tensions within the global system. These last two themes are grouped under the term of 'critical geopolitics',[31] a label which is likely to disappear as the singular use of the name 'Geopolitics' reasserts its academic legitimacy.

5. The 're-territorialisation' of the state and the emergence of new ethnic, national and territorial identities. As globalisation and boundary permeability affect the state at one end of the spectrum, so too do the emergence of new states and the associated creation of new boundaries affect the lower end of the system. Globalisation itself is partly responsible for a parallel increase in ethnic identities at local and regional levels, with the demand for autonomy, self-government, secession and independence becoming stronger, rather than weaker. This is as true of such 'stable' political units as Western Europe and the emergence of 'fourth world nations'[32] (Basques, Catalonians, Scots), as it is, albeit at a different intensity, of state-less nations, such as the Kurds, Palestinians and other ethnic minorities. Territorial ideologies remain strong at both the concrete and symbolic levels.[33] Ethnic and national groups are still prepared to fight and die for their territorial homelands, as well as to practice policies of ethno-territorial exclusion, cleansing and purification as they seek to erect new territorial boundaries and fences of separation. Geopolitics should focus on the geographic differentiation of these processes, along a continuum from de-territorialisation to re-territorialisation[34] and the way in which globalisation affects different state activities unevenly,[35] if it seeks to reflect the whole global picture rather than regional and time-specific case studies.

Globalisation, Deterritorialisation and the Postmodern Discourse of Geopolitics

The title of this volume begs the question: is there such a thing as a postmodern geopolitics discourse? To the extent that the 'end of the nation state' thesis[36] is perceived as being part of the postmodern discourse, then the answer is affirmative. To the extent that the same thesis is simply an additional cog in a process of spatial and territorial reconfiguration, a process which has been taking place throughout history – albeit at greater and lesser levels of intensity – then the answer must be more reserved. The principles of this discourse are briefly presented here and in the papers which appear in this volume, with a diversity of response concerning the extent to which this discourse does indeed represent the reality of the changing world political map, and the degree to which contemporary processes of global change are significantly more, or less, structural than past changes which have also signalled the heralding of new world orders by contemporary observers.

A major part of the postmodern geopolitical discourse concerns the changing functions and roles of international boundaries as the lines which demarcate and enclose the territory of the State. Westphalian notions of territorial fixation and demarcated compartmentalisation of State sovereignty is, it is argued, falling apart, while the nation state is supposed to be a politico-territorial feature of the past. The impact of economic globalisation and information cyberspace are seen as being the major factors bringing about the deterritorialisation of the state and the associated removal of boundaries. The State has been experiencing significant spatial reconfiguration as State sovereignty is weakened by both pan-national global, and intra-state regional forms of territorial/spatial organisation. Pan-national activity is reflected in new economic and political associations, most notably the European Community and NAFTA, while intra-state regional activity is, in turn, reflected in the renaissance of dormant ethnic and national identities as part of an increasing demand for self government and territorial autonomy, if not independence and secession from the existing State structure. Intra-state regions often bypass the State as they seek their own external economic and political alliances, leaving the State policy makers to bemoan their loss of sovereignty and independent decision-making power.

The changing function of boundaries does not, by definition, mean a 'borderless' world. It is questionable as to whether the notion of a 'borderless' world is even applicable with respect to economic flows and transactions, [37] while the transfer of certain elements of state sovereignty to supra-national organisations by no means signals the end of territorial sovereignty in the traditional Westphalian sense.[38] But changes are taking place in the world political map which affect the relationships between territory, sovereignty and boundary demarcation. From a legal perspective, state sovereignty continues to apply within the demarcated, and recognised, boundaries of the State while, at the same time, sovereignty may also be expressed through some form of *de facto* control – which may be either territorial or expressed through virtual communities – as contrasted with *de jure* international recognition. This has been described as constituting 'nominal' sovereignty,[39] dealing directly with the exercise of power, deriving from the German doctrine of *Gebietshoheit*. For geographers, the idea of nominal sovereignty may be seen as a modern version of the notions expressed some sixty years ago by Derwent Whittlesey in his study of the impress of effective authority upon the landscape,[40] or 25 years ago in David Knight's study of the impress of authority and ideology upon human territories.[41]

At the same time as boundaries are becoming more permeable to the movement of goods and people, and diffusion of ideas and transactions, the fences of national and ethnic separation continue to be erected in other parts of the world. The re-emergence of nation states in the wake of the collapse of the Soviet Union, the redrawing of the lines of separation between the Czech republic and Slovakia, and the desire for clearly defined separate national territories on the part of Bosnians and Croats, Israelis and Palestinians, Turkish and Greek Cypriots, to name but a few, are indicators of the continued power and importance of territorial lines. The desire for self-government and independence are tied up with the concrete formation of national identities and the way in which these are linked to the territorial demarcation of national homelands, as reified in the socialisation processes of these same groups. It may not be the classic Westphalian state model, but territorial dominance and, in some cases extreme exclusivity resulting in ethno-territorial cleansing, remain the order of the day in many parts of the non-Western European, non-North American world. In this sense, the nature of territories and boundaries, their respective roles and functions, may be changing as they are impacted by gobalisation and cyberspace, but they are certainly not at 'their end', nor are they disappearing from the changing world map. Territorial change is geographically differentiated as processes of globalisation and deterritorialisation impact different places unevenly, determined by a multitude of social, economic, political and demographic processes at the local level.

Will globalisation end up having a truly global impact? The answer to this will only be determined over a relatively long time span, during which time these processes will become diffused to other places and cultures, particularly in post-conflict societies, where the inherent desire for ethno-territorial separation is not felt as strongly and where the economic processes of shared spaces are allowed to flourish as they have done in western Europe and North America. At the same time, it would be erroneous to assume that a single model of political organisation will affect the entire globe at one and the same time. Geographic differentiation will continue to take place. The notion of fixed territories and the Westphalian model of territorial sovereignty only reached much of the non-European world when it was superimposed through the colonialism of the last century, two to three hundred years after it was adopted in Europe itself. It is somewhat ironic to see how Europe and North America are now exporting new narratives of globalisation and deterritorialisation to areas which have not yet fully adapted to notions of territorial fixation which, as we continue to see in contemporary Africa and Asia, still clash with the territorial behaviour of many indigenous and nomadic or tribal societies. While globalisation may be a relatively new phenomenon, concepts of deterritorialisation and shared spaces are, in some ways, similar to those which were common to the pre-Westphalian era in Europe and to much of Asia and Africa as recently as fifty years ago. A cynic would argue that the territorial changes brought about by the impact of globalisation and boundary penetration is simply the re-introduction of a pre-modern (pre-Westphalian) system of spatial organisation in a post-modern (post-Westphalian) era.[42]

An alternative way of understanding contemporary territorial change is through the glocalisation model. This describes the parallel impact of the global (macro) and local (micro) at the expense of the meso (state) level of political and territorial ordering. It is reflected in the global impact of economic and information spaces on the one hand, and the emergence of local and regional ethnic identities, on the other. No better example of glocalisation would serve than the impact of the 1998 Mondial, a truly global expression (with the single notable exception of the United States of America) of world interest while, at the same time, the local/national identities of the participants and their supporters became strongly focused as they became engaged in their tribal battles for dominance on the soccer field.[43] Rather than understanding territorial change as part of a 'zero sum' game in which global spaces expand, at the expense of the relative power of State spaces, the notion of 'glocal' spaces is seen as part of a process through which territorial reconfiguration takes place at a number of scales.[44]

The Papers in This Volume

The papers in this volume both present and, to a certain extent, deconstruct much of the contemporary discourse of a postmodern geopolitics, inasmuch as this discourse relates to a deterritorialised world in which the nation state is no longer, boundaries have disappeared or, at the very least, are in the process of disappearing, and the world is searching for a new form of post-Westphalian system of territorial ordering which reflects new patterns of sovereignty, control and power hegemonies.[45] The papers focus around two interrelated themes: the deterritorialisation of the state as characterised by the increased permeability of boundaries in the face of economic and information globalisation, and the impact of these changes, to the extent that they really occur, on the role and functions of the post-Westphalian state, particularly as it relates to the changing nature of State sovereignty.

With the exception of the first and last paper, the contributions are written by political geographers. The papers are largely conceptual, while drawing on a diversity of empirical case studies, ranging from Israel-Palestine to the Moldovan republic, and from the Finnish border to the Caribbean as a means of highlighting some of the more abstract themes that are developed in the volume. For both geographers and IR scholars, it is an attempt to achieve a synthesis between the realist and critical schools of thought, with an attempt to place a focus on the latter, which has been severely neglected in both traditional disciplines of Geopolitics and International Relations.

In the opening chapter, Mathias Albert discusses the role of 'postmodernist' analyses in the discipline of international relations. He also elaborates some central tenets of poststructuralist philosophy. Taking these perspectives together, he shows how 'postmodern' ways of thought can be utilised for the study of borders and boundaries. In particular he argues that seemingly small changes in bordering processes can serve as indicators for far-reaching structural change. Albert concludes by identifying the merits of 'postmodernism' not in providing a coherent approach, but opening the inquiry into borders and boundaries to theoretical pluralism, much in the same way that has been posited by David Newman and Anssi Paasi in their proposed agenda for the study of boundaries.[46] Albert's thesis is part of a broader International Relations approach to the study of identity and territory, known as 'Identity, Borders, Orders' which seeks to integrate the various disciplinary perspectives on area studies in general, and the territorial reordering of the world in particular.[47] It is, he argues, through a post-modern analysis that International relations scholars and Political Geographers can find common ground and semantics in the study of territory, sovereignty and boundaries.

The next three papers discuss diverse aspects of the impact of globalisation on state organisation. In asserting that the Westphalian state system was itself no more than a fiction which perpetuated the conditions needed for the continued inequalities in power between states, Fabrizio Eva takes the argument one stage further. Rather than seeing notions of state sovereignty simply as social construct,[48] Eva builds on the notion of the Westphalian system as being 'ordered anarchy'. With the world no longer 'balanced' between the superpowers, and with the (apparent) instability this caused now behind us, Eva discusses the notions of supranational bodies and the setting up of world government. He focuses on four principles of state transition, namely: stability, the territorial containment of conflict, economic and financial globalisation, and the maintenance of Western democratic values. Eva posits that, in effect, an informal system of world government is already in place founded on the principle of hegemony. He further argues that current geopolitical dynamics foretell a move away from the concept of organised anarchy towards one which is characterised by democratic (hierarchical) order. But within this system, the establishment of supranational governmental bodies is hampered by contradictions between principles (democracy, the common good, human rights and so on) and the need – created by the state of hegemony – to act hierarchically and 'from above'.

Gerard Toal questions what he sees as the binary distinction between modern and postmodern (Westphalian and post-Westphalian) classifications of the world political map, past and present. He argues that the processes of globalisation, informationalisation and the end of the Cold War have wrought many changes in the conceptualisation and practice of geopolitics. During the Cold War, the discourse of threats and risks was predominantly a territorial one and, while this practice persists in 'rogue state' rhetoric, a discourse of 'deterritorial threats' and 'global dangers' has become much more salient in US foreign policy conceptualisations and strategy. This paper interprets this discourse within the terms of Ulrich Beck's theorisation of 'risk society,' particularly his notion of reflexive modernisation as an alternative to the modern/postmodern distinction. It concludes by highlighting some general contradictions in the reflexive modernisation of geopolitical threats and risks by Cold War-era bureaucracies.

Simon Dalby contrasts the models of globalisation and global apartheid as explanations of the global political situation in the postmodern world. He suggests that boundaries are best understood in relation to the larger geopolitical frameworks within which they function. The global apartheid literature condemns the inequities in the current global economy and analogises the homelands in South Africa with the poorer states in the underdeveloped world that are both a source of labour, and simultaneously viewed by the beneficiaries of their labour as a problem and source of politically threatening and destabilising population mobility. The importance of flows across boundaries and the impossibilities of spatially constraining cultures and economies suggests that both globalisation and the model of global apartheid have some explanatory usefulness as heuristic devices to challenge the persistence of unreflective spatial thinking in trying to understand contemporary social processes

This globalisation theme is continued in the next three papers, albeit with a more specific focus on issues of territorial compartmentalisation and the changing role of boundaries. In particular, they examine the extent to which boundaries have become more permeable as a result of transboundary flows of capital markets (Hudson), information cyberspace (Brunn), and identities (Paasi).

In his study of 'regulatory landscapes' Alan Hudson offers a conceptual framework for thinking about globalisation, sovereignty and boundaries in the contemporary international political economy. Two moments of geo-regulatory change are described before the paper explains how extra-territorial jurisdictional disputes arise. Processes of globalisation lead to geo-political conflicts as regulatory authorities seek to extend their rules beyond their borders. The paper then turns to consider how such jurisdictional disputes are dealt with, and argues that rather than simply celebrating the dismantling of boundaries and the sharing of spaces in a supposedly postmodern world we ought to pay more attention to the institutional mechanisms through which border disputes and competing jurisdictional claims are managed. It is through the development of such mechanisms that spaces and rule-making authority can be shared.

Building on his previous work dealing with the impact of cyberspace on territorial organisation,[49] Stan Brunn discusses the ways in which information and communication technologies are shaping and reshaping the internal policies and external relations of states. The rapid dissemination of faxes, email, listserves, and the World Wide Web call into question the definitions and significance of boundaries, sovereignty, power, representation, and interdependence. There is a need to consider how space-adjusting technologies affect the world's political regions and how the Internet is ushering in a world characterised by rapid speed, the demise of distance, new and powerful state and nonstate actors, and increased flows of transborder information. Brunn argues that features of these evolving contemporary worlds, where nodes become more important than territory, suggest the need for a Treaty of Silicon to replace the Treaty of Westphalia.

Finnish geographer Anssi Paasi builds on his previous work concerning the relationship between territory, boundaries and the social construction of national identities.[50] Paasi discusses the changing meanings of territoriality and state boundaries where nationalism and ethno-regionalism seem concomitantly to be establishing new boundaries and giving rise to conflicts between social groups (re-territorialisation) at the same time as the processes of economic globalisation are reducing their effect (deterritorialisation). Instead of perceiving boundaries merely as fixed products of the modernist project, Paasi attempts to conceptualise them as social processes. He argues that instead of analysing how boundaries distinguish social entities, we should concentrate on how social action and discourse produce diverging, continually changing meanings for boundaries and how these are then used as instruments or mediums of social distinction. The changing meanings of the Finnish-Russian border are used as empirical illustrations of this approach. The history of this border suggests that instead of understanding the idea of territoriality as one form of control used in strictly bounded territorial units, several forms of territoriality exist concomitantly in diverging social practices and discourses.

The volume ends with two case studies which focus on the ethno-territorial, rather than economic or information, dimensions of the changing world political map. John O'Loughlin and Vladimir Kolossov examine the formation of what they term 'pseudo states' in the Transdniester Moldovan Republic (TMR), while Mira Sucharov discusses the attempts at peacemaking in Israel/Palestine. While the two papers reflect the different disciplinary tools used by Political Geography and International Relations scholars respectively, they both demonstrate the continued importance of boundaries and territorial demarcation in regions where ethnic conflict results in the strengthening, 'reterritorialisation', rather than weakening, of separate national identities.

O'Loughlin and Kolossov show how, in addition to economic globalisation, continued attempts to form independent states offer another challenge to the stability of the existing state system. A growing number of self-declared states are now becoming semi-permanent features of the world system as a result of incomplete and contested state-making. Minority groups, dissatisfied with perceived limitations on cultural and economic expression, have been able to carve out what they term as pseudo-states, especially in the geopolitical debris of the Soviet Union. As in the previous use of such terms as 'quasi states',[51] 'insurgent states',[52] or 'ghetto states',[53] this concept relates to the *de facto* exercise of control, as contrasted with the full *de jure* international attainment of sovereignty. A comparison of the causes and courses of conflicts in four pseudo-states (Transniestria, Abkhazia, Chechnya and Nagorno-Karabahk) is presented, followed by a detailed account of the Transdniester Moldovan Republic (TMR). The authors argue that evolving geopolitical relations between the TMR, Moldova, Ukraine and Russia will determine the course of the conflict and set the terms of the pseudo-statehood of the TMR.

Political scientists and International Relations scholars are showing a renewed interest in territorial and spatial issues.[54] Sucharov's study of the Israel-Palestinian peace process suggests that the pursuit of territorial conflict resolution is largely propelled by ideational and discursive factors. The author seeks to explain and predict the prospects for territorial conflict resolution. Through an examination of the decision by Israel and the PLO to enter into negotiations surrounding the 1993 Oslo accords, Sucharov argues that 'national role conception', stemming from a state's conception of its own sovereignty, helps to predict relative levels of hawkishness or dovishness regarding territorial disputes. In an examination of three 'sovereignty indicators' – pan-national versus state sovereignty, symbolic attachment to land, and degree of exclusionary discourse used to consolidate political community – Sucharov concludes that the latter indicator is the more important determinant of territorial conflict resolution. This draws attention to the relative importance of elites in bringing about initial foreign policy change and contrasts with the argument that the slow down in the progress of the Israel-Palestine peace process following the election of the right wing administration in 1996, was not just because of a change in policy as practiced by the political elite, but more significantly because these same political elites had failed to inculcate a solid following for the peace process amongst the grass roots population, preferring to emphasise the concrete steps to be negotiated, while ignoring many of the deeply rooted symbolic dimensions of the conflict.[55] Sucharov concurs in her conclusion that for comprehensive peace to be reached, the entire polity must be mobilised towards such an end.

Concluding Comments

Many changes have taken place in the world political map during the past decade, not only in pattern (the collapse of the Soviet Union, the formation of new states), but also in process (the impact of globalisation on information and economic flows, the emergence of non-territorial communities). But the impact of these changes does not back up the 'end of the nation state thesis', or the associated notions of deterritorialisation and a borderless world. The papers in this volume demonstrate that the impact of globalisation and the extent to which territorial boundaries have become more permeable is geographically differentiated throughout global space, and that what is relevant in Western Europe and North America (if indeed it is relevant even there) does not necessarily apply to other regions. In particular, the relative impact of increased economic and information flows over and beyond boundaries, by no means applies to ethnic and national boundaries. The social construction of national identities is still inherently tied up with the notions of territory, space and place. For geopolitics, it is important to understand the spatial reconfiguration of the world political map and the extent to which the previous dominance of the state as the supreme player in this map is now being shared with the supra-state and intra-state levels of territorial ordering. It is a more complex world, with power being diffused both upwards and downwards from the State, and with boundaries taking on multi-dimensions of bordering, excluding and including, not only territories but also social groups and virtual communities. This is the 'new world order' which, some would argue, is post-Westphalian. Herein lies the study of geopolitics into the next millennium.

Notes

1. Exceptional in this respect has been the work of Saul Cohen and his discussion of shatterbelts and gateway states. See S. B. Cohen, *Geography and Politics in a World Divided* (New York: Random House, 1963); 'A New Map of Global Geopolitical Equilibrium; Developmental Approach', *Political Geography Quarterly*, 2 (year), pp.223–41.
2. P. O'Sullivan, *Geopolitics* (London: Croom Helm, 1986); G. Parker, *Geopolitics: Past, Present and Future* (London: Pinter Press, 1998).
3. J. O'Loughlin and H. Heske, 'From "Geopolitik" to "Geopolitique": Converting a Discipline for War to a Discipline for Peace', in N. Kliot and S. Waterman (eds) *The Political Geography of Conflict and Peace* (London: Belhaven, 1991) pp.37–59.
4. Ibid. See also: S.B. Cohen, 'Geopolitics in the New World Era: A New Perspective on an Old Discipline', in J. O'Loughlin and H. van der Wusten (eds) *The New Political Geography of*

Eastern Europe (London: Belhaven Press, 1993) pp.15–48.
5. Tuathail's definition of critical geopolitics draws on various authors in the field of International Relations and Political Geography to include diverse notions, such as the spatialisation of global politics, and geopolitics as spatial exclusion. See: G. O'Tuathail, *Critical Geopolitics: The Politics of Writing Global Space* (Minnesota , Univ of Minnesota Press, 1997), Chapter 5, pp.141–86.
6. World Political Map (WPM) is the name given to the political geography speciality group of the International Geographic Union (IGU).
7. Editorial essay, 'Political Geography: Research Agendas for the Nineteen Eighties', *Political Geography Quarterly*, 1/1 (1982), pp.1–17.
8. See, for instance: O'Loughlin and van der Wusten (eds) *The New Political Geography of Eastern Europe* (note 4); G.J. Demko and W.B. Woods, (eds), *Reordering the World: Geopolitical Perspectives on the Twenty First Century* (Boulder, CO: Westview Press, 1994):
9. J. O'Loughlin, 'Political Geography: Returning to Basic Conceptions', *Progress in Human Geography*, 15/3 (1991), pp.322–39.
10. D.R. Reynolds, 'Political Geography: Thinking Globally and Locally', *Progress in Human Geography*, 16/3, (1992), pp.393–405.
11. G. O'Tuathail, 'Political Geography I: Theorizing History, Gender and World Order Amidst Crises of Global Governance', *Progress in Human Geography*, 19/2 (1995), pp.260–72.
12. Held in Trieste, 10–13 December 1997.
13. F. Ratzel, *Politische Geographie* (Munich, Oldenbourg, 1897).
14. M. Bassin, 'Friedrich Ratzel', in T.W. Freeman (ed.) *Geographers: Bibliographical Studies*, Vol.11. (London: Mansell, 1987).
15. Held in Israel, 25–31 January 1998.
16. See: O'Tuathail, *Critical Geopolitics* (note 5); G. O'Tuathail, S. Dalby and P. Routledge (eds) *The Geopolitics Reader* (New York: Routledge, 1998); J. Agnew, *Geopolitics: Revisioning World Politics* (New York: Routledge, 1998); S. Dalby and G. O'Tuathail, *Rethinking Geopolitics* (London: Routledge, 1998).
17. This journal, formerly known as Geopolitics and International Boundaries, was launched as recently as 1996. The inclusion of the term 'International Boundaries' was a form of softening the impact of a journal which included the name 'Geopolitics'. Not only is this no longer deemed as necessary, but it is also appreciated that the topic of international boundaries is but one of a multitude of topics subsumed under the more general term.
18. The study of geopolitics is presented in this way by Glassner in his undergraduate text on Political Geography, probably the most widely used text of this sort in the English speaking world. See: M. Glassner, Political Geography (New York: John Wiley, Fourth Edition, 1996).
19. O'Loughlin and Hesse (note 3).
20. For recent IR approaches to geopolitics, see: J. George, *Discourses of Global Politics: A Critical (Re)Introduction to International Relations* (Boulder CO, Lynne Reiner, 1994).
21. See: J. Agnew and S. Corbridge, *Mastering Space: Hegemony, Territory and International Political Economy* (New York: Routledge, 1995).
22. For the use of the term 'glocalisation' see: B. Axford, *The Global System: Economics, Politics and Culture* (Cambridge: Polity Press, 1995) p.156: U. Ram, 'Post-Nationalist Pasts: The Case of Israel', *Social Science History*, 22/4 (1998); N. Brenner, 'Global cities, Glocal States: Global City Formation and State Territorial Restructuring in Contemporary Europe', *Journal of International Political Economy*, 5/1 (1998), pp.1–37.
23. P. Taylor, 'Territorial Absolutism and its Evasions', *Geography Research Forum*, 16, (1996), pp.1–12.
24. The study of international boundaries has continued to occupy an important place in political geography. See, for instance: D. Rumley and J.V. Minghi (eds) *The Geography of Border Landscapes* (London: Routledge, 1991); C.H. Schofield (ed.) *Global Boundaries: World Boundaries Vol.1* (London: Routledge, 1994); D. Newman and A. Paasi, 'Fences and Neighbours in the Postmodern World: Boundary Narratives in Political Geography', in *Progress in Human Geography*, 22/2 (1998) pp.186–207; M. Pratt and J. Brown (eds) *Borderlands Under Stress* (Kluwer Law International, London, forthcoming).
25. For a discussion of the deterritorialisation thesis, see: G. O'Tuathail, 'Political Geography

III: Dealing with Deterritorialisation', *Progress in Human Geography*, 22/1 (1998), pp.81–93; R. Mansbach, 'Deterritorializing Global Politics', in C. Kegley and D. Puchala (eds), *Visions of International Relations* (Colombia, SC: University of South Carolina Press, forthcoming); D. Newman, 'Territory, Boundaries and Postmodernity: Towards Shared or Separate Spaces?', in M. Pratt and J. Brown (eds), *Borderlands Under Stress* (note 24).
26. See, for instance, the collection of papers in K. Dodds and D. Atkinson (eds), *Geopolitical Traditions? Critical Histories of a Century of Geopolitical Thought* (London: Routledge, 1999): G. Dijink, *National Identity and Geopolitical Visions: Maps of Pride and Pain* (London: Routledge, 1998).
27. The study of maps as political and historical narrative has emerged as an important area of study in the 1990's. Recent books on this topic include: D. Wood, *The Power of Maps* (London: Routledge, 1993); M. Monmonier, *Drawing the Line: Tales of Maps and Cartocontroversy* (New York: Henry Holt, 1995); G.H. Herb, *Under the Map of Germany: Nationalism and Propaganda, 1918-1945* (London: Routledge, 1997); J. Black, *Maps and Politics* (Chicago: University of Chicago Press, 1997); J. Black, *Maps and History: Constructing Images of the Past* (New Havan, Yale University Press, 1997).
28. See, for example, P. Girot and E. Kofman (eds) *International Geopolitical Analysis* (London: Croom Helm, 1987), which consists of a selection of papers which appeared in the French journal, Herodote, or a forthcoming theme issue of this journal which will focus on French geopolitical writings of the past decade.
29. B.Anderson, *Imagined Communities: Reflections on the Origin and Spread of Nationalism* (London,Verso Books, 1983).
30. M. Billig, *Banal Nationalism* (London: Sage Publications, 1995).
31. G. O'Tuathail (note 5).
32. The notion of 'fourth world' nations in Western Europe is discussed by: B. Nietschmann, 'The "Fourth World': Nations Versus States', in G.J. Demko and W.B. Woods, (eds), *Reordering the World: Geopolitical Perspectives on the Twenty First Century* (Boulder CO: Westview Press, 1994); R. Griggs and P. Hocknell, 'The Geography and Geopolitics of Europeans Fourth World', *Boundary and Security Bulletin*, 3/4, (1995), pp.59-67.
33. A.B. Murphy, 'Territorial Ideology and International Conflict: the Legacy of Prior Political Formations', in N. Kliot and S. Waterman (eds) *The Political Geography of Conflict and Peace* (London: Belhaven, year), pp. 126-41; D. Newman, 'Real Spaces - Symbolic Spaces: Interrelated Notions of Territory in the Arab-Israel Conflict', in P. Diehl (ed.), *A Road Map to War: Territorial Dimensions of International Conflict* (Nashville, TN: Vanderbilt University Press, 1999).
34. G. O'Tuathail and T. Luke (1994) 'Present at the (Dis)integration: Deterritorialisation and Reterritorialisation in the New World (Dis)order', *Annals of the Association of American Geographers*, 84 (year), pp.381–98.
35. J. Anderson, 'The Shifting Stage of Politics: New Medieval and Postmodern Territorialities?', *Society and Space*, 14, (1996), pp.133–53.
36. K. Ohmae, *The End of the Nation State. The Rise of Regional Economies* (London: Free Press, 1995).
37. Henry Wai-Chung Yeung argues that the notion of a borderless world does not even apply to the flow of capital. See: H. Wai-chung Yeung, 'Capital, State and Space: Contesting the Borderless World', *Transactions of the Institute of British Geographers*, 23/3, (1998), pp.291–309.
38. M.G. Kohen, 'Is the Notion of Territorial Sovereignty Obsolete?', in M. Pratt and J. Brown (eds) *Borderlands Under Stress* (note 24); See also, C. Murray Austin and M. Kumar, 'Sovereignty in the Global Economy: An Evolving Geopolitical Concept', *Geography Research Forum*, 19 (1998).
39. Ibid. M. Kohen.
40. D. Whittlesey, 'The Impress of Effective Central Authority Upon the Landscape', *Annals of the Association of American Geographers*, 25/2 (1935), pp.85–97.
41. D. Knight, 'Impress of Authority and Ideology on Landscape', *Tijdschrift voor Ecnmische en Sociale Geografie (TESG)*, 62 (1971), pp.383–7.
42. This is similar to Anderson's combining of 'new medieval' and 'postmodern

conceptualisations of territoriality and sovereignty'. See J. Anderson (note 34).
43. For a study of the relationship between national identity and soccer, see: B. Carrington, '"Football's Coming Home" but Whose Home? And do we Want it? Nation, Football and the Politics of Exclusion', in A. Brown (ed.) *Fanatics: Power, Identity and Fandom in Football* (London: Routledge, 1998) pp.101–23.
44. Brenner (note 22).
45. D. Newman, 'Territory, Boundaries and Postmodernity: Towards Shared or Separate Spaces?', in M. Pratt and J. Brown (eds) *Borderlands Under Stress* (note 24).
46. See: D. Newman and A. Paasi, 'Fences and Neighbours in the Postmodern World ...' (note 23).
47. M. Albert, D. Jacobson and Y. Lapid, Identity, *Borders, Orders: New Directions in International Relations Theory* (London: Macmillan, 1999).
48. See T.J. Biersteker and C. Weber (eds) *State Sovereignty as Social Construct* (Cambridge: Cambridge Studies in International Relations, Cambridge University Press, 1996).
49. S.D. Brunn and J.A. Jones, 'Geopolitical Information and Communication in Shrinking and Expanding Worlds: 1900–2100', in G.J. Demko and W.B. Woods (eds), *Reordering the World: Geopolitical Perspectives on the Twenty First Century* (Boulder CO: Westview Press, 1994). See also: D. Morley and K. Robins, *Spaces of Identity: Global Media, Electronic Landscapes and Cultural Boundaries* (London: Routledge, 1995).
50. A. Paasi, *Territory, Boundaries and Consciousness* (New York: John Wiley, 1996); see also G. Dijink, *National Identity and Geopolitical Visions* (note 25); G. Herb and D. Caplan (eds), *Nested Identities: Nationalism, Territory and Scale* (USA: Rowman & Littlefield, 1999).
51. M.G. Kohen (note 36).
52. R.W. McColl, 'The Insurgent State: Territorial Bases of Revolution', *Annals of the Association of American Geographers*, 59/4, (1969), pp.613–31.
53. R.W. McColl and D. Newman, 'States in Formation: the Ghetto State as Typified in the West Bank and Gaza Strip', *Geojournal*, 28/3 (1992), pp.333–45.
54. See: G. Goertz and P. Diehl (eds), *Territorial Changes and International Conflict* (New York: Routledge, 1992); J. Coakley (ed.) *The Territorial Management of Ethnic Conflict* (London: Frank Cass, 1993); I.S. Lustick, *Unsettled States – Disputed Lands: Britain and Ireland, France and Algeria, Israel and the West Bank-Gaza* (Ithaca, NY: Cornell University Press, 1993); P. Huth, *Standing Your Ground: Territorial Disputes and International Conflict* (Ann Arbor: University of Michigan Press, 1996); P. Diehl (ed.), *A Road Map to War* (note 33).
55. T. Herman and D. Newman. 'A Path Strewn with Thorns: Along the Difficult Road of Israeli-Palestinian Peacemaking', in J. Darby and R. McGinty (eds) *Coming Out of Violence: A Comparative Study of Northern Ireland, South Africa, Israel-Palestine, Sri Lanka and the Basques* (London: Macmillan Press, 1999).

De-Territorialised Threats and Global Dangers: Geopolitics and Risk Society

GEARÓID Ó TUATHAIL (GERARD TOAL)

As we approach the twenty-first century, the quidity of boundaries, borders and territory, and the geopolitical practices organised around them, in a world of turbulent financial flows, instantaneous telecommunications, and transnational dangers, is very much in question. What is the status of the state border in a world where states appear to be overwhelmed by transnational flows of capital, information, and commodities?[1] What does geopolitics mean in a world where there is no dominant territorial antagonism, where many states are failing as a consequence of ethnic wars and institutional collapse, and where those states that have not failed are increasingly preoccupied by the transnational threats posed by environmental degradation, global webs of crime, and the proliferation of weapons of mass destruction?[2] What is the significance of territory in a world where power appears to reside in technological capability not territorial mass, and where military war machines strive to dominate speed not space?[3]

One approach to these questions, an approach appealed to in this volume, is to operationalise a distinction between the modern and the postmodern in order to make sense of the present. This narrative has a certain heuristic value. In a prevalent geopolitical version of this narrative, the modern is associated with the establishment of the Westphalian state system in sixteenth and seventeenth Europe. It gave rise to what Agnew terms the 'modern geopolitical imagination'.[4] One of its most distinguishing features is 'a state-centric account of spatiality' characterised by three geographical assumptions: first, that states have exclusive sovereign power over their territories; second, that 'domestic' and 'foreign' are separate and distinct realms; and third, that the boundaries of a state define the boundaries of 'society'.[5] Modern geopolitics, according to this logic, is a discursive formation, which privileges sovereign states, bordered realms and distinct territorially delimited societies. The postmodern in this narrative is a post-Westphalian world where states are no longer as sovereign as they once were, where transnational actors and forces are problematising domestic/foreign borders, and where transnational media and networks are creating a 'global society'.[6] Postmodern geopolitics is a new moment in the relationship of geography to power, a new discursive formation concerned with the problems generated by the breakdown of the Westphalian model (state implosion and failure), the globalisation of economies and the advent of a 'borderless world' in many domains and, finally, the emergence of a new 'global' category of threats, dangers and risks associated with globalisation, informationalisation, the end of the Cold War, and the contradictions, broadly described as 'environmental', generated by the triumphs of modernity. In contrast to a modern geopolitical imagination dominated by state-centric spatiality (bordered, sovereign, territorially delimited states) the postmodern geopolitical imagination grapples with borderlessness, state failure, and deterritorialisation.

Operationalised as a binary narrative this modern/postmodern distinction invites sweeping generalisations, simplistic contrasts, and forced totalisations about the present. The messiness of the contemporary geopolitical conjuncture can not be reduced to a conceptually clean story of modern past and a postmodern now; rather the present is much more complex and confused. Even in the past, the Westphalian model of the interstate system, and the subsequent hegemony of the normative ideal of a 'nation-state' (a state characterised by a homology between cultural identity and political institutions) was never an adequate representation of the complexity of political organisations across the planet.[7] The modern geopolitical imagination is not a correspondence conceptualisation of world politics but a powerful eurocentric discourse of power that seeks to interpret world politics within territorial, nation-state and strategic categories. Confidently asserted and imposed upon world space in the past, the modern geopolitical imagination has recently lost some of its power and legitimacy as geopolitical practitioners and commentators have become more willing to acknowledge the limitations of state-centric conceptualisations of world space. Today, how practitioners, strategists and defense planners in the developed world think about world politics is changing as they try to make sense of the apparent chaos of international affairs at the end of the twentieth century. In the US, a postmodern geopolitical imagination attuned to a post-Westphalian story of globalisation, informationalisation and scientific-environmental challenges is increasingly evident in the public thinking, strategic conceptualising and security planning of leading decision-makers, alongside its traditional concerns with territorial enemies, security alliances and balance of power politics. While concerned still with territorial threats from so-called 'rogue states', US security discourse during the Clinton administration has expanded to include threats which are not necessarily territorial and dangers which are global and planetary in nature. A plethora of 'de-territorialised threats' and 'global dangers', from transnational terrorism and proliferating weapons of mass destruction to environmental degradation and ethnic nationalism, are now regularly evoked as serious security challenges to the prosperity and well being of the United States of America. Yet, that these 'de-territorialised threats' and 'global dangers' are understood as threats to the United States is indicative of the 'in-betweenness' of the current geopolitical condition. On the one hand, many of the processes and dramas characterising world politics are acknowledged as being global, transnational and post-territorial, yet, on the other hand, these same processes and dramas are rendered meaningful as threats to the 'national security' of the US and its allies. A postmodern geopolitical imagination is evident but it still resides in a world established by the modern geopolitical imagination. Transnational threats are specified, but layered upon a state-centric and territorially delimited 'national security' problematic.

To explore this curious condition further, this article leaves the overdetermined modern/postmodern distinction aside in favour of the interpretative schema offered by the German sociologist and theorist of 'risk society', Ulrich Beck.[8] Beck's work has considerable implications for understanding and interpreting twentieth century geopolitics, particularly the late twentieth century 'post-Westphalian' concerns with 'de-territorialised threats' and 'global dangers'. The paper is organised into three parts. Part one documents and delineates the emergence of the discourses of 'deterritorialised threats' and 'global dangers' in late twentieth century US foreign policy. Part two outlines some of Beck's ideas and links the emergence of these new discourses to Beck's notion of 'reflexive modernisation'. Part three points to contradictions in the reflexive modernisation of geopolitics. In all instances the argument is necessarily brief due to limitations of space.

'De-Territorialised Threats' and 'Global Dangers' Discourse in US Foreign Policy.

Unlike the Bush administration, which tended to adhere to a territorial conceptualisation of geopolitics, the Clinton administration entered office with a distinctive vision of how globalisation and informationalisation were transforming the borders of the world political map. The world, Clinton believed, was in a transition away from Cold War geopolitical concerns to a new era which would be dominated by geo-economic and geo-finance.[9] In his first inaugural address, in 1993, President Clinton signalled a recognition of the changing condition of states, borders and security in the post-Cold War world.

Communications and commerce are global; investment is mobile;

technology is almost magical; and ambition for a better life is now universal... There is no longer division between what is foreign and what is domestic – the world economy, the world environment, the world AIDS crisis, the world arms race – they affect us all.[10]

This late twentieth century condition of economic (particularly financial) globalisation, intense technological change, global environmental transformations and the borderless world of opportunities and dangers produced by it became the meta-narrative of US foreign policy during the Clinton-Gore administrations. Foreign policy bureaucracies – the State Department, the Central Intelligence Agency and the Defense Department – all established new programs and divisions to study the various diplomatic and security dimensions of this metanarrative.[11] The State Department created a new bureaucratic post, Under Secretary of State for Global Affairs, and formally incorporated consideration of globalisation issues and environmental problems into its policy planning operations.[12] The CIA began conducting studies on the environmental origins and causes of civil conflicts across the globe in order to predict where new crises might erupt. Pentagon planners began to conceptualise and operationalise how they should be dealing with informational warfare, failed states, proliferating toxic substances and peacekeeping operations in environmentally-stressed regions. The US foreign policy community in general debated the 'coming anarchy' of global change, 'postmodern terrorism', and 'managing global chaos'.[13] Within these debates and discussions, 'de-territorialised threats' and 'global dangers' emerged as related but occasionally distinct themes. De-territorialised threats were modified traditional national security threats, so-called 'hard' threats involving weapons and violence posed by transnational networks of terrorists and cyber-criminals, or threats posed by proliferating weapons of mass destruction. 'Global dangers' comprised 'softer' less traditional national security threats posed by global environmental problems (access to scarce resources, population pressures and environmental stress), international migration and violent ethnic nationalism.[14] In practice, the term 'global dangers' often functioned as a catch-all term for both types of security threats, the emphasis between them varying depending upon the institutional and policy context.

Discourses on 'deterritorialised threats' and 'global dangers' found frequent expression in the speeches of the vice-president and president. In an address to the United Nations General Assembly in September 1997, for example, President Clinton described both the promises and dangers posed by a world where national borders are falling and fading. 'Bit by bit,' Clinton declared, 'the information age is chipping away at the barriers – economic, political, and social – that once kept people locked in and ideas locked out.'[15] The emergence of a borderless world, while generally positive, also holds many dangers. 'We are all', he noted, 'vulnerable to the reckless acts of rogue states and to an unholy axis of terrorists, drug traffickers, and international criminals. These twenty first century predators feed on the very free flow of information and ideas and people we cherish. They abuse the vast power of technology to build black markets for weapons, to compromise law enforcement with huge bribes of illicit cash, to launder money with the keystroke of a computer. These forces are our enemies.' A few months later, in February 1998, Clinton re-iterated this passage in an address to Pentagon personnel on Iraq, representing that state as just such a 'twenty-first century predator' which must not be allowed to build an arsenal of nuclear, chemical and biological weapons.[16] In a borderless world, the territorial authority and military might of the United States are still needed to keep world order and contain 'rogue states and nuclear outlaws.'[17]

This discourse of 'deterritorialised threats' that are sometimes territorialised in the actions of rogue and outlaw states dominates the 1997 policy document *A National Security Strategy for A New Century*, an inter-agency document that is produced annually under the co-ordinated supervision of the National Security Council.[18] It begins from the premise that acknowledges no border between the domestic and the foreign: 'Our strategy recognises a simple truth: we must lead abroad if we are to be secure at home, but we cannot lead abroad unless we are strong at home.'[19]

The document identifies three intertwined categories of threats to the United States and to the world. The first category is 'regional or state-centered threats', a seemingly traditional territorial conceptualisation of the threat of coercion or cross-border aggression by states. Yet, this category of threats is not as traditional as it seems because no state is specified by name as a threat and the specific threat is the efforts of certain states to obtain offensive technological capabilities, such as their acquiring nuclear, chemical or biological weapons. This first category of threats, consequently, is deeply entwined with the remaining two, both of which are worldwide and trans-territorial.[20]

The second category is what the document terms 'transnational threats' and these include 'terrorism, the illegal drug trade, illicit arms trafficking, international organised crime, uncontrolled refugee migrations, and environmental damage.'[21] These are threats in the form of dangerous flow-mations, semi-permanent yet fluid structures of movement, transit and flow that challenge, erode and undermine the jurisdictional power and authority of states. They are often difficult to combat because they are amorphous and decentralised, mobile and shifting webs that cannot be discretely located on a map. Advances in technologies of transportation, transmission and communication have made these threats more potent.

The third category of threats are weapons of mass destruction.[22] Because of their potentially catastrophic effects on the planet as a unified ecosystem, weapons of mass destruction have globalised the US 'national security' problematic. Security is held to be indivisible and global, hence the construction 'global security' which the document uses. Weapons of mass destruction 'pose the greatest potential threat to global security'. They do not respect international borders and constitute a threat to all. The US 'must continue to reduce the threat posed by existing arsenals of such weaponry as well as work to stop the proliferation of advanced technologies that place these destructive capabilities in the hands of parties hostile to US and global security interests. Danger exists from outlaw states opposed to regional and global security efforts and transnational actors, such as terrorists or international crime organisations, potentially employing nuclear, chemical or biological weapons against unprotected peoples and governments'.[23] In the post-Cold War world US 'national security' requires 'global security.' Weapons of mass destruction are threats to the United States and the globe, so America must act for itself and for humanity as a whole. It must be an engaged global leader promoting arms control and nonproliferation initiatives. It needs to shape, with its allies, the international environment to prevent or deter threats while retaining its own ability to respond to the full spectrum of potential crises and security challenges of the twenty-first century. It, the document implicitly suggests, must retain its own weapons of mass destruction in order to protect the world from weapons of mass destruction.

Finally, the national security document notes so-called 'soft' threats such as 'climate change and ozone depletion' which are given a harder edge in the text by combining them with 'the transnational movement of dangerous chemicals'. All three are held to 'directly threaten the health of U.S. citizens'.[24] New infectious diseases are also mentioned as threats to developing countries. (The Clinton administration has formally designated emerging infectious diseases as a national security issue).[25]

Deterritorialised Threats, Global Dangers and Risk Society

Behind these discourses on 'deterritorialised threats' and 'global dangers' are important shifts in the condition of modernity, transformations suggestively interpreted by Ulrich Beck.[26] Instead of using the dichotomy modern/postmodern, Beck's schema juxtaposes industrial society to risk society to move, he suggests, 'the future which is just beginning to take shape into view against the still predominant past.'[27] Beck's argument is not that modernity is over but that it is currently undergoing a rupture and that a new modernity is emerging which can be distinguished from classic industrial modernity. His argument develops two overriding sets of distinctions.

First, industrial society, he argues, is a society of scarcity dedicated to the production of wealth and primarily organised around the distribution of 'goods' (commodities but also positive goals like capital accumulation, technological progress and income growth). Risk society, by contrast, is an affluent society no longer defined by scarcity but by risks. It is primarily organised around the production, distribution and management of 'bads' (pollutants, toxins, hazardous materials and ecologically destructive practices) (see Figure 1). Wealth and risks are not mutually exclusive but in a historically oscillating relationship. In classical industrial society the logic of wealth production dominates the logic of risk production whereas in risk society the condition is the reverse.[28] As societies become more affluent and the spectre of scarcity begins to fade, previously repressed questions concerning the design, operation and maintenance of advanced techno-industrial production systems are raised. Productive forces lose their innocence as awareness grows that advances in techno-industrial 'know how' also ends up producing 'latent side effects' and inescapable risks which are more daunting and dangerous than any ever previously faced by human societies. Risk society is the 'age of side-effects.'

FIGURE 1
ULRICH BECK'S UNDERSTANDING OF RISK SOCIETY

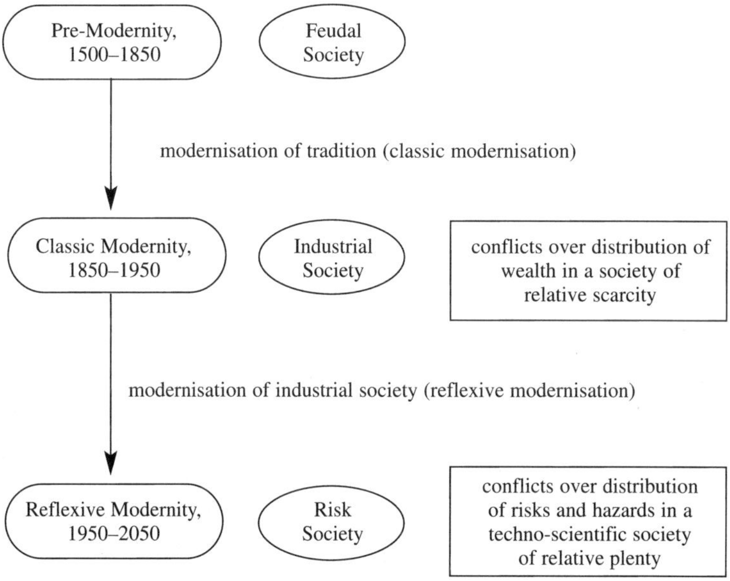

Pre-Modernity, 1500–1850	Feudal Society	
↓ modernisation of tradition (classic modernisation)		
Classic Modernity, 1850–1950	Industrial Society	conflicts over distribution of wealth in a society of relative scarcity
↓ modernisation of industrial society (reflexive modernisation)		
Reflexive Modernity, 1950–2050	Risk Society	conflicts over distribution of risks and hazards in a techno-scientific society of relative plenty

Second, Beck argues that industrial society is a consequence of an initial modernisation of the traditional values of feudal society. It is a society where modern science and reason have displaced religion and rank as the organising principles of society. Bureaucratic and techno-scientific elites begin to occupy positions of expertise and power in the society. Their command decisions and technological innovations have tremendous consequences for the organisation of work and everyday life in industrial society. Risk society, however, is a consequence of a second modernisation: the modernisation of the initial modernisation that brought industrial society into being. A second wave of rationality and science begins to question the previously unchallenged instrumental rationality and elite science of industrial society. The notion of 'what is rational' becomes a matter of debate between competing camps, each laying claim to the Enlightenment ideal of reason. Science starts to question its own methods and procedures, subjecting them to skeptical scientific critique. The notion of the scientific itself, like rationality, begins to fragment. Expertise and authority come into question. The origins of this second wave of modernisation can be traced to the first half of the twentieth century but its full ramifications are still only unfolding. Beck terms it 'reflexive modernisation', namely a modernisation that is about itself and contrasts it to 'classic modernisation', the initial modernisation of traditional values that produced industrial society.

Beck's argument seeks to break the automatic association of modernity with industrial society, arguing that we need to begin conceiving of modernity beyond the categories and experience of industrial society, 'beyond its classical industrial design'.[29] Risk society is so named because it is 'a developmental phase of modern society in which the social, political, economic and individual risks increasingly tend to escape the institutions for monitoring and protection in industrial society.'[30] Beck identifies two phases in its development, a first stage "in which the effects and self-threats are systematically produced but do not become public issues or the center of political conflicts. Here the self-concept of industrial society still predominates, both multiplying and 'legitimating' the threats produced by decision-making as 'residual risks' (the 'residual risk society').[31] The second stage is when the dangers of industrial society begin to dominate public life and policy discourse. 'Here the institutions of industrial society become the producers and legitimators of threats they cannot control. What happens here is that certain features of industrial society become socially and politically problematic. On the one hand, society still makes decisions and takes actions according to the pattern of the old industrial society, but, on the other, the interest organisations, the judicial system and politics are clouded over by debates and conflicts that stem from the dynamism of risk society.'[32]

It is this unfolding of the logic of reflexive modernisation *within a still predominantly industrial society* that is of particular interest in helping explain our contemporary geopolitical condition, one facing global challenges with Cold War institutions. The unforeseen unfolding of the second modernisation transition and the conflicts it provokes with the residual institutions of industrial society are what is crucial. This transition is unforeseen, ironically, because of the tremendous organisation and technological triumphs of industrial society. The institutions of industrial society begin to fail under the strain of their own success. The autonomised dynamism of classic modernisation produces latent side effects which can remain latent and merely side effects no longer. The 'constellations of risk society are produced because the certitudes of industrial society (the consensus for progress or the abstraction of ecological effects and hazards) dominate the thought and action of people and institutions in industrial society. Risk society is not an option than one can choose or reject... . It arises in the continuity of autonomised modernisation processes which are blind and deaf to their own effects and threats.'[33] Risk society's modernisation is reflexive because it is dealing with problems, risks and dangers created by its own modernity. Reflexive modernisation 'means self-confrontation with the effects of risk society that cannot be dealt with and assimilated in the system of industrial society as measured by the latter's institutionalised standards'.[34]

We can understand the emergence of 'deterritorialised threats' and 'global dangers' discourses as a long-delayed unfolding of a logic of reflexive modernisation in geopolitical theory and practice at the end of the century. This logic of reflexive modernisation is not necessarily reflective and it is consequently mired in contradictions and ironies that critical geopoliticans need to expose and deconstruct.[35] Ostensibly and unsurprisingly, contemporary US geopolitical discourse still articulates the mythic system of industrial modernity. In Beck's characterisation of this mythic system it 'asserts that developed industrial society with its pattern of work and life, its production sectors, its thinking in categories of economic growth, its understanding of science and technology and its forms of democracy, is a *thoroughly modern* society, a pinnacle of modernity, which it scarcely makes sense to even consider surpassing.'[36] In its multiple celebrations of American democracy, capitalist enterprise and free markets, US foreign policy discourse continues to trumpet its own hyper-modern society as the pinnacle of modernity, the modernity myth in national exceptionalist wrapping. Globalisation and informationalisation are articulated as the newest fulfillments of an already self-evidently superior way of life. The historical experience of the US is transformed into a story of the inevitability and beneficent progress of modernity.

Yet, the very same US foreign policy is now giving voice to anxieties and concerns about the byproducts of the modern project. Globalisation and informationalisation may be celebrated but US foreign policy-makers now recognise the plethora of risks and dangers which accompany these processes. 'Deterritorialised threats' and 'global dangers' discourse can be interpreted as the reflexive modernisation of geopolitical theory. These discourses have their origins not with the end of the Cold War but much earlier in the century at the end of the First World War, when the destructive consequences of modern industrialised war were first seen on a large scale. The effort, in the 1920s, to ban war did not succeed and the problem of modern techno-industrial war (total war) remained. As a problematic, it became more complex with the Second World War and the development of the atom bomb. One single weapon could wreck indiscriminate havoc on major metropolitan areas. A technological pinnacle to techno-industrial society could destroy the home of techno-industrial society, the modern city. Enough nuclear weapons used in a co-ordinated way could potentially threaten nearly all forms of life on the planet and radically alter the future of the human species. Indeed the consequences soon became incalculable.

The rationality of using nuclear weapons and developing other chemical and biological weapons of mass destruction was widely questioned from the outset.[37] Science began to fragment as some scientists formed groups like the Union of Concerned Scientists to challenge what they saw as the military-industrial distortion of science.[38] The Cold War raised the stakes in the struggle to manage the deadly risks produced by modern industrial civilisation but it also institutionalised a workable albeit highly dangerous regime of control over the distribution and risk of nuclear weapons: deterrence by mutually assured destruction. During the Cold War, the mythic self-concept of 'industrial society' was contested but still prevailed while 'national security' discourses rhetorically contained unprecedented techno-scientific risks within its dominant Cold War narratives.

With the end of the Cold War, this regime of risk containment and management has broken down. Consequently the problem of the control of the most deadly products of techno-industrial civilisation has entered a more fluid and uncertain phase. Scientific and technical knowledge is globalising, and so too are the components needed to construct weapons of mass destruction. Cold War technologies like nuclear, chemical and biological weapons of mass destruction have become global hazards. Blindly produced and conveniently legitimated during the Cold War, these techno-industrial achievements have diffused beyond the laboratories and states that did the initial pioneering work. Now these states are dealing with a boomerang effect as their own soldiers face enemy states suspected of having stockpiles of nuclear, chemical and biological weapons their own scientists invented and their own corporations helped build. In Iraq, for example, the US faced a state suspected of having the capability of manufacturing weapons of mass destruction because of technology supplied by commercial US labs and German chemical corporations amongst others. Key personnel in its weapons programs were trained in US universities.[39]

Environmental degradation, transnational crime, informational vulnerabilities (the Y2K problem) and the threat of information warfare ('netwar' and 'cyberwar') are other indicative features of risk society that have forced themselves into 'national security' discourse.[40] Previously 'latent side effects' of advanced industrial society have proved themselves to be neither latent nor marginal but pervasive and profound dangers. The dormancy of techno-industrial risk production has ended. The reputation of science as a source of progress is increasingly in doubt as is the possibility of rational governance and controlled development. Uncertainty has returned in the form of a widely perceived ecological crisis, emergent informational vulnerabilities, and increasingly manifest institutional failures of states, military alliances, financial markets, and proliferation regimes. The very foundations of the modern project are being questioned. The modern industrial institutions that have helped create our ongoing ecological, informational and security crises – the transnational capitalist market system, techno-scientific culture and the 'national security' state – are having to confront what they have unleashed. In adjusting their missions and re-legitimating their mandates they are reflexively modernizing. This process, however is fraught with contradictions.

Contradictions in The Reflexive Modernisation of Geopolitical Risks

Beck has noted that the pervasive and globalised risks of risk society 'are particularly *open to social definition and construction*. Hence the mass media and the scientific and legal professions in charge of defining risks become key social and political positions.'[41] No risk is self-evident in and of itself; it must be described, represented and constituted as part of a larger narrative. During the Cold War, geopolitical risk analysis was the monopoly of an establishment community of intellectuals of defence and statecraft. It was their job to survey the surface of world affairs, identify dangers and calculate risks. The larger narrative that enframed their work as risk analysts was the struggle between the two geopolitical superpowers and their allies. Risks within this narrative were mapped onto both territory and otherness, the clearly identifiable territorial home of one's geopolitical antagonist, and the overdetermined otherness that made this antagonist 'the enemy.'

Geopolitical risks were predominantly threats of territorial expansionism and threats to the balance of military power. Professional analysts in intelligence agencies developed refined conceptual systems of knowledge to study such geopolitical risks (like Sovietology), appraise the intentions and capabilities of 'the enemy' (through use of human, photographic and other forms of intelligence), and to assess effective institutional ways of responding to these territorial geopolitical risks.

Since the end of the Cold War the pluralised, globalised and deterritorialised character of geopolitical risks has been harder to deny. New forms of expertise and knowledge in global civil society – in academia, the media, the legal profession, and private insurance and risk assessment industries – now compete with the state's geopolitical experts to represent the post-Cold War world of risks. The monopoly of Cold War professionals over 'national security' has been profoundly challenged. Post-Cold War risks are no longer adequately represented and stabilised as territorial threats from recognizable enemies; rather post-Cold War risks have become amorphous and pervasive dangers. 'National security' has become a problematic of 'global security'. Cold War institutions have attempted to re-invent themselves by creating new bureaucracies, pluralising their understanding of security, and developing discourses like 'de-territorialised threats' and 'global dangers' in respond to the late twentieth century world.

However, this attempt by Cold War institutions reflexively to modernise themselves is burdened with contradictions. For a start, while the universe of geopolitical risks during the Cold War could be disciplined into a narrow military paradigm of 'national security', the universe of risks today is not so easily contained and disciplined. From the military's point of view, 'national security' during the Cold War was a clearly identifiable problematic that could be addressed with clarity, decidability and resoluteness. Geopolitical risks were problems that could be 'controlled' by established institutions with the application of instrumental rationality. 'Global security' is an amorphous set of global problems which contain many ambivalences and undecidables. No unambiguous solutions are apparent. The ability of Cold War institutions, organised originally in opposition to territorial enemies, to address the plural challenges of risk society is questionable.

Beck suggests it is virtually impossible for modern institutions to conceptualise the problems of risk society using only the conceptual imagination provided by industrial society. By this logic, the reflexive modernisation of geopolitics by industrial age geopolitical institutions will inevitably been superficial and partial. It will attempt to reduce the irredeemably global problems of risk society to an 'either/or' logic of representing risks as enemies, drawing boundaries against this enemy, and then applying instrumental rationality to 'solve' the threat.[42] Consequently, 'global dangers' are configured in practice as a parade of enemies like 'terrorists,' 'rogue states' and 'nuclear outlaws' that need to be isolated, contained and defeated.

In responding to the security challenges of late twentieth century risk society by modernizing enemies, the complicity of the nuclear security state itself in creating these security challenges is marginalised. Broader questions concerning the triumph of the West's Cold War way of life in producing the difficulties it now faces are usually disallowed for this way of life is considered non-negotiable. Yet, reflexive modernisation unleashes questions and issues which problematise the national security state and the West's way of life. Can the Pentagon be a credible force in addressing the problem of environmental degradation when it is one of the largest polluters in the US? If nuclear, chemical and biological weapons of mass destruction are a global problem why does the US retain stockpiles of these weapons (in some instances, in conditions that are very hazardous)? Are not these weapons a threat to the US itself? In attempting to grapple with risks that refuse easy conceptualisation and categorical containment, the limits of the industrial society (techno-military) nature of security become more evident and problematic.[43]

Beck's writings suggest that in risk society institutions of order will become overwhelmed by the immanent pluralism of risk. As industrial accidents, state failures, market meltdowns, and environmental catastrophes multiply, the power and legitimacy of aging industrial society institutions of security and order is likely to be exposed and challenged. The crucial question is whether this already apparent 'crisis of security' will be an occasion to re-invent modernity in a radical fashion (by creating new global institutions fit to address the challenges of 'risk society'), or whether it will be a stimulus for a dangerous counter-modern modernity, a modernity that refuses to accept the contingencies and ambivalences of living in a world of its own making.

NOTES

1. M. Castells, *The Rise of the Network Society* (Oxford: Blackwell, 1996).
2. A. Herod, G. Ó Tuathail and S. Roberts (eds), *An Unruly World? Globalization, Governance and Geography* (London: Routledge, 1998).
3. C.H. Gray, *Postmodern War: The New Politics of Conflict* (New York: Guilford, 1997); P. Virilio and S. Lotringer, *Pure War* (New York: Semiotext(e), 1983).
4. J. Agnew, *Geopolitics: Re-Visioning World Politics* (London: Routledge, 1998).
5. Agnew, *Geopolitics*.
6. For a fuller discussion of the concept of postmodern geopolitics see G. Ó Tuathail, 'At the End of Geopolitics? Reflection on a Plural Problematic at the Century's End', *Alternatives* 22 (1997), pp.35–56 and 'Postmodern Geopolitics? The Modern Geopolitical Imagination and Beyond', in G. Ó Tuathail and S. Dalby (eds) *Rethinking Geopolitics*, pp.16–38

(London: Routledge, 1998).
7. D. Newman and A. Paasi, 'Fences and Neighbours in the Postmodern World: Boundary Narratives in Political Geography', *Progress in Human Geography*, forthcoming; J. Agnew and S. Corbridge, *Mastering Space* (London: Routledge, 1995).
8. U. Beck, *Risk Society* (London: Sage, 1992).
9. M. Walker, *Clinton. The President They Deserve* (London: Vintage, 1997).
10. W. Clinton, Inaugural Address, 1993. Available from http.//www.whitehouse.gov
11. S. Greenhouse, 'The Greening of U.S. Diplomacy: Focus on Ecology', *New York Times*, 9 October 1995.
12. W. Christopher, *In the Stream of History: Shaping Foreign Policy for a New Era* (Stanford: Stanford University Press, 1998), pp.412–24.
13. R. Kaplan, 'The Coming Anarchy', *Atlantic Monthly* 273/2 (1994), pp.44–76; W. Lacquerer, 'Postmodern Terrorism', *Foreign Affairs* 75/5 (1996) pp.24–36; C. Crocker, F.O. Hampson and P. Aall (eds) *Managing Global Chaos: Sources of and Responses to International Conflict* (Washington, DC: US Institute of Peace, 1996).
14. S. Lynn-Jones and S. Miller (eds) *Global Dangers: Changing Dimensions of International Security* (Cambridge: MIT Press, 1995). This 'hard' versus 'soft' distinction is used widely within the policy community, with traditionalists often disparaging the 'soft stuff' involving the environment, humanitarian crises and peacekeeping. Discussing the rationale for a significant speech on diplomacy and the environment that he gave in April 1996, former US Secretary of State Warren Christopher argued that "We needed to foster a conceptual transformation, showing how what some considered to be a 'soft' issue had a place in US diplomacy alongside the more traditional 'hard' foreign policy concerns." Christopher, in *The Stream of History* (note 12), p.414.
15. W. Clinton, Remarks by the President to the 52nd session of the United Nations General Assembly. 1997. Available from <http.//www.whitehouse.gov>.
16. W. Clinton, Remarks by the President on Iraq to Pentagon Personnel. 1998. Available from <http.//www.whitehouse.gov>.
17. M. Klare, *Rogue States and Nuclear Outlaws* (New York: Hill and Wang, 1995).
18. The White House, *A National Security Strategy for a New Century*, May 1997. Available from <http.//www.whitehouse.gov>. The writing of this document was co-ordinated by Major James Seaton who is on the National Security Council staff. Many thanks to him for discussing its creation with Virginia Tech students and I at the White House in February 1998.
19. Ibid., p.2.
20. Ibid.. pp.5–6.
21. Ibid., p.6.
22. See R. Betts, 'The New Threat of Mass Destruction', *Foreign Affairs*, 77/1 (1998), pp.26–41, and J. Sopko, 'The Changing Proliferation Threat', *Foreign Policy* 105 (1997) pp.3–20.
23. *National Security Strategy* (note 18), p.6.
24. Ibid., p.11.
25. See L.Garrett, 'The Return of Infectious Disease', Foreign Affairs 75 (1996), pp.66-79 and 'Runaway Diseases', Foreign Affairs 77 (1998), pp.139-142.
26. See U. Beck, *Risk Society; Ecological Politics in an Age of Risk* (Cambridge: Polity, 1995), and *The Reinvention of Politics* (Cambridge: Polity, 1997).
27. Beck, *Risk Society*, ibid., p.9. Beck rejects the 'postmodern' as a concept because it is both vague and overloaded with a weight of meanings. It gestures at a beyond it cannot name. The concept can be saved and brought into harmony with Beck's own arguments, however, by thinking of its 'post' not as a beyond but as a 'new modernity'. His argument that new social movements do not stand in opposition or contradiction to modernity is also true of many notions of postmodernism which seeks not to reject the Enlightenment and modernity but to radicalise it.
28. Ibid., p.12.
29. Ibid., p.10.
30. U. Beck, 'The Reinvention of Politics', in *Reflexive Modernisation: Politics, Tradition and Aesthetics in the Modern Social Order* (Stanford: Stanford University Press, 1994), p.5.

31. Ibid., p.5.
32. Ibid., p.5, emphasis in original.
33. Ibid., pp.5–6.
34. Ibid., p.6.
35. Beck takes great care to distinguish reflexive–self-referentiality from reflective–conscious and sometimes critical thought and reasoning. See ibid., pp.5–8.
36. Beck, *Risk Society* (note 26), p.11.
37. See R. Rhodes, *The Making of the Atomic Bomb*,(New York: Simon and Schuster, 1986).
38. See Solly Zuckerman, *Nuclear Illusion and Reality* (London: Collins, 1982) and Robert Jay Lifton and Richard Falk, *Indefensible Weapons* (New York: Basic Books, 1982). Cold War geopoliticians also challenged the rationality of nuclear weapons. See George Kennan, *The Nuclear Delusion: Soviet American Relations in the Atomic Age* (New York: Pantheon, 1983).
39. For example, Nassir Hindawi, the so-called 'father of Iraq's germ weapons program', was trained as a microbiologist at Mississippi State University. See J. Miller, 'Iraqis Jail "Father" of Toxic Arms Program', *International Herald Tribune* 25 March 1998, A1, 12.
40. See G. Rochin, *Trapped in the Net: The Unanticipated Consequences of Computerization* (Princeton: Princeton University Press, 1997) and J. Arquilla and D. Ronfeldt (eds), *In Athena's Camp. Preparing for Conflict in the Information Age* (Santa Monica. Rand Corporation, 1997).
41. U. Beck, *Risk Society* (note 26), p.23.
42. U. Beck, 'The Reinvention of Politics' (note 30) pp.1–10.
43. The furore over the US military's efforts to dispose of leaking and aging napalm is a good example. Even strong Congressional supporters of the military, for example, are taking the US military to task for shipping hazardous materials into their constituencies. Other examples include controversies over the US military's storage of its chemical weapon arsenal and its lagging clean-up efforts at its bomb making facilities at Hanford in Washington state and Rocky Flats in Colorado.

International Boundaries, Geopolitics and the (Post)Modern Territorial Discourse: The Functional Fiction

FABRIZIO EVA

Despite the end of the Cold War, the world is a no less unsettled place; conflicts continue and even appear to be multiplying. But the nature of these conflicts has changed. Rather than conflicts predominantly *between* states, there are more conflicts *within* states; rather than armed ideological uprisings, there has been an increase in ethno-nationalist revendication.

With the world no longer 'balanced' between the superpowers, and with the (apparent) instability this caused now behind us, increasingly authoritative voices are calling for supranational rules and bodies and the setting up of a true world government. There is a call to move on from the current 'anarchic' Westphalia System to a world order that is accepted by all and governed for all.

In this paper I will demonstrate that the Westphalia System is based on a fiction, and that the acceptance of this fiction perpetuates the conditions needed for inequalities in power between states to continue. In effect, an informal system of world government is already in place founded on the principle of hegemony. But within this system, the establishment of supranational governmental bodies is hampered by contradictions between principles (democracy, the common good, human rights and so on) and the need – created by the state of hegemony – to act hierarchically and 'from above'.

As the prevailing nature of international relations is substantially state-centric, it is unlikely that a new or balanced system will come into being in the near future. Today's main schools of thought – liberal democracy, which currently dominates; Marxism, at present on the defensive; and postmodernism with its many shortcomings – are unlikely to help in this direction.

However, certain theories and lines of thought on international relations, postmodernism included, unwittingly draw upon concepts that are typical of anarchic thought. In some cases these ideas were developed more than a century ago. Given the non-state-centric premises of anarchism, extracting those elements from it that are still valid today may contribute to constructing a true dialectic in the science of international relations and formulating new solutions.

The Fiction

Relations between states as they have developed since the Peace of Westphalia in 1648 are increasingly the subject of investigation by scholars of international relations and geopolitics. The collapse of the USSR and the growing importance of globalisation have undermined traditional concepts and methods of analysing world geopolitical dynamics. This forces us either to search for new interpretive frameworks or to reconsider everything from different perspectives.

The so-called Westphalia System has been widely analysed and often forms a point of reference in geopolitical discussion and writings. Danilo Zolo has attempted to pinpoint its essential elements through reference to the works of Falk, Cassese, and others.[1] He identifies five fundamental points: first, the subjects of international law are exclusively states; second, an 'international legislator' does not exist; third, the Westphalia model does not provide for any form of obligatory jurisdiction nor the legitimate use of force; fourth, the equality of states is absolute; and fifth, recourse to war for defence and/or the pursuit of a state's interests is not subject to international or supranational judgement.

Reducing things still further than Zolo, I propose that the two fundamental premises of the Westphalia System are: first, there is no authority above the level of the system of states; second, this system operates on the basis of equalities of power – that is, the recognition of the equality and incontrovertible sovereignty of individual states within internationally recognised borders.

Only anarchic thought has postulated the political value and desirability of the absence of institutionalised government for free and equal individuals. For this reason, the Westphalia System has been defined as an *anarchic system*. However, since it possesses rules (customs), principles, and procedures, the more accurate term *ordered anarchy* has also been used. Arrighi attributes the coining of the latter term to anthropologists in the study of the generation of order through conflict or in the absence of a central government – as is the case with various 'tribal' systems, for example.[2] Zolo[3] attributes the term to Kenneth Waltz,[4] but still in the context of the same issue: the ability for a system to remain stable in the absence of centralised authority. It is worth remembering that noted anarchic thinkers of the past and present have always maintained that the negation of authority renders necessary the setting in place of dynamic relationships and principles of negotiation so that the anarchic (not chaotic) system may continue.⁵ This is a vision of anarchy as a system that is without hierarchical power, but is *organised*: 'nothing in anarchic thought precludes a minimal institutional presence at every level of society, provided that this presence stems from popular rather than elitist pressure'.⁶

'Borders and frontiers are cultural constructs that can take on many different meanings,'⁷ and throughout history they have principally had the function of 'selection' that is, as conceptual and concrete points of reference for establishing what is internal and what is external, what can come in and what must stay out. Within the Westphalia System, borders play a fundamental role in that they identify states, that is, the basic building block of the system. Separation by borders should have the effect of preventing conflict, while with rights equal between states thus separated prevarication should be halted. The principle of non-interference into internal affairs has been constantly confirmed by current geopolitical dynamics – Algeria being a case in point.

Any school history book will reveal a story of continual conflict, for the most part over borders. This state of conflict, however, has not destroyed the system; rather, it has perpetuated it. There has been an ongoing fluctuation between crisis and stability stemming from the existence of another dynamic force: the more powerful states aiming to achieve hegemony and greater power.

Ratzel postulated the organic need of the state with a growing population to expand. And this was supported, more categorically, two decades later by Kjellen in *Lebensraum*. Similarly, in his dissertation on the pivots of history, Mackinder deals with geo-strategy, power, and hegemony, but certainly not equality between states.

Europe founded the Westphalia System on the 'modern' concept of the state and its centrality. And over the last two centuries it has exported the system, along with it the proof of its fiction, all over the world.⁸ Colonialism was the clearest example of inequality between states. Europe's internal conflicts of the nineteenth century were to a great extent the result of confrontation between a few major powers, which, although stating they desired stability and peace for the continent, actually worked to maintain, or achieve, a state of hegemony. The Congress of Vienna in 1815 and the constitution of the Holy Alliance represented the formalisation of the hegemonic role of a few powers.

In practice, the Westphalia System is functionally hierarchical and fictionally anarchic. It presupposes the existence of a hegemonic state or states. Changes in the hegemonic role can come about through conflict (two-sided or many-sided) or decline/accession. This hegemonically-led system still operates today, and it is no coincidence that it has been compared to the constitution of the Holy Alliance after the Congress of Vienna.⁹

Although immersed in an economic–ideological dichotomy, after 1945 the confrontation between the USA and USSR evolved along lines that were typical of this system, eventually developing into an equilibrium between the two superpowers at the highest level of the hierarchy – that is, the effective joint management, including through conflict, of the entire world-system. 'Wallerstein maintains that the United States and the Soviet Union were involved in a conflict that was highly structured, carefully contained, and, above all, formal ... The Soviet Union worked to guarantee order and stability within its area of influence and acted as an ideological shield for the United States through which its capacity to preserve world hegemony grew. As bizarre as it may seem, Wallerstein therefore maintains that, from 1945 until its collapse, the Soviet Union can be seen as a sub-imperial power of the United States.'[10]

From the outset of the Cold War, the two superpowers asserted their positions of hegemony by failing to respect the borders or sovereignty of other states. There are numerous examples, ranging from the US's interventions in Latin America and Asia, through the 'aid' given by the USSR to its 'sister countries' in 1956, 1968, and so on. In this regard, it is possible to interpret the joint Great Britain–French military occupation of the Suez Canal in 1956 as one of the last attempts at a display of hegemony on the part of the shrinking colonial (super)powers.

For forty-five years, the US and the USSR represented a kind of informal world government that was operated bilaterally and from within the formal sphere of the UN Security Council by vetoes.

The decolonisation process very much put the Westphalia System to the test for two principal reasons:

- the high number of states that almost simultaneously claimed equality and sovereignty, and
- uncertainties regarding the real acceptance by the new states of the fiction – that is, of the existence of a hierarchy within which by necessity the most recent arrivals occupied a marginal and/or subordinate position.

On the practical front, disputes – occasionally bloody at the local level – between the two superpowers over drawing newly independent states within their spheres of influence developed like a kind of systemic container that perpetuated, through necessity, the acceptance of the functional anarchy/hierarchy fiction. During his visit to Africa in March/April 1998, President Clinton admitted that during the Cold War the choice to support or abandon African countries was often dictated by decisions that had nothing to do with the fate or problems of that continent (*Il Sole 24 Ore*, 3 April 1998). The great USA–USSR game continued, and countries' attempts to remain unaligned were in vain, partly because some of the states championing non-alliance actually belonged to an alliance themselves (Cuba, for example). The confrontation between powers continued, occasionally becoming more conspicuous when borders or sovereignty were violated.

In some cases border violations took place that were not directly related to the bipolar clash, but nevertheless could be seen after the event to fit into the global strategy. Examples include Cuba's intervention in Ethiopia following the Somali attack on Ogaden, the Six Day War of 1967 in Israel, the invasion of Lebanon, and the air strikes on Iraqi nuclear sites. In other cases – such as the annexation of East Timor by Indonesia, the Turkish occupation of Northern Cyprus, and US and allied intervention in Grenada – the violation of borders and sovereignty was formally condemned, but with no real international action taken. This generally occurred – and continues to occur– when the geographic location of the area affected allows a convenient territorial isolation from the issue.

The various proposals for new world orders advanced in the 1980s did not question the internal hierarchy of the system, even tending to justify and stabilise it in the name of the common good. The conflict between blocs, however, rendered the success of these proposals impossible.

Objective: A World Order

The end of the bipolar world order has resulted in the US becoming the sole superpower, thus creating a state of 'unnecessary' hegemony contrary to the premises of the Westphalia System and the democratic values at the basis of international relations. These ideals have been reaffirmed in recent times in the preamble to the Charter of the United Nations, a body that officially operates on the basis of the equality of states (all Member States have one vote each at the General Assembly) and the inviolability of sovereignty within borders (the principle of non-interference). However, the structure of the UN, particularly as regards the constitution and operation of the Security Council, contravenes these general principles since the five permanent members obviously have a privileged position relative to the other states.

While the Cold War lasted, it was possible to disguise this contradiction since, on the one hand, the USA–USSR clash blocked the operation of the Council (declarations based on Chapter VII of the Charter, which authorises the use of force, were unthinkable) and, on the other, it acted as a *force majeure* that made a world organised according to democratic principles unworkable.

The current debate on the functions of the UN and the constitution of a world government suggests that it is necessary to find a new justification for inequality between nations that also takes into account the dynamics set in motion by globalisation and new technologies. Fifty years of the UN and the constitution of numerous other organisations for international negotiation (GATT-WTO, G7, OECD etc.) have changed certain aspects of the Westphalia System, not only creating a huge body of accepted international regulations, but also a desire to project an interiorised image of order at the supranational level; that is, a variety of global state led by a world government.[11]

The objective is to establish a world order that is stable, shared, and/or accepted by all, that is, with centralised formal jurisdiction and a government with executive power and the means for the legitimate (possibly exclusive) use of force. Before this objective is met, however, 'the *status quo* is the only solution that we can allow ourselves at this time'.[12]

Since 1989–91 (the period that saw the fall of the Berlin Wall and the collapse of the USSR) the interventionist role of the UN has increased in situations of international crisis and tension because of decisions made by the Security Council. Military intervention in Iraq in 1991, based on Chapter VII of the Charter and in response to the violation of a state's borders and sovereignty, is one example. The composition of the Council has become the subject of discussion and even political clashes among members. It is significant that the US is proposing a simple increase in the number of permanent members (without the right to veto) based on factors (economic power and regional importance) that are in line with the above-mentioned concepts of Holy Alliance and inequality. The alternative, championed by an unusually high-profile Italy, does not question the privileged positions of the permanent members, but proposes a rotation system based on different periods, areas, and levels of importance. Such a system can be defined as a broader and more democratic Holy Alliance. The internal diplomacy of the UN is unused to conflicting views of such importance when they are not ideologically different, and for this reason the debating of the issue at the General Assembly has thus far been deferred.

Pending the definition of the new role of the UN, and the resolution of the yet to be confronted contradictions in its operation (for example, the respective powers of the Security Council and the International Court of Justice), the world order remains in a state of transition that is developing according to certain key principles – namely, *stability*, the *territorial containment of conflict*, *economic–financial globalisation*, and the maintenance of *Western democracy* and its values.

The Four Key Principles

Stability is meant here in the sense of action to maintain the current geopolitical world map—that is, to keep existing states within their current borders. One would imagine that this should permit negotiation with recognised leaders in the case of crises or to arrange 'easy outcomes' should a crisis degenerate into armed conflict. Events in the former Yugoslavia, however, are proof of how false such expectations can be, with the obstinate initial defence of the integrity of the Yugoslav territory by the international community actually worsening the situation. After four years of bloody conflict, however, the external and internal borders of the former Yugoslavia are still certain and accepted points of reference, including by the internal protagonists.

The defence of existing borders permits the application of the strategy of *territorial containment*, this consisting of preventing crises and tensions from escalating beyond the state in which they originated and guaranteeing that neighbouring countries and the rest of the world are in no way affected. More importantly, territorial containment does not negatively influence overall economic activity and under some circumstances may even produce economic benefits – illegal markets, increases in prices for certain products, new cash flows, and so on. The conflict in the Balkans, the civil war in Afghanistan, and the Algerian crisis are all examples of this. The Rwanda–Burundi regional emergency, which resulted in hundreds of thousands of refugees, and deaths approaching the levels of genocide, ceased to be a matter of concern for the international community when Laurent Kabila took control of Zaire in only three months. In so doing, he guaranteed both stability and territorial containment, as well as the respect of mining contracts. Also, the last troubles in Zaire/Congo confirm the relevance of the *territorial containment*; the so-called international community accepted even external armed (troops from Zimbabwe!) intervention in order to reach *stability*.

Having definite borders also allows the resolution of logistics problems and helps in the decision as to whether, and to what extent, to intervene in disputes. The defeat of Iraq in 1991 is paradoxical in that while the country was partially occupied by the military and forced to endure two no-fly zones, it was possible to resolve the internal conflict with the Shiite minority – which is, however, a majority in Bassora area, which is within a non-fly zone – with the intervention of tanks and guns.

As regards borders, the functional fiction makes it possible to officially ignore events such as Turkish troops crossing Iraq's borders to fight the Kurds and Somaliland's declaration of independence, while skirmishes over a handful of islands in the Aegean Sea between Greek and Turkish ships have been described in certain newspapers as 'a threat to peace in the Mediterranean'.

In view of this observance of the 'border-based' principles of stability and territorial containment, it figures that in today's world internationally recognised borders are under no real threat. 'The territorial configurations of the contemporary world order are undergoing functional, rather than spatial, changes. Boundaries remain important lines of demarcation'.[13]

The other two of the four key principles might appear to operate independently of borders: the speeding up of the communications and finance sectors (both of which are essential to *globalisation*) and the maintenance of *Western democracy* and its values (including unlimited private property, the rights of the individual, and multiparty elections). In practice, however, these two principles are closely connected to the existence and defense of the nation-state as a fundamental political structure. And the modern state insists on undisputed land surrounded by undisputed borders.

'The defense of the right of freedom, the rules of the market, and private property within liberal-democratic countries would be impossible without the presence of a power structure capable of guaranteeing political order.'[14] Even in an economically globalised world, stock exchanges must still have 'protected' seats. The development of the Peking and Shanghai exchange— and the tranquility of the Hong Kong exchange after the reunification with China—were and are guaranteed by the Chinese government, which, although declaring itself to be communist, has been working for some time to protect its domestic financial markets.

For transnational corporations to operate beyond their borders, they must have branches (holding companies or affiliates) in physical and not virtual locations: '90 per cent of TNCs are headquartered in the advanced capitalist states (five major home countries account for over half of the developed country total).'[15] In addition, they control production and cash flows that cross, or are in, specific territories. The state system guarantees the economic system. What is fundamental is the openness of the system, but we certainly would not want to see its disappearance. 'The mode of regulation at the global scale is constituted in large part by the actions of states.'[16]

The current Westphalia System, with its functional fictions, is fertile ground for the world economy. A hypothetical world government could create excessive inflexibility and possess excessive power unless clear roles and limits are defined, and this could only occur after intense international dispute. For this reason, we can assume that the creation of a world order with its own system of government will be a long time coming.

There is a call for strong leadership from many quarters. This is because strong leadership is an effective solution since it is ideologically acceptable, and it is seen as a lesser evil than the much-feared chaos.

How a World Government Might Come Into Being

If the above-mentioned principles are the instruments for guiding the transition towards a stable and shared world order, it is obvious that such a world order will be the product of the methods used. The means become the ends.

Current geopolitical dynamics foretell of a move away from the concept of 'organised anarchy' towards one of 'democratic (hierarchical) order'.
'Stable and universal peace tends to coincide with the freezing of the [world] geopolitical, economic, and military map.'[17] This freezing also becomes a prospect and an end, sanctioning the acceptance of the current state of inequality: 'trans-state organisations are not extra-state organisations. They do not mark the eclipse of the state. [They] reflect the unequal power relations between states.'[18]

'There is a kind of awakening on the part of all states to the varying importance of each within the international hierarchy . . . The criterion of economic and strategic importance has gotten the better of the occasionally too rigid rules of the Statute of the United Nations.'[19] This statement suggests a positive position as regards the enforcing of the rules – including that of equality – so as to set up a truly global government.

In 1992, the Security Council declared an air embargo on Libya following the Lockerbie disaster on the basis that two Libyan citizens were believed to be responsible. Libya applied to the International Court of Justice stating that the grounds of the embargo were legally unjustified. Recently the Court ruled that the application was admissible. Should the Court find in favour of Libya, the question would arise of the relative importance of the different agencies of the UN. Is there a separation of powers? Which of the two – Council or Court – should have the greater authority? Delegations of certain 'permanent' countries have already responded quickly to support the pre-eminence of the Security Council, while many diplomats from countries that are economically and strategically less important have stated their belief that the Court has the ultimate authority. In the latter case, we must ask ourselves, however, which agency of the UN would be able to and/or have the authority to oblige a permanent member with the veto right to enforce measures against themselves, even in the case of measures under Chapter VII that would involve armed force.

The International Court of Justice's influence seems greater now than in the past. The US and the UK have accepted neutral ground (the Hague) and a Scottish court for the Lockerbie disaster trial. The two accused Libyans have been guaranteed that they will not be extradited from the Netherlands until the end of the trial. This situation demonstrates an entirely different attitude to the decisions of the International Court of Justice compared to the mid-1980s, when the Court condemned the US's sanctions against Nicaragua.

Perhaps it is no coincidence that this coincided with the world conference held in Rome during June and July 1998, which concluded with 120 nations signing the act for the establishment of the International Criminal Court. A formal ratification process within the parliaments of the signatory countries has now commenced, and the Court will begin operating once a minimum of 60 countries approve its statute. The secretary of the UN, Kofi Annan, has described the creation of the ICC as a 'giant step forward'.

Seven states voted against the statute: the USA, China, the Philippines, India, Turkey, Israel, and Sri Lanka. Together these states represent almost half the world's population. This diplomatic defeat of the USA, which was unable to stop the establishment of the Court, stands out in particular.

Albeit slowly, international relations are evolving, and countries that are in a position of power or who can act with greater freedom must work to maintain their position.

Regarding the establishment of a world government, the present situation would indicate a reassertion of the functional fiction through a bending of the rules of procedure—that is, the strongest would hold the upper hand. 'In my opinion, this [bending of the rules] is an important sign that places a new perspective on the vitality of an organisation [the UN] that is all too often criticised for its procedural immobility.'[20] Playing for time and freezing up the current situation would allow discussion to be steered toward adjusting the UN and stabilising it through a continual bending of the rules. Until such a time as the UN is recognised as having rights that cross borders – that is, the right to interference based on a formal process – the world's 'shadow government' (G7/8, IMF, Security Council) will oversee this transition and influence the outcomes of debate. The underlying idea would appear to be the establishment of a mega-(meta)-state that will institutionalise as democratic entities the current decision-making centres and recognise NATO as an instrument that may legitimately use force to protect global security.

Problems arise from the fact that as organisms founded on territory and absolute sovereignty, nation-states are the structure on which other organisms that are 'a-territorial' and with limited/conditional sovereignty are based (the UN and IMF, for example). The attribution of greater sovereignty to such organisms presupposes the attribution of authority over actual territories. This creates both a conceptual and practical conflict with the political structures that control these territories. Defining limits to the actions of a-territorial organisms directly flies in the face of the meaning we give borders today.

There are three main issues that diplomats and experts in international relations have been debating for some time: the functionality of the UN, the effectiveness of the decisions made by a potential world government, and ideological points of reference.

As regards the functionality of the UN, for quite some time, and in many quarters, there has been criticism of the UN's bureaucracy on the grounds that it is dysfunctional, too expensive, has too many bureaucrats, and is too slow. The US is the main critic – particularly when the Republicans have a majority in the US Congress. The Republican Party has never concealed its increasing impatience with an organisation of 'politicians' who, among other things, have shown themselves to have diminishing levels of respect for the United States. The General Assembly voted no less than three times against the US embargo of Cuba, and since Reagan was in office UNESCO has received no funding from the US since this organisation was perceived as being too left-wing. In terms of the amounts involved, the United States has the worst payment record as regards its share in the UN's expenses.

The most interesting issue, however, is the role to be attributed to the Secretary and a broader Security Council. The Security Council is the only UN agency with the power to intervene in countries' affairs, and from this perspective it is already in a position to transform itself into a world government. It would, however, be necessary to better define its relationship (and relative powers) with the Secretary and widen its field of action, which is currently 'limited' to the non-specific maintenance of peace and international security. Without further concessions, the rigidity of procedures obstructs interference in the sovereignty of individual states and, therefore, requires that borders be respected.

The issues under discussion at present are increasing numbers in the Council and the declaration of new motivations for the interventions now in place. In essence, there is an attempt to define which universally shared objectives allow the crossing of a state's borders and the limitation of sovereignty. For such a definition to be universal, it would require a broader Council than the one we have at present.

The universal principles currently upheld are 'humanitarian grounds' and the 'defence of global security'. Examples of the defence of human rights, and/or assistance to ease the suffering of populations include the situation in Somalia some years ago and current events in Algeria. The UN did intervene in Somalia, but the newly accepted bending of the rules was able to occur not only because of the pressure applied by President Bush and the mass media of the developed nations, but also because in effect Somalia no longer existed and, therefore, the question of sovereignty was not involved. Because of continuing conflicts between armed clans, a new and peaceful state of Somalia does not exist today. Nevertheless, the borders of the old Somalia remain and are officially recognised by bordering nations – the new, self-proclaimed independent republic of Somaliland having retained the boundaries of the ex-British colony overthrown more than fifty years ago. This situation remains on hold (the principle of stability) thanks to the respect of recognised borders (principle of territorial confinement).

Intervention in the Algerian Civil War was justified on humanitarian grounds. However, to date, the existence of a state with full powers and the fact that the conflict has remained exclusively within the country's borders (stability and containment) have hampered the bending of the rules.

Humanitarian grounds are beginning to be accepted as a justification for UN intervention even by certain non-governmental organisations, religious groups, and theorists with progressive and/or liberal platforms. The concept is now even being discussed in the media, which are increasingly becoming the preferred instrument for requesting intervention by the international community. The defence of global security would still appear to remain the province of government and the military, however. It would not appear to be seen as sufficient grounds for interfering in the sovereignty of states or the crossing of borders.

The US bombardment of Sudan and Afghanistan, in retaliation against attacks on US embassies and as a measure against terrorism, can be seen as a bending of the rules made possible by the US's political–military leadership. Although the UN did not take an official position on the matter, by and large the international community's response was negative.

For the time being, global security is regarded as being sufficiently well protected by the freezing of the current geopolitical situation. As mentioned, debate on the broadening of the Security Council is now livelier than ever, but the unexpected presence of opposing views has frozen discussion.

On the level of ideals – which must also be universal – the demise of the ideological communist–capitalist conflict has opened the field to capitalism. And this system – known as the 'market' – is increasingly laden with values, including of a politico-ideological nature: there is 'increasing confusion between democracy and economic liberalisation.'[21] Globalisation is championed by its enthusiastic supporters (first among them, Renato Ruggiero, the Italian director of the WTO) as a means of spreading well-being and freedom throughout the world; and increasingly a close connection between individual freedom, democracy, and the market is being asserted. In the case of states that do not uphold human rights as they are understood in the West, it is hoped that they join the capitalist system since in this way Western-style human rights and democracy will spread. The faith that this can take place stems from a vision of democracy for 'collective groups' and a failure to address the question: 'Is democracy compatible with systems of hierarchical subordination such as some churches and most large business enterprises?'[22]

This was the stance taken relative to the Asian NICs and has had ample confirmation in the macroscopic case of relations with China following the events in Tian An Men Square. While the Chinese Communist Party did not renounce exclusive control of power nor of information (for example, the control of Internet access and the expulsion of opponents), this did not prevent the newly sworn-in Premier Rongji being received with every honour in Europe during the China–EU and Asia–Europe economic summits held in London in April 1998. Nor did it prevent his economic pragmatism creating a flurry of activity in the stock exchanges.

During this transitional phase the International Monetary Fund is the UN agency that is most rapidly broadening its functions and jurisdiction. The IMF has already played an important role over the past two decades because a bending of the rules has allowed it to take action at the economic level in states in debt or crisis to such an extent that its actions have been seen as interfering with the sovereignty of those nations; 'social rights tend to be neglected in order to attract international investment'.[23] What is new about the current phase stems from the crisis that swept through the Asian stock markets in late 1997 and early 1998; that is, the stabilising role it plays by providing funding is required by the entire globalised economic system. It was no coincidence that the Asia–Europe summit concluded with a declaration that openly spoke of a wish for greater and more transparent global surveillance by the Fund combined with the creation of a new mechanism for regional surveillance.[24] The desire is that the IMF be transformed from financier to a global controller, and this will probably be the essence of discussions at the next meetings of the IMF and the G7 countries. It is significant that to combat the stock market crises of August 1998 (in Japan, Russia, and elsewhere), the British prime minister, in agreement with the US president, took the initiative of calling a summit with the G7 nations (an extra-UN organisation)[25] and the IMF and WB (both UN organisations) at a time when the media reflected a growing call for authoritative control and international regulations.

It is appropriate at this point to mention that voting rights within the IMF are not equal, but proportional on the basis of payments and economic importance. For this reason the USA holds around eighteen percent of voting rights. In addition, the IMF must officially and absolutely act in respect of the principle of sovereignty since it deals exclusively with governments and economic structures on the national level. Its actions are therefore in line with the principles of stability and territorial containment.

The strategies of the Fund and its restructuring plans have always born the imprint of defending and furthering a *laissez-faire* economic system founded on containing state spending, the freedom of private initiative, and the free circulation of goods and capital. The economic instrument is increasingly becoming a strategic political instrument – China saw this clearly when it supplied four billion dollars to help the countries suffering under the Asian economic crisis, this placing it in third position behind the United States and Japan.[26]

Giovanni Arrighi has reconstructed the hegemonic phases of the international economic–political system since the thirteenth century.[27] He convincingly identifies the hegemonic states throughout history, including cities in northern Italy, the Netherlands, Great Britain, and finally the United States. At the end of the book the question is posed as to which country will act as the hegemonic state during the next phase, which, according to Arrighi, is imminent. The author suggests the decline of the US and the ascension of a Japan in control of the world's liquid assets.

Political and economic events over recent years, however, suggest that the US will be able to maintain its leading role in the near future since both the world political situation and the dynamics of global economics are working in its favour. The freezing of the current geopolitical situation based on hierarchically unequal nation-states allows the US to both maintain its position as a superpower and influence the setting up of international organisations (the UN and IMF, for example) that in turn perpetuate this role. The Anglo-American influence in the maintaining and widening of a cultural hegemony in the international geo-strategic field should not be underestimated. If language plays a decisive role in 'national imaginings',[28] it also plays a similar part in the construction of dominant roles and ideas. 'Today's theories of international ethics were conceived to perpetuate the supremacy of English-speaking countries.'[29]

For historical and cultural reasons, Japan would not appear to be in a position to undermine the United States – in the space of only four years the country having partially lost control of the international liquid assets Arrighi attributed to it. In addition, Japan has traditionally placed itself in a position of isolation by assuming superiority. In much the same way as it was closed for hundreds of years to relations with other states, over the past century it has developed aggressive, control-oriented policies that prevent it from aspiring to a role as a hegemonic state without provoking a serious backlash. Strong social cohesion, which does, however, also take the form of cultural inflexibility, has proved very useful in developing the Japanese economy, but would prevent the country from efficiently managing a position of hegemony, which, since it is a global role based on the control of money, presupposes flexibility and the art of compromise. The immobility of the Japanese government as regards the stock market crisis of August–September 1998 is the most recent example of this.

Over the past twenty years, China, on the other hand, has brushed down many of those characteristics that for centuries allowed it to occupy a hegemonic role in eastern Asia: a historical capacity to manage huge areas and populations; a widespread acceptance of a hierarchy that extends from the nucleus of the extended family outwards to include respect for authorities; an undisputed skill with handling money and business; and close ties to the country (the Middle Kingdom) that have nevertheless not prevented the spread of Chinese communities to all over the world who maintain links to the native country that are based more on family than nostalgia. Thanks to the four 'modernisations' introduced by Deng Xiaoping and the acceptance of market-based socialism by the Communist Party, China has begun to develop a highly pragmatic international policy that is seeing the country occupy an increasingly important role.

Through diplomatic means, China has reconquered Hong Kong (which has one of the most important stock exchanges in the world) and re-established relations with the important Chinese community in Singapore as well as other Chinese living abroad. In just a few years it has acquired a certain international importance in various manufacturing sectors and demonstrated a shrewd capacity for economic–financial management during the recent Asian currency crisis. China avoided devaluing the *yuan* during the 1998 market crisis for reasons of political advantage (and honour) over economic interests, thereby demonstrating its ability to act as an authoritative and stable nation.

China entirely satisfies three of the four key principles: it is stable in its pragmatic foreign policy, it limits internal problems to within its boundaries, it is rapidly adjusting itself to globalised economic mechanisms. It does not adhere to the fictional elements of Western democracy, but this would appear to be the least important of the four key principals. All these factors would suggest that China may, with the US, be the joint leader of the future international state system.

Conclusions

Although a summarised view, the above discussion is intended to demonstrate the existence of a geopolitical reality based on the dominance of a few states over others – a situation that is increasingly difficult to justify. Current debate on the future of international relations is spirited and will presumably grow since we are in a transitional phase.

There is a 'realist' school of thought that recognises hegemony as being both good and necessary. For those subscribing to this view, it is sufficient that this dominance is wielded by democratic states through international bodies engaged in negotiation. There is another line of thought that rejects hegemony and propounds models for supranational structures/orders that are 'democratic', co-operative, polycentric, and so on. This line of reasoning proposes that these models will help us move on from the Westphalia System and that these same bodies must act to balance out world economic inequality.[30]

The model for democracy nevertheless remains the Western version, which is tied in with capitalist economics. There is an acceptance, therefore, of the central ideology of liberal democracy – a system that may more accurately be termed 'capitalist democracy'. Capitalist democracy is a social order in which the 'buying mentality of the market' and the 'tendentially egalitarian mentality of political rights' coexist within a 'functional tension'.[31] The clash between these two contradictory mentalities is countered within the structure of the Western nation-state, which defends unlimited ownership (the principle of inequality), but allows dynamic policies (the principle of equality in political rights).

The acceptance of capitalist democracy renders the link between the global economic aspect of power and efforts to formalise the power of international supranational institutions clearer. Although they do not deny states and borders, such institutions remove some powers from the former and see the latter as serving a function rather than signifying a demarcation. Since the collapse of the USSR, no alternative form of economic organisation, other than capitalism, has been proposed; or more accurately, the media and intelligentsia have not been willing to give any real attention to other forms. Thus the hegemonic world system of the Holy Alliance can tolerate nation-states that are barely, or not at all, democratic, provided they permit ownership or, at least, freedom for capital flows.

The new world orders that have been proposed tend to favour a world mega-state based on the following premises:

- substantial preservation of the current world geopolitical map;
- preservation of borders and the principle of non-interference, other than in the case of decisions taken by legitimate supranational bodies;
- ethnicities, nationalities, identities, religions and so on are controlled ('confined') by individual states in the interests of maintaining the stability needed for a borderless economy;
- formalisation of supranational powers (such as for legal intervention, including armed, for humanitarian reasons, the maintenance of global security, the regulation and control of markets and international capital flows, or the defence of human rights);
- the primary role of the Security Council, G7/8 (G9 with China?), IMF-WB, and WTO as formal spheres for supranational decision-making;
- the International Court of Justice as the court of last (very remote) resort;

and
- the desirability of a single president of a world federation of states who has at his or her disposal a supranational military structure along the lines of the NATO model.

As the sum of its nation-state parts, the world mega-state would include that functional tension between the equality of formal political rights (for example, the one-vote-per-state of the UN) and inequality of economic conditions. The new fiction would be supranational democracy, the function (not new) would be hierarchical order.

Is there a conceivable alternative?

TABLE 1

	Individual	State	Ownership	Inequality	Society seen as:
Capitalism	●	✘	●	● (competition)	○ Market
Marxism	(✘)	●	✘	✘	● Community
Postmodernism	●	✘ (representation)	?	?	○ Mosaic of diversity
Anarchism	●	✘	✘	✘	● Cooperation

Legend: ● = positive value; ✘ = negative value, ○ = relative position.

For decades, the only alternative to capitalism that played a major role was Marxism. This was because it was a mirror image of capitalism (see Table 1). With the collapse of its practical application (that is, of the so-called 'real-socialism') Marxism has today been placed on the defensive. It is unlikely that it could again become 'competitive' since it continues to be obsessed with the state, an area in which today it must compete with nationalism, ethnicity, religions, and various groups united by a common concept of collective identity that have as their foremost goal the claiming of their right to a homogenous nation-state. Today all such groups wield high emotional impact.

In addition, 'the socialist–communist movement has never managed to develop, in political or theoretical terms, its own satisfactory interpretation of the geographic dynamics of capitalist accumulation and the geopolitical foundations of class struggle.'[32] Added to the excessive rigidity of the party orthodoxy, this limited concern with the spatial dimension and has seen many Marxists take an interest in the deconstructive flexibility of postmodernism.

Postmodernism is flexible and dynamic because it rejects representation (discourse). However, since its premises do accept the borderlessness of the globalised economy, it is not seen as an alternative and does not itself offer any alternative solutions as far as political representation is concerned.

Harvey explicitly declares his desire to fill a void in the Marxist conceptual framework, namely, the absence, or shortcomings, of its approach to space. He believes that 'A new theory of socialism must today have space as its central issue' since 'when capital is in movement, the importance of space becomes much clearer.'[33] As a geographer, Harvey sees space as central not only to analysis, but also as a starting point for the political class struggle against capitalism. His in-depth analysis of the spatial–economic dynamics of globalised capitalism, however, does not lead to an alternative view from the spatial perspective. The state still must be created before it can be destroyed.

Postmodernism would not appear concerned with political models derived from spatial analysis. It analyses the local and the particular. It semiologically constructs and/or deconstructs spaces, places, and situations. But since it does not concern itself with representations of the world, it does not attempt to represent space or the theories surrounding it. Nor does it have any geopolitical vision.

To propose alternatives, we must envisage metageographies. 'Metageography is a crucial semic point that, like all crucial semic points, the dominant classes attempt to control because it is through them that the geostructure produced by it is accepted.'[34] Geographers build images of the world and 'since they satisfy the function of legitimizing power, images of the world are always ideological.'[35]

An alternative school of thought which may be able to trigger a real dialectic with the dominant capitalist democracy is anarchism. Despite the fact that postmodernism has many elements derived (unknowingly?) from anarchism, this could only come about if the traditional and generalised dismissal of anarchism can be overturned and some leeway made against the widespread lack of intellectual esteem with which it is regarded. Anarchic thought is so socially dangerous that in the past it has even forced capitalists into defending the state. This is another factor that has led to its 'criminalisation'.

Since its conception, anarchism has produced metageographies because it has attempted to imagine future society within the context of real spaces. It is no coincidence that the philosophies of anarchism and modern geography have been intertwined since the beginning. 'A major coming together between geographic and anarchic thought appears fundamental to me. Many authors have been struck by the fact that Reclus and Kropotkin were both great theorists of this political scheme and great geographers.'[36]

'Anarchism and geography have more than casual relations – there are structural similarities between the two in terms of anarchism's naturalistic interpretation of the human character (as essentially cooperative) and the spatial form of its decentralised vision of an alternative society.'[37]

The most interesting geographic aspect of anarchism is its flexible view of political space – in other words, what we now call the *glocal*. This flexibility stems from the dynamic and permanent relationship between the macro and micro. It means promoting relations, analyzing, and conceiving systems that grow outward from the local to the global and vice versa. As ecologists say, 'think globally, act locally'.

While Ratzel represented the embodiment of bourgeois geographic thought[38] and set in stone the geopolitical land–population–state triad, Reclus, even earlier, regarded land as a space with which individuals and groups have a changing and dynamic relationship. Ratzel saw time as bringing about the organic growth of states towards a better civilisation. Reclus, however, saw it as bringing about changes in relations, habits, and territorial positioning within organised political spaces whose size may change according to historic events or the will of humans.

Reclus saw history (and language) as one of the components to be combined with *genre de vie* for pinpointing what he termed 'natural regions'.[39] Today, therefore, although basing our view on the current configuration of the states (the result of history), we can see the basic building block of political communities not as nation-states, but as smaller organisms, such as communes, municipalities, cantons, and districts. This leads to a view of the borders of current states as *temporary and movable demarcations* – 'but this very freedom of the individual group necessitates a flexible border; in reality, how little the manifest will of inhabitants is actually in agreement with official conventions!'[40] Provided it occurs from the bottom up, the reaching of specific objectives at the macro level creates a push towards the setting up of groups, the stipulation of agreements, and the pooling of resources and skills. To some extent, this is happening with the Euroregions, certain supranational bodies, and twinnings between regions that consider themselves similar (such as the Lombardy–Catalonia–Baden Wuerttemberg–Lyon region agreement).

All current relations – supranational, cross-border, subnational, or variations thereon – can be regarded as concrete spaces for broader self-determination. Not only anarchists have this vision; authors such as Nozick, for example, regard 'mixed governments in mixed territories'[41] in a favourable light, meaning by this, territories with residents of different nationalities who vote and make decisions together on common questions and separately on separate questions. A solution of this type was recently proposed for the negotiated solution in Jerusalem.[42]

The international community can and must, however, arrive at a basic ethical stance that is not merely formal, but substantial – that is, 'the substitution of justice for order as the primary test of the adequacy of a given arrangement of power in world society'.[43] A key concept here is confederation, which 'is in reality a community based on human rights and clearly defined ecological imperatives'.[44]

'The primary world order need is to find an alternative to statism. Anarchism, despite its limited political success in the statist era, provides the most coherent, widespread, and persistent tradition of antistatist thought. It is also a tradition that has generally been inclined toward world-order values: peace, economic equity, civil liberties, ecological defense.'[45]

Harvey's doubt as to whether current changes make necessary 'a radical revision of our theoretical concepts and political machinery (not to mention our aspirations)'[46] finds a complete and affirmative response in the conceptual framework of anarchic thought. Using Gottmann's categories, the current dominant iconography must have a truly antagonistic movement factor to trigger a dialectic and a dynamic movement that will produce a future that is more functional and less fictional.

NOTES

1. D. Zolo, *Cosmopolis*, (Milan: Feltrinelli 1995) pp.117–9; English version: Polity Press, Cambridge. Referred to in R.A. Falk, *The Interplay of Westphalia and Charter Conceptions of International Legal Order* (Princeton: Princeton University Press, 1969). A. Cassese, *Il diritto internazionale nel mondo contemporaneo* (Bologna: il Mulino, 1984).
2. G. Arrighi, *Il lungo XX secolo* (Milan: il Saggiatore 1996) p.53; English version: *The Long Twentieth Century*, 1994 (London: Verso, 1994).
3. Zolo (note 1) p.128
4. K. Waltz, *Theory of International Politics* (New York: Newbery Award Record 1979).
5. P. Kropotkin, *Mutual Aid: A Factor of Evolution* (London, 1915). E. Malatesta, Organizzatori e antiorganizzatori, *Umanità Nova*, 20 June 1922; 'Un progetto di organizzazione anarchica', *Risveglio* 1–15 October 1927; C. Ward (1979), *Anarchia come organizzazione* (Milan: Edizioni Antistato 1979) (English title: *Anarchy in Action*, 1973)
6. R. Falk, 'Ordine mondiale e federalismo', Vol. 4, (1995), Editrice A, Milano, from (In?) R. Pennock, J. Chapman (eds.), *Anarchism* (New York: New York University Press 1978).
7. P. Zanini, *Significati del confine* (Milan: Ed. Scol. Bruno Mondadori 1997) p.28.
8. D. Newman, 'Borderlands under Stress', paper presented at the Fifth International Conference of the IBRU, Durham, England, 15–17 July 1998.
9. Zolo (note 1), p.22
10. M. Di Meglio, *Lo sviluppo senza fondamenti* (Trieste: Asterios Editore 1997), p.138
11. R. O. Lourau, *Lo stato incosciente* (Milan: Eleuthera, 1988).
12. D. McHenry, interview in *liMes*, Jan. 1998, p.215
13. Newman, (note 8), p.9

14. Zolo (note 1) p.93
15. R.J. Johnson, P.J. Taylor and M.J. Watts (eds.), *Geographies of Global Change* (Oxford: Blackwell, 1996) p.13
16. S.M. Roberts, 'Global Regulation and Trans-state Organisation', in Johnson, Taylor and Watts (eds.), *Geographies of Global Change* (Oxford: Blackwell, 1996), p.113
17. Zolo (note 1), p.33
18. Roberts (note 16), p.126
19. McHenry (note 12), p.215
20. Ibid.
21. J. Agnew, 'Democracy and Human Rights after the Cold War', in R.J. Johnson, P.J. Taylor and M.J. Watts (eds.), *Geographies of Global Change* (Oxford: Blackwell, 1996), p.93.
22. Ibid., p.83. F. Eva, 'Public Space, Private Space: One Territory, two rule systems', paper presented at the Inaugural International Conference on Critical Geography, Vancouver, Aug. 1997. Published on the conference World Wide Web page.
23. Agnew (note 21) p.88.
24. *Il Sole 24 Ore*, 3 April 1998.
25. A. Cerretelli , 'Russia, è G7 straordinario', *Il Sole 24 Ore*, 6 September 1998.
26. *Il Sole 24 Ore*, 3 April 1998.
27. G. Arrighi (note 2).
28. N.C. Johnson, 'The Renaissance of Nationalism', in R.J. Johnson, P.J. Taylor and M.J. Watts (eds.), *Geographies of Global Change* (Oxford: Blackwell, 1996).
29. E.H. Carr, *The Twenty Years' Crisis 1919–1939*, quoted in Zolo (note 1), p.75.
30. For an exhaustive analysis of both positions, see Zolo (note 1).
31. Zolo, ibid., p.159.
32. D. Harvey, *Il problema della globalizzazione* (Milan: Edizioni Punto Rosso, 1997), p.82
33. Ibid., p.81–2.
34. C. Raffestin (ed.), *Geografia Politica: teorie per un progetto sociale* (Milan: Unicopli, 1983), p.16.
35. Habermas, quoted by Raffestin, ibid., p.26.
36. J.P. Ferrier 'Geografia Politica avete detto? Ovvero le lezioni particolari del territorio', in *Raffestin*, ibid., p.112.
37. R. Peet, *Modern Geographical Thought* (Oxford: Blackwells, 1998), pp.71–2.
38. F. Farinelli, 'Alle origini della geografia politica borghese', in *Raffestin* (note 36).
39. E. Reclus (1905–1908), *L'Homme et la Terre* (Paris: Librairie Universelle).
40. Ibid.
41. R. Nozick, 'Privatizziamo lo stato', interview by S. Vaccaro in *Volontà*, 4 (Dec. 1995) Milan: Editrice A, p.29.
42. S. Hasson, 'The Municipal Organisation of the Jerusalem Metropolitan Area', paper presented at the Third Israeli Seminar in Political Geography, Haifa and Beer Sheva, 25–31 January 1998.
43. Falk (note 6), p.181.
44. M. Bookchin, *Democrazia diretta* (Milan: Eleuthera, 1993), p.91.
45. Falk (note 6), p.189.
46. Harvey (note 32), p.99.

On Boundaries, Territory and Postmodernity: An International Relations Perspective

MATHIAS ALBERT

As the disciplines most explicitly dealing with the role and function of territorial boundaries in the social world, International Relations and Political Geography have witnessed – or are indeed continuing to witness – numerous new approaches and criticisms informed by so-called 'postmodern' ways of thinking. Reactions to postmodern contributions have ranged from a cautious to an enthusiastic welcome on the one hand, and from mild to fervent criticism on the other.[1] In spite of the discussion surrounding 'postmodernity', indeed its proliferating use even in public debate, the main issues and theses underpinning postmodernist thought remain little-known. The present contribution seeks to elucidate some of these underpinnings and explore some of the implications of postmodern thought and criticism for the study of boundaries and geopolitics. In so doing, it does not attempt to provide a comprehensive overview of the vast array of contributions that employ the term even in the two disciplines that are of particular interest here. What can be done, however, is briefly to sketch the discussions as they have been conducted especially in the academic field of International Relations. As will be seen, despite the vast differences between the various approaches, the main denominator of postmodern thought is that it provides a criticism of the epistemology of our age, the way we make sense of things and the way in which this in turn shapes social reality.

In the eyes of many observers as well as critics of postmodern contributions, the main problem with this kind of epistemological questioning is that it does not lend itself easily to be translated into the analysis of more or less narrowly defined, 'practical' issues. However, this article proceeds from the assumption that this problem should not serve as a basis for derogating this (or for that matter any) kind of epistemological criticism as irrelevant for singular fields of inquiry, but rather takes the view that more thorough efforts are warranted to provide exactly the kind of translation work that many find missing (or even to be impossible).

A main methodological problem that has to be faced in trying to meet this task consists in the vast (dis-)array of approaches that can be subsumed under the 'postmodern' label. The present contribution will seek to address this problem by a 'return to philosophy', as it were. Instead of going through contribution after contribution that may or may not be relevant for judging the influence of postmodernism for the study of geopolitics and boundaries, it will directly relate to some of the main arguments of the philosophical debate that informs postmodernism throughout various disciplines. This course of presenting the argument follows from the impression that from some of these philosophical contributions very important and more or less 'direct' insights can be inferred that may help to gain a fresh perspective on the role and function of boundaries and the meaning of geopolitics in a changing world.

The following section will provide an overview on how the issues of postmodern epistemological criticism and the renewed interest in the concept of territoriality relate to each other in the discipline of international relations. Readers from the field of political geography will find a significant similarity to the debates as they are conducted in their field (something which, it may be added, bears witness of the amount of cross-disciplinary fertilisation that has occurred between these two disciplines in recent years). The article's second section will present some central theses of poststructuralist philosophical thought. The main issue of interest here is how perceiving the world in spatial categories and actually creating social structures and orders such as territorial boundaries are closely related to each other. The third section will develop some thoughts as to how these philosophical positions can be seen to enable a fresh perspective on the study of boundaries.

Postmodernism in International Relations

It is fair to say that the study of territorial boundaries and territoriality as the primary differentiating principle of the international system of states has been marginalised in most post-war analyses of international relations.[2] The dominant paradigm in the discipline, political realism, more or less took the foundations on which the post-war world order rested for granted.[3] Issues of boundary disputes or more general questions on territoriality that might have arisen in relation to the process of decolonisation in particular were by and large relegated to specialists of international law.[4] However, what applies to the explicit study of territorial boundaries does not hold true equally for thinking in 'geopolitical' terms in general. Although the term may have been discredited politically, various 'geopolitical visions' certainly continued to lie behind a number of conceptualisations of world politics, especially in the field of 'strategic studies'.[5] Nevertheless, only recently and retrospectively has the presence of such 'geopolitical visions' in some schools of thought of international politics been uncovered and analysed explicitly (not least by political geographers).[6]

This situation of a relative indifference towards questions of territoriality and international boundaries changed profoundly after the Cold War came to an abrupt end – an end not anticipated by a discipline whose main business was to study the basic constellation of international politics.[7] Even after that, it took the majority of students of international politics quite a while to realise that the new era of 'postinternational politics', which James Rosenau heralded in 1990, entailed a more profound reconfiguration of world order than many were prepared to admit.[8] However, today it seems clear that what is at stake is not merely the configuration of the international system after the Cold War. What is at stake are the very foundations of the 350 year-old Westphalian system of states, which uses territorial demarcation and control as its prime differentiating and organising principle.[9]

It seems surprising that the discipline of international relations did not take up the issue of substantive change in the quality, shape, and construction of territorial spaces earlier. After all, a number of political geographers and sociologists had already provided thorough analyses about the historically contingent and socially constructed character of political and social spaces.[10] Nonetheless, it seemed as if the basic differentiating principle of the international political system, territoriality, would remained unchanged. This is not to say that the great structural displacements that occurred in the world system, even despite the continuation of the East-West conflict, were not taken up and assessed, such as the restructuring of the world economy (the influence of transnational corporations, regional trading blocs etc.), the emergence of new global problems and agendas (environment), or the growing influence of non-governmental organisations on the international floor. However, these developments were *either* seen as not affecting the character and predominance of the territorial state as the defining element of international relations at all,[11] *or* seen as more or less directly challenging it in a sort of zero-sum game.[12] What largely escaped the attention of most analysts was the possibility that the very meaning of statehood, the principle of territoriality that underpinned it, and the international structure it supported, were undergoing a qualitative transformation. Such a transformation renders it largely meaningless to simply juxtapose 'states versus markets' or 'geopolitics' versus 'geo-economics' in attempts to make sense of the new global order's structures and dynamics. It rather requires fresh conceptual approaches that consciously reflect on the restraining effects of traditional analytic notions and on possibilities of moving beyond them.[13]

In a way things have changed quite profoundly at the end of the 1990s. Increasingly, analysts are beginning not only to acknowledge the radical nature of the changes that can be witnessed, but also to devise new strands of analysis that seem more apt to explain the new than the theories traditionally dominant in International Relations, such as realism and neorealism.[14] The main issue in this respect may be seen to lie in the question of what constitutes 'international relations' or the 'international system'. It seems quite clear the traditional state-centric view becomes less and less tenable in an era of transnational migration and the formation of stable transnational communities, the intangibility of international financial markets and the globalisation of consumption, labour and production, and the emergence of new political forms of organisation such as the European Union. Given the changing meaning of territorial boundaries, reference is frequently made to a 'new medievalism', an overlapping of various authorities on the same territory, in turn giving rise to the idea that empire-like structures are reappearing in the most 'advanced' parts of the world (such as Western Europe).[15] In addition, various conceptualisations of 'international society' and 'world society' receive renewed attention as it becomes increasingly clear that the traditional sociological notion of 'society' itself carries the image of a society bounded by the boundaries of the territorial state, an image which becomes untenable in an era of globalisation.[16] This is neither to say that analysts would be blind to countertendencies – whilst nation-states may be superseded in Western Europe by empire-like structures, the implosion of the Soviet empire has led to many new projects of exclusionary nation-state-building. Nor is it to say that the metaphor of 'neo-medievalism' should be taken too literally. Of course no one suggests a return to social and political structures that characterised the pre-modern world. What the use of concepts such as 'neo-medievalism' seeks to express is merely the fact that changes in the world are of such a character that a reliance on established vocabularies to explain them would not do them justice, while the new vocabularies needed to provide the proper explanation are as yet only in the process of being devised and searched for.

While this observation merely reflects the fairly commonsensical wisdom of a necessary time-lag between changes in social structure and changes in the according semantics,[17] it bears an as yet little noticed consequence for the importance and impact of so-called 'postmodern' contributions in the field. The more the contours of a new semantic begin to emerge, a semantic that would be able to take account of the changed form of the world system, the more it appears as if 'postmodernist' accounts of radically deterritorialised orders seem to have concentrated on only one dimension of these very changes, systematically underestimating the self-reproductive and adaptive capacities of the old orders. Nonetheless, they have concentrated and indeed continue to concentrate on that dimension of change that constitutes the most radical break with previous orders and therefore appears as the most incomprehensible to traditional analytical techniques. In fact, postmodernist contributions in International Relations have repeatedly emphasised that if these techniques are understood as knowledge structures, then it is part of their self-reproduction to exclude and deny fundamental changes in the studied field.[18]

'Postmodernist' analyses have been of considerable value in helping many of the social sciences to open up 'thinking spaces'.[19] In fact, major intellectual developments such as the increasing impact of constructivist, feminist, or 'critical' thinking may not have had their origins in postmodernist theses, but definitely may have been helped in making the impact they had by the fact that postmodernism contributed to a fundamental questioning of authorities and concepts that also hindered a more widespread engagement with these directions of inquiry.

This observation can be illustrated well by turning to the particular issues of interest here – boundaries and territoriality. While at least some political geographers were for a while already deliberating the socially constructed and therefore contingent nature of spaces, places and their interrelation, the idea was until recently not widely discussed or its full implications received in IR. Today, and particularly due to the 350th anniversary of the Peace of Westphalia, the business of trying to *imagine* what an international political order that is not clearly differentiated territorially might look like has moved to the discipline's centre stage. And this development has to a significant extent been enabled by the preparatory work of postmodernist criticism in the discipline.

Postmodernist contributions in IR began to emerge in the discipline of international relations during the second half of the 1980s, initially more focused on the agendas of 'mainstream' IR theories in particular,[20] but soon coming to perceive these agendas as endemic to 'modern' ways of thinking in general.[21] At first, and in what in comparison to the French philosophers fluent in this technique initially appeared to be a number of fairly clumsy exercises,[22] postmodernist scholars would 'deconstruct' well-known, 'canonical' texts of international relations theory.[23] It thereby became possible to show that these texts relied on a number of presuppositions typical for a modernist understanding of science. One example here would be the way that even theories which purport to operate on a 'systemic' level rely, or in fact depend, on treating 'the state' as a given unchanging unit (thereby stripping themselves of possibilites to account for historical change).[24] Pertinent to the understanding of boundaries it was shown by the postmodern critics that the representation of the social world in terms of inside and outside, privileging the former over the latter (in a normative as well as in an analytic sense) was in fact constitutive of most of the discipline's inquiries. This, it was forcefully argued by Walker, was however not to be blamed on the peculiarities of the discipline of international relations in particular; rather, the discipline thereby only mirrored one of the main themes of Western, and particularly modern political thought.[25] After the ground had been prepared, more specialised studies on certain aspects of international relations and international relations theory began to emerge. Inquiries took up subjects such as to which extent the institution of diplomacy had developed through a set of power relationships and thus must not be seen as a neutral mechanism for communication between the 'real' actors, i.e. states,[26] or the way that the extensive use of multimedia-images during the Gulf War contributed to the construction of a new notion of the realities of war, one detached from 'real' war on the spot,[27] etc. In the meantime, studies of this kind have proliferated and now occupy a more prominent position in the discipline's research programmes.

It will be immediately clear to the political geographer that many of the issues raised in the context of postmodernist contributions in IR bear relevance to the analysis of the transformation of territory and boundaries through a geographical lens. Nonetheless, even upon superficial inspection it appears as if there are more commonalities between those inclined towards postmodernist thinking in both disciplines than there are commonalities and critical engagements between 'postmodernist' and more 'traditional' approaches within the disciplines themselves. A productive engagement with postmodernist approaches is still, by and large, missing in international relations as well as in political geography. This is particularly deplorable given the fact that postmodernist thinking not only has important things to say about epistemological issues, but also about the issues of territoriality and boundaries. It thus touches on a subject which constitutes a marker of the dramatic changes underway and which is in need of fresh conceptualisations. As mentioned above, it is also suspected that the communicative barriers existing in this regard may in part be due to a lack of understanding of some important concepts utilised by 'postmodern' philosophy. The lowering of these communicative barriers is the main idea behind the following presentation of some of the philosophical thoughts underpinning 'postmodernist' thought.

Poststructuralism and (De-)Territorialisation

There are probably as many answers to the question of what 'postmodernism' or 'postmodernity' mean as there are people employing the terms. This has sometimes led to the criticism of a lack of standards and an arbitrariness regarding the use of these concepts. Yet it is possible to discern some common thematics, especially from the philosophical considerations that sparked these concepts in the first place. It goes without saying that the degree to which individual postmodernist contributions in the social sciences reflect on these themes varies to a significant extent.

At the heart of postmodern thought lies philosophical poststructuralism which, as the name suggests, developed out of the tradition, in criticism and as a radicalisation, of structuralist thought, primarily in French philosophy.[28] One of its main ideas was to show that most structuralist thinking still implied the notion of a centre, some kind of fixed point without which a structure would not be meaningful, and that this notion was a remnant of modern subject-centred thinking against which structuralist thinking originally set out.[29] However, similar arguments were brought forward, not only against structuralism, but against a whole range of influential philosophical and linguistic approaches. In a sense, the aim is always the same: to show how these approaches utilise, rely on and thereby reproduce, fundamental figures of thought that are taken to be typical, not only of modern thinking, but of the tradition of Western metaphysical thinking since Greek philosophy as such. Thereby it is also meant to show that some constraints of thought which appear to be 'given' or 'natural' are in fact contingent. Though very elaborate and successful in pointing out these traits, which regulate what can count as meaningful at a very fundamental level, the 'alternatives' offered by poststructuralist philosophy are very 'modest'. It first of all acknowledges the fact that it is a practical, if not a logical impossibility to criticise a certain mode in which meaning is produced (in and through language and signs) without at the same time employing this very mode and thereby contributing to its reproduction.[30] This is where the technique of 'deconstruction' is introduced. Put very simple, it works like follows: a trace of the 'logocentric' universe of Western metaphysical thought is identified within a text; it is then shown that some of the very claims put forward by the text in fact work against these very deeply ingrained underlying assumptions; from thereon, the entire text can be shown to basically 'deconstruct' itself by exhibiting these 'deficiencies' through and through. This point must not be mistaken: the issue is not if contradictory arguments are used; the issue is if an argument, in order to count as meaningful and valid, does not rely on criteria of what constitutes meaning and validity that it purports not to rely upon.[31] Also, the issue is not to 'destroy' the text. Endemic to poststructuralist texts is the notion that deconstruction can be used against any text which at a certain point in time can claim to be meaningful. The purpose of deconstruction is thus destruction and reconstruction at the same time. By conducting such an exercise, the 'centre', 'meaning', the 'reflexivity' of a text will have changed to a degree, if only immeasurably small. In that sense, the purpose of deconstruction is an enlightenment different from modernity's enlightenment of grand design, full-fledged rationality and 'great stories', but more some kind of a 'postmodern enlightenment' of small heuristic steps.[32]

The link of such a kind of thought to the study of international boundaries may not be immediately visible, except that poststructuralist criticism may be read as a general call on all kinds of scientific inquiry to become more sensitive towards its own fundamental embeddedness in a way of thought and an awareness about the possibilities that such an embeddedness may foreclose. Nonetheless, there is a more direct relevance of poststructuralist thought to the study of international boundaries and geopolitics. This becomes particularly visible in Gilles Deleuze and Félix Guattari's *A Thousand Plateaus*.[33] In this very abstract, yet historically-empirically rich study, Deleuze and Guattari show how society's need to affix itself to territory and to draw territorial boundaries is in itself part of the very way of claiming that something is meaningful in the 'logocentric' universe of Western metaphysics, which actually makes it worthwhile to examine and interpret this work in more detail than will be possible here:

As outlined by Jacques Derrida's study of modern Saussurian linguistics,[34] language is structured in such a way that a sign or a 'signifier' (which can be a symbol, an utterance etc.) is only seen as meaningful because it is taken to signify something that 'exists' in reality (the 'referent', or 'signified'). As much as the latter can be a very abstract thing, such as an idea, it is nonetheless the guarantor for there being meaning. The meaning that is thereby attached to something may change according to the way it is represented through language etc.; but the referred-to, the signified is there independently of this very representation, there could be no sign and no language if it didn't refer to something external to the sign and to language at some point. What Deleuze and Guattari show is how this very fundamental logic underlying the way in which we make sense of things works specifically in the realm of human practice that has to do with territory. As shall be well-known to geographers, a 'space' of any kind can be represented in very different ways.[35] However, the very fundamentals of our epistemologies work in such a way that these representations only count as meaningful and are therefore only legitimised by the idea, 'the alibi', so to speak, that in the end it refers to something which is 'real', independent of these representations, a set of places, a territory.[36] Thus, for example, it is possible to read Deleuze and Guattari in way that shows how ideas like sovereign statehood were not and continue not to be constituted by relying on some abstract representation of their legitimatory origin (such as a national founding myth). Rather, sovereignty is something that has to be *practised* through 'marking' space by boundaries of various kinds – and by mapping these boundaries in an exact science. Space and boundaries are thus seen as something that can never be seen or studied as some kind of status. Rather, and this is shown by Deleuze and Guattari through the employment of poststructuralist philosophy, for territory to be meaningful (for individuals as well as for states defining themselves through it) it is necessary that a continuous *process* of *territorialisation* takes place. This process of territorialisation is dialectic in the way that it consists of processes of deterritorialisation on the one hand and processes of reterritorialisation on the other. For territory to be meaningful it has to be reproduced by the enactment of challenges to it, by questionings and erasures of boundaries as markers of space, but also through the inscription of new boundaries.[37]

Quite a few of 'postmodernist' contributions in the social sciences have focused on the issue of where 'deterritorialisations' occur and how these change a world order that has primarily been differentiated by territorial demarcations. Quite correctly it is asserted that innovations of technology (virtual reality), the general acceleration of communication and the creation of profit on international financial markets that do not deal with 'real' use-value all form instances of where 'deterritorialisations' take place.[38] Most of theses observations would probably agree on the characterisation of current changes as challenges to the space of clearly demarcated places by a (global) space of flows. In a way then, radical postmodernist analyses, which seek to identify processes of deterritorialisation, and 'traditional' analyses of the location and the movement of international boundaries are not incompatible with each other; they rather form but two sides of the same coin. They both study the on-going process of (re- and de-) territorialisation which, given the philosophical argument portrayed above, is the primary mode available in order to ascribe meaning to places. This of course does beg the question *if* (and how) a waning importance of territoriality could be observed at all. If territorialisation as a practice of producing and reproducing meaning for social practice is so deeply embedded in and reflective of very fundamental undercurrents of the building of 'Western metaphysics', then the answer to that question would seem to be negative. If it is only possible to refer to a waning importance of territorialisation or the drawing of spatial boundaries by employing, so to speak, 'territory talk', then the very practice of diagnosing a waning importance of territorial boundaries would mean engaging in their reproduction. Thus, one could always make the argument that functional boundaries become more important than territorial ones in today's world. But to understand the implication of such an observation for place and space, one still would be forced to point to a territorial dimension of these functional boundaries – even if they are of a more fuzzy kind than for example international boundaries.

Still it could be argued that one could study this kind of philosophical thought and gain an insight into the logical and historical difference and contingency of very different orders and perceptions of the world, yet that this does not bear immediate consequences for the study of specific boundary issues. I argue that this is and should not be the case. If something can be learned from poststructuralist philosophy in general and its account of territoriality in particular, it is that fundamental changes in world views and changes between what – with some hesitation – might be termed 'epochs' do not show themselves as grand designs on the wall.[39] However, it is possible to analyse indicators and get a glimpse of such changes through seemingly 'small' developments. In that sense, indicators of the quality of change on a macro-scale are not to be found by observing radical and comprehensive redrawings of the world's territorial-political map, such as in the wake of the Cold War's ending. Rather, such indicators are to be found exactly in singular places where small changes do occur, small changes that nonetheless alter the way in which the dialectic of re- and deterritorialisation is played out. The final section will try to point out some research issues that arise from such a reading.

De-Borderings, Re-Borderings

From the above depiction of a 'postmodernist' perspective on boundaries, it is possible first of all to correct a common misperceptions about such a perspective that quite often seem to arise. 'Postmodernist' thought is not about a breakdown of boundaries and a deterritorialisation of statehood in the sense that space would be entirely displaced by time.[40] Except in some very crude adaptions of postmodern philosophical thought, reterritorialisation is always conceived to form a necessary part of deterritorialisation. What is changing in the process are the exact mode and the relative importance of certain kinds of borderings. Thus, the 'boundary differentiation' thesis can indeed be seen to be compatible with a postmodern perspective on boundaries.[41] In contrast, the 'end of boundaries' thesis is nothing particularly 'postmodern'; quite to the contrary, it is extremely modern in the sense that it forms a normative claim of cosmopolitan and universalistic positions in political philosophy. It would be more in line with postmodern reasonings to describe the boundary changes underway as 'deborderings'.[42] What this term suggests is that we currently witness a continuing functional differentiation on a worldwide scale, with an ensuing incongruence of functional boundaries that cease to overlap on one line (the territorial state's boundary). These functional boundaries do always also possess a territorial expression, however not necessarily in the form of sharp demarcation lines. Such processes of debordering do follow from structural shifts that can be observed sociologically, primarily the continuing functional differentiation of world society and the ensuing increased operative autonomy of the various functional subsystems.[43] However, the kind of new borderings and modes of differentiation as well as separation that emerge in the process of debordering cannot be logically inferred from observing these macroscopic processes of change. They rather require to be observed and analysed individually, bearing in mind that even seemingly liminal changes may carry the potential for severe structural displacements, literally 'deconstructing' structures that appear to be rigid. At this point, looking for new kinds of borderings must not be limited to the traditional field of view of international relations or political geography but requires to take the perspectives of other disciplines into account.

Thus it appears that new modes of inclusion and exclusion as well as the breakdown of such modes in cultural practices can be equally telling about new structural features of a 'postmodern' world as can be solely political-spatial demarcations. It is in particularly this sense that a 'postmodern' transformation must not be seen as confined to the Western world. Quite to the contrary, it seems as if developments in non-Western cultural practices in particular provide a number of offers as on how to 'deconstruct' Western representations of cultural, political and other spaces.[44]

It is by now very well understood that the appearance, function, and even the location of territorial boundaries can usually not be pinned down in a simple manner: 'The boundary does not limit itself merely to the border area or landscape itself, but more generally manifests itself in social and cultural practices, in legislation but also in movies, novels, memorials, ceremonies and public events, which are expressions of narratives connected with boundaries and border conflicts as well as definitions of the Other'.[45] What is striking indeed is that a similar awareness about boundaries more or less simultaneously emerged in a number of disciplines. While the background of the authors just cited is in geography, IR scholars have come to study the cross-links between processes of identity-formation, boundary-drawing and the establishment of order;[46] anthropologists and ethnographers have come to perceive culture not as an object to be studied but as a boundary-construction exercise which can only be understood by studying the way that cultural reality is expressed through symbolic markers;[47] philosophers and theorists of science have made the argument that it may be more appropriate to study relations and boundaries in the first place rather than pretend that there are given entities which take logic precedence over their boundaries.[48]

As much as various disciplines and approaches therefore converge on providing fresh perspectives on the study of territorial boundaries in a changing world order, as much can their insights benefit the analysis of particular boundary problems.[49] This first of all calls for taking into account the variety of meanings that are invested in a particular boundary; only then can one hope to judge the micro-problem at hand in its connection to structural macro-settings. Such an approach could and should, however, be encouraged also to work the other way around. The task then would not be to look at a particular boundary and the analyses conducted thereupon in order to find possible models for new forms of territoriality. The indicators that need to be looked after in this respect might be seemingly marginal: the task here is, first of all, to sieve through the manifold proposals and think-pieces regarding, for example, the resolution of territorial disputes, in order to identify deviations from the way that territorial delimitations were conceived of previously. In addition, one could systematically analyse models of cross-border co-operation which are already enacted and tried out in practice and that may therefore serve as an indicator for future transformations on a larger scale (for better or worse). It would thus be perfectly legitimate to ask if the various forms of private or semi-private cross-border co-operations between public entities all over Europe (the 'Euregios') could provide a model for future interaction between states on a larger scale. Empirical studies about these cross-border linkages on the micro-scale can be very telling about various possible ways to map and represent the social world in the future. One example of where this question achieves very direct relevance would be the hotly debated issue of the possibilities for transnational forms of democracy. Up to now the consensus seems to be that democracy is so intrinsically linked to, even dependent on, territorial demarcation, that no true public sphere, no democratically organised political community, is possible beyond the territorial state, lest it be organised as a cosmopolitan democracy.[50] Looking not at new grand designs, but at various small-scale examples, this diagnosis might have to be rephrased. These examples may not sound very dramatic. And in fact, they may not be. However, they might show the possibility, if nothing else, that the meaning of boundaries can and does change without this being necessarily an instance of the evaporation or reassertion of territorial boundaries as such, but maybe a slight alteration in the practice of territorialisation that may in the long run lead to its demise.[51]

Numerous examples that may provide indicators for such a development could be enumerated. In that respect the local sewage system that extends to two towns on two different sides of an international boundary is as interesting as the increasing willingness of states to subject themselves to private laws in transnational commerce. Both developments are not statements of irreversible change, nor are they the sole or even primary signs which would allow to judge the direction of changes. They are, however, sites in which the practices of de- and reterritorialisations are played out and thus they form potential sources which, taken together with many others, may allow us to get a glimpse of future structures and organisational forms of the social world.

Conclusion

This article has tried to elaborate some aspects of a 'postmodern' perspective on borders and (international) boundaries. It has done so, first, by introducing the way in which similar attempts have been made in the academic field of international relations and, second, by pointing towards some important tenets of poststructuralist philosophy. What follows from this is not a call to adopt a 'postmodern approach'. Quite to the contrary, what follows from the reading provided above is that a postmodern perspective should not be confused with a single or coherent theory or analytic strategy. It rather entails a call for and an acceptance of theoretical pluralism. Such a theoretical pluralism must not be misunderstood as being theoretical relativism. It simply reflects the conviction that the complexities of today's social world and the boundaries structuring this world cannot be recaptured in one approach or perspective, but that only a variety of such approaches and perspectives can do justice to such a complexity. This also means that the quite often heard argument, according to which the same analytic results that are reached by inquiries informed by postmodernist thought could be reached without reference to such thought, misses the point. In terms of theoretical plurality and inter-paradigmatic competition, the interesting thing is not that the same results can be reached without a 'postmodern' perspective, but that they can be reached *with* it.[52]

It is not by accident that so many disciplines focus their attention to questions of boundaries and boundedness on the one side and possible uses of 'postmodern' routes of inquriy at roughly the same time. This development reflects the fact that we are in the midst of processes of change that not only affect the ways in which the social world is structured, but also require a restructuring of spaces of imagination and representation that are used to make sense of such a changing world. As witnessed by this volume, the term 'postmodernism' provides a focal point for cross-disciplinary debate on how to come to terms with these changes. As such, it is not a conceptual remedy for all analytic problems associated with these changes, but a point of analytic departure. Any attempt to fix it and turn it into *a* 'postmodern approach' would be counterproductive. Like 'borders' and 'boundaries' the term 'postmodern' lends itself to many metaphorical uses which may at first seem to dilute analytical clarity. Nonetheless, it is exactly through the use of metaphors that new semantics can emerge that are adequate to newly emerging social conditions.

Notes

1. See, for example, the less than polite debate that has been fought out in the *Journal of Peace Research*, initiated by Ø. Østerud, 'Antinomies of Postmodernism in International Studies', *Journal of Peace Research* 33/4 (November 1996), pp.385–90.
2. A notable exception can be found in the works of John Herz; cf. J. Herz, 'Rise and Demise of the Territorial State', *World Politics* 9/4 (1957) pp.473-9; 'The Territorial State Revisited', *Polity* 1 (1968), pp.11–34.
3. For an overview, see R. Spegele, *Political Realism and International Relations* (Cambridge: CUP 1996).
4. These issues have only been taken up to a significant extend after Robert Jackson drew attention to the character of some ex-colonies as 'quasi-states', i.e. states that possess *de jure*, but not *de facto* sovereignty and control over territory; see R. Jackson, *Quasi-States. Sovereignty, International Relations and the Third World* (Cambridge: CUP 1990).
5. One of the few examples of explicit geopolitical reasoning in this realm would be C. Gray, *The Geopolitics of the Nuclear Era. Heartlands, Rimlands, and the Technological Evolution* (New York: Crane, Russak and Company 1985).
6. See G. Ó. Tuathail, S. Dalby and P. Routledge (eds.), *The Geopolitics Reader* (London: Routledge 1998); G. Ó. Tuathail, *Critical Geopolitics* (Minneapolis: University of Minnesota Press 1996).
7. See J.L. Gaddis, 'International Relations Theory and the End of the Cold War', *International Security* 58/1 (Winter 1992), pp.5–58.
8. J.N. Rosenau, *Turbulence in World Politics* (Brighton: Harvester Wheatsheaf 1990); also: *Along the Domestic-Foreign Frontier. Exploring Governance in a Turbulent World* (Cambridge: CUP 1997).
9. The pathbreaking article that set the agenda was: J.G. Ruggie, 'Territoriality and Beyond: Problematizing Modernity in International Relations', *International Organisation* 47 (Winter 1993), pp.139–74.
10. See, in particular: D. Harvey, *The Condition of Postmodernity* (Oxford: Basil Blackwell 1989); also R. Sack, *Human Territoriality: Its Theory and History* (Cambridge: CUP 1986).
11. See S. Krasner, 'Compromising Westphalia', *International Security* 20/3 (1995), pp.115–51.
12. S. Strange, *The Retreat of the State: The Diffusion of Power in the World Economy* (Cambridge: CUP 1996).
13. The term 'geo-economics' was introduced by E.N. Luttwak, 'From Geopolitics to Geo-economics: Logic of Conflict, Grammar of Commerce', *The National Interest* 20 (Summer 1990), pp.17–24.
14. Good overviews over the variety of approaches that try to go beyond the traditional realist/neorealist agenda can be found in: S. Smith, K. Booth and M. Zalewski (eds.), *International Theory: Positivism and Beyond* (Cambridge: CUP 1996).
15. See O. Wæver, 'Imperial Metaphors: Emerging European Analogies to Pre-nation-state Imperial Systems', in: O. Tunander, P. Baev and V. I. Einagel (eds.), *Geopolitics in Post-Wall Europe. Security, Territory and Identity* (London: Sage 1997), pp.59–93; the term 'neo-medievalism' was coined by Hedley Bull in his classic *The Anarchical Society* (London: Macmillan 1977).
16. Attempts to draw up analytically useful notions of 'world society' that do not rely on territorial understandings of 'society' are to be found in the German debate; see: N. Luhmann, 'The World Society as a Social System', in R. F. Geyer and J. van der Zouwen (eds.), *Dependence and Inequality: A Systems Approach to the Problems of Mexico and Other Developing Countries* (Oxford: Pergamon Press 1982), pp.295–306; World Society

Research Group, 'In Search of World Society', *Law and State. A Biannual Collection of Recent German Contributions to these Fields* 53/54 (1996), pp.17–41; also M. Albert, L. Brock and K.-D. Wolf (eds.), 'Civilizing World Politics. Society and Community Beyond the State' (Lanham: Rowman and Littlefield, forthcoming).
17. See N. Luhmann, *Die Gesellschaft der Gesellschaft* (2 vols; Frankfurt/M.: Suhrkamp 1997).
18. Cf. R. Ashley, 'Political Realism and Human Interest', *International Studies Quarterly* 25 (June 1981), pp.204–36.
19. J. George, 'International Relations and the Search for Thinking Space: Another View of the Third Debate', *International Studies Quarterly* 33 (September 1989), pp.269–79; Y. Lapid, 'The Third Debate: On the Prospects of International Theory in a Post-positivist Era', *International Studies Quarterly* 33 (September 1989) pp.235-49.
20. Cf. R. Ashley, 'The Poverty of Neorealism', *International Organisation* 38 (Spring 1984), pp.225–86.
21. Cf. R.B.J. Walker, *Inside/Outside: International Relations as Political Theory* (Cambridge: CUP 1993); James Der Derian and Michael Shapiro (eds.), *International/Intertextual Relations* (Lexington: Lexington Books 1989).
22. This not at all meant to suggest a deficiency of the arguments presented, but rather point to the lack of stylistic elegance typical for most 'postmodern' philosophers in France.
23. Ashley, 'Poverty of Neorealism' (note 20).
24. See ibid., with particular reference to K. Waltz, *Theory of International Politics* (New York: Random House 1979); it should be noted, however, that a number of attempts have been made recently to modify neorealist theory in a way that it is able to account for historical change in and of the international system; cf. B. Buzan, C. Jones and R. Little, *The Logic of Anarchy: Neorealism to Structural Realism* (New York: Columbia University Press 1993).
25. Walker, *Inside/Outside* (note 21).
26. J. Der Derian, *On Diplomacy. A Genealogy of Western Estrangement* (Oxford: Basil Blackwell 1987).
27. J. Der Derian, *Anti-Diplomacy. Speed, Spies and Terror in International Relations* (Oxford: Basil Blackwell 1991); T. Luke, 'The Discipline of Security Studies and Codes of Containment: Learning from Kuwait', *Alternatives* 16 (Summer 1991), pp.315–44.
28. For an overview of structuralist thinking, cf. F. Dosse, *History of Structuralism* (2 vols; Minneapolis: University of Minnesota Press 1997). There are of course many who will not feel at ease with portraying poststructuralist thinking as the main philosophical underpinning of postmodernism; for a more elaborate presentation of my argument in this regard, see M. Albert, *Fallen der (Welt-)Ordnung. Internationale Beziehungen und ihre Theorien zwischen Moderne und Postmoderne* (Opladen: Leske+Budrich 1996).
29. See J. Derrida, *Writing and Difference* (Chicago: University of Chicago Press 1980).
30. Attempts to go 'beyond' this circle of the self-reproduction of the standards of meaning through language then usually result in very difficult, almost illegible texts; cf., for example, J. Derrida, *The Postcard. From Socrates to Freud and Beyond* (Chicago: University of Chicago Press 1987).
31. Deconstruction, in a way, works like continuously reapplying Gödel's proof to various texts; in his famous proof, Gödel showed that no axiomatic system can be without self-contradiction if it does not rely on assumptions which themselves cannot be derived from within the system; K. Gödel, 'Über formal unentscheidbare Sätze der Principia Mathematica und verwandter Systeme I', *Monatshefte für Mathematik und Physik* 38 (1931), pp.173–98.
32. See M. Albert, 'Postmoderne' und Theorie der internationalen Beziehungen', *Zeitschrift für Internationale Beziehungen* 1 (June 1994), pp.45–63.
33. G. Deleuze and F. Guattari, *A Thousand Plateaus* (Minneapolis: University of Minnesota Press 1987); this is the second volume of *Capitalism and Shizophrenia*, the first volume of which was the influential *Anti-Oedipus* (Minneapolis: University of Minnesota Press 1985).
34. See J. Derrida, *Of Grammatology* (Baltimore: Johns Hopkins University Press 1977).
35. D. Gregory, *Geographical Imaginations* (Oxford: Basil Blackwell 1994); locus classicus (although itself strongly set in a Marxist theoretical framework): H. Lefebvre, *The Production of Space* (Oxford: Basil Blackwell 1991).
36. For a formal elaboration of these issues, see J. Baudrillard, *For a Critique of the Political*

Economy of the Sign (St. Louis: Telos Press 1981).
37. 'The territorial texture can not be separated from the lines or coefficients of deterritorialisation, from passages and relais to other textures' (G. Deleuze/F. Guattari, Tausend Plateaus (Berlin: Merve 1992), p.454 [translation my own]).
38. See S. Lash and J. Urry, *Economies of Signs and Space* (London: Sage 1994); M. Featherstone, *Consumer Culture and Postmodernity* (London: Sage 1992).
39. Rather, it only seems possible to identify or reconstruct such grand epochal designs in retrospective; for a fascinating example of this, see G. Deleuze, *Le pli. Leibniz et le baroque* (Paris: Minuit 1988).
40. D. Newman, 'Boundaries, Territory and Postmodernism: Towards Shared or Separate Spaces?' Paper presented to the 5th International Conference of the International Boundaries Research Unit, Durham (14–17 July 1998).
41. See ibid.
42. M. Albert and L. Brock, 'Debordering the World of States: New Spaces in International Relations', *New Political Science* No.35 (Spring 1996), pp.69–106.
43. See Luhmann, *Gesellschaft der Gesellschaft* (note 17).
44. Even the theoretical literature on these issues is much too vast to be referred to here; a leading outlet of relevant contributions with a particular view on issues of structural change in international relations/political geography is the journal *Alternatives. Social Transformation and Human Governance* (Boulder, CO: Lynne Rienner).
45. D. Newman and A. Paasi, 'Fences and Neighbours in the Postmodern World: Boundary Narratives in Political Geography', *Progress in Human Geography* 22 (June 1998), pp.187–207.
46. See Y. Lapid and F. Kratochwil (eds.), *The Return of Culture and Identity in IR Theory* (Boulder, CO: Lynne Rienner 1995); M. Albert, D. Jacobson and Y. Lapid (eds.), *Identities, Borders, Orders: New Directions in IR Theory* (in preparation); M. Shapiro and H. Alker (eds.), *Challenging Boundaries: Global Flows, Territorial Identities* (Minneapolis: University of Minnesota Press 1996).
47. See M. Kearney, 'Borders and Boundaries of State and Self at the End of Empire', *Journal of Historical Sociology* 4 (1991), pp.52–74; U. Hannerz, 'Borders', *International Social Science Journal* 194 (December 1997), pp.537–48.; A.P. Cohen, *The Symbolic Construction of Community* (Chichester and London: Ellis Horwood and Tavistock 1985); A. Appadurai, *Modernity at Large: Cultural Dimensions of Globalisation* (Minneapolis: University of Minnesota Press 1996).
48. Cf. A. Abbott, 'Things of Bundaries', *Social Research* 62 (1996), pp.857–82; M. Emirbayer, 'Manifesto for a Relational Sociology', *American Journal of Sociology* 103/2 (September 1997), pp.281–317.
49. An excellent example of the type of study I have in mind here is A. Paasi, *Territories, Boundaries and Consciousness. The Changing Geographies of the Finnish-Russian Border* (Chichester: John Wiley 1996).
50. See D. Held, *Democracy and the Global Order: From the Modern State to Cosmopolitan Governance* (Stanford: Stanford University Press 1995); W. Connolly, 'Democracy and Territoriality', *Millennium* 20 (Winter 1991), pp.436–84; A. McGrew (ed.), *The Transformation of Democracy?* (Cambridge: Polity Press 1997).
51. In a way, this is also to say that there can be no 'theory of international boundaries' without it being embedded in a larger theory of society and social change. Most attempts to construct far-reaching conceptualisations of international boundaries fail exactly because they lack such an embeddedness; cf., for example O. Martinez, *Border People. Life and Society in the U.S.-Mexico Borderlands* (Tucson: University of Arizona Press 1994).
52. Equally, no one in physics would proclaim the theory of relativity useless because in most cases Newtonian mechanics will lead to the same results.

Boundaries as Social Processes:
Territoriality in the World of Flows

ANSSI PAASI

Political geographers and political scientists have for a long time perceived boundaries as fixed, stable empirical entities which divide the global space into bounded units that change mainly as a consequence of conflicts. Sibley points out that the boundary question has been a traditional but undertheorised concern in human geography.[1] Perhaps this is the reason why geographers have not traditionally paid much attention to the meanings of boundaries in the construction, organisation and reproduction of social life, territoriality and power, but rather have understood boundaries as forming categories of their own and then classified them on diverging grounds.[2] This has been linked with the fact that the state-centred system of territories and boundaries largely defines how we understand and represent the world and how knowledge of the geography of the world is produced, organised and used in the reproduction of the nation-state system. The logic of this maintains that all individuals should belong to a nation and have a national identity and state citizenship and that the bordered state sovereignties are the fulfillment of a historical destiny. This view has become pivotal in defining not only our world-views but also human identities.

National identity is only one of many, often coexisting and overlapping identities (religious, tribal, linguistic, class, gender, etc.) but it is perhaps the most fundamental in the modern world. Greenfeld and Chirot argue that this identity actually defines the very essence of the individual, which the other identities only slightly modify.[3] States are in a decisive role in the production and reproduction these manifestations of territoriality, particularly through spatial socialisation and territorialisation of meaning, which occur in many ways through education, politics, administration and governance.[4] This territorialisation takes place through physical and symbolic violence, and states everywhere attempt to control, marginalise or destroy various aspects of centrifugal otherness, such as instances of ethnic solidarity or indigenous movements.[5]

Researchers have not been innocent regarding this territorialisation of the world. They continually produce statistical information in a state-based framework and construct narratives on how the ideas of sovereignty and the system of states have developed in relation to changing physico-material, economic and technological circumstances.[6] They also recount how the ideology of nationalism and ideas of the nation as a manifestation of this ideology gradually emerged and spread to replace absolutist rule, and how the rise of the modern territorial system of (nation-) states finally fixed the network of diffuse, permeable frontiers to form a grid of exclusive territorial boundaries.[7] Agnew discusses this acceptance of state and nation as given and calls it *methodological nationalism*, noting that this idea has lain behind both mainstream and much radical social science.[8]

Boundaries in the 'World of Flows'

Many contemporary discourses have began to challenge the state-centred conceptual narratives during the last decade or so – and to provide new ones in their place. The strongest challenges have emerged from overlapping discourses on postmodern aesthetics, style and culture, the epoch – particularly the socio-economic condition of postmodernity, with its emerging 'flow' rhetoric – and, finally, a postmodern (or rather post-structuralist) understanding of the constructed and contested nature of identities, knowledge and 'truth'. In particular, dissident international relations theorists and critical geopoliticians, often drawing on post-structuralist argumentation, have aimed at rendering 'theoretically visible' the constituents of the *territorial trap* – the traditional assumptions of state territoriality and fixed images of the bordered world of nation-states and identities.[9] As Shapiro writes; 'The assumption that bordered state sovereignties are the fulfillment of a historical destiny rather than a particular, and in some quarters controversial, form of political containment has been challenged.'[10] An increasingly critical attitude exists towards the state and boundaries as categories that are taken for granted, and this can also be seen in a new interest in boundary literature, which seems to be emerging on the basis of both theoretical motives and concrete border cases.[11]

The second challenge for border studies has been more practically based, often emerging from the context of post-Cold War Europe and from concrete efforts to expand various forms of cross-border co-operation.[12] This is linked with a broader context, i.e. the processes of globalisation. It is now increasingly being argued that capitalism and the processes of globalisation will give rise to new global geographies and increase all manner of links (cultural, political, economic, informational) across boundaries. This will detract from the role of state boundaries and sovereignty and lead to the de-territorialisation and re-territorialisation of the territorial system. Boundaries (and nation-states) are comprehended as fading dimensions in socio-spatial transformation rather than fixed physical lines. The ideas of de-territorialisation and re-territorialisation come originally from the psychoanalytically-laden works of Deleuze and Guattari,[13] but in the current geopolitical literature they seem to be much used metaphors for cultural, social and spatial change. ÓTuathail, following the philosopher Virilio, argues that de-territorialisation is a question: it 'evokes the challenges posed to the status of territory, our territorially embedded understandings of geography, governance and geopolitics, states, places and the social sciences, by planetary communication networks and globalising tendencies'.[14]

Researchers in economics, cultural studies and international relations are engaged today in evaluating the changing roles of state, sovereignty and boundaries, and in extreme cases their disappearance. Much of this discourse is linked with ideas of globalisation, but scholars are not unanimous about this phenomenon and its effects on global-local relations and on boundaries. Amin and Thrift, for example, argue that 'globalisation does not represent the end of territorial distinctions and distinctiveness', rather it means 'an added set of influences on local economic identities and developing capacities'.[15] In any case, the new rhetoric reflects changing global links, and boundaries are increasingly being understood as symbols of a past, fixed world that will be replaced by a more dynamic one. Accordingly, this process will reduce the roles of the sovereignty and identities of states and therefore also challenge national identities and boundaries. Few have been more explicit than Ohmae, who declares that 'in terms of real flows of economic activity, nation states have *already* lost their role as meaningful units of participation in the global economy of today's borderless world'.[16]

In spite of globalisation, many authors argue that the state will still be the major context in which we organise our daily lives in the future, and it is important to note that territorial states are now operating in a different, global context.[17] Hirst and Thompson in particular remind us that despite the rhetoric of globalisation, the bulk of the world's population live in closed worlds and are 'trapped by the lottery of their birth'. Boundaries will continue their existence and will continue to be linked with the idea of sovereignty. Hirst and Thompson maintain that states remain sovereign, not in the sense that they are all-powerful or omnipotent within their territories, but rather because they police the boundaries of these territories.[18] Anderson, for his part, has noted that 'in some ways the modern nation-state, with its sovereignty defined by familiar territorial boundaries, seems as firmly rooted as ever', and he goes on, 'tax-collectors stop at the border, immigrants are stopped at the same border and transnational (or, more strictly speaking, trans-state) linkages can still be snapped off by independent state power'.[19]

The Purpose and Empirical Context of this Article

This paper will continue from the arguments set forth by Hirst and Thompson and by Anderson. Its argument will be that the debates on globalisation, de-territorialisation and re-territorialisation have raised serious questions for border scholars, but the idea of a boundary has been understood rather vaguely in these debates. Scholars have considered various social and cultural phenomena and their effects on boundaries rather than the changing meanings of boundaries as manifestations of territoriality. Territoriality is, as Sack defines it, a spatial strategy which can be employed to affect, influence, or control resources and people, by controlling area.[20] It is obvious that this strategy is still in use 'in the world of flows', but the forms in which it occurs must be much more complicated than before and there are obviously many coterminous strategies in operation, some of them overlapping and some even conflicting. This is what several authors mean when they argue that we are now moving to *new medievalism* typified by overlapping authorities and contested loyalties between nation-states and other agencies – with the EU as perhaps the most commonly used example of this.[21]

Therefore, instead of repeating much used arguments showing how nation-states and boundaries are disappearing, the aim of this paper is to scrutinize recent theoretical discourses presented in social and cultural studies and on this basis to suggest some new perspectives for boundary studies. The current confusion on the roles of boundaries is easier to understand if we consider the roles of boundaries as *institutions* and *symbols*.[22] This helps us to realise the increasingly complicated meanings of boundaries and the fact that the same symbolising element may have variegated meanings for different people in different contexts.[23] It is obvious that the arguments provided by the extreme globalisation theoreticians have also reflected the traditional meanings of boundaries, interpreting them as fixed, absolute, almost material entities. Nevertheless, one of the major challenges is to note the fact that boundaries are contextual phenomena and can vary from alienated to co-existent, or from interdependent borderlands to integrated ones, to employ the concepts of Martinez. This variation may be seen even in the case of single boundaries when they are analysed in a historical perspective.[24]

Therefore, instead of comprehending boundaries merely as stable, fixed lines and products of a modernist project, the aim of this paper is to conceptualise them as *processes* that exist in socio-cultural action and discourses. While state boundaries still have many of their traditional functions, e.g. as the territorial limits of sovereign states, this paper tries to broaden the understanding of these functions and meanings. This is due to the fact that social action, discourse and ideologies produce diverging, perpetually changing meanings for boundaries and these are then used as instruments or mediums of social distinction and control. Boundaries are institutions, but they exist simultaneously on various spatial scales in a myriad of practices and discourses included in culture, politics, economics, administration or education. If some of these practices and discourses, e.g. in the fields of economics, foreign policy or identity, happen to change, this does not inevitably mean the disappearance of boundaries. It is portentous to note that the meanings of sovereignty and territoriality are also perpetually changing, implying that territoriality is not just a static, unchanging form of behaviour for a state.[25]

Taylor has argued that as a political, economic and cultural container, a state has diverse orientations.[26] As a power container it strives to preserve existing boundaries. This will usually be done by organising foreign and defence policies, a police force and an army, together with education and various forms of legislation, on a basis which reflects state-centred forms of territoriality. As a wealth container, a state will strive to enlarge its territory, i.e. to strengthen its economic space of links and flows outside its existing territory, while conversely, as a cultural container it will tend towards smaller territories, although it will concomitantly aim to maintain the national identity space and, linked with the economic space, this may again presuppose a larger territory.

We will look here at three challenging themes which seem to be arising in the field of contemporary boundary studies, and will develop an approach that identifies boundaries as complicated social processes and discourses rather than fixed lines. Firstly we will discuss the discursive construction of boundaries and the role of narratives in this process. This is linked with the relation between boundaries and identity, the second theme. Thirdly, we will consider the links between boundaries and power.

Even though this paper is mainly theoretical and conceptual in its aims, each of these perspectives will be illustrated by using concrete examples. These examples concern the Finnish-Russian border area, but they also draw on broader contexts, particularly the EU, to shape the contemporary meanings of this area. Both the theoretical discussion and empirical examples are aimed at illustrating the complicated forms of territoriality that exist in the contemporary world and at suggesting some alternatives for traditional boundary studies.

The Finnish-Russian border is a good example of various forms of de-territorialisation that have occurred since the collapse of the rigid East-West dichotomy, and also shows that it is essential to consider the multidimensionality of borders and approach them contextually. A longer historical perspective, beginning from the period when Finland was an autonomous state within the Russian Empire (1809-1917) before gaining its independence in 1917, shows the importance of understanding boundaries contextually.[27] During the autonomy period the border was very much an open one and there was a great deal of cultural and economic cross-border interaction. Using the categories of Martinez, this may perhaps be labelled as an interdependent borderland.[28] When Finland gained its independence, the territorial strategy of the state changed radically: the border became an *ideological* one, a much used example in textbooks of political geography, and there was a minimal amount of interaction across the border – it was a typical alienated borderland. Furthermore, the border itself became a decisive symbol in the Finnish national identity, since it distinguished Finland from the Soviet Union, typically represented as the Other, or the Evil One.[29] After the Second World War, Finland had to cede more than 12 per cent of its territory to the Soviet Union and the border became a strictly guarded line. Finland's position in western geopolitical images also changed, so that where it had been classified in the western bloc before the Second World War, it was represented in textbooks of political geography after the war as an eastern European state. This was very much based on the changes in the country's international geopolitical position that followed from the pacts that it was forced to enter into with the Soviet Union. The Finnish state adopted a very cautious foreign policy, and all cross-border trade was organised formally at state level.[30]

After the demise of the Soviet Union this strictly closed boundary between a small, western capitalist state and the leading socialist state changed rapidly and became much more open to all kinds of flows. It is still strictly guarded on both sides, however, illustrating in a sense the arguments set out by Taylor on the diverging, coexisting territorial strategies that nation-states may practice.[31] Finland's entry into the European Union at the beginning of the 1995 has changed the meanings of this boundary still further, since it is now the only border between the EU and Russia. This fact has given it new functions and meanings that actually operate on spatial scales larger and smaller than the state. The former is accentuated by the forecasts of those Finnish social scientists who claim that during the next decade Europe will be a federal state and that the European Economic and Monetary Union (EMU) is the first step in that direction. This would imply a very radical change in the territoriality of the state. On the other hand, concrete cross-border spatial planning and development projects are now occurring on a sub-state scale, which again 'transcends' the former territorial exclusiveness of the border.[32]

Boundaries as Knowledge, Narratives and Institutions

It was Gottmann who pointed out that political and economic interests are combined in a complex way to form a trilogy of territory, population and governmental organisation, and he reminded us at the same time of the power of symbolism, values, beliefs and ethics.[33] This indicates the point of departure selected for the present paper: that states continue to play a significant role in the popular politics of place-making and in the creation of naturalised links between places and people.[34] Boundaries are therefore not merely lines on the ground but, above all, manifestations of social practice and discourse. The construction of the meanings of communities and their boundaries occurs through *narratives:* 'stories' that provide people with common experiences, history and memories, and thereby bind these people together. Narratives should not be comprehended only as modes of representation but also as discourses that crucially shape social practice and life. Somers points out how social life is commonly 'storied'.[35] A narrative is for her an ontological condition of social life: it is through narrativity that people come to know, understand and make sense of the social world, and it is through narratives that they constitute social identities. Somers and Gibson write that all people come to be what they are by locating themselves in social narratives, which are rarely of their own making.[36] This is particularly the case with separate generations, which may differ greatly as far as their collective experiences are concerned.[37] Great importance, therefore, has to be attached to public narratives associated with cultural and institutional formations and inter-subjective networks and institutions. From the perspective of this paper, it is narratives connected with the institutions of nation, state and territory that are of vital importance. These are typically linked with ontological narratives – stories that actors use to make sense of their lives as members of social collectives and to define who 'we' are. Boundaries between 'us' and 'others' are critical elements in establishing 'us' and excluding 'others'.

Boundaries are therefore one specific form of institution.[38] The major function of institutions is perhaps to establish stable structures for human interaction and thus to reduce uncertainty and increase ontological security, but they can vary greatly in nature. As North points out, formal rules in a society may change rapidly as a consequence of political or judicial decisions, but informal constraints embedded in customs, traditions and codes of conduct are usually considerably more impervious to deliberate policies.[39] All institutions are perpetually developing and being transformed, however, and the boundaries of territorial communities and the narratives constitutive of collective identities are also constantly changing.[40]

Ashley remarks that the important question is not where a boundary is, but how, by what practices and in the face of what resistances, this boundary was imposed and ritualised.[41] This is a strong and somewhat 'non-geographical' argument. We should perhaps point out – as Giddens does – that while borders are in principle nothing more than lines drawn to demarcate the sovereignty of states, their location may be significant for the fortunes of states in the event of territorial disputes.[42] This is the case also with the history and symbolic meanings of boundaries and how these manifest themselves in the territorial identities of the inhabitants of states and in the iconographies of states. This means that we should understand boundaries more broadly than traditional studies suggest. A boundary does not exist only in the border area, but it manifests itself in many institutions such as education, the media, novels, memorials, ceremonies and spectacles, etc. These are effective expressions of narratives linked with boundaries and border conflicts and serve as references to the Other. These mediums are also the essence of the institutionalisation of the border symbolism and perform the key functions of symbolism; that is, social control and communication.[43] As far as nationalism is concerned, particularly challenging objects of research are the practices and discourses that territorialise memory and transform it as part of the civil religion.[44] The latter is important in the spatial socialisation process of the citizens and occurs most effectively in education.

Education in geography and history in particular typically produces and reproduces the *iconography of boundaries*; that is, the symbols that essentially construct the history and meanings of a territory. This iconography forms an entity that can be scrutinised using many types of concrete material, since boundaries exist in various practices and discourses: in politics, administration, economics, culture or the organisation of ethnic relations. These have both material and textual manifestations (newspapers, books, drawings, paintings, songs, poems, various memorials and monuments, etc.), which reveal and strengthen the material and symbolic elements of historical continuity in human consciousness. Particularly challenging objects of research are maps, which are often the results of deeply institutionalised practices of power and representation. *Geography* is therefore exploited in many senses in these boundary producing practices.[45]

The construction of identity narratives is a contested political process and part of the distribution of social power in society. 'Struggles over narrations are thus struggles over identity', write Somers and Gibson.[46] The narrative constitution of identities points to the fact that language is a fundamental element in the nature of identity, where language is understood broadly as including other language-like systems which mean, represent or symbolise something 'beyond themselves'.[47] This is the case with most national symbols and the iconography that is used to communicate territoriality and boundaries. As Smith remarks, 'the boundaries of nations and national states may be determined by military, economic and political factors, but their significance for their inhabitants derives from the joys and sufferings associated with a particular ethnoscape',[48] i.e. ethnic landscape. This has become obvious all over the world in places where various minorities have began to raise their voice and where the dominating majorities have aimed at keeping their control in the definition of the relations between physical and social spaces.

Boundary narratives have to be examined in connection with broader national and state narratives. In Finland, for instance, the border with Russia has been an indispensable part of many state narratives since the gaining of independence (e.g. national identity, or links with the West), and it also has a number of material and symbolic manifestations which differ radically from Finland's other borders; that is, with Sweden and Norway. Even though the Soviet collapse has radically altered the roles of the Finnish-Russian border and a total of 26 crossing points over the border have now been opened – six of them to international traffic – the border landscape still includes a strictly controlled frontier zone which can be entered only with special permission (Figure 1). This zone was established after the Second World War on the Finnish-Russian border, but no corresponding arrangement exists on the Swedish or Norwegian border.[49] While as many as four million Finns and Russians per year cross the border at present, and goods traffic is increasing, a similar, very effective border patrol system still exists as during the Soviet period, and new, increasingly technical, surveillance mechanisms are being introduced. New electronic monitoring systems have been installed which permit more effective governance and control of space. In spite of the increasing flows of people and goods, very much the same system of border signs still exists, including material and symbolic elements from watchtowers, customs houses and flags to barbed wire and uniforms.[50] Most these elements are lacking on the Swedish and Norwegian borders.

All this means that the de-territorialisation of the Finnish-Russian border has occurred in discrepant ways and in the context of different social practices. In some practices the border is still largely a closed one and territoriality as control over space is effectively enforced. Customs operations and control over migrants and refugees are very effective; i.e. although the flow of people has radically increased, control over who these people are has also increased. On the other hand, numerous cross-border planning projects, partly established with the support of EU structural funds, indicate that the formerly almost totally closed border is relatively open in these areas of activity. The Finnish-Russian border is among the

FIGURE 1
CROSSING POINTS ON THE FINNISH–RUSSIAN BORDER (1998)

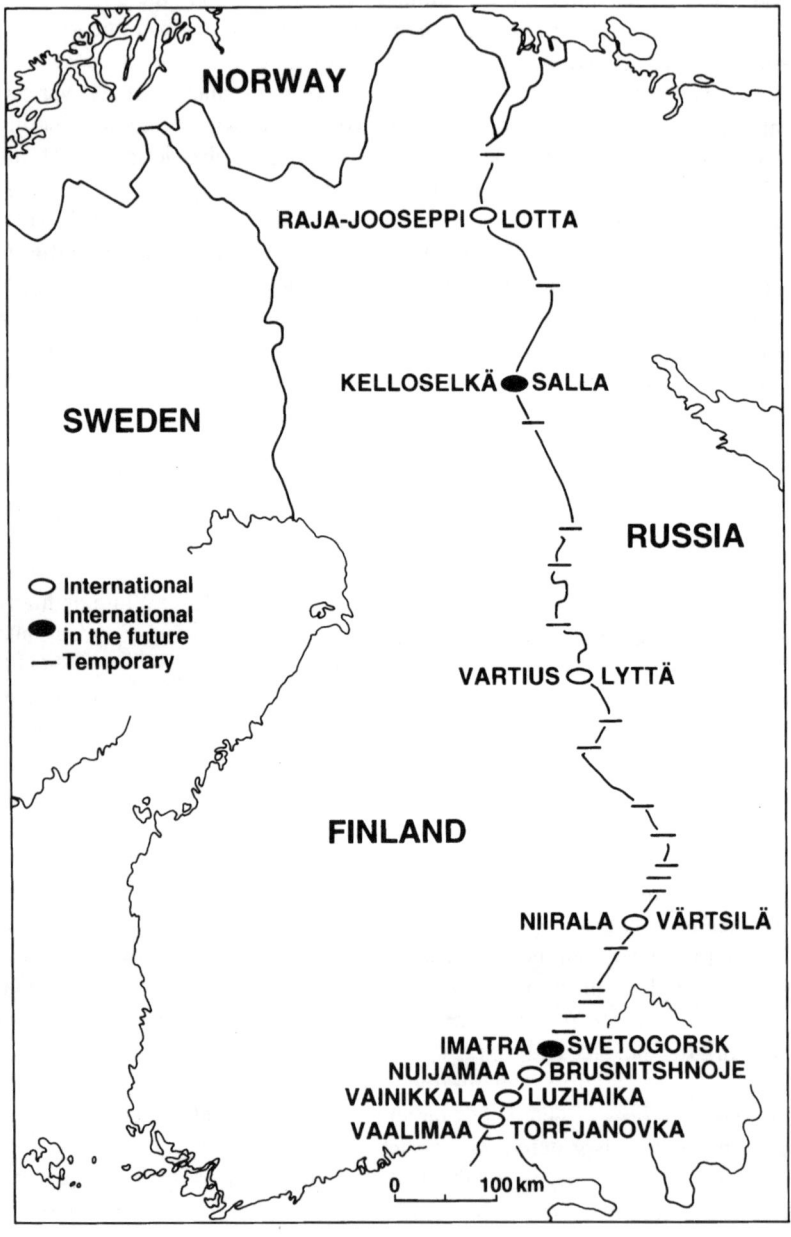

largest thresholds in the world as far as standards of living are concerned, and both of the these strategies aim at controlling and governing the situation in the border area.[51]

Territorial power and control manifest themselves not only in the border landscape but also in places, practices and discourses in which violence, the possibility for violence or memories of violence are implicitly or explicitly present. Typical examples include such elements as national armies, memorials to the Unknown Soldier and military cemeteries in general, military parades, days on which flags are flown, etc. Border landscapes and border guard systems are thus only one manifestation of boundaries, although they may, of course, be of crucial importance. Battlefields in particular, which are typically located near border areas, are often significant sites of territorialised memory, and these may occupy a pivotal position in the national iconography.[52]

All these elements have deep institutional roots. In principle, all of them are connected with the idea of offering or preparing to offer oneself in war for a collective ideal that is greater than the individual, and they form one part of the moralising aspect of the state which Émile Durkheim, for example, saw as one of its major functions.[53] As Gottmann has pointed out, the principle of dying for one's country was already accepted in some parts of Western Europe by the fifteenth century, as was the link between the defence of a country, a specific piece of territory, and the defence of a faith.[54] This idea is still deeply embodied in military and religious practices that effectively symbolise, produce and reproduce territoriality and boundaries, endowing them with a transcendental aura. In many states – as in Finland or Israel – the national army, linked to a religious rhetoric, has a fundamental role in national socialisation.[55]

The narratives attached to boundaries change perpetually along with developments in interterritorial socio-political relations and the internal relations within specific states. One challenge is to study the changing interpretations given to boundaries and how these express inter-state ideologies and links with the international geopolitical landscape. This approach is inevitably historical and non-essentialist: territoriality, boundaries and identities should not be understood as something primordial but rather *situational* and *contextual*.[56]

The Finnish-Russian border provides a fitting example of this contextuality. The meanings of the border have always been historically contingent and contextual, and these meanings have gained varied forms in social actions. While the border is still strictly controlled, the previous forms of territoriality have been changing since the Soviet collapse, indicating de-territorialisation of the border, so that Russia is partly excluded from these new territorialisations and partly included in them.

Territorial discourses and practices at the state level are now diverging. In the broader context, territorial Finland is part of western Europe and the EU (and now also the forthcoming EMU zone) and speculations on possible NATO membership occupy a significant position in current Finnish society, all of which in a sense constructs an exclusive border between Finland and Russia. On the other hand, Finland has been very active in the EU context in opening links with Russia and including that country in a larger European space. Finland was particularly active in efforts to have Russia accepted as a member of the Council of Europe. Similarly, current efforts to develop a Northern Dimension in European Union policy have the same aim: to create economic links, particularly with north-western Russian, in order to prevent environmental problems and to integrate Russia into the larger European space. These links are therefore not merely economic ones but also deep reflections of the aims of security policy elites.[57] In spite of the still strict territorial control maintained at the border, the new spatial planning practices established by the Finnish and Russian authorities are producing new regionalisations that span this border. Thus the border region is now divided into four development zones, Southern Finland-St. Petersburg, Karelia, Arkhangelsk and Barents, each of which has its own problems and its own planning strategies based on cross-border co-operation. Increasing cross-border links are not looked on favourably everywhere. There has been deep scepticism in the Baltic countries, notably Estonia and Latvia, where the Finns are accused of 'unscrupulous efforts to consider only Finnish interests', intrigues with the Americans and attempts to capture transport contracts with Russia. The Finnish perspective is completely opposite.

Boundaries and the Construction of Identity

Boundaries are both symbols and institutions that simultaneously produce distinctions between social groups and are produced by them. Nevertheless, they not only separate groups and social communities from each other but also mediate contacts between them. As Mach states, borders provide normative patterns that regulate and direct interactions between members of social groups, rules on how to cross boundaries and rules governing the exchange of people, goods and symbolic messages.[58]

As symbols, boundaries are mediums and instruments of social control and the communication and construction of meanings and identities.[59] As institutions, they link the past, present and future together, i.e. they construct a continuity for social interaction. This makes the links between boundaries, nationalism and identity particularly strong. Since identity – or the *representation* of identity – is achieved through the inscription of boundaries, the question of power is essential. Cultural researchers in particular have studied the struggles and symbolic links between social groups, and this question is becoming an increasingly challenging one in a world of voluntary and forced movement and exile.[60] Barth, for instance, puts more emphasis on boundaries than on identity, since the classifications constituting the grounds for identity mean in fact the construction of boundaries.[61] Calhoun points out that although the concern for distinction may be universal, identities themselves are not.[62] Neither are they free-floating. Collective identity is not generated naturally but is socially constructed and produced by the social construction of boundaries.

The meanings of boundaries are thus underlined by the fact that identities are produced through these boundaries. They become part of collective identities, shared memories and the sense of continuity between generations. Identities are often represented in terms of a difference between Us and the Other, rather than being something essentialist or intrinsic to a certain group of people.[63] While identity is based on differentiation, this should not inevitably take the form of opposition, of drawing a hard boundary between 'us' and 'them'.[64] This has been the case, however, in many realist international relations studies, in political geography, and more importantly, in the operation of contemporary states.

It should now be evident that boundaries are not 'constants' but mean different things for different actors and in different contexts. The production of boundaries is linked effectively with the social and spatial division of labour, the control of resources and social differentiation. Military leaders and statesmen all produce representations and visions of the meanings of boundaries, and these are all historically contingent. How does this take place? Eisenstadt and Giesen claim that constructing boundaries and demarcating realms presupposes symbolic codes of distinction. They argue that the core of all codes of collective identity is formed by a distinction between 'us' and 'others'. Identity codes are linked in discourses with other social and cultural distinctions such as sacred-profane, centre-periphery, past-present-future or inside-outside.[65]

Recent studies on the construction of foreign policy discourses, understanding them as boundary-producing practices developed by the state, provide one interesting approach. Campbell, for instance, has examined the relations between identity and difference and how they are exploited in the construction of threats in foreign policy discourses. The representations of threats serve in turn to secure the boundaries of a state's identity.[66] The Finnish-Russian border illustrates Campbell's argument. The Soviet Union was the Other for the Finns, and before the Second World War this image held good both at the political level and in the national process of socialisation. After the war, Finnish foreign policy towards the Soviet Union was very cautious, and both the official 'geopolitical truths' and, for example, the representations of Finland's huge neighbour in national socialisation – school textbooks – became much more neutral. The boundary-mediated interpretations of the geopolitical context thus changed radically. This example illustrates why it is of great importance to examine how state boundaries become a part of the everyday life and the (contested) identity narratives existing in a state. This also makes it possible to understand why various generations living in the same spatial context may have quite different identities – they simply have different spatialised memories.[67] Therefore, as far as spatial identities, memory and experience are concerned, territoriality is never a static phenomenon but rather one that is perpetually changing.

Boundaries and Power

Boundaries are expressions of power relations. As institutions, they embody implicit or explicit norms and values and legal and moral codes. They are hence constitutive of social action and may be both obstacles and sources of motivation. The Finnish-Russian border is a good example of this duality. During the Soviet period the border areas on both the Finnish and the Soviet side became typical examples of alienated borderlands, peripheral areas where all links were directed towards their own national centres. The border is the same today, and border patrolling practices are still very strict, but since the collapse of the Soviet Union the border has no longer been a serious obstacle to co-operation, which now takes place across it in forms varying from environmental to cultural and from economic to regional planning projects.[68]

The arguments of (postmodern) globalisation theorists and the representatives of IR make out that the spatiality or geographical organisation of power is not merely connected with the territorial state but may also 'flow' and manifest itself on all geographical scales. Power should not be understood merely as a commodity to be wielded by agents, usually the dominant social group, in order to control all the places and localities within a given territory. Power is diffused in global networks of wealth, information and images 'which circulate and transmute in a system, of variable geometry and dematerialized geography'.[69] Power 'flows' in the codes of information and in the 'images of representation around which societies organize their institutions, and people build their lives and decide their behavior'.[70] Agnew notes that 'forms of power are generated, sustained and reproduced by historically and geographically specific social practices, rather than given for all time in one mode of spatial organization: that of state territoriality'.[71] Power is therefore present in all relationships among people and the power of the state relies on the wide range of sources that it can tap.

What, then is 'power' in the case of boundaries? The major challenge for boundary studies is to analyze how the state-centred naturalization of space is produced and reproduced, and how the exclusions and inclusions between 'We' and 'Them' that it implies are historically constructed and shaped in relation to power, various events, episodes and struggles.[72] Therefore one logical object of study is geographical concepts and terms, particularly boundaries, and how they have historically functioned within national discourses. An analysis of the activities of Finnish academic geographers and geography teachers, for instance, has shown that they have done much to shape people's understanding of the national territory through their representations and conceptualisations, and that they have also effectively developed diverging concepts and categories to represent the boundary in specific ways. In a word, they have produced geopolitical scripts that have at times been put to effective use by the political and military elites of the state.[73]

Campbell points out that states are never finished as entities and the tension between the demands of identity and the practices that constitute it can never be completely resolved, because the nature of identity can never be fully revealed.[74] Massey similarly remarks that identities are never 'pure' even though they are often represented as such.[75] It is a challenging task to trace this process and to see how the *purification of space* takes place through the construction of exclusions and boundaries.[76] Since boundaries are an expression of the power structures that exist between societies, a major challenge for boundary research is to deconstruct such power relations in the form of boundary narratives. Boundaries may therefore be comprehended as flows of power in which memories are transformed into things of the present and future. It is of vital importance to analyze how certain rituals and symbols, discourses and practices of power have emerged, taken their current shape, gained in importance, and affected political decisions. This puts the accent on a contextual, culturally and historically sensitive approach to boundary studies.

Epilogue

'The rise and fall, the construction and deconstruction of various types of boundaries', Oommen writes, 'is the very story of human civilization and of contemporary social transformation'.[77] This argument lends support to the key conclusion of the present paper: instead of simply accepting rhetorical comments on how boundaries are disappearing in the 'world of flows', boundary scholars should be more sensitive to the changing meanings of boundaries. They also should pay more attention to the contextual nature of boundaries and to developing approaches that are based on recent social, political and cultural theory.

Despite the effects of globalisation, changing power relations and the meanings of sovereignty, environmental problems and the post-nationality arguments of postmodern theoreticians, the state will apparently continue to be the ideal form of organisation for most nations at the turn of the millennium. This argument does not take for granted the much criticised realist viewpoint or the ideas on an anarchical world that exists outside organised states. It is based on the fact that the increasing complexity of the institutional organisation and networks of the contemporary world will continue to be mainly organised by the state in the near future. Hirst and Thompson emphasise that the state may now have less control over ideas, but it remains in control of its borders and the movements of people across them.[78] A large majority of the world's people want – voluntarily or by force – to understand themselves as nations or to struggle to create their own sovereign states. It is also obvious that the majority of political, economic and military elites in the already existing states aim to maintain their state and its apparatus in order to retain or increase their own power and symbolic capital or that of their political parties or corporations.

The contemporary system of states entails more than 300 land boundaries, which means that there must be more than 600 collective narratives of their meanings in national discourses and practices. These exist and are reproduced in science, art, atlases and textbooks, national symbols, monuments and rituals, norms and legislation. There must also be more than 600 nationalised or naturalised networks or constellations of power through which these boundaries become parts of national(ist) discourses, practices and rituals, and parts of processes of national socialization which aim at social integration, cultural signification and political legitimation. There must be more than 600 strategies of power, probably far more, through which narratives of boundaries will become part of the everyday practices of life on every spatial scale. Boundaries are hence one part of the 'discursive landscape' of social power, which is decisive in social control and the maintenance of social order. This landscape is not limited to border areas, but extends into society and its social and cultural practices, wherever it is produced and reproduced. This landscape usually exposes the power relations between territorial structures and aims at legitimating them.

Boundaries play a dual role, reflecting both collective and individual practices, discourses and memory. The latter occur on all spatial scales and reflect the division of labour in the social construction of territoriality and its meanings. Territoriality and boundaries may be present in social and cultural practices in which power is virtually invisible. This is obvious in cases such as legislation, geography and history textbooks in education, atlases, songs, hymns or pledges, values, norms and rituals or naturalised images of external threats and in the meanings of these for the respective identities. The boundaries of the identity of a state (or a group of states as a 'we') are typically secured by the representation of danger which is an integral part of foreign policy. All these phenomena are illustrations of the anonymous authority discussed by Fromm.[79] They are examples of invisible sources of norms that constitute the discipline that frames the formation of a collective identity.

It is of vital importance to note that various conceptualizations of boundaries are themselves products of diverging, contested discourses. As Massey points out, boundaries are one means of organizing social space, part of the process of place-*making*.[80] This means that questions of power, knowledge, agency and social structures become decisive. State boundaries probably mean diverging, at times contrasting, things for international capitalists, military leaders or ordinary people – or for scientists coming from various states. One task is therefore to examine how they become a part of the everyday practices of life and of collective, contested identity narratives.

The conceptualisation of spatial scales provides one tool for overcoming abstract dichotomies between global/local or abstract/concrete phenomena. Everyday life does not consist only of a local context but also of national socialisation (knowledge, values, rituals, memory) and participation in a broader division of labour and a struggle over meanings through locally embedded institutional practices. It is through these practices that the forms and rules of territorial discourses are mediated and sedimented in the practical consciousness of individuals, to become one part of their local daily routines and their social identities. All spatial scales from local to global are involved in all forms of territoriality in the contemporary world. Therefore the link between national and local identity narratives provides one prominent topic for boundary studies. Boundaries are always an important element in local action and the discourses of daily life, and in this sense they cannot be reduced to collective, historical meanings that express themselves in collective representations of national identity. At the level of local experience, national symbols become expressions of banal nationalism that are, as Billig writes, 'flagged' in daily life.[81] A particularly visible role in boundary research should be assigned to education and other forms of national socialisation – which are well-known basic factors in most theories of nationalism. This is the foundation on which foreign policy and military discourses rest, and it is crucial to the understanding of how boundaries, territoriality and the nation-state are linked together.

A further portentous challenge is that of searching for new conceptualizations by which to comprehend the changing meanings of boundaries. The latest interdisciplinary literature on boundaries makes it clear that the answers to questions regarding their disappearance are not simple ones of the either-or type, because boundaries are no longer understood as physical, immovable spatial entities. The questions of context, knowledge, representation and power become crucial. Thus, in addition to empirical case studies on boundaries – which continue to be of crucial importance – researchers will also have to develop abstractions to make the multi-dimensional character of territory and boundary building 'theoretically visible'.[82] This will help us to realise that traditional territoriality is increasingly turning into *territorialities*, i.e. more vague, overlapping spaces of dependencies and constellations of power. Hence, whereas authors like Ohmae are ready to declare the death of the nation-state and of boundaries, pointing mainly to economic practices, boundaries still make a difference in the spheres of governance (including the governance of economic flows), culture and spatial identities and will continue to provide interesting challenges for researchers in the future.

NOTES

1. D. Sibley, *Geographies of Exclusion* (London: Routledge, 1995), p.32.
2. Examples of more sensitive boundary studies in geography are e.g. A. Murphy (1988), 'The Regional Dynamics of Language Differentiation in Belgium: a Study in Cultural-Political Geography', *The University of Chicago, Geography Research Paper No.227*. Chicago; D. Rumley and J. Minghi (eds.), *The Geography of Borderlands* (London: Routledge 1991); A. Paasi, *Territories, Boundaries and Consciousness: The Changing Geographies of the Finnish-Russian Border* (Chichester: John Wiley 1996); see also M. Anderson, *Frontiers: Territory and State Formation in the Modern World* (Cambridge: Polity Press 1996).
3. L. Greenfeld and D. Chirot, 'Nationalism and Aggression', *Theory and Society* 23 (1994), pp.79–130.
4. A.D. Smith, 'Culture, Community and Territory: the Politics of Ethnicity and Nationalism', *International Affairs* 72 (1996), pp.445–58.
5. M. Shapiro and H. Alker (eds.), *Challenging Boundaries* (Minneapolis: UMP 1996); M. Guibernau, *Nationalisms* (Cambridge: Polity Press 1996).
6. A. Murphy, 'The Sovereign State System as Political-Territorial Ideal: Historical and Contemporary Considerations', in T.J. Bierstaker and C. Weber (eds.), *State Sovereignty as Social Construct* (Cambridge: CUP 1996).
7. P.J. Taylor, *Political Geography* (Longman: London 1993).
8. J. Agnew, Transnational Liberalism and the New Geopolitics of Power, Paper presented at the Annual Meeting of the International Studies Association, Toronto 20 March 1997.
9. J. Agnew, 'The Territorial Trap: the Geographical Assumptions of International Relations Theory', *Review of International Political Economy*, 1, (1994), pp.53–80; D. Campbell, *Writing Security. United States Foreign Policy and the Politics of Identity*, (Bloomington: IUP 1992); G.ÓTuathail, *Critical Geopolitics: The Politics of Writing Global Space*, (London: Routledge 1996); T. Kuehls, *Beyond Sovereign State* (Minnesota: UMP 1996); M.J.Shapiro and H.R.Alker (note 5).
10. M.J. Shapiro, 'Introduction', in M .J .Shapiro and H. R. Alker (note 5), pp.xvi.
11. A. Paasi, 'The Political Geography of Boundaries at the End of the Millennium: Challenges of the De-Territorializing World', in H. Eskelinen, I. Liikanen and J. Oksa (eds.), *Curtains of Iron and Cold. European Peripheries and New Scales of Cross-Border Interaction*

(Aldershot: Ashgate Publishers 1999); D. Newman and A. Paasi, Fences and Neighbours in the Postmodern World: Boundary Narratives in Political Geography, *Progress in Human Geography* 22 (1998), pp.186–207; M. Anderson (note 2); M. Anderson and E. Bort (eds.), *The Frontiers of Europe* (London: Pinter 1998).
12. L. O'Dowd and T. Wilson (eds.), *Borders, Nations and States* (Aldershot: Avebury 1996); Anderson and E. Bort (eds.), *The Frontiers of Europe* (London: Pinter 1998); H. van Houtum, *The Development of Cross-Border Economic Relations* (Center for Economic Research, Tilburg University 1998).
13. G. Deleuze and F. Guattari, *A Thousand Plateus. Capitalism & Schizofrenia* (London: Athlone Press 1988).
14. G.ÓTuathail, 'Political Geography III: Dealing with Deterritorialization', *Progress in Human Geography* 22, p.82.
15. A. Amin and N. Thrift, 'Living in the Global', in A. Amin and N. Thrift (eds.), *Globalization, Institutions and Regional Development in Europe* (Oxford: OUP 1994), p.2.
16. K. Ohmae, *The End of the Nation State* (New York: Free Press 1995), p.11.
17. J. Agnew (note 8).
18. P. Hirst and G.Thompson, *Globalization in Question* (Cambridge: Polity Press 1996).
19. J.Anderson, 'The Exaggerated Death of the Nation-State', in J. Anderson, C. Brook and A. Cochrane, *A Global World? Re-ordering Global Space* (Oxford: Open University 1995) p.67.
20. R.D. Sack, *Human Territoriality* (Cambridge: CUP 1986), p.1.
21. J. Anderson, 'The Shifting Stage of Politics: New Medieval and Post-Modern Territorialities?' *Environment and Planning D: Society and Space* 14, pp.133–53.
22. A. Paasi (note 2).
23. Z. Mach, *Symbols, Conflict and Identity* (Albany: SUNYP 1993) p.43.
24. O. Martinez, 'The Dynamics of Border Interaction. New Approaches to Border Analysis', in C.H. Schofield (ed.), *Global Boundaries, World Boundaries, Vol.1* (London: Routledge, 1994), pp.1–15.
25. A. Murphy (note 6).
26. P. Taylor, 'The State as Container: Territoriality in the Modern World-System', *Progress in Human Geography* 18 (1994), pp.151–62.
27. A. Paasi (note 2).
28. O. Martinez (note 24).
29. A. Paasi, Geographical Perspectives on Finnish National Identity, *Geojournal* 43 (1997), pp.41–50.
30. A. Paasi (note 2).
31. P. Taylor (note 26).
32. A. Paasi, 'Boundaries as Social Practice and Discourse: The Finnish-Russian Border as an Example', *Regional Studies* (forthcoming).
33. J. Gottmann, *The Significance of Territory* (Charlottesville: UVP 1973).
34. A. Gupta and J. Ferguson, 'Beyond "Culture": Space, Identity, and the Politics of Difference', *Cultural Anthropology* 7 (1992), pp.6–23.
35. M.R. Somers, 'The Narrative Construction of Identity: a Relational and Network Approach', *Theory and Society* 23 (1994), pp.605–49.
36. M.R. Somers and G.D. Gibson, 'Reclaiming the Epistemological "Other": Narrative and the Social Constitution of Identity', in C. Calhoun, (ed.) *Social Theory and the Politics of Identity* (Oxford: Blackwell 1994).
37. A. Paasi (note 2).
38. See also M. Anderson (note 2).
39. D. North, *Institutions, Institutional Change and Economic Performance* (Cambridge: CUP 1990), p.6
40. H. Bhabha (ed.), *Nation and Narration* (London: Routledge 1990).
41. R. Ashley, 'Untying the Sovereign State: A Double Reading of the Anarchy Problematique', *Millennium* 17 (1988), pp.227–62.
42. A. Giddens, *The Nation-State and Violence* (Berkeley: University of California Press, 1987), p.51.
43. A. Paasi (note 2).

44. A. Gamoran, 'Civil religion in American Schools', *Sociological Analysis* 51 (1990), pp.235–56.
45. A.Paasi (note 2).
46. M. Somers and G.D.Gibson (note 36), p.74
47. J.R. Searle, *The Construction of Social Reality* (New York: Free Press 1995).
48. A. D. Smith, 'Culture, Community and Territory: the Politics of Ethnicity and Nationalism', *International Affairs* 72 (1996), pp.445–58.
49. A. Paasi (note 32).
50. Ibid.
51. Ibid.
52. A. Smith (note 48).
53. M. Guibernau (note 5).
54. J. Gottmann (note 33), p.35.
55. G. Falah and D. Newman, 'The Spatial Manifestation of Threat: Israelis and Palestinians Seek a 'Good' Border', *Political Geography* 14 (1995), pp.189–206; A. Paasi (note 29).
56. J.L. Comaroff and P.C. Stern, 'New Perspectives on Nationalism and War', *Theory and Society* 23 (1994), pp.35–45.
57. A. Paasi (note 32).
58. Z. Mach (note 23), p.55.
59. R. D. Sack (note 20), A. Paasi (note 2).
60. A.Bammer, *Displacements: Cultural Identities in Question* (Bloomington and Indianapolis: IUP, 1994).
61. F. Barth, 'Introduction', in F. Barth (ed.), *Ethnic Groups and Boundaries: The Social Organization of Culture Difference*, (London: Allen and Unwin 1969).
62. C. Calhoun, 'Social Theory and the Politics of Identity', in C. Calhoun (ed.), *Social Theory and the Politics of Identity* (Oxford: Blackwell 1994).
63. S.N. Eisenstadt and B. Giesen, 'The Construction of Collective Identity', *Archives Européennes de Sociologie* 36 (1995), pp.72–102.
64. D. Massey, 'The Conceptualization of Place', in D. Massey and P. Jess (eds.). *A Place in the World* (Oxford: The Open University 1995).
65. S.N. Eisenstadt and B. Giesen (note 63).
66. D. Campbell (note 9).
67. A. Paasi (note 2).
68. A. Paasi (note 32).
69. M. Castells, *The Power of Identity* (Oxford: Blackwell 1997), p.359.
70. M. Castells (note 69), p.359.
71. J. Agnew (note 8), p.9.
72. A. Paasi, 'Inclusion, Exclusion and Territorial Identities: The Meanings of Boundaries in the Globalising Geopolitical Landscape', *Nordisk Samhällsgeografisk Tidskrift* 23 (1996), pp.3–17.
73. A. Paasi (note 2).
74. D. Campbell (note 9), p.11.
75. D. Massey (note 64).
76. D. Sibley (note 1); G. Falah and D. Newman (note 55).
77. T. K. Oommen, 'Contested Boundaries and Emerging Pluralism', *International Sosiology* 10 (1995), pp.251–68, p.251.
78. P. Hirst and G. Thompson (note 18).
79. E. Fromm, *Escape from Freedom* (New York: Holt 1994).
80. D. Massey (note 64), p.68.
81. M. Billig, *Banal Nationalism* (London: Sage 1995).
82. D. Newman and A. Paasi (note 11).

Beyond the Borders: Globalisation, Sovereignty and Extra-Territoriality

ALAN HUDSON

Introduction: Sovereignty and Beyond

Sovereignty, the bundling of rule-making authority within bounded territories, is the hallmark of the modern international political economy. Globalisation, signifying an increase in the importance, volume, speed and scope of cross-border flows of ideas, money, commodities and people, challenges the exclusive territorial authority of sovereign states. Rules and regulations have historically referred to activities and/or the spaces where the activities are conducted. In an era when activities increasingly cross borders – lines which separate different regulatory environments – and regulators seek to maintain some control over these activities, the spatial organisation of rule-making authority is brought into question. Issues of extra-territoriality or disputes of jurisdictional authority inevitably come to the fore as spaces and the rules which govern them are contested. Spaces and rule-making authority may come to be shared, but the ways in which they are shared and the outcomes of such sharing depend upon the institutional mechanisms which are established to deal with jurisdictional disputes.

In the context of contemporary challenges to sovereignty, increased attention has been given to the historical geography of state power.[1] Until recently however, scholars, particularly but not exclusively in International Relations, have tended to take 'sovereignty' – the bounded territorialisation of power and social relations – as an adequate description of the spatial organisation (spatiality) of regulatory authority, falling into the 'territorial trap'.[2] The discourse/practice of sovereignty has provided the link between regulation and geography, or power and space, linking power with space in bounded sovereign state-territorial parcels. Sovereignty sets up a dichotomy of inside/outside: inside is the domestic arena of politics and community; outside is characterised by anarchy and international relations.[3] Externally, territories are defined through mutual recognition in the inter-state system; internally, sovereignty allows the state to shape what goes on within its territory. Discourses and practices of sovereignty mark out territories in space and confer the power to regulate what takes place within them. But, as history shows, other spatialities of power and social relations are possible.[4] As social processes change, the spatial organisation of power and social relations may be expected to change too. It is important not to accept sovereign state territoriality as an unchanging principle of the international political economy. As Ruggie complains: 'it is truly astonishing that the concept of territoriality has been so little studied by students of international politics; its neglect is akin to never looking at the ground that one is walking on'.[5]

This paper seeks to put territoriality and borders at the heart of a spatialised International Political Economy. The paper begins by offering a conceptual framework – the idea of 'regulatory landscapes' – for thinking about the spatiality of rules and the activities which the rules seek to regulate,[6] before using this framework to describe two moments of geo-regulatory change and to explain how extra-territorial jurisdictional disputes arise. Processes of globalisation lead to geopolitical conflicts as regulatory authorities seek to extend their rules beyond their borders. The paper then turns to consider how such jurisdictional disputes are dealt with, and argues that rather than simply celebrating the dismantling of boundaries and the sharing of spaces in a postmodern world – which is not a universal process anyway – we ought to pay more attention to the institutional mechanisms through which border disputes and competing jurisdictional claims are managed. It is through the development of such mechanisms that spaces and rule-making authority can be shared.

Regulatory Landscapes

Geographers might be expected to focus on the spatialities of power and social relations in trying to understand processes of social change,[7] but scholars of International Relations, Political Science and Sociology too have begun to appreciate that in order to understand processes of globalisation we must explore their geographies.[8] Globalisation, for a variety of commentators, is best understood in terms of changes in the importance and meaning of space, place, distance and borders; the spatialities of power and social relations. Globalisation, fundamentally, refers to the stretching of social relations across space and time,[9] to 'processes which are not hindered or prevented by territorial or jurisdictional boundaries'.[10]

Cerny develops a spatialised political economy approach with his discussion of globalisation and the changing logic of collective action.[11] In this framework, globalisation is about a shift in the appropriate scale for the provision of public goods. Political economies of scale are 'particular historical matrices or patterns of imbrication between economic-organizational and political-institutional structures'.[12] These political economies of scale change over time, as the nature and spatial mobility of the goods, assets and resources which are central to the international political economy change in a dynamic technological environment. As the scale of goods and assets produced, exchanged and used in an economic sector diverges from the scale of the state, the authority, legitimacy and effectiveness of the state as a regulatory authority is brought into question. Such processes of structural differentiation require new political economies of scale.[13]

Agnew and Corbridge develop a similar approach to understanding changes in the international political economy with their concept of 'geopolitical order'.[14] By order they mean 'the routinized rules, institutions, activities and strategies through which the international political economy operates in different historical periods'.[15] They argue that orders are necessarily geographical, involving particular spatialities of power and social relations; that orders can be distinguished by their geographies;[16] and that changes in the geopolitical order involve changes in the differentiation of the spatial fields of practice, that is, changes in the location, function and understanding of borders. Geopolitical orders are organised in terms of two dimensions: the scale of accumulation or economic activity; and the scale of political regulation. It is this sort of approach which I develop with my concept of 'regulatory landscapes'.

In using the term 'regulatory landscape' I mean to suggest that the international political economy in some ways resembles the physical landscape. It is a landscape of places and actors; a landscape which is re-shaped by actors within it, at the same time as the actors' behaviour is shaped by the existing landscape; a landscape made up of individual places and actors and the connections between them; a landscape which is uneven; a landscape in which there are flows of people, goods, money, and other types of assets and information which flow in different ways depending upon their characteristics, particularly, their spatial mobility or immobility; and, finally, a landscape which is reproduced and transformed by the flows of these goods and assets. Most importantly, regulatory landscapes are socially constructed or constituted,[17] and scaled in particular ways.[18]

The concept of scale is crucial here: 'geographical scale is the focal setting at which spatial boundaries are defined for a specific social claim, activity or behaviour'.[19] The politics of scale provides an important tool to help us to understand processes of globalisation;[20] scale is about boundaries, and boundaries are about power. The location, function and understanding of boundaries that separate different regulatory environments is part of a social process involving contests for power or authority. But scales, and the borders which constitute them, change only intermittently because they are institutionalised, for a time, through the discourse and practice of law.[21] The politics of globalisation, then, is all about who has the power to draw boundaries around places and peoples, at what scale such boundaries are drawn, and what the boundaries signify. If we neglect the politics of scale and boundaries we miss the central feature of processes of globalisation, the reshaping of regulatory landscapes, shifts in the stage on which the play of power politics is performed.[22]

To put the 'regulatory landscapes' approach to work, we need to disaggregate and recombine the component parts of regulatory landscapes, develop a typology of landscapes, and generate testable hypotheses about their dynamics. Regulatory landscapes are organised in terms of two dimensions or axes: the degree of boundedness of economic activity; and the degree of boundedness of political regulation. Each of these axes stretch from 'bounded' to 'trans-boundary' poles. 'Bounded' economic activity refers to the production, distribution and consumption of commodities within a defined territory, for instance the state; 'trans-boundary' economic activity refers to situations where commodity flows cross (state) borders. The scale and hence boundedness of economic activity depends upon the technological environment and the characteristics – particularly the potential spatial mobility – of the commodities in question. 'Bounded' regulation means that rules refer to specific defined territories or jurisdictions; 'trans-boundary' regulation signifies that rules extend beyond national borders. The scale and boundedness of political regulation depends upon the technological environment and decisions made by national regulators about the optimal scale of political regulation for the commodities in question. Combining these two dimensions generates a typology of regulatory landscapes, or geo-political economies, as illustrated by Figure 1. Regulatory landscapes can be differentiated in terms of the ways in which scales of economic accumulation and political regulation are combined. That is, in terms of the degree of boundedness or territoriality of activities and rules. In a regulatory landscape of 'domestic political economies', borders are all important. This ideal type landscape – pre-dating the development of transport and communications technologies – is one of economic autonomy and political sovereignty in which communities are self-contained and de-linked from the international political economy. In a 'global political economy', borders are unimportant; this is a borderless world in which neither activities nor rules pay much attention to territorial limits; some aspects of internet commerce perhaps come closest to this ideal. In the case of 'political globalisation', rules transcend borders whilst commodity flows do not; this is a landscape characterised by extra-territoriality or efforts to apply rules to activities that do not take place

FIGURE 1
A TYPOLOGY OF REGULATORY LANDSCAPES

	Political regulation	
	Bounded	**Trans-Boundary**
Bounded	Domestic political economies (sovereignty and autonomy)	Political globalisation (extra-territoriality)
Economic accumulation		
Trans-Boundary	Economic globalisation (competitive deregulation)	Global political economy (borderless world)

within the territory of the regulatory authority which seeks to extend its rules. Efforts by northern countries to impose minimum environmental or labour standards on domestic industries in the south would come close to this landscape. In the case of 'economic globalisation', commodity flows cross borders whilst rules do not; this is a landscape characterised by tendencies towards competitive deregulation and regulatory under-provision. The development of Caribbean offshore financial centres and tax havens in the 1960s and 1970s, when the centres were largely able to preserve their autonomy to regulate their own territories and the transnational banking which made use of them, provides a good example of this type of regulatory landscape.[23] In short, regulatory landscapes are socially constructed spatial configurations or scalings of economic activity and political regulation, in which borders are more or less important; particular spatialities of power and social relations, particular geographies.

Geo-Regulatory Change

The theory of regulatory landscapes generates a series of research questions about the production of regulatory landscapes, their dynamism, and the implications which follow from the development of different types of landscape. Processes of geo-regulatory change involve two analytically separable moments – the trans-boundary extension of economic accumulation and the trans-boundary extension of political regulation – both of which lead to potential problems.

Regarding the first moment of geo-regulatory change, the theory suggests that: increased potential spatial mobility of the assets or commodities in question, in conjunction with the potential for greater profitability, leads to an extension of economic activity beyond the existing borders. This first moment of geo-regulatory change is well-illustrated by the development of new forms of money such as Eurodollars from the 1960s, although we could also examine the transnationalisation of manufacturing and other forms of economic activity. Beginning particularly from the 1960s, US Dollars moved out of the USA to European, Caribbean and other offshore financial centres, due to a combination of technological change and the existence of regulatory differentials which made potential profits greater offshore. This extension of financial activity offshore generated a process of competitive deregulation. Offshore states were able to regulate their own territories, and created attractive regulatory environments for transnational banking, a process which, in the absence of central co-ordination, led to a game of competitive deregulation and regulatory underprovision. The globalisation of economic activity and the resultant scale mismatch with the states' basis of political authority made the provision of territorial regulation by individual states problematic and insufficient for activities which spanned state boundaries.[24]

The second moment of geo-regulatory change is illustrated in the 1990s by the USA's Helms-Burton Act concerning trade with Cuba which seeks to include non-US businesses in the continuing economic embargo, and perhaps most clearly in US efforts to restrict the activities of Caribbean offshore financial centres through the 1980s. The US feared that the laxity of regulation in the offshore centres was leading to processes of competitive deregulation which increased the likelihood of the centres facilitating tax evasion, tax avoidance, financial fraud and money laundering by US corporations, organisations and citizens. Perceiving this threat, the USA sought to extend its regulations into the formally sovereign Caribbean territories, interestingly by holding transnational banks accountable across borders. However, as US regulators sought to catch up with the scale of economic accumulation and extend their rules offshore, the Caribbean centres defended their sovereignty, leading to border skirmishes. Border skirmishes are legal battles, often characterised as 'extra-territoriality', over the location, role, meaning and porosity of boundaries.[25] As states attempt to extend their laws extra-territorially, to catch up with their economic activity or to prevent competitive deregulation, conflicts of jurisdictional authority or sovereignty result.

Extra-Territoriality and Jurisdictional Conflicts

Jurisdiction involves powers exercised by a state or other regulatory authority over persons, property or events. So, the question is: which state or regulatory authority has the legitimate power to set the rules of the game for the particular activity within the territory in question? Border skirmishes are the result of competing claims to jurisdiction. International Law distinguishes between different varieties of jurisdiction: legislative or prescriptive jurisdiction – the power to set the rules of the game; adjudicative or judicial jurisdiction – the power given to the state's courts to judge between competing interests; and, enforcement jurisdiction – the power to police and enforce the rules of the game through arrest, seizure of property and so on.[26] However, for the purposes of understanding extra-territoriality, it is not the varieties of jurisdictional claim which matter; rather, it is the fact that claims to jurisdiction – of whatever variety – can be based on more than one principle, and that these principles can and do produce conflicts. To put it simply, do the rules refer to fixed bounded territories, or potentially mobile trans-boundary activities and commodities? International Law, in principle and practice, allows that claims to jurisdiction may be based on a variety of principles: the territorial principle; the nationality principle; the protective principle; and, the principle of universality. This is clearly seen in the United States' 1987 Restatement (Third) of Foreign Relations Law.[27]

The territorial principle allows that states have the right to exercise their power legitimately when the events, persons or property in question are physically placed within their territory. This is the principle of jurisdiction upon which sovereign statehood is fundamentally based. Closely linked to ideas of private property,[28] the territorial principle of jurisdiction organises power and regulatory frameworks through the use of clearly defined spatial borders – that is, exclusive territoriality.[29] However, even this first principle of jurisdiction is not clear cut. If a man standing in France shoots a man standing across the border in Germany, both states have jurisdiction. France has jurisdiction under the subjective territorial principle because the shot was fired from France; Germany has jurisdiction under the objective territorial principle – the effects doctrine – because the injury was felt in Germany.[30] In an increasingly globalised world in which money, goods, pollution (as well as bullets) flow across borders, the importance of this tension within the territorial principle is clear.

Nationality provides the second principle upon which jurisdictional claims may be based within international law. Put simply, this means firstly that the US retains some right to legitimately exercise its power over a person or corporation of US nationality even if that 'person' is located beyond US territorial borders. The US may prosecute its nationals for crimes committed anywhere in the world. Secondly – at least in regard to terrorist activities and other serious crimes – the US may legitimately claim jurisdiction over activities and persons beyond its borders which affect its nationals.[31]

Thirdly, the protective principle allows that a state – the US for example – may legitimately seek to regulate activities which take place beyond its territorial borders and which are not conducted by US nationals if those activities pose a threat to the security of the state. For instance, plots to overthrow the government, espionage, currency counterfeiting and plots to break immigration regulations would be covered by this principle.[32] Clearly this leaves much room for interpretation; it might be clear that US security is threatened by the production of nuclear weapons targeted on New York, but it is less clear that the production of training shoes by child labour in Pakistan poses a threat to US security. The line has to be drawn somewhere. Universality provides the fourth principle upon which claims to jurisdiction may be based. A state may legitimately claim jurisdiction over activities which take place beyond its borders if those activities – war crimes, genocide, piracy, hijacking, international terrorism – are universally viewed as harmful or illegitimate.

To summarise, claims to jurisdiction may be based on a variety of principles and so states and regulatory authorities may disagree over who has the right to regulate the events, persons, or property in question. As Trachtman clearly puts it, '[t]he problem results from the fact that each state, or jurisdiction, may have multiple relations with a particular activity, asset, or person'.[33] The increasing prominence of issues of so-called extra-territoriality (more precisely, conflicting jurisdictional claims), can be seen in, for instance: the USA's Helms-Burton Act concerning trade with Cuba which seeks to force other states and their nationals to join the US economic embargo of Cuba;[34] the Massachusetts Burma law which seeks to persuade corporations of whatever nationality not to deal with the current Burmese government; and, attempts – such as in the Tuna-Dolphin and Shrimp-Turtle cases – to unilaterally apply environmental or labour standards extra-territorially, in apparent contravention of the General Agreement on Tariffs and Trade (GATT) and World Trade Organization's multilateral framework. As economic activity spreads increasingly across the borders which have marked the limits of national laws, and states attempt to retain some control over these transnational activities, these laws are likely to come into conflict. The US particularly, in defining its interests as regional or global and scaling the regulatory landscape in a particular way, comes into conflict with other jurisdictions which are keen to defend their sovereignty and regard US efforts to regulate their territories as illegitimate interference. Palan suggests that, 'the transnationalization of economic activities has created in effect a situation whereby the right to devise the laws as expressed in the concept of sovereignty is increasingly "shared" among many polities'.[35] In the absence of a clear hierarchy of principles of jurisdiction the issue is how the international community should decide which rules apply to which events, persons, property and territories? How should power over space be shared? Where and how should the border be drawn?

Allocating Authority

Border skirmishes are the primary process through which the regulatory landscape is transformed and power and authority are reallocated. In all jurisdictional conflicts the question is how to accommodate overlapping claims to jurisdiction. Border skirmishes are the primary mechanism of change because in modernity, power, communities and their values have tended to be horizontally organised into territorial parcels.[36] It is worth reiterating however that border skirmishes include conflicts over the role, meaning and porosity of borders as well as their geographical location. In fact, as we shall see, one of the ways in which horizontal/spatial jurisdictional conflicts are resolved is through the unbundling of authority or sovereignty into various vertical issue areas.[37] Challenges to sovereignty as an historically specific spatial organisation of power are most apparent at the margin; power may be everywhere, but it is most clearly contested at the margin. In the transition from a modern to a postmodern regulatory landscape the margin is frequently a spatial border. As Rosenau puts it: 'the political space opened up by the erosion of the boundaries between domestic and foreign affairs emerged as the frontier where most of the action on the global stage unfolds'.[38] Border skirmishes are central to processes of geo-regulatory change.

Borders are the dividing lines between cultures, communities and value-systems. As competing communities seek to extend their value-systems or rules they will eventually clash. Border skirmishes are negotiations about which/whose rules should rule over which activities in which spaces; they are battles over the appropriate scope and scale of political regulation. Conflicts over the allocation of authority may involve horizontal and vertical elements. Horizontally, is the US or Mexico the appropriate regulatory authority for the Eastern Tropical Pacific? Vertically, does the US have the authority to regulate all activities in the Eastern Tropical Pacific, or just dolphin-unfriendly tuna-fishing, or no activities whatsoever?

The horizontal and vertical reallocation of power and authority, is fundamentally political, with the outcomes of border skirmishes often determined by the relative powers of the protagonists. In practice, the US is frequently able to get away with the extra-territorial application of its laws. However, with the international community looking on, brute force may not suffice. States are increasingly forced to justify their jurisdictional claims; to give persuasive reasonable accounts as to why their rules and values should win out over those of competing regulatory authorities. In order to redraw the borders, to reallocate regulatory authority, decisions have to be made, jurisdictional claims and the values upon which they are based must be compared.

Reallocating Jurisdictional Authority in Theory

Reallocating jurisdictional authority involves comparing the values upon which competing jurisdictional claims are based. As Trachtman puts it, there is a need 'to compare different reasons and integrate them in order to indicate where jurisdiction should be allocated in particular circumstances'.[39] In an interesting and provocative article, Trachtman draws on the transactions costs approach to Law and Economics, after Coase, Demsetz and Williamson, suggesting that the allocation of prescriptive jurisdiction is usefully thought of in terms of a market for property rights. The first move in this argument is the suggestion that 'claims of prescriptive jurisdiction may be regarded as analogous to claims to property rights, insofar as the bundle of prescriptive jurisdiction rights that a particular state has in a particular activity, asset or person is comparable with the property rights that an individual has with respect to a particular activity, asset, or person within a domestic legal system'.[40] Just as markets work to allocate property rights and resources, the allocation of regulatory authority as a set of property rights can also be conceptualised in terms of transactions between actors with different preferences or values.

For instance, the Helms-Burton law dispute involves two 'transactors' – the US and the EU – with different preferences or values concerning trade with Cuba. The US values the transition to a post-Castro democratic regime highly and believes that isolating Cuba through an economic embargo is the best way to achieve this; the EU values its authority to regulate the activities of its corporations' Cuban-related trade and investment, believing that the transition to democracy can best be achieved through integrating Cuba into the world economy. In a transactions costs approach, the socially optimal allocation of regulatory authority is achieved through comparing these values on a common metric and drawing the line accordingly. In the language of transactions costs economics, externalities should be internalised to the marginal point; the border should be shifted – and authority reallocated horizontally and vertically – to the point where net gains are maximised.[41]

The transactions costs approach is – as Trachtman recognises and the US-Cuba example makes clear – extremely problematic. Firstly, in claiming that allocations of authority exist because they are the most efficient solution, and that they are arrived at through maximising the efficiency of allocation, the transactions costs approach is tautological. Secondly, it takes a leap of faith to view states as unified actors with clear bundles of preference and values. Thirdly, there are clear practical and moral problems with placing values on preferences. Can and should values – monetary or otherwise – be placed on the wish to see a post-Castro Cuba; can and should environmental preferences be measured? Finally, even if we can value different preferences using a common metric, we are still faced with the problem of inter-personal, or inter-national comparisons of utility or values. Although it may be that the US values the economic embargo of Cuba, and the EU values its approach to Cuba, each to the tune of $1bn, this does not necessarily mean that their preferences are equal.

Despite these problems the transactions costs approach usefully emphasises the necessity of choice. It may be difficult to compare values but such comparisons and choices cannot be avoided. The question is: which institutional mechanisms should be used to make decisions about the allocation of jurisdictional authority.[42] Trachtman suggests that the transactions costs approach can be rescued and operationalised through an institutional analysis which compares the cost and benefit profiles of various institutional mechanisms.[43]

Reallocating Jurisdictional Authority in Practice

In recent years, as levels of interdependence between states have increased and become institutionalised – for example in the EU, NAFTA and the WTO – the necessity of establishing institutional mechanisms for deciding upon the allocation of regulatory authority and the legitimacy of jurisdictional claims has become apparent. Where and at what level, should power lie in relation to which activities? Within these inter-state clubs the constitutional rules which govern the allocation of authority are particularly important. As with any club, if a member-state isn't satisfied with the way the club works the state may choose to exercise its exit option, to the detriment of the club as a whole. Such issues have assumed particular prominence in recent years as the WTO – and now the proposed and recently (April 1998) postponed Multilateral Agreement on Investment (MAI) – has come under scrutiny due to its apparent prioritisation of the values of free trade and investment.[44] Environmentalists and labour groups have often claimed that the WTO allows little room for the consideration of environmental values and labour rights.[45] This may be so, but the WTO, the EU, the USA as a federal system, and other inter-state organisations, necessarily include mechanisms for comparing different sets of values and allocating jurisdiction. From an environmental perspective the objection to the WTO is perhaps more that environmental protection is not viewed as a value worthy of comparison, rather than a fundamental objection to the mechanisms through which values are compared and decisions made.[46] In the spirit of comparative institutional analysis it is worth examining the different ways in which jurisdictional claims – and hence values – are evaluated and compared in these inter-state organisations.

In a recent paper Trachtman (1998) examines the ways in which jurisdictional disputes about the values attached to trade and other issues are settled: within the WTO, by Dispute Resolution Panels; within the EU, by the European Court of Justice; and within the USA, by the Supreme Court.[47] The constitutions of each of these organisations provide decision-making guidelines for cases when there is an apparent conflict between trade and other values such as environmental protection or labour rights. Although these guidelines are primarily about the vertical allocation of power in trade disputes, they also provide the framework for resolving extra-territorial disputes or border skirmishes, which are conceptually similar in that they are about the horizontal allocation of power or authority. In fact, in practice, jurisdictional disputes often involve both horizontal and vertical elements, with the vertical re-allocation of power providing one mechanism through which horizontal disputes are settled. In the WTO, Article XX of GATT is the meta-rule for deciding on the rules of the game; in the EU it is Articles 30 and 36 of the Treaty of Rome; in the US it is the Commerce Clause. Despite their differences it is possible to see a similar range of mechanisms for deciding on the legitimacy of jurisdictional claims operating in each organisation.

Ideally and by definition, decisions would be made on the basis of a comprehensive cost-benefit analysis which would maximise social welfare, at least among the members of the club. In practice, because of measurement and administrative difficulties, distributive, moral (should you value dolphins?) and theoretical (can you make inter-personal comparisons of utility?) concerns, these international organisations have tended to shy away from strict cost-benefit analysis. Rather, as Trachtman outlines, they make use of a variety of trade-off devices which retain some of the strengths of cost-benefit analysis and avoid some of the weaknesses. The first guideline or trade-off device is the test of 'National treatment'. Such a rule is an anti-discrimination device which looks at whether different regulatory standards are applied to comparable cases, which vary only in terms of the nationality of the regulatees. A jurisdictional claim which treats Mexican fishermen less favourably than their US counterparts by virtue of their nationality is disallowed under this rule. Simply put, this rule says: treat foreigners and their goods at least as well as you treat locals and their goods. A second guideline for the allocation of jurisdiction is the 'simple means-ends rationality test'. Is an import restriction on dolphin-unfriendly tuna a reasonable way of protecting dolphins?; if not, the jurisdictional claim is illegitimate. A third test, the 'necessity or least trade-restrictive alternative', asks whether the extra-territorial jurisdictional claim – the US attempt to protect dolphins through import restrictions – was the only way of achieving the goal, or whether there was a different less trade-restrictive way of achieving the same goal, a multilateral agreement for instance. Fourthly, the 'proportionality' test asks whether the jurisdictional claim is reasonable given the importance of adequately regulating the issue area in question. Finally, coming closest to a full cost-benefit analysis is the 'balance of interests' trade-off device in which the legitimacy of the jurisdictional claim is evaluated by taking all factors and interests into account even if they are not strictly amenable to monetisation or comparison.

Despite their differences, all of these trade-off devices or guidelines for deciding about the legitimacy of jurisdictional claims have one thing in common, a willingness to juxtapose, and in many cases compare, trade and non-trade values. They are all institutional mechanisms used in the process of evaluating competing claims and values. None of them are perfect – in the real world of transactions costs and trade-offs how could they be? – but they do face up to the inevitable problem of choice. The EU, the GATT/WTO and the US Federal System use different mixtures of trade-off devices in different ways. The EU and the US make limited use of balancing and cost-benefit analysis, whilst the GATT/WTO does not as yet require such a test. Proportionality tests are employed by the EU, occasionally considered by the US, but not required by the GATT/WTO. Necessity testing is required by the EU and used in certain limited circumstances by the GATT/WTO and the US. Simple means-ends rationality tests are required by both the EU and the US and are frequently employed by the GATT/WTO. National treatment however, is central to the decision-making of all three inter-state organisations. This principle of non-discrimination is the fundamental principle upon which these inter-state clubs are based; it is the institutional mechanism which makes them more than just a collection of states. The national treatment trade-off device institutionalises principles of impartiality and fairness amongst the members of the inter-state clubs. In the absence of such principles, club members would likely exercise their exit option and leave the club; in fact the club would more closely resemble an imperial project in which the values and jurisdictional claims of the most-powerful state would always take precedence. The institutional mechanisms employed by these inter-state organisations for the allocation of jurisdictional authority commit the organisations and their participants to some conception of impartiality, fairness and justice.[48]

Institutional mechanisms are central to the evaluation of competing jurisdictional claims and the reallocation of regulatory authority. It is through these mechanisms that the borders are re-drawn and jurisdictional authority is reallocated. Once the borders have been re-drawn and authority has been reallocated, the regulatory landscape enters another period of temporary stability, stability which is codified in legal institutions and norms.[49] The nature of the geo-regulatory landscape and the meanings attached to borders have been transformed. A new regulatory landscape of values institutionalised through temporarily scaled spaces and borders has been constructed.

Conclusions

This paper has offered the idea of 'regulatory landscapes' as an approach to thinking about processes of globalisation and the ways in which such cross-border processes challenge sovereignty as the basic principle of the international political economy. As activities spread across borders and regulators seek to maintain some control of these activities, overlapping and competing claims to jurisdictional authority are almost inevitable. Currently, extra-territorial disputes and competing claims to jurisdiction proliferate and assume ever greater prominence in relations within and between the WTO, NAFTA and the EU. Sovereignty as a particular spatiality of power and authority seems unsuitable for an increasingly globalised world. As Spruyt puts it: '[g]lobal ecological problems, international financial transactions, unprecedented human migration, the potentially disastrous effects of nuclear force, and growing economic interdependence cast doubts upon the sovereign, territorial state as the system of rule most appropriate to deal with such issues'.[50]

Extra-territorial disputes arise due to competing jurisdictional claims, in which multiple regulatory authorities seek to set the rules of the game for a particular space and/or issue area. These disputes are settled, and the competing jurisdictional claims evaluated, through specific institutional mechanisms. Although extra-territorial disputes may seem marginal to the workings of the international political economy, changes by definition occur at the margin. Competing jurisdictional claims and the resultant reallocations of jurisdictional authority are both marginal and central. The allocation of jurisdiction, spatially and otherwise, is never socially neutral. When borders are re-drawn and authority reallocated the geo-regulatory landscape is transformed. Different regulatory landscapes institutionalise different value systems. Processes of re-scaling are simultaneously processes of re-valuing. If spaces are to be shared and jurisdictional authority is to be allocated in fair and sustainable ways, rather than simply celebrate the development of a so-called borderless world, careful attention must be paid to the nature of the institutional mechanisms through which the regulatory landscape is transformed.

NOTES

1. J. Anderson, 'The Shifting Stage of Politics: New Medieval and Postmodern Territorialities', *Environment and Planning D: Society and Space* 14/2 (1996), pp.133-53; J. Barkin and B. Cronin 'The State and the Nation: Changing Norms and the Rules of Sovereignty in International Relations', *International Organization* 48/1 (1994), pp.107-30; T. Biersteker and C. Weber (eds.), *State Sovereignty as Social Construct* (Cambridge: Cambridge University Press 1996); J. Camilleri and J. Falk, *The End of Sovereignty? The Politics of a Shrinking and Fragmenting World* (Aldershot: Edward Elgar 1992); D. Elkins, *Beyond Sovereignty: Territory and Political Economy in the Twenty-First Century* (London: University of Toronto Press 1995); F. Kratochwil, 'Of Systems, Boundaries and Territoriality: an Inquiry into the Formation of the State System', *World Politics* 39/1 (1986) pp.27-52; R. Lapidoth, 'Sovereignty in Transition', *Journal of International Affairs* 45/2 (1992), pp.325-46; S. Rosow, N. Inayatullah, and M. Rupert (eds.), *The Global Economy as Political Space* (London: Lynne Rienner 1994); J.G. Ruggie, 'Territoriality and Beyond: Problematizing Modernity in International Relations', *International Organization* 47/1 (1993), pp.139-74; P. Taylor, 'The State as Container: Territoriality in the Modern World System', *Progress in Human Geography* 18/2 (1994), pp.151-62; P. Taylor, 'Beyond Containers: Internationality, Interstateness, Interterritoriality', *Progress in Human Geography* 19/1 (1995), pp.1-15; R.B.J. Walker, 'State Sovereignty and the Articulation of Political Space/Time', *Millennium* 20/3 (1991), pp.445-61.
2. J. Agnew, 'The Territorial Trap: the Geographical Assumptions of International Relations Theory', *Review of International Political Economy* 1/1 (1994), pp.53-80.
3. R.B.J. Walker, *Inside/Outside: International Relations as Political Theory* (Cambridge: Cambridge University Press 1993), p.46.
4. Y. Ferguson and R. Mansbach, *Polities: Authority, Identities and Change* (Columbia: University of South Carolina Press 1996); H. Spruyt, *The Sovereign State and its Competitors: An Analysis of Systems of Change* (Princeton: Princeton University Press 1994).
5. Ruggie (note 1), p.174.
6. See also: A. Hudson, 'Reshaping the Regulatory Landscape: Border Skirmishes around the Bahamas and Cayman Offshore Financial Centres' *Review of International Political Economy* 5/3 (1998), pp.534-64.
7. K. Cox (ed.), *Spaces of Globalization: Reasserting the Power of the Local* (New York: Guilford Press 1997); P. Dicken, *Global Shift: the Internationalization of Economic Activity* (London: Paul Chapman 1992); D. Harvey, *The Condition of Postmodernity* (Oxford: Blackwell 1989); E. Kofman and G. Youngs (eds.), *Globalization: Theory and Practice* (London: Pinter Publishers 1996); E. Swyngedouw, 'Neither Global nor Local: "Glocalisation" and the Politics of Scale', in K. Cox (ed.), *Spaces of Globalization: Reasserting the Power of the Local* (New York: Guilford Press 1997), pp.137-66.
8. P. Cerny, 'Globalization and the Changing Logic of Collective Action', *International Organization* 49/4 (1995), pp.595-625; A. Giddens, *The Consequences of Modernity* (Cambridge: Polity Press 1990); J. Rosenau, 'The Dynamics of Globalization: Toward an Operational Framework', Paper presented at the Annual Meeting of the International Studies Association (1996); J. Rosenau, *Along the Domestic-Foreign Frontier: Exploring Governance in a Turbulent World* (Cambridge: Cambridge University Press 1997); Ruggie (note 1); J. Scholte, 'Globalisation and Modernity', *Paper Presented at the Annual Meeting of the International Studies Association* (1996).
9. Giddens (note 8).
10. Rosenau (note 8 – 1996), p.5.
11. Cerny (note 8).
12. Cerny (note 8) p.598.
13. See also Spruyt (note 4).
14. J. Agnew and S. Corbridge, *Mastering Space: Hegemony, Territory and International Political Economy* (London: Routledge 1995).
15. Ibid., p.15.

16. Ruggie (note 2).
17. K. Burch and R. Denemark (eds.), *Constituting International Political Economy* (London: Lynne Rienner Publishers 1997).
18. D. Harvey, *Justice, Nature and the Geography of Difference* (Oxford: Blackwell 1996).
19. J. Agnew, 'The Dramaturgy of Horizons: Geographical Scale in the "Reconstruction of Italy" by the New Italian Political Parties, 1992–1995' *Environment and Planning A* 16/2 (1997), pp.99–121, 100.
20. N. Smith, 'Geography, Difference, and the Politics of Scale', in J. Doherty, E. Graham and M. Malek (eds.), *Postmodernism and the Social Sciences* (London: Macmillan 1992), pp.57–79; E. Swyngedouw, 'The Mammon Quest: "Glocalisation", Interspatial Competition and the Monetary Order: the Construction of New Scales', in M. Dunford and G. Kafkalas (eds.), *Cities and Regions in the New Europe* (London: Belhaven Press 1992), pp.39–67.
21. Rosenau (note 8 – 1997), p.217.
22. Ruggie (note 1).
23. A. Hudson, 'Globalization, Regulation and Geography: The Development of the Bahamas and Cayman Islands Offshore Financial Centres' (Cambridge: Unpublished Ph.D. Dissertation 1996).
24. Cerny (note 8), p.598.
25. P. Gann, 'Issues in Extraterritoriality – Foreword', *Law and Contemporary Problems* 50/3 (1987), pp.1–10; K. Meessen, *Extraterritorial Jurisdiction in Theory and Practice* (London: Kluwer Law International 1996); S. Picciotto, 'Jurisdictional Conflicts, International Law and the International State System', *International Journal of the Sociology of Law* 11/1 (1983), pp.11–40; P. Slot, E. Grabandt, 'Extraterritoriality and Jurisdiction', *Common Market Law Review* 23/3 (1986), pp.545–65.
26. J. Griffin and M. Calabrese, 'Coping with Extraterritoriality Disputes', *Journal of World Trade Law* 22/3 (1988), pp.5–25; F. Mann, 'The Doctrine of Jurisdiction in International Law', in F. Mann (ed.), *Studies in International Law* (Oxford: Clarendon Press 1973), pp.1–139; F. Mann 'The Doctrine of International Jurisdiction Revisited after Twenty Years' in F. Mann (ed.) *Further Studies in International Law* (Oxford: Clarendon Press 1990), pp.1–83.
27. J. Trachtman, 'Externalities and Extraterritoriality: The Law and Economics of Prescriptive Jurisdiction', in J. Bhandari and A. Sykes, (eds.), *Economic Dimensions in International Law: Comparative and Empirical Perspectives* (Cambridge: Cambridge University Press 1997), pp.645–86.
28. K. Burch, 'The "Properties" of the State System and Global Capitalism', in S. Rosow, N. Inayatullah and M. Rupert (eds.), *The Global Economy as Political Space* (London: Lynne Rienner 1994), pp.37–59.
29. R. Sack, *Human Territoriality: its Theory and History* (Cambridge: Cambridge University Press 1986).
30. P. Malanczuk, *Akehurst's Modern Introduction to International Law* (London: Routledge 1997).
31. Ibid.
32. Ibid.
33. Trachtman (note 27), p.645.
34. A. Lowenfeld, 'Congress and Cuba: The Helms-Burton Act', *American Journal of International Law* 90/3 (1996), pp.419–34; S. Lisio, 'Helms-Burton and the Point of Diminishing Returns', *International Affairs* 72/4 (1996), pp.691–711.
35. R. Palan, 'Having Your Cake and Eating it: How and Why the State System has Created Offshore', *Paper Presented at the Annual Meeting of the International Studies Association* (1996), p.6.
36. Anderson (note 1); Ruggie (note 1).
37. J. Trachtman, 'Trade and ... Problems, Cost-Benefit Analysis and Subsidiarity', *European Journal of International Law* 9/1 (1998), pp.32–85, esp.33.
38. Rosenau (note 8 – 1997), p.xiv.
39. Trachtman (note 27), p.653.
40. Ibid., p.647.

41. J. Trachtman, 'The Theory of the Firm and the Theory of the International Economic Organization: Toward Comparative Institutional Analysis', *Northwestern Journal of International Law and Business* 17/2 (1997), pp.470–555.
42. Trachtman (note 37), p.85.
43. Trachtman (note 41), p.502.
44. It is interesting to note that one of the stumbling blocks to the completion of the MAI is the question of extra-territoriality and how jurisdiction should be allocated.
45. D. Esty, *Greening the GATT: Trade, Environment and the Future* (Washington, DC: Institute for International Economics 1994).
46. This is not entirely correct as the mechanisms through which decisions are made are not environmentally neutral. For instance: trade restrictions on the basis of Process and Production Methods are WTO-illegal; WTO disputes can only be brought by states; and, NGOs do not have any legal standing within the WTO. These factors are unlikely to be environmentally neutral.
47. Trachtman (note 37).
48. B. Barry, *Justice as Impartiality* (Oxford: Clarendon Press 1995).
49. Rosenau (note 8 – 1997), p.217.
50. Spruyt (note 4) p.183.

A Treaty of Silicon for the Treaty of Westphalia? New Territorial Dimensions of Modern Statehood

STANLEY D. BRUNN

The fact that politics has to be framed in the language of electronically based media has profound consequences on the characteristics, organizations, and goals of political processes, political actors, and political institutions.
Castells, 1996, p.476

The convergence of computers and telecommunications has made us into a global community, ready or not ... Ideas move across borders as if they did not exist.Indeed, time zones are becoming more important than borders.
Wriston 1997, p.175

The flowmations of industry, investment, individuals, and information (the global 'I's') have been eroding nation-states, and now leave the world political map as a 'cartographic illusion'.
Luke and Ó Tuathail, 1998, p.79

Three distinctive features highlight the current world political map. First is the speed with which huge volumes of national and international information (words, numbers, images, money) are conveyed from almost anywhere to potentially everywhere. Second is the fuzziness of local, regional, and global politics. And third is the desired access and aspiration to power and decision making by a diverse set of state, interstate, and non-state actors. At the root of these features are basic issues about their *raison d'être*, viz.: territory and boundaries, sovereignty, representation, citizen rights, and security. These are many of the same issues that were raised in the Treaty of Westphalia in 1648 when economies were rural, cities were few, population growth was slow, most travel was short-distance, land transportation was slow, royalty and nobility were important in state leadership, conflicts were rampant, and religion was a binding force among peoples.

The contemporary political map has some distinguishing features that differentiate it from the map that ended the Thirty Years War (1618-1648) and the colonial/territorial land wars of the past several centuries in Europe and elsewhere. The map before Westphalia showed hundreds of small civil and ecclesiastical units in central and southern Europe, including almost a thousand German states alone. Confederations and empires after the treaty consolidated the number of states, for example within Germany and Italy, to more manageable numbers. The world map today has many more officially recognised world states than existed in the mid-seventeenth century and they are scattered on five continents. The world population has increased sharply as have the mixes of populations that comprise the world's states. The distribution of power and influence is more than Eurocentric; rather there are very strong and very weak countries among the nearly two hundred world states that are distributed not only on major continents, but in insular areas of the Caribbean, South Indian Ocean, and Pacific Basin. There is a global awareness of many social, economic, and environmental problems by all world states and their leaders. This fact is evident in the growth of regional compacts and alliances, increased number of thematic world conferences held annually, global topics debated before the United Nations, and references to global topics among leaders celebrating the institution's fiftieth anniversary in 1995.

On the world map there are many new 'actors' or groups interested in politics and the state, some with substantial influence on regional and international issues, others with more local agendas. Both the new states that have been created, and the new actors leading governments or those supporting independence, are often marked by conflict, sometimes short-term and with low levels of violence, and others protracted and with heavy human and property losses. The political world is more than a two-dimensional (length versus breadth of land territory) world, rather politics have become concerned about volume (defining and defending water, air, and planetary spaces). And finally, the linkages, networks, and webs of communication among states are being promoted and developed by the technologies of speed. These advances in transportation, information and communication technologies are affecting all states on the world map, including how they view themselves and others in the world, how they address their own and others' problems and issues, and the form and frequencies of information exchanges. The Internet is often used as the descriptor of these new worlds.[1]

The focus of this essay is on the last point, viz., how the introduction and diffusion of 'speed' technologies are changing the role of states, those residing within state boundaries, and regional and global governmental organizations. The technologies I am discussing include those information and communications technologies (ICT) that 'bridge' space or spatial differences and that reduce the amount of time to transact political space.[2] The 'space adjusting' technologies include not only the introduction and use of telephones and television, but more recently the diffusion of fax machines, video conferences, and the Internet. These latter innovations are associated with cyberspace and virtual space in the rapid (and nearly becoming global) dissemination of email, community bulletin boards, listservs, and the World Wide Web (WWW).[3] These developments account not only for changes in the ways states perceive themselves and others, but how they govern and how they transact state business with their own citizens and other organisations and governments, many which are 'close' in communication time, but 'distant' in ways traditionally places have been separated.

The changes described below at the state and international level are associated with new terms and labels, many of which did not exist five or ten years ago. One hears in the popular media and scholarly circles about 'the virtual state' or the 'cyberstate' or the 'electronic or wired state' or the 'Internet state'. All are associated with a new lexicon about how these time- and space-shrinking advances are affecting the ways states conduct their business and the ways those within these 'state spaces' perceive government and politically related issues. Below I use these electronic, wired, and cyberspace terms interchangeably, as they reflect ways in which units on the world political map need to be considered in a world of instant and rapid communications, and one where the volume and content of information transmitted between states, IGOs, and NGOs exceed that of any time in human history. Authors from various disciplines and perspectives have contributed valuable materials to these topics such as the future of the state and society, ICT innovations and the state, reconfigured and restructured economies, cultures, and cities, and the spatial impacts of shrinking worlds.[4]

The title of this paper stems from what I perceive is the importance of considering evolving geopolitical structures and international politics within the context of information and communications technologies. The Treaty of Westphalia represents one of the major political watersheds in human history. It became the basis for our current thinking and rationale about how states are defined, the legal definitions of sovereignty and territory, the rights of states and of those within its boundaries, and formal relations with other states. Changes in communications and information technology have always been important in the political organisation of states and interstate relations, but in the past two decades the introduction and diffusion of new technologies have called into question many of the traditional definitions of states, their reasons for existence, their uniqueness in a world of greater transborder information flows,[5] and their effectiveness in being able to solve pressing regional and global problems. My argument is that what is needed in scholarly and government circles at this time is more discussion and debate about how instant communications, the rapid diffusion of information from anywhere, the new holders and purveyors of power (those investing in ICT) in the world are affecting political spaces and peoples in those spaces. These themes I place under the label Treaty of Silicon, the word 'silicon' is associated with the computerised worlds of the Internet. The concept of treaty suggests the importance of global debate and consensus on such issues as sovereignty, boundaries, privacy, representation, governance, political actors, and power in a time- and space-compressed world.

I first discuss the nature of transborder information flows and the salient attributes of what I call the 'electronic or wired political map'. These discussions are followed by a description of the major features of those Internet states, that is, those that have experienced or are experiencing the impacts or consequences of the electronic speed technologies. Next I examine major problems confronting the electronic political worlds and describe the key features of this 'electronic political map'. I conclude by suggesting a number of issues that might be debated and discussed in any international conference devoted to a 'Treaty of Silicon'.

The Transborder Politics of Information

The world's major problems are information based. It might well be argued that information has always been the source of problems facing states. That is, when aggressive states were seeking ports, strategic military sites, agricultural land for expansion, and potential energy and industrial resources, what they were looking for was information about where these features or resources (which are information on materials useful to society) existed on the world or continental map. But in the Information Age economies of the Europeanised worlds, information is perceived in a different light.[6] Rather than the location of specific naturally occurring commodities (water, soils, forests, arable land, minerals, etc.), information or knowledge is produced by individuals for human consumption. The state itself is in the 'business' of producing, consuming, disseminating and even manipulating information about a multitude of products, including those about the natural and knowledge-Research and Development worlds.

If we consider the major transborder issues that will confront states in

TABLE 1
EXAMPLES OF MAJOR TRANSBORDER AND GLOBAL PROBLEMS THAT ARE
INFORMATION-BASED

- Sovereignty
- Reported environmental catastrophes (floods, droughts, etc.) that cause widespread destruction to life, crops economic livelihood
- Crop production; mineral output
- Reserves (arable land, energy and industrial minerals, etc.)
- Industrial output
- Global warming and consequences (sea level rise, anomalous seasonal weather, etc.)
- Spread of AIDS
- Monetary crises and economic collapse of states
- Outbreaks of diseases (crops, livestock, humans)
- Empowerment of women
- Exploitation of children
- Plight of refugees (civil wars, ecocatastrophes, ethnic cleansing)
- Reports of civil war and state/civilian clashes
- State's treatment of minorities
- Havoc raised by nuclear weapons testing (previously threats of nuclear war)
- Threatened loss of endangered species
- Human rights violations
- Stemming and monitoring the flow of drugs
- Thwarting regional and global terrorism
- Transborder issues (refugees, pollution, drugs, human rights violations, minorities)
- Cyberweaponry (production and acquisition) computers, viruses, (data on weather, stockmarkets, personality profiles of leaders)

the early twenty-first century, many will relate to questions about individual and group rights, human resources, the investment in human talent (education, reskilling, etc.), the quality of life, and natural and human environments (Table 1). Their salience surfaces when we recognise the amount of legislation, regulation, financing, and organisation that is devoted to the collection and reporting of information on these topics. Examples that illustrate the extent of a 'global information oriented world' include the importance that many groups, especially new ones, attach to issues about the elderly and youth, but also documented and undocumented aliens, the victims of abuse and oppression and exploitation, the marginalised urban and rural poor, the landless, the homeless, underemployed and unemployed women and men. State and interstate and non-state organisations issue reports, with tables and maps, detailing the exploitation of children and women, the treatment and discrimination of racial and ethnic minorities, political prisoners, the victims of AIDS, smoking-related cancer deaths, injuries from firearms, pesticides, and unsafe technologies in the workplace. Economic and environmental information is another major topic of information produced by and for the state. Reports are issued on the outbreaks and impacts of crop and livestock diseases, the short- and long-term consequences of aseasonal weather and long-term global warming, and the consequences of increased losses of cropland and water resources by urban and suburban development, amenity parks and landscapes, and unique plant and animal species. Political-military issues also highlight the transborder information world for many states and regions. These include the legal and illegal sales of weapons, including nuclear weapons, to rogue states and paramilitary groups, the importation of drugs, and the efforts to thwart regional and international terrorists. During the 1970s and 1980s there was much concern among states, scientists and citizen organisations about the effects of a nuclear war and nuclear winter on the world's population and ecosystems. Futuristic information concerns of individual states and multistate organisations will not be limited to terrorism, drugs, and weapons sales, but also will include the producers and disseminators of computer viruses, efforts by computer vandals to manipulate the world's stock markets, and in depth reporting and analysis of world events by major and minor non-state actors.

A variety of interstate and inter-regional information moves across international borders daily, weather systems and forecasts and analyses of regional and global stock markets, investments, exchange rates, and sporting events among them. More specific political information is provided for the state's farmers, industries, and scientific communities. Also accounts are provided of diplomatic visits, coups, revolutionary and counter-revolutionary activities, trade missions, and prices of raw materials and finished products. States that have large number of foreign workers (legal and illegal) discuss legislation on defining and redefining citizenship, granting citizenship for asylum seekers, information of interest to those living beyond the state's borders. States depending on tourism to bolster their economies will publish and disseminate information about tourist arrivals, temperatures, available accommodations and health and safety conditions. Export and import businesses also rely on information produced by the state and for the state. Whether they import or export films, television programs, videos, computer software, books, or magazines, these businesses must comply with certain requirements of state or multistate organisations.

The Current 'Electronic World Political Map'

World political maps that are constructed and used at any point in time have a number of salient features. They contain names of states, boundaries, capital cities, major physical features (rivers, lakes, and seas), and other noted centers of economic and political activity. Depending on the cartographer or cartography agency preparing the map for the state, there may be places on the map that reflect disputed claims and undemarcated territories. An official map identifies the names and boundaries of other states that it recognises thus official maps vary in content, especially when territorial and ideological disputes erupt. Maps are products of the state.[7] State maps may also convey overt and subtle propaganda messages through the use of colours, symbols, names, and materials in the margins and legends.[8]

The standard world political map that appears in most school textbooks and classrooms, and the one appearing in major government offices is a map that displays the world's continents and states in their absolute position. The image that comes from these maps, which are produced by cartography firms in Europe or North America, is Eurocentric, that is, Europe is in the middle. Asia is often split. These maps show the physical territory of the states, that is, the areal or territorial spaces. These same maps, which are ideal for showing land area, have been used by governments for the past several centuries, especially the ever-popular Mercator projection, which conveys accurate shape, but not land area.[9]

The Eurocentric maps and those that display absolute country and continental locations have two distinct shortcomings when considering current interstate relations. First, they convey nothing about the linkages between and among states, whether those be trade, transportation, or communication. These linkages are very important in understanding how states interact with each other for political, cultural, and economic reasons. Second, the maps reveal nothing about the role of speed, which has emerged as a very significant feature in human and institutional relations the past couple decades. Some states, especially those that are connected by information and telecommunications technologies, are in close or the same political and social spaces. Formal distances, measured in kilometers, separating capital cities and major population centers mean nothing. The formal barriers that divided states or precluded interaction, be they physical barriers, ideological barriers, or even expanses of distance, have been reduced in importance. Faster planes and automobiles, widespread national telephone services, global television news from anywhere, and fax machines and email, which permit instant contact, have reduced the formal significance of states. In short, it is a world where states are close in 'electronic space' but distant in formal space.

Boundaries, sovereignty, and capital cities are three of the distinguishing features of states. As noted above, these were important in the Treaty of Westphalia and have remained so since, even with new states being carved out of others during the 1980s and 1990s. Boundaries do not disappear in the electronic or Internet State. In short, the 'end of the state' is not accompanied by the 'end of boundaries'.[10] Sovereignty also exists, although it too is a concept that is being redefined and reinterpreted in the worlds of electronic transborder politics and electronic commerce. Capital cities as well remain as distinctive features of each state, but they also are assuming different roles, not only within their own state, but also as concentrations of information industries and services and communication linkages with other states.

There are many new and more actors participating or interested in participating in state decisions than one or two centuries ago. And many of these are networked by electronic technologies which reduce the significance of boundaries. They include formally recognized groups by the state, that is, those with some official sanction, such as corporate and transnational groups, but also others that are more grassroots and local in origin and structure. Both new 'top down' and 'bottom up' groups have specific agendas, some which converge. The specific causes include the rights of women, minorities, children and the disabled, the protection of endangered ecosystems, fair labour practices by transnational corporations, access to media by under-represented groups, official approval of opposition political parties, quality of life (health care, education, safety) issues, and the production of consumer products that are safe and healthy, whether food, computers, household appliances, cars, or toys.

Many of these interest and politically oriented groups are organised and networked across state boundaries. Their influences are often felt far beyond the state where they have their headquarters, or where they are contesting or protesting a specific issue. They are networked by electronic communication (fax, email, etc.), sometimes in ways more advanced than states they seek to influence. Their electronic networks may influence decisions made by the state through communications with friends and groups in other states; or they may provide financial assistance to supporting organisations. These states not only have to deal with groups beyond the state who seek to influence human rights, environmental, and trade legislation, but also those seeking influences in the political parties themselves. Irredentism, a phenomenon associated historically with supporters living in unofficial territory in adjacent states, now has an electronic dimension. In electronic geopolitics groups have the ability to generate and disseminate information electronically. Thus the supporters of regional or oppressed minorities may reside in another continent and are able to send electronic messages or money (which is really information) to organisations and groups across multiple international borders simultaneously. The above questions raise the issue of governance, viz.: how it is defined and what it means in the electronic political world?

The electronic world has one final distinctive feature that is a departure from the mid-seventeenth century: its nodal structure. Places, be they capital cities, regional administrative centers, universities, offices, departments, and even households, are nodes that are 'wired' to each other for quick and easy connection; that is, to places close by and those a long distance away. A nodal world is connected by information and communication technologies described above. A nodal-information world relays vast amounts of information between and among places about people and human institutions, not primarily about agricultural or industrial products or land and water transportation systems.

The nodal state has a different geometry than the two-dimensional state in existence following the Treaty of Westphalia and the one used to demarcate and identify states on the world political map. Whereas land boundaries were important prior to and following the Thirty Years War, the electronic state is one that is highly connected instantly to places of power anywhere. One of the major contemporary problems is 'fitting' nodal problems into an areal state structure. Laws, legislation, rights, and policies are area and region-defined, not nodal. Thus the appearance of the highly electronically integrated and connected state will not be evident on a world map where states and continents (length and breadth) are displayed. This networked nature of states and global communities is also not readily evident in those maps produced by the state or the private sector and sold to the general public, or that is included in school texts. The powerful ICT state may be defined as the one most connected with access to huge financial markets, competitive markets for goods and services, global decision making, active non-governmental organisations, and with close ties to centers of innovation for information and communications technologies.

Distinctive Features and Problems of 'the Internet State'

There are seven major features of the Internet State. The first is associated with *speed*, a theme understudied in the social and policy sciences.[11] Speed becomes a major element in the reporting, receiving, sending, and analysing information and an element in almost all decisions future states and states in the future will have to cope. And it may be that time zone borders will be more important than state boundaries.[12] A major challenge facing the state is how it can and will be able to adjust to new meanings of time zones (in commerce and diplomacy) and boundaries that have different meanings. These problems face states that have a long history of being connected by speed technologies, such as phone, radio and television, and more recently by fax, email, and the Internet. But it also is a challenge to those states, including new states on the map, that for the first time can be connected elsewhere to the new information-communication technologies. How can they 'catch up' quickly and learn to cope with these new space-adjusting technologies? The importance of speed and its governance call for new forms of legislation, negotiation, and diplomacy. It affects the process of making decisions and setting deadlines, deadlines that sometimes place a premium on reaching a quick solution rather than processes where deliberation, reflection, and patience are in order.

A second feature is the density of information and communication *networks*.[13] These include the standard networks for telephone and telegraph usage, but also those that use radio and television and reporters to send, receive, and collect information. Large government offices have banks of telephones and many television sets that receive information from major national and global news networks and organisations and private corporations. Networks extend to fax machines which send and receive information from multiple locations. The Internet provides instant or nearly instant contact with embassies and consulates around the world. Government offices and military and intelligence centers connected to the Internet also subscribe to various listservs, as do many IGOs and NGOs. The WWW is used by the state to publish information about itself for its own citizens as well as for tourists, investors, other governments and NGOs. Many state agencies and non-state organisations receive the same information at the same time.

A third feature of the electronic world is the growing importance of *visual information*. The 'visual' replaces the word as the most important way of presenting and relaying information, that is, informing the public.[14] Evidence of this phenomenon comes from the importance of television (public and private ownership) in a culture, not only in the number of television sets per household and the number of hours individuals watch television during a week, but in licensing multiple television channels offering highly specialised programming. Governments also seize the importance of 'the visual' by using photographs of events, whether of leaders, conflicts or commemorations, to build allegiances and foster stronger identities to the state.[15] The 'power' of the television lies in its presenting images effectively to many sectors of society at the same time; for many viewers 'seeing is believing'. Groups protesting that states can use television to inform supporters and to engender support far beyond their state boundaries.[16] The photograph, especially the state produced photograph, is also considered a symbol of 'power', because it also conveys what the state wishes others to 'see' (in short 'to know') about an event or problem or personality. The map is another powerful image that can present information of a deceptive nature, or material that is colorful, seductive, and manipulative.[17] The WWW is a major innovation that is used by states to display what information they wish and how they want it presented. This information potentially is consumed or 'seen' by individuals living in many different cultures, political systems, and economies. The state is able, using highly choreographed Web technology, to visually present its own version of history, culture, economy, and human landscapes; in short, to present 'official' information in an ever-popular medium.[18] 'Niche marketing' or advertising is another facet of this visual-oriented world. States as well as NGOs and IGOs can prepare and disseminate information for a specific clientele, be they foreign investors, adventure tourists, human rights advocates, environmental activists, or the corporate sector marketing new information technologies.[19] The question of authenticity and accuracy is often left unanswered, as there is no 'global gatekeeper' or treaty affecting the subject matter or quality or truth of what is displayed or described.

A fourth feature relates to the *new actors* that emerge in and with the electronic state. These are groups and organisations that are using many of the same information and communications technologies as the state to inform various constituencies. IGOs and NGOs are using more than telephone surveys and 'hot lines' and sponsorship of television programmes. They are using listservs, email, fax and the WWW to generate support for their objectives, agendas, and missions, to increase membership, to solicit monies for their activities, and to influence legislation being discussed by states, regions, and international organisations. They are in the business of collecting, presenting, and disseminating information, even it is biased and anti-state. And they want and choose to write their own histories, geographies, and interpretations of events. These new actors are using many of the same technologies of the state, or perhaps even before the state acquires them, to report and disseminate massive amounts of information, including tables, references, and maps, on human rights violations or to alert the public to pending environmental disasters. Some organisations are overtly revolutionary in nature; they may be anti-state, that is, terrorist, paramilitary and revolutionary in nature. Other groups seek to promote change by less violent means; they call attention to legislation promoting women's access to improved health care and education, language training for new immigrant groups, and stronger safety and environmental standards in the workplace. New actors in the electronic state have networks that may be local, national, regional, and international. Local ones may use the phone lines, fax machines, community bulletin boards, listservs, email, and WWW to present information on controversial development projects (expanded airports, megahydroelectric projects, and expanded military training facilities). International ones may use the same technologies to generate support for resettling political refugees, providing sanctuary for undocumented aliens, and for halting the dumping and trade of toxic and hazardous substances. The developers of Web sites and the managers of listservs may reside within the state, an adjacent state, or in multiple states. The time-line of these new 'electronic actors' will also vary, some being of a permanent nature; that is, with powerful lobbies, thousands of members and hundreds of chapters in dozens of countries worldwide. Others will be more *ad hoc* and fade out once their specific cause has been aired or a decision reached that satisfies their objectives. Examples of *ad hoc* 'information' groups are those associated with the cleanup following natural disasters, the deportation of 'high profile' political leaders, and the showing of a Hollywood film unflattering to a state.

The fifth element is *scale*. Scale issues underpin the above-mentioned elements; that is, it relates to speed, networks, and actors. In a tightly networked political and social world where speed is a paramount feature, scale questions become fuzzy. The question arises: what is local? What is regional and what is global? In short, they become mixed and somewhat confused, which poses a problem for the local state, the national state and also interstate relations. The reason is that local issues, events or problems have or can have far-reaching impacts that may extend not only into local areas in an adjacent state, but into states and territories in another part of the world region or in another part of the world. The result is that 'the local becomes global', and 'the global becomes local'. Examples of these mixed scales are recognised in the decisions made by governments (local or national) on education requirements, air and water pollution, species protection, investment and credit. National government decisions made about immigration quotas, loans and credit, business subsidies, and favoured nation trade affect local and regional decisions far distant from the official seat of national legislation. Transnational corporations also enter the scale picture, as they also make decisions about investment, markets, and futures that affect small towns and large cities wherever they have holdings or influence. TNCs often work in close alliance with states at all scales, local, regional, and global. NGOs are other actors that through their own networks and chapters co-ordinate activities. News organisations (print and visual) dispatch reporters to widely scattered locations who send information (film footage, live interviews, commentaries) to large and small states, economic core and peripheral regions, and local and global markets. Their reporters provide information from local places to national capitals to their own international headquarters.

Related to scale is the sixth major feature of the electronic political map, *distance and proximity*. Both are directly related to the technologies of speed and the consequences of a highly networked and integrated information and communication systems.[20] Distance on this electronic map is measured in relative distance; that is, how long it takes to transmit messages from one place to another. Absolute locations, that is, the geometric co-ordinates of a location, are not that important. Places that were once far distant in time can be reached as quickly as places close by with speed-oriented communication technologies. Cities in time zones six or ten hours different from the headquarters office of a TNC or NGO or a state capital are just as easy to contact as those in the same time zone as one resides. Having access to information is important for those making political decisions or seeking to influence political decisions, but more important is having access to the desired information at the same time as those who make those decisions. That government and non-government organisations have and can have access to the exact same information (photographs, words, images, and new Web pages), which may come from distant sources, means that proximity is no longer an issue in acquiring information. Information can come from a neighboring state or an organisation in an adjacent state in the same time as that coming from a government office or NGO regional chapter half a world away.

TABLE 2
MAJOR LOBBY AND INFLUENCE GROUPS IN EARLY 21ST CENTURY

Descending in Importance	Ascending in Importance
Fishing	Health
Agriculture	Banking
Mining	Biomedical & genetic
Oil & gas exploration	Alternative energy resources
Forestry	Entertainment (leisure, tourism)
Auto Manufacturing	Computer hardware & software
Steel Manufacturing	Telecommunications
Textiles	Education
Shipbuilding	Television
Railroads	'Green' industries & services
Military hardware	Military software
Construction equipment	Satellite products
Industrial Machines	Knowledge industries
Traditional Western religious faiths	Worldwide religious/rights groups

The seventh and final feature is that of *economic sectors and institutions* that have a direct interest and impact on the proceedings and shaping of electronic state policies. The major institutions that were important a century ago in the rich world were the railroads, mining companies (especially coal, and then oil, and iron), producers of agricultural products, and the banking community (Table 2). These institutions were related to the production of raw materials for various industrial products. Later the major institutions included those producing petroleum and natural gas, but also farm, construction, and mining machinery, household appliances, motor vehicles and later aircraft. More recently, in a service economy, the chief institutions are those responsible for providing a variety of services to the population, industries, and the state. These include highly networked financial establishments, but also recreation and entertainment (Hollywood, Disneyworld, sports, etc.), environmental monitoring, health and health care, conferencing, and education.[21] The education institutions are those devoted to training and retraining professionals and paraprofessionals, but also co-operative research and development initiatives for the government and private sector. Universities today have networks of faculty and students that are as international as many international corporations. Private companies and 'think tanks' are included in the powerful information economies, be they Microsoft, IBM, CNN, ATT, and Rand, all of which have major national, transnational, and international investments and agendas which influence legislation and markets outside their home bases. How these corporations influence political decisions today is similar to that of the IGOs and NGOs; that is, through information (power and money – both which are information) which is conveyed by speed. These new postindustrial sectors seek to influence state and interstate regulations and to promote the expansion of their own products.

The evolving electronic political world is not without some problems, some which were not conceived of a century ago. At the base of many problems, however, are questions that have long plagued states, before and after the Treaty of Westphalia. These include defining boundaries and the meaning of sovereignty, security, identity, and power, which are not mutually exclusive concerns, especially in a cyberworld. The resolutions to some of the problems may be unknown at present (Table 3). Those that relate to the state include the following. How does the state define and identify itself in the electronic world, a world that is more than a two-dimensional piece of land territory on the world political map? Many state interests extend far beyond those of adjacent states; they extend worldwide for many states and for major TNCs within them. Related to the question of territory is sovereignty. What does sovereignty mean in the electronic world? Does sovereignty extend to a state's citizens who use the Internet for their communication and employment? Are a state's interests only confined to its official land or land and water territory? Or do the legal limits of electronic territorial differ from air space? How do those within a state identify themselves in an electronic world? Are those identities stronger to the state in which they reside, the state they came from, or to non-state actors? And how are those identities measured? Are symbols and images assuming greater importance in cyberworlds and in newly imagined communities. to generate state loyalty?[22] Another question facing the electronic state relates to security. What does security mean? Does it mean

TABLE 3
PROBLEMS OF THE INTERNET STATE

- Government and governing
- Regulating the flow of information
- Responding to new 'electronic' state actors: inside and outside
- Inability to fund connections to reduce Internet inequities: social and spatial
- Inability to compete in electronic commerce using WWW
- Computer viruses
- Spying and surveillance (on the ground; satellites, etc.)
- Empowerment of traditionally disenfranchised groups: women and minorities
- Transmission of misinformation and false information from known (rogue) and unknown states and organisations
- False message, symbols
- Ownership of the Internet (states, IGOs, NGOs, etc.)
- Justice and equity issues: access, availability, cost
- Priorities for use and access and criteria for values and ethics
- Identity (state, multistate, primary loyalties)
- Instilling civic virtue and values (who defines and defends them?)
- Ownership of one's body, DNA, and artificial parts
- Regulating commerce in information
- Compensating victims whose personal information is sold, misused, maligned
- Whether rules of Internet state and Internet commerce are loosely or strictly enforced
- Terrorist bases beyond the state (can be anywhere)

protection from computer hackers and spreaders of viruses or does it also relate to the jamming of telephone, fax, and television networks by knowledge terrorists or the invasion of unwanted information?

There are also questions about citizenship, the rights of citizens, and changes in international law.[23] What exactly does citizenship mean in the 'electronic political world?' Is a citizen defined by place of birth or place or residence or length of residence? Do the world's states need new categories of citizenship? And what are the rights of citizens in a multistate economic union? Or those with a stronger allegiance to TNCs or NGO than a state? Or those with multiple state allegiances? Can one hold multiple citizenships? These questions are significant when issues surface such as refugee status, involuntary diasporas, and temporary workers.[24]

New communities also are appearing with keen interests in state matters. In an electronic world and the Internet state they include more than those physically residing within a state's legal two-dimensional territorial boundaries. They include 'electronic communities' of students, scholars, environmental scientists, refugees, exiles, investors, and retirees (corporate, military, and professional) who may reside in an adjacent state, but also in dozens of states halfway around the world.[25] They seek through electronic communications to influence the selection and election of leaders, the platforms of political parties, and the agendas of non-governmental organisations. Some in academic settings become part of what are referred to as 'invisible colleges'.[26] These electronic communities serve multiple purposes, including cutting-edge scientific research important to states and non-states, moral leadership, financial assistance, information disseminated on listservs which they initiate and monitor, and the construction of WWW pages. They also may generate global support for antigovernment activities, revolutionary groups, and causes in support of leading dissidents and on pressing issues, such as genocide. The extraterritorial bases of these individuals and cyberspace communities, may contain supporters of the existing state, but also opponents who are forced into voluntary exile. They represent an important force or influence in future electronic state politics.

There are also the concerns about state economies in the electronic world. The postindustrial world is one associated with growth in the production and consumption of a plethora of human services. The service economies include real estate, finance, tourism, telecommunications, conferencing, environmental quality, health, and education – all sectors that are information based. At issue are whether states, independently or in tandem with the private sector, will able to develop competitive positions in the emerging worlds of electronic commerce. State-assisted initiatives will be needed not only to guarantee entry into these electronic information-communication fields, but also to retain competitive roles. The uses of the WWW by states to promote these fast-growing service sectors are already apparent. Without state or interstate support in these ventures, some states may fall farther behind and never catch up, or be dominated by other more powerful and richer states or regional and global transnational corporations.

The growing importance of information and communications producers is positioning a new group of actors who will have a great influence on state and non-state decisions. These producers are of television programming and news reporting and computer hardware and software, but also those marketing information and information products for those pursuing leisure, sports, and entertainment, investment, shopping, and education.[27] When global media producers are producing the news and programmes for groups of states, not for an individual state or portions thereof, what are the consequences? Is Western influence increasing its dominance over non Western cultures?[28] Will these producers replace the state as major actors in the electronic political state? And at what costs? Those media products generated and disseminated by local and grassroots groups are also a concern to states, not just those on interregional and transnational levels. These may present challenges to the state, as they have networks that may be more international than officials in a given state. Local groups may appear anywhere on the electronic world map and they may support specific legislation and decisions or they may express disapproval by various means, including financially supporting opposition political parties and candidates, calling for the removal of specific leaders from office, or even engaging in terrorist and counter-revolutionary activities, some of a cyberworld nature.

A series of problems specifically related to the technologies of information and communication and nationalism and regionalism are likely to surface.[29] These include coping with the introduction and dissemination of computer viruses, including those from unknown origins, and dealing with Rogue Internet States who are bent on destroying the computer systems of 'wired' governments, corporations, organisations, and households. A series of legal questions will arise regarding how to detect and thwart such efforts, how to punish perpetrators, and how to obtain international agreement on the producers and transmitters of unwanted, undesirable, unwholesome, and illegal information. States that engage and will engage in 'electronic' or 'wired diplomacy' will likely be faced with the consequences of making decisions quickly, often with incomplete and potentially inaccurate information. They also may question the merits of 'virtual diplomacy' to solve ticklish economic and political problems, perhaps choosing to rely on face-to-face and shuttle diplomacy instead of close circuit television or teleconferencing or exchanging a blizzard of faxes. Two related problems that electronic states will face deal with the values one might instill with the introduction and diffusion of these ICTs and with the 'social gaps' that emerge with the adoption of these technological innovations. Is it possible for a state to use the WWW, electronic listservs, and technologies of the Internet to foster new and renewed identities? Or will users of these services become less attached to states and more to non-state or trans-state organizations or no identity whatsoever. Regarding technology 'gaps', will states be able to reduce the social and spatial 'gaps' that will emerge with uses and users? Or will they choose not to, with the result being others, perhaps corporations and NGOs, assuming the role of providing strategies to reduce the differences? The social implications of these state and private supported technologies, including GIS and the constraints on its diffusion, are worth examining just as much in newly independent states as in the early stages of cyberdemocracy.[30]

A final problem is that not all states will choose to or be able to enter the Internet world. That is, future world political maps will still contain states and regions within them that are not receiving or benefiting from the recent and anticipated advances in electronic information and communication. Their leaders may choose not to participate for ideological or personal reasons. Governments may not be able to afford the infrastructure that is required to be linked and become competitive. And some governments may also refuse proposals and incentives by interstate and inter-regional governmental and non-governmental organisations to assist their entry into an Internet world. The result of these variances in adoption and adaptation will be political worlds in which many or most places will be connected, and other places will not.

What the 'Electronic Political World Map' Would Look Like

The electronic political world map will have a different appearance than the world projections we are used to, with Europe or North America in the centre and a 'split'Asia. They will also be different from maps of the European impress on major world regions.[31] It is best not to consider only one map, but several (Table 4). In a highly connected electronic state that is wired for multiple uses, there will be information transmitted through a variety of different modes. These include telephone and television as well as fax, e.mail, and the growing popularity of wireless communication. There will be some states that will have well-developed and integrated information and communications networks. Their largest cities and largest universities and military/security bases will be connected, as will cities with large corporate offices.[32] The resulting electronic political map will have a patchwork quilt pattern; that is, some depressions, perhaps even deep 'sinks' that reflect places that are not connected. These state disparities will also exist among NGOs and IGOs. While there will be some states that are highly developed, the 'peaks' on the map, there will be others that have many fewer connections. These may be states that do not have the financial resources to invest in internet connections, or places that assign it a low priority for investment, or those that have not been provided for such investments by international organisations and lending institutions. These little or unconnected states may only have their capital cities, or portions thereof, military bases, selected universities, and residences of key political figures connected. This unevenness, even though it exists today, may become more irregular in the next twenty-five years.[33]

One might consider a seven-fold classification of states: innovative ICT states, heavily linked, meso-linked states, unlinked states, rogue (terrorist) states, rump (*ad hoc* states), laggards or luddites (among the last to have ICT). The last category would include those states that refuse for religious, ideological or cultural reasons. This is only a projected classification and proposed labels; it is doubtful if they would be accepted by the international community. But what is probably more significant is how the powerful states, where power is defined in the sense of producing and disseminating ICT and directing global ICT policies, would look at the world. One might even contemplate those powerful states and major IGOs, which are connected with global issues of human welfare and environmental protection as well as finance, policing, military/security, using these labels

TABLE 4
WHAT THE ELECTRONIC POLITICAL WORLD MAP WOULD LOOK LIKE

- Great unevenness in governments: clashes, conflicts, stability, rigidity
- Some places in states (cities, military sites, R and D facilities) heavily connected; others not; some states will be more connected to other states than to regions in their own state
- Patchwork pattern of connected states (some heavily connected; dense patterns; others 'deep' holes)
- Major information and communications flows between rich states and between world capitals
- Emergence of 'electronic irredentism' (places connected to areas beyond official state territories)
- Various boundaries: new boundaries for new states; relict; artificial, permeable, impermeable
- Reconfiguration of states: some new; some parts of old states in new states; some parts of new states in old states; existing states; renamed states
- Variety of networks: local, national, regional and global; intra and interregional and multiregional; temporary and permanent; top-down and grassroots
- Multiple information classifications: innovative, heavily linked; unlinked; rogue; rump (ad hoc); laggards, luddites
- Various gatekeepers: regional, interregional, global; inside and outside states
- Global intelligence agencies
- Ultranationalist groups: to retain the past and identities; preserve boundaries, traditional loyalties
- Transnational corporations in some states more powerful than some states; they are connected before many states and use ICTs more than states
- Distribution of power: ICT linkages; information produced, consumed, and moved

of states and peoples within them to promote their own agendas regarding acceptable 'information economies and cultures'. A result might be assisting those they like and agree to their 'norms', and initiating punitive actions against whose ideologies and information geopolitics run counter to their 'info rich' agendas. (A parallel might be the uses of various 'World' classes used by states and scholars between the 1960s and 1980s, remnants of which thinking still persists today.)

A second feature of these electronic political maps will identify the various actors that will become a part of state and interstate dialogue and decisions. These will include organisations and groups within a state itself, but increasingly those in adjacent states and far beyond. The phenomenon of 'electronic territorial aggrandisement' described above will become a more dominant feature in the political landscape. These may be comprised of exiles in widely scattered locations or non-state actors with strong interests in a state's human rights, religious, environmental, and cultural decisions. These can and could be located anywhere. These groups, IGOs and NGOs, will be successful in part because of their ability to provide information for groups within a state, financial resources to support their initiatives, and electronic communication modes which may be in excess what a given state can or will be able to do.

This last point raises the issue about who will be the important actors in the electronic political world? There are likely to be several. Some rich and large states will continue to be important, but they will be challenged by powerful, influential and well-organised groups and actors who have a strong interest in the state. Included will be major information and communications corporations that have extensive global connections. They will be providing hardware and software for ICT, leisure and entertainment (films, videos, etc.), seductive advertising campaigns (perhaps even for the state), and organisations committed to selected agendas, for example, improving the human rights of oppressed people, preserving biodiversity, eliminating the testing of laser weapons, and removing trade barriers with those of differing ideologies. One might even consider a political map as displaying the gatekeepers of information, the producers, the consumers, the transmitters (how information is moved), and the manipulators. It is also very likely that transnational corporations in some states will be stronger than individual states, and even stronger than these TNC are currently. That situation will become more widespread because many TNCs will have the technology before states and because states require time and legislation to invest in the technology and to devise and use it effectively for the purposes of government.

The unevenness feature described above will be a feature similar to the present world of electronic politics and commerce. Another striking feature of the map will be the permanency of some boundaries and state names. New names of political units will certainly appear and new states (smaller) will be carved out of existing ones, because of the successes (revolutionary and non-violent) of autonomous groups who desire their own space and to have control of their own destiny. There will be many states that will have the same name as today, even if their territory is reduced or they have a 'pockmarked' or archipelagic appearance. Boundaries will persist on the world map, even though some will devolve in importance with electronic communication and selected relict features (state boundaries, names, and capital cities) will be much in evidence, as they are today.

Elements of a Treaty of Silicon

Treaties emerge when multiple states have conflicting views on how to resolve conflicts, when states recognise the need for a diverse set of states to have a role in international or regional agreements, and when large powerful and dominant states seek to impose their 'national interests' to regions they wish to control. International treaties during the last quarter of the twentieth century have covered issues about the world's oceans, biodiversity, global warming, and ozone depletion, to name but a few.

Global conferences have also been held on these topics, as well as human settlement, refugees, women, children, and the disabled. Resolutions passed at these conferences often become the basis for resolutions appearing in regional and international treaties. Heightened international interests in information processing and telecommunications by government and TNCs are among the items currently discussed in state and interstate conferences and conventions.

The idea of a Treaty of Silicon signals the need for an international discussion around the issues raised above. A number of issues will need to be discussed among the world's states, IGOs and NGOs (Table 5). Twelve that appear to be of crucial importance for wired and non-wired states, rich and poor states, old and new, powerful and powerless states, are the following:

1. The ownership (intellectual property) of information, information resources (data banks, etc.), and communications delivery systems.
2. Surveillance and spying, by and for the state, by and for non-state actors, including NGOs with good intentions, IGOs with an interest in citizen opinions, and pro- and anti-state actors.
3. Policing, monitoring, and regulating the producers and providers of information and communications technologies to prevent destabilisation of the state, control of information economies globally and violation of individual and group privacy.
4. Preventing and combating a series of cybercrime issues, including crimes by "fiber vandals" (against individuals and property), cyberterrorism and cyberwar, which promise to become realities with each successive decade and greater uses of the Internet by individuals, groups, companies, and states.
5. Issues of equity, to ensure that states and citizens are not shut out or eliminated from access to and availability of the Internet, an issue that will be a social and political problem in many states, from wired to unwired.
6. Establishing security pacts among states, non-state actors, and transnational corporations for protection from rogue states, terrorist organisations, and knowledge vandals.
7. Regulating the production and flow of information that moves across interstate and interregional boundaries of a violent, exploitative, vituperative, and insensitive nature.
8. Deciding whether the rules of Internet use by the world's states and non-states will be loosely or strictly enforced and how this is to be done – by implanting viruses or destroying the infrastructure?
9. Compensating victims (individuals, groups, and states) whose lives,

livelihoods, and cultures have been destroyed, manipulated, or persecuted by the misuse (privacy, exploitation, threat) of information technologies.
10. Ownership of personal information, including one's genetic code, body and artificial parts.[34]
11. Establishing cross-cultural and international codes of conduct for Internet use that will apply to individuals, non-state groups, and states participating in interstate, inter-regional, and transnational commerce and communication.
12. Strategies to resolve territorial and extraterritorial disputes arising from questions of cyberpolitics and cyberculture, especially whether we will be discussing increasingly shared or separate spaces.[35]

TABLE 5
MAJOR ELEMENTS IN A TREATY OF SILICON

- How power will be defined (information, communication, access and accumulation)
- Violators of electronic space: states, NGOs, IGOs, revolutionary groups, rouge groups and states
- Spying and surveillance
- Policing and monitoring the state
- Policing, monitoring, and regulating ICT producers and providers
- Security pacts (controls, regulations, etc.)
- Prevention of cyberterrorism
- Combating cyberwar
- Equity issues: availability and accessibility
- Ownership issues of information, resources, delivery systems
- Role of gatekeepers
- Access to data banks (collected by states, for states, by and for individuals)
- Non-state actors (state supporters and revolutionaries; permanent or *ad hoc*)
- Regulating the production and flow of data and information commerce
- Codes of conduct for Internet use

Two additional and significant questions (perhaps these should be in the 'problem' discussion above) about a Treaty of Silicon that need to be addressed are: who will sign it and where will it be signed? (If 'signing' in a traditional sense will be done in the world of the Internet!) The signatories will not be the same as those who fashioned the Treaty of Westphalia, who were heads of states, but also military heroes, royalty and nobility, landed gentry, and church leaders. In view of the many parties that would have an interest in the geopolitical issues of cyberspace, I would suggest that the signatories would include more than heads of states, but also producers of global information and communication technologies, and leaders of large regional and global NGOs concerned with issues facing the information economies. Those in the later group might include groups with strong human rights, women and children, environmental, spiritual, security, and representation interests. Also those with interests in the preservation of sacred spaces and traditional *genre de vie*, newly 'electronically' tribalised spaces, vast holdings in finance, entertainment, and data collection, and newly franchised groups need merit inclusion. In regards to location, in one sense it might be argued that location is irrelevant, as, in a cyberspace world, any place would be as appropriate as any other. But a stronger and probably more convincing position might be to identify some new place on the planet that symbolises electronic politics, commerce, and society and also has an image for the future. Among the possible sites to sign a Treaty of Silicon would be major international information cities, such as Brussels, Geneva, Los Angeles, or New York, or sites that are the current and emerging locales of global information and communication technology production. The treaty might be signed in Silicon Valley, California, but also similar high-tech sites in Brazil, South Asia, Japan, and Europe. Or best might be to have a treaty (whether 'paper' or in digital form) signed in multiple locations simultaneously.

Summary and Looking Ahead

The technological innovations associated with information production and dissemination and the rapid and instant communication networks are affecting the role of the state and its functions at local and global scales. While issues of boundaries, sovereignty, identity, representation, power, and alliances remain important, they assume some additional significance in a world where speed, instant communication, new and multiple state and non-state actors are characteristic. What is discussed above is the need for social and policy scientists to explore the underpinnings of these Internet worlds and their impresses of those information and communication developments on individuals, groups, and states. The thesis advanced is that there is a need for a Treaty of Silicon, a concept characterising these developments, in which the existing and potential developers and adopters of these technologies begin to address crucial questions about rights, representation, sovereignty, and boundaries. Through such deliberations will the states fashion their roles in the next century.

Three questions merit the attention of those social, policy, and environmental scientists interested in the interfaces between the Internet and geopolitics. The first is how states will address sovereignty, boundary, human rights, and governance in a world where global information systems and increased volumes of information are challenging the very nature of identity, loyalty, and allegiance to state-centred political units. The second is whether international and inter-regional aid programmes that are designed to reduce the 'information and communication gaps' across regions, classes, and cultures will be successful. If not, what realistic alternative scenarios can be implemented to bring about more evenness? The third tantalising question is whether there will be a backlash against these ICTs by non-European cultures, whose presence is increasing on the world's economic, cultural, and political scenes.[36] And if this occurs, what will be the ramifications of these clashes on existing states, pan-regions, and global policy making? Anticipated answers to these and other questions raised above suggest the need for increased scholarly and policy discussion on the geopolitics of the Internet state and world.

NOTES

1. S. D. Brunn, 'The Internet as "The New World" of and for Geography: Speed, Structures, Volumes, Humility and Civility', *GeoJournal* 45 (1998), pp.5–15.
2. R. Abler *et al.*, *Human Geography in a Shrinking World* (North Scituate, MA: Duxbury Press 1974); S.D. Brunn and T.R. Leinbach (eds.), *Collapsing Space and Time: Geographic Aspects of Information and Communication* (New York: HarperCollins and Routledge 1991); and D.J. Janelle, 'Global Interdependence and Its Consequences', in S.D. Brunn and T.R. Leinbach (eds.) ibid., pp.49–81.
3. B. Gates, *The Road Ahead* (New York: Viking 1995).
4. S.D. Brunn, 'Future of the Nation-State System', in P.J. Taylor and J. House (eds.) *Political Geography: Recent Advances and Future Directions* (London: Croom-Helm 1984), pp.149–67; S.D. Brunn and J.A. Jones, 'Geopolitical Information and Communication in Shrinking and Expanding Worlds: 1900-2100', in G.J. Demko and W.B. Wood (eds.) *Reordering the World: Geopolitical Perspectives on the Twenty-first Century* (Boulder, CO: Westview 1994), pp.301–22; D. Porter, *Internet Culture* (London: Routledge 1997); K. Ohmae, *The Borderless World: Power and Strategy in the Interlinked Economy* (New York: Harper and Row 1990) and his *The End of the Nation State. The Rise of Regional Economics* (New York: Free Press 1995); D. Holmes (ed.), *Virtual Politics. Identity and Community in Cyberspace* (London: Sage 1997).
5. T.W. Luke and G. O'Tuathail, 'Global Flowmations, Local Fundamentalisms, and Fast Geopolitics: "America" in an Accelerating World Order', in A. Herod, G. O'Tuathail and S. M. Roberts (eds.), *Unruly Worlds: Globalization, Governance, and Geography* (New York and London: Routledge 1998), pp.72–94.
6. M. Poster, *The Mode of Information: Poststructuralism and Social Context* (Chicago: University of Chicago Press 1990) and *The Second Media Age* (Chicago: University of Chicago Press 1995).
7. A.K. Henrikson, 'The Power and Politics of Maps', in Demko and Wood (note 4), pp.49–70.
8. J. Pickles, 'Hermeneutics and Propaganda Maps', in T.J. Barnes and J.S. Duncan (eds.) *Writing Worlds: Discourse, Text, and Metaphor in the Representation of Landscape* (London and New York: Routledge 1992), pp.192–230.
9. M. Lewis and K. Wigen, *The Myth of Continents: A Critique of Metageography* (Berkeley: University of California 1997).
10. D. Newman, 'Boundaries, Territory and Postmodernism: Towards Shared or Separate Spaces', in G. Blake *et al.* (eds) *Borderlands Under Stress*. (Kluwer Law International, London, forthcoming).
11. P. Virilio, *Speed and Politics: An Essay in Dromology*. Trans. M. Polizzotti (Minneapolis: University of Minnesota Press 1986) and *The Art of the Motor*, trans. J. Rose (Minneapolis: University of Minnesota Press 1996).
12. W.B. Wriston, 'Bits, Bytes, and Diplomacy', *Foreign Affairs* 765 (1997), pp.172–82.

13. M. Castells. *The Rise of the Network Society* (Malden, MA and Oxford, UK: Basil Blackwell 1996).
14. J.B. Harley, 'Maps, Knowledge, and Power', in D. Cosgrove and P. Daniels (eds.) *The Iconography of Landscape* (Cambridge: Cambridge University Press 1988), pp. 277–312 and 'Deconstructing the Map', in Barnes and Duncan, op. cit., pp.221–47; M. Wark, *Virtual Geography. Living with Global Media and Events* (Bloomington, IN: Indiana University Press 1994).
15. J. Neuman, *Lights, Camera, War: Is Media Technology Driving International Politics?* (New York: St. Martin's Press 1996).
16. P. Adams, 'Protest and Scale Politics of Transformation', *Political Geography* 15 (1996), pp.419–44.
17. Harley, 1988, 1992, op. cit.; K.C. Clarke, 'Maps and Mapping Techniques of the Persian Gulf War', *Cartographic and Geographic Information Systems* 19 (1992), pp.80–7.
18. M.J. Cronin, *Global Advantage on the Internet: From Corporate Connectivity to International Competitiveness* (New York: Van Nostrand Reinhold 1996); S.D. Brunn and C.D. Cottle, 'Small States and Cyberboosterism', *Geographical Review* 87 (1997), pp.240–58.
19. S.M. Roberts and R.H. Schein, 'Earth Shattering: Global Imagery and GIS', in J. Pickles (ed.) *Ground Truth: The Social Implications of GIS* (New York and London: Guilford Press 1996), pp.171–95.
20. A. Toffler, *Future Shock* (New York: Random House 1976); Janelle (note 2); F. Cairncross, *The Death of Distance* (Boston: Harvard Business School Press 1996).
21. D.L. Garcia, 'A New Paradigm for Electronic Commerce', *Information Society* 13 (1997), pp.17–31.
22. B. Anderson, *Imagined Communities* (New York: Verso 1989).
23. H.H. Frederick, *Global Communications and International Relations* (Belmont, CA: Wadsworth Press 1993); and S.D. Brunn, 'Human Rights in the Evolving Electronic State,' in M. Wilson and K. Corey (eds.) *Information Tectonics: Space, Place, and Technology in the Information Age* (Chichester: John Wiley, forthcoming).
24. S.D. Brunn, 'The Internationalization of Diasporas in a Shrinking World', in G. Prevelakis (ed.) *Les Reseaux des Diasporas. The Networks of Diasporas* (Nicosia: Cyprus Research Center 1996), pp.259–72.
25. H. Rheingold, *The Virtual Communities. Homesteading on the Electronic Frontier* (Reading, MA: Addison-Wesley 1993); S.D. Brunn, J.A. Jones, and D. Purcell, 'Ethnic Communities in the Evolving "Electronic State": Cyberplaces in Cyberspace', in W. Gallusser *et al.* (eds.) *Political Boundaries and Coexistence* (New York and Vienna: Peter Lang (1994), pp.415–24; S.D.Brunn, K. Husso, P. Kokkonen and M. Pyyhtia, 'The GEOGRAPH Electronic Mailing List: the Emergence of a New Scholarly Community', *Fennia* 175 (1997), pp.97–123; S.R.M. O'Lear, 'Using Electronic Mail (E-mail) Surveys for Geography Research Lessons from a Survey of Russian Environmentalists', *The Professional Geographer* 48 (1996), pp.209–17; S.D. Brunn, GEOGED as a Virtual Workshop, presented at National Council for Geographic Education, November 1998, unpublished paper.
26. S.D. Brunn and S.R. O'Lear, 'Research and Communication in the "Invisible College" of the Human Dimensions of Global Change', unpublished paper.
27. E. Carmel, 'American Hegemony in Packaged Software Trade and the "Culture of Software"', *Information Society* 13 (1997), pp.125–42.
28. A. Smith., *The Geopolitics of Information. How Western Culture Dominates the World* (New York: Oxford University Press 1980).
29. R. Maxwell, 'Technologies of National Desire', in M.J. Shapiro and H.R. Alker (eds.) *Challenging Boundaries: Global Flows, Territorial Identifiers* (Minneapolis, MN: University of Minnesota Press 1996), pp.329–58.
30. Pickles (note 19); S.D. Brunn, Carl Dahlman and Jon Taylor, 'GIS Uses and Constraints on Diffusion in Eastern Europe and the Former USSR', *Post-Soviet Geography and Economics*, 39 (1998), pp.566–87.
31. W. Zelinsky, *A Prologue to Population Geography* (Englewood Cliffs, NJ: Prentice-Hall 1966), pp.74–5.

32. M. Batty and B. Barr, 'The Electronic Frontier: Exploring and Mapping Cyberspace', *Futures* 26 (1994), pp.699–712; S.D. Brunn (note 1), *GeoJournal*. See also the various cyberspace maps and schematics developed by Martin Dodge; he can be reached at ucfnmad@ucl.ac.uk
33. Luke and O'Tuathail (note 5).
34. R. Shields (ed.) *Cultures of Internet. Virtual Space, Real Histories, Living Bodies* (London: Sage Publications 1996).
35. Newman (note 10).
36. S. Huntington, *The Clash of Civilizations* (New York: Norton 1994); Lewis and Wigen, op. cit.

Globalisation or Global Apartheid? Boundaries and Knowledge in Postmodern Times

SIMON DALBY

By acquiring earth-spanning technologies, by developing products that can be produced anywhere and sold everywhere, by spreading credit around the world, and by connecting global channels of communication that can penetrate any village or neighbourhood, these institutions we normally think of as economic rather than political, private rather than public, are becoming the world empires of the twenty-first century. The architects and managers of these space age businesses understand that the balance of power in world politics has shifted in recent years from territorially bound governments to companies that can roam the world.
Richard J. Barnet and John Cavanagh[1]

We live in a world that is one-fifth rich and four fifths poor; the rich are segregated into rich countries and the poor into poor countries; the rich are predominantly lighter skinned and the poor darker skinned; most of the poor live in 'homelands' that are physically remote, often separated by oceans and great distances from the rich. Migration on any great scale is impermissible. There is no systematic redistribution of income. While there is ethnic strife among the well to do, the strife is more vicious and destructive among the poor.
Thomas Schelling[2]

Globalisation has been the political buzzword of the 1990s. It implies all sorts of economic, political and cultural challenges and changes. Economic decisions are supposedly slipping beyond state control. Sovereignty is being

---

Earlier versions of this paper were presented as a seminar to the Geography Department at the University of Witwatersrand in March 1998, and to the Annual Meeting of the Canadian Association of Geographers in Ottawa June 1998. My thanks to the participants at these sessions and to Belinda Dodson, Gernot Kohler, David Newman, Alan Mabin, David McDonald, Peter Vale and to one journal referee for their comments, criticism and assistance.

compromised as international arrangements supplement, and in places substitute for, state control of economic decisions and regulations. Transnational corporations are supposedly the wave of the future; global commerce will in the process remake societies, or at least those that get on the bandwagon and participate in the new transformations. 'McWorld' has arrived.[3] Intel is inside everywhere. Bill Gates is more wealthy than the whole populations of some of the poorer states on planet Reebok. Cultures are melding, 'world beat' and other syncretic cultural forms are emerging in the virtual cyberspaces of trans-boundary 'third nature.' Boundaries are fossils of an earlier age according to the *diktats* of the information highway and 'cyberspace'. This international free market is supposedly the route to prosperity for all. Neo-liberalism has 'mastered space' and reduced the whole world to a market for global products.[4]

But the skeptics are vocal too. To its critics globalisation can be a frantic acceleration of the processes of dispossession of the poor and enrichment of the already wealthy. Cultures are being destroyed, identities shattered by the power of advertising and the rapidly extending reach of post-modernity. Citizenship is less important to the jet-setting executives and the media moguls of technological hype. In all this who 'we' are is less and less dependent on where 'we' live than on which brand 'we' buy, and which satellite feeds 'we' watch on our new advanced technology televisions. Niche marketing supplies identities that tradition and locality used to provide. States are falling apart in violent struggles in the new zones of turmoil where ethnic identity is supposedly everything.[5]

Coupled to the challenges to the epistemological certainties of modern science, and the knowledge of classical physics that underlies so many claims to 'objectivity', these changes have been invoked under the term of the postmodern. Whether as artistic pastiche, cultural syncretism, or the end of modernity's 'metanarratives', in Jean Francois Lyotard's oft cited formulation, the term 'postmodern' simultaneously suggests a new period of human experience, a decentring of the privileged vantage points of Western knowledge and radical doubts about knowledge claims.[6] The postmodern is about juxtapositions and epistemological skepticism, about cultural innovation and the difficulties of living in times of rapid cultural change.

Many contemporary commentators suggest that these questions of politics, knowledge and cultural identity are best understood as complex contestations, in which struggles are simultaneously about political power and claims to identity. The postmodern is not just a matter of media, migrants and modernisation, but also of complex arrangements of diasporic communities and decontextualised claims to identity. Crucially, the ruptures between different facets of human experience give us not only a postmodern world in the sense of juxtapositions and doubts about social knowledge, but a global one in motion too:

> This mobile and unforeseen relationship between mass mediated events and migratory audiences defines the core of the link between globalisation and the modern. ... (T)he work of the imagination, viewed in this context, is neither purely emancipatory nor entirely disciplined, but is a space of contestation in which individuals and groups seek to annex the global into their own practices of the modern.[7]

This multiplicity of voices and their multiple claims to identity have called into question stable and univocal accounts of history, culture and identity and especially the crucial modern formulation of political identity in the sovereign nation state. We live in a postmodern age. Boundaries and identities are not what they once supposedly were. Lines of demarcation around precisely defined sovereign states are an increasingly unconvincing description of contemporary political life and an unconvincing answer as to how politics ought to be thought and practiced.[8] States persist, often violently, but trans-national flows of trade, communications, media, finance, crime and culture suggest that in the information age politics can no longer be understood in terms of locations, places, boundaries and state sovereignty.[9]

And yet, in so much of the world the aspirations of the state makers and citizens apparently remain those that globalisation or the post-modern is supposedly rendering redundant. Citizenship in the zones of affluence is a luxury that the rapidly growing number of forced migrants in this world can often only dream about; a passport is only really understood when one doesn't have one and needs to travel for pressing reasons. The migrants and the numerous impoverished people in the face of the extreme wealth of the world's commercial elite suggests to other commentators a more appropriate descriptive term to designate the global polity of the end of the century: apartheid.

As will be argued in this article the debate about which term most adequately captures the political realities of the moment also implies an epistemological question – one that suggests that boundaries between states are also about boundaries of categories of political actors and between political identities. How identities are constructed and secured in the processes of boundary drawing and policing is very much the stuff of contemporary geopolitical investigations. The consequences of understanding both boundaries and identities as contingent and changing, rather than given and determined, are considerable.[10] More than this, the geopolitical categories are themselves part of the contemporary changes and, as such, need to be a focus of analysis for understanding the changing significances of contemporary geopolitical imaginaries.[11] How the world is politically specified, and places given significance in these specifications at the largest scale, is a matter of geopolitics. These places and the political significance of their interconnections and relationships is a matter of geopolitical reasoning.[12] So too is the important matter of the overall construction of the world in terms of 'them and us', developed and underdeveloped, North and South, primitive and modern, which are so frequently structured within the broad spatial categorisations of the contemporary geopolitical imaginary.[13]

What many of the boundary studies and discussions of identity and culture in contemporary political discussions and social science analyses ignore are these macro-scale considerations, and the specificity of where exactly these flows and territorial transgressions occur.[14] This is especially necessary as a counter argument to the cruder 'homogenisation' interpretations of globalisation. The alternative model of 'global apartheid' might well offer further insights into the arguments made by the critics of the practices and theories of contemporary international relations and discussions of boundaries in contemporary geopolitics. In acting as a heuristic device it extends the arguments that suggest that much of contemporary scholarship takes for granted the very categories that it ought to examine. The assumption of the importance of boundaries is one such argument; focusing on the constructions of boundaries in the different descriptions of globalisation and of global apartheid suggests that their importance is directly related to the larger practices of geopolitical reasoning.

However, as the argument later in this article suggests, the question in the title may be a false dichotomy. The processes in motion might, perhaps, be best understood in terms of both globalisation and global apartheid. This is because the de-territorialisation, commercialisation, media fluxes, accelerations and challenges to conventional accounts of sovereignty are part and parcel of the same processes that are increasing the inequities between peoples and, often, between places. The crucial point, however, is that boundaries play very different roles for people and for images, commodities and financial flows, dependent on which larger framework is invoked as the overarching spatial architecture of politics. In other words, the significance of these differences, indeed their visibility in the first place, is related directly to the largest scale geographical assumptions used in constructing accounts of the world.[15] The analogy of global apartheid is but one conceptual device to challenge the conventional epistemological practices of geopolitical reasoning, but as the argument below suggests, it has considerable efficacy as an alternative framework for thinking about global politics.

Global Apartheid and Geopolitics

When it was official South African government policy 'apartheid' had many facets. The overall pattern of 'grand apartheid', built on the spatial segregation of people on the basis of their racial categories, was of prime importance. Its function to promote the 'separate development' of the races operated to maintain control over the economy, and over most of the wealth, which was in the hands of the white minority. The black majority population was limited to the urban townships, or banished to the rural 'homelands', which consisted of a small percentage of the territory of the state. Migrant labour from the homelands and sometimes further afield in Southern Africa was an important factor in providing the labour for white-owned businesses and the domestic labour needed to maintain an affluent lifestyle. The homelands suffered serious problems of poverty and environmental degradation as people tried to gain a living from the land and the remittances sent there from the cities and mines. The violence involved in maintaining such inequities and the violation of the principles of human rights, as well as the basic liberal assumption of human equality, brought condemnation of the regime from many places both inside and outside South Africa. Political reform eventually abolished at least the formal structures of the apartheid state, if not many of the profound structural inequities of the system.

The term 'global apartheid' has had limited circulation in academic circles at least since the appearance of Gernot Kohler's formulation of it in 1978.[16] More recently it has been used by a number of writers considering international politics after the Cold War. Fantu Cheru uses the phrase as a synonym for North-South divisions in the title of a recent chapter.[17] Titus Alexander's introduction to international politics invokes apartheid as an overarching framework for understanding global politics.[18] In discussing changing global patterns and policies of migration Anthony Richmond formulates the post-cold war world order in terms of 'global apartheid.'[19] Writers connected to the World Order Models Project have also recently reworked the formulation as a way of focusing on the patterns and practices of contemporary global politics.[20]

The global apartheid theme is captured in Thomas Schelling's 1992 reflections, written at the end of the Cold War but before the election of Nelson Mandela's government:

> If we are to think about a 'new world order' that might embark on the gradual development of some constitutional framework within which the peoples of the globe would eventually share collective responsibility and reciprocal obligations, somewhat analogous to what we expect in a traditional nation state, and if we were to think

about the political mechanisms that might be developed, what actual nation, existing now or in the past, might such a world state resemble? If we were to contemplate gradually relinquishing some measure of sovereignty in order to form not a more perfect union, but a more effective legal structure, what familiar political entity might be our basis for comparison? I find my own answer stunning and embarrassing: South Africa.[21]

The provocative suggestion in these formulations is that apartheid, as formerly practiced in South Africa, offers a microcosmic model of the current global polity. The implications of such a formulation are obviously powerful when questions of governance and international policy are considered.

Kohler's more recent elaboration of the concept argues that it can be understood in three ways, first, as an empirical concept that describes the structure of the global society; second, as a normative concept implying a negative judgment on that order; and, third, as an existential category encompassing experience of the world and the lived identities constructed on the basis of this experience by participants in the global polity.[22]

As an empirical concept, global apartheid offers an addition to the conventional geopolitical vocabularies which construct the world in terms of developed and underdeveloped, first world and third world, world system, core and periphery, North and South. The term apartheid has been variously applied to inequities in economics, technology, salaries, technology and gender at the global scale to emphasise the different facets of inequality across the globe. They add a racial dimension to the geopolitical categories, emphasising the affluence of the white races and the relative poverty of most of the rest. These formulations point to the structural dimensions of these divisions and to the overt racism that may be part of the political system.

Of special importance for the argument here, Kohler draws attention to some of the consequences of these formulations relating to international boundaries:

> In the global apartheid perspective, nation-states are compared to South African homelands; that is territories reserved for non-whites. National boundaries, passports, border patrols and fortifications function as reinforcements of racial segregation at the world level, since they provide effective control mechanisms for keeping non-whites (of the South) out of white areas (of the North) of the world if so desired.[23]

'Northern' fears of Southern population explosions and migrations suggest that this is widely desired by some people in the affluent parts of the world. One of the important consequences of this is that low wage labour is held captive in certain parts of the world. People are much less mobile than capital, and the global economy is in part structured by these patterns of inequality. Northern states' attempts to restrict immigration and to choose carefully who can settle in the states of the North continues to be a tempting strategy to deal with the 'problems' of mass migration which are already underway. The migration controls in South Africa under apartheid were extensive; segregation and limited mobility produced a very distinctive political geography of apartheid.

While labour resides in the homelands, economic control and the ability to employ it and to extract resources for international markets, by contrast rests with the Northern 'white' population, or at least with its international institutional creations such as the International Monetary Fund, rather than the Southern populations that can be easily analogised with people of the South African homelands and townships. Another parallel formulation, suggesting that some African states are analogous to South African 'Bantustans,' has provoked a debate in recent issues of the *Review of African Political Economy*.[24] The argument for this conceptualisation is that, given the dominance of foreign financial control, the role of aid donors and 'puppet' regimes in determining economic policy are similar to the homelands of South Africa within the apartheid arrangements. The status of sub-Saharan former colonies is a reasonable analogy to apartheid era arrangements in South Africa. The dominance of external control, through political and economic processes sometimes summarised as 'recolonisation,' mirrors the effective control of the Pretoria administration over the homelands. While the utility of the term 'Bantustan' is contested, it has, so the argument goes, the virtue of reminding readers that Northern conceptions of the South, and of Africa in particular, are both racist and colonial constructions.

It is also easy to analogise the enclaves of guest workers in the cities of the North with the enclaves of non-white domestic workers in the white part of South Africa or even with the segregated arrangements of the urban townships. The constraints on these people are similar to the visa restrictions on numerous people in the international flow of labour. Indeed the analogy may be closest in the field of international domestic labour and the migratory patterns of nannies and maids from the poor to the rich parts of the planet. The economic importance of remittances sent back by these employees is also important, as are the international relations difficulties caused by incidents involving migrant workers. Migration has both diplomatic and social change consequences on both ends of these flows.[25]

Considering the apartheid analogy in terms of the natural environment, it is again easy to read global patterns into the Apartheid state. Homelands often became seriously degraded while 'white' areas were maintained in much better ecological shape.[26] The analogy can be further extended when global resource control is worked into the picture. These patterns parallel the patterns of North-South relations. Perhaps the most salient case is the relationship between Japan and South East Asia, where Japan has maintained relatively intact forests on its islands but imports timber products that cause clear-cut logging and the displacement of indigenous peoples in Indonesia and Malaysia.[27] While in historical terms the analogy does not hold exactly, in that people have not been displaced from Japan onto the forest lands of South East Asia, and the population density patterns are not similar, the pattern of resource flows and degradation is instructive. The resource exploitation of South East Asia is not sustainable. The damage happens in areas inhabited by poor people who cannot easily move, but works to the benefit of the wealthy living at a distance from the destruction. This pattern extends to many facets of the global political economy where, in part, environmental destruction in rural areas is driven by the commodity demands of the metropoles.[28]

The moral force of condemnation invoked by the term 'global apartheid' implies a radical unfairness in the world, and one supported by the dominant political and legal structures of the present global order. It points to the spatial arrangements that are codified by borders and the political and economic consequences of the various functions that boundaries of various sorts play in specific contexts. Above all the metaphor draws attention to the practices of boundary making and the policing of political identities. If the current geopolitical situation fits the analogy of global apartheid reasonably closely then there are at least half a dozen grounds on which a moral indictment can be constructed. Kohler lists six: justice and fairness, basic needs, human rights, equality, democracy, and racial non-discrimination.

Just about any politics premised on notions of social justice and democracy suggests that global apartheid arrangements are objectionable on these normative principles. The condemnation of South Africa's policies on this basis suggests that there are good reasons to criticize the current global polity on similar grounds. In Kohler's terms the case for the 'prosecution' in the court of world public opinion involves both the history of colonisation since at least the beginning of the sixteenth century with all the appropriations and dislocations that have resulted, and the current practices of economic control and selective access to markets and economic conditionalities that some argue are effectively recolonising parts of the 'South'.[29]

But, and this is the crucial point about using global apartheid to think about boundaries and the knowledge practices of contemporary geopolitics, to issue such condemnations requires rethinking the taken for granted categories of states as sovereign entities.[30] It also requires rethinking politics and obligation across boundaries and taking seriously the social and economic consequences of the current global division of labour. In addition it requires challenging the assumptions that economic growth can solve the problems that centuries of development seem to have aggravated. As the United Nations Development Program figures cited by Alexander suggest, the disparities in income between the poorest and the richest on the planet have increased dramatically in the past few decades of economic growth.[31]

In doing any of these things the global apartheid formulation requires a challenge to the identities of modernity in the North. Here the existential challenge to the North implicit in the concept of global apartheid connects up to the question of geopolitical imaginaries and the political functions of boundaries. Where the advocates of globalising neo-liberalism emphasise the beneficial effects of free trade and often the benefits of multi-culturalism in many places, the global apartheid framework suggests very different questionings of geopolitical identity. Viewed at the largest geopolitical scale, identity is not a matter only of national imaginaries and the construction of neighbouring nations as the difference against which identity is formulated.[32] Now Kohler issues the challenge to identity at the largest scale. The moral superiority of the developed, the civilised, the advanced, the democratic and so on, is challenged by the re-imagination of boundaries as temporary arrangements at best administering the current flows of wealth and resources around the world. Rather than the fixed structures that must be defended to maintain some semblance of political stability in the face of globalising instabilities, they are understood as a tactic of rule, an administrative contrivance by the rich and powerful for the maintenance of a political order of drastic and increasing inequity.

In addition taking states, or even such geopolitical labels as the 'North' or the 'West,' as eternal entities obscures the patterns of conquest and control that have historically constituted the wealthy political states that claim sovereignty as a mode of controlling what are now deemed to be undesirable flows of migrants and refugees across these boundaries.[33] The treatment of states as equals in the United Nations, and in the formal recognition of sovereignty in international relations, often obscures the patterns of inequity and the very different histories of various states.[34] It suggests that causes of disparities are endogenous rather than at least in part caused by cross-border relations. But if the underdeveloped parts of the world are understood as having a broadly similar relationship to the developed world as the homelands did to white South Africa under apartheid, then a very different understanding of international relations emerges. The analytical and political importance attributed to boundaries are dependent on these larger geopolitical assumptions about world order.

Global Social Change and the End of Apartheid

The analogy of global apartheid and its contrast to themes of globalisation is especially suggestive when the causes of the end of apartheid government are closely examined. While the political transformation is a very complex matter, and no single explanatory factor can account for what happened, the failure of the policy of spatial segregation is an important part of the story that is relevant here. In the words of former South African foreign minister Pik Botha: 'The government began to shift away from apartheid when it realised that it was impossible to stem the tide of Africans moving to the urban areas in search of employment, signaling that the homeland system did not work.'[35] The migrations of workers and their families suggested that the spatial delimitation of the apartheid migration control was incapable of controlling peoples' movements.

While the influx control arrangements shaped the patterns of South African urbanisation, and sometimes prevented the emergence of migrant slum settlements by the simple expedient of bulldozing them, the crucial point is that the development of the economy depended on labour that could not be neatly contained within the geographical structures of grand apartheid.[36] Without this spatial control the whole geographical logic of separate development could not be maintained in the long run. 'Black people have been paradoxically trapped between the economic imperatives of urbanisation and the political obstacles of the system that helped to create these imperatives. In order to subsist, they have been compelled to live on the fringes of urban life, commuting across homeland boundaries to places of work in white areas or living in peri-urban "squatter camps" characterized by squalid, crowded conditions.'[37] In the face of large-scale urbanisation processes, the spatial containment of the population proved impossible.

This is a theme parallel to what some contemporary analysts of international migration are suggesting in discussing matters at the global scale.[38] The structural changes involved in the processes of global change are changing labour force requirements rapidly. Migration is an inevitable part of the process. But the dislocations of refugees are also rapidly increasing in recent years. Whether due to violence, or social disruption and dispossession in the face of encroaching commercial developments, people are on the move.[39] This is portrayed as a threat by many politicians in Northern states. The Schengen and Dublin agreements in Europe tighten co-operation by European states to deal with refugees and to limit access.[40]

Debates about immigration in the United States often invoke fear of all manner of disease and social disruption attributed to migrants. Apart from the obvious irony of a state built by immigrants now portraying them as a threat, the effect of these restrictions on mobility, and the construction of foreigners as threats, has numerous repercussions on the welfare of migrants and the political tolerance of all communities involved. Given the demographic changes in the 'North' with its aging population, and the need in future for numerous services, it is likely that labour forces will often be based on the availability of either immigrants or temporary workers.

As Nigel Harris suggests, the key to much of this may be to unravel the links between migration, citizenship and employment.[41] The assumption that immigration is a permanent process is part of the political arrangement that renders trans-border flows as a threat. If it is necessary to get work then people seeking work will seek immigrant status; if not temporary employment status may well satisfy many people. This is especially the case given the changes wrought by globalisation, which allow media to simultaneously broadcast across many state boundaries and allow telecommunications quickly to connect people across distances. Diasporic communities and return migration suggest a much less stable and settled population. Territorial administrative systems are inevitably challenged by these social arrangements.

Understanding migrants as threats to the political order of sovereign states relies on the assumption that such states are the only possible political arrangement. But as the example of South Africa and the failure of influx control in the face of economic demands suggests, such territorial strategies of state control may be doomed to failure in the long run in a world of flows and geographic change. As temporary expedients, migration controls and movement restrictions apparently reinforce state control and constrain population flows up to a point. But in causing numerous legitimacy crises by dealing with migrants in inhumane ways, the political costs of such strategies suggest that a more flexible administrative structure for dealing with migrants is likely preferable in most situations.[42]

The possibilities of international labour codes and international corporate practices to guarantee standards of human rights might also work to reduce the fraught security and identity frameworks for considering these matters. In the process the assumptions of exclusive territorial sovereignty and linkages between citizenship and the right to work will have to be rethought. Until they are, they will remain obstacles to political progress on numerous fronts in ways analogous to the restrictions of apartheid influx control.

Dealing with these restrictions on migration does not of course guarantee that the structural inequalities in the global economy will be ameliorated. The end of grand apartheid in South Africa has not led to either widespread land or wealth redistribution, nor to the emergence of an economy that produces greater social justice. It has however reduced the control of movement and some of the more pernicious practices of the apartheid state, although other difficulties concerning both internal and international migration and the application of people's rights remain urgent social issues.[43] Skilled and professional black people have undoubtedly benefited from the end of apartheid restrictions, and their success is mirrored on the world scale in the 1990s where talented software engineers and entrepreneurs usually manage to find ways to circumvent border controls and citizenship limitations when working for transnational corporations.[44]

Identity, Territory and Sovereignty

Considering the possibility of dealing with people rather than citizens suggests immediately the constraints on the political imaginary of contemporary times where flows are discussed within the assumption of sovereign states inhabited by political subjects who are citizens rather than people. This is not to doubt the power of states or their potential for extreme violence. It does however suggest that understanding boundaries and citizenship based on territorial criteria is a poor fit for the social dynamics of globalisation.[45] It acts as a powerful constraint on what is deemed politically appropriate in many places. All these considerations apply very immediately to the fate of the dispossessed, be they traditional political refugees, or those that now fall into the larger category of displaced peoples as a consequence of various 'humanitarian' disasters and complex emergencies. The confused debates about humanitarian interventions and United Nations peace keeping missions emphasizes the difficulty of dealing with pressing human needs in a framework that defines matters in static categories.[46]

The apartheid analogy can be further extended to reconsider the larger discussions of globalisation and the changing roles of states in the international system. Just as the homelands and the white areas of South Africa were interconnected and linked together, despite the claims to sovereignty that were only recognised within South Africa, it is easy to construct the argument that numerous states are not effectively sovereign in today's globalised world. This appears in the international relations literature on 'failed states' and, in particular, the problems within many of the African 'quasi-states' in the 1990s that have suffered severe violence and the collapse of centralised control.[47] Siba Grovogui's argument, that such a formulation assumes incorrectly that these spatial entities had the necessary attributes of modern sovereign statehood in the first place, can be read as an analogy with the apartheid homelands, states without many of the capabilities or attributes of statehood and recognised as such only by the white apartheid regime.[48] This use of the apartheid analogy suggests once again the crucial point of understanding the cartographic representations of administrative areas as suggesting equivalent social entities across the globe, a mode of representation that is often a very useful political fiction for obscuring the larger patterns of inequality.[49]

Such musings also raise questions about how to tackle Benjamin Barber's principal concern, which is not, as many commentators and critics have assumed, with whether McWorld or *Jihad* will win a contest between them to shape the future of politics, but rather about the demise of the possibility of democracy when tribal identities are competing with each other in a world shaped by global patterns of consumption.[50] In this scenario, the possibility for civil societies, the *fora* for debate, discussion and decision on matters of collective concern, are removed by either corporate control or violent assertion of tribal identities. The tribal identities are now reinforced at long distance by expatriate fervour for causes in far away homelands. The images and messages are transmitted by the communications infrastructures of the large corporations.

Assertions of political identity may not, however, directly feed into political claims on territories. Numerous collectivities are possible, many of them may operate to make political demands in non-territorial manners. Assertions of identity are complicated by these factors, but the crucial point that is in danger of being lost in these discussions is that not all assertions of national identity are related to ethnic antagonisms or political violence. Race, nationality and identity are fraught constructs, but they are in part and in places negotiable and changeable and can be appropriated in support of such cultural themes as national soccer teams and other sporting achievements in relatively non-antagonistic ways. The domestic analogies of nations as sacrosanct autonomous spheres of private space persist as powerful tropes, but the social changes of globalisation suggest that both families and nationalities are changing, and with them the possibilities of new political forms of community and identity.[51]

The model of apartheid may suggest that the particularities of localities and the common patterns of globalisation can be better understood as capturing parts of the processes in motion. While multi-culturalism has come to the fore in North America recently and is advocated as a solution to numerous social difficulties, the capabilities of migrants to express themselves and their identities varies widely from one locale to another. The trans-national class which, as some writers now suggest is in the making – the 'white' population of privileged, and mobile wealthy beneficiaries of global markets – dominates and controls many of the flows that cross the boundaries of the geopolitical imaginary. But the crucial lesson from the end of the apartheid system may simply be that it does not control all of them. While it is not at all clear which flows might have the transformative potentials that might eventually subvert the existing geopolitical patterns, the flows clearly matter in terms of social change and the politics of resistance.

On the largest scale the emergence of numerous global institutions suggests that it may be much more useful to emphasise the importance of the mutual enmeshment of states within larger networks of economic flows, communications networks, trans-boundary criminal schemes and non-governmental organisations. 'Nation states may retain their decision making capacity, but, having become part of a network of powers and counter-powers, they are powerless by themselves; they are dependent on a broader system of enacting authority and influence from multiple sources.'[52] If they ever were, states are now no longer what most social science theories have assumed them to be.

Postmodern Geopolitics?

Whether we, who read and write in scholarly publications on geopolitics, understand ourselves as part of a rich white minority in a radically divided global system, or as victims of homogenous processes of globalisation, matters both in terms of scholarship, and politically, in terms of how we teach, write and live our lives. Unconventional geopolitical categories, such as the interpretative scheme implied by 'global apartheid', have considerable utility as heuristic devices to tackle the contemporary narratives of globalisation, and to reveal the assumptions about sovereign states that structure conventional thinking. Such intellectual exercises extend the critiques of conventional geopolitical reasoning that have been the mainstay of critical geopolitics for the past decade. They do so in a 'postmodern' way, confronting the accepted categories with different understandings and rendering the obvious strange so as to investigate the cultural antecedents that make specific geopolitical imaginaries possible.

Political space may now be 'closed', as Halford Mackinder observed a century ago, in so far as all habitable territory has been claimed by a state, but the way that international political processes operate no longer feeds into the European inter-imperial rivalries of his time. Political closure had very different effects then in comparison to the global situation of a century later. The important point is simply that geopolitics is about change, and political ordering principles, as well as the discourses they embody, change in complex ways.

Both the globalisation literature and the global apartheid analogy suggest that models of states and their boundaries are inadequate assumptions for understanding contemporary geopolitical processes. The global apartheid model also emphasises the point that sovereign states are cartographic devices which often conceal the nature of the states and the relations between them that cross their boundaries. More specifically the models of globalisation and global apartheid have at least three crucial dimensions in common which are useful in considering how we think about boundaries and what role they might have in considering how we might (re)think geopolitics in the new millennium.

First, both globalisation and global apartheid models assume that the conventional assumptions of states as the containers of politics and of world politics reduced to the matters of 'high politics' between states are inadequate. Both refuse to accept the 'territorial trap' in understanding the inadequacies of the contemporary focus on sovereign states as the conceptual basis for the analysis of contemporary realities.[53] Hence their geopolitical frameworks suggest both the transience and the importance of thinking very carefully about boundaries and what they can constrain and control.

The converse of this, and the second factor that both models have in common, is the emphasis on the importance of flows that traverse these boundaries. In the long run the changes are more important than the temporary controls offered by boundaries. This is not to suggest that state boundaries ought to changed or that they will be frequently changed in the future. The weight of evidence suggests that established boundaries are likely to remain, not least because of the dangers of serious violence where they are changed. But what is more important is that the functions they serve may change quickly, drastically and with little advance warning. It is also worth emphasising that much of the discussion of globalisation works to reinscribe statist territorial assumptions of political identity precisely by constructing them as that which is being transcended by contemporary processes.

The third theme that the models have in common is the importance of the imagination in the construction of identity and political possibility in postmodern times. Information, images, advertising and the scripts of soap operas viewed by millions all over the world are now part of the social imaginary. Linked to migration, and despite the obvious limits on how politics is reported on the global scale, the media is still often a force for political change in many places that is hard to constrain even in the most repressive of political states. The collapse of the Warsaw Pact and the demolition of the Berlin wall were powerful symbols of change that acted as examples across the world, although local interpretations of these are obviously highly diverse.

The simple theories of cultural globalisation and McWorld assume homogenisation is a process that is inevitable. But what the more complex models of globalisation, and also apartheid, as a model of world politics assume, is that the processes in motion have specific albeit changing geographies. The consequences of a particular cultural or technological innovation will not be felt similarly in different places. Place matters in the contestation of political and social change. Resistance and appropriation of universal symbols is not the same in different cultures where these symbols are invoked, used and resisted in different ways dependent on the local histories and cultural opportunities. Quite how this occurs is an empirical question that needs detailed research in particular cases.[54]

But tragically, despite the discussions of globalisation and assumptions of new forms of postmodern politics, these acts of resistance often do remain trapped in the linguistic constraints of conventional understandings of geopolitics.[55] Boundaries and identity challenges become fraught with danger when the conventional political understanding of community as inside is contrasted to danger and threat specified as outside a territorially demarcated area.[56] As Appadurai puts it:

> This incapacity of many deterritorialised groups to think their way out of the imaginary of the nation state is itself the cause of much global violence because many movements of emancipation and identity are forced, in their struggles against existing nation states, to embrace the very imaginary that they seek to escape. Postnational or nonnational movements are forced by the very logic of actually existing nation-states to become antinational or antistate and thus to inspire the very state power that forces them to respond in the language of counternationalism. This vicious circle can only be escaped when a language is found to capture complex, nonterritorial, postnational forms of allegiance.[57]

Specifying the world in particular ways is therefore a profoundly political act. Postmodernism suggests the decline of the importance of state boundaries, but the celebration of difference also suggests the contemporary political importance of cultural distinctions and identities. Who 'we' are is, as argued above, partly about the commodities we buy and the cultural experiences we purchase in the global economy, but these are intimately connected to the geopolitical categories and the related knowledge practices that specify the world in which that 'we' lives and enters into relations with others. In so far as these categories remain specified within the conventional understandings of geopolitical boundaries and modern sovereign states the potential for violence remains a spectre haunting the search for identity.

NOTES

1. Richard J. Barnet and John Cavanagh *Global Dreams: Imperial Corporation and the New World Order* (New York: Simon and Schuster 1994), p.14.
2. T. Schelling, 'The Global Dimension' in G. Allison and G.F. Treverton (eds.), *Rethinking America's Security* (Norton, New York 1992), p.200.
3. To use Benjamin Barber's formulation in his *Jihad vs. McWorld: How Globalism and Tribalism are Reshaping the World* (New York: Ballantine 1996).
4. J. Agnew and S. Corbridge *Mastering Space: Hegemony, Territory and International Political Economy* (London: Routledge 1995).
5. Gearóid Ó Tuathail, and T.W. Luke 'Present at the (Dis)integration: Deterritorialisation and Reterritorialisation in the New Wor(l)d Order' *Annals of the Association of American Geographers* 84/3 (1994), pp.381–98; Jan Arte Scholte 'The Geography of Collective Identities in a Globalizing World' *Review of International Political Economy* 3/4 (1996), pp.565–607.
6. Jean Francois Lyotard, *The Post-Modern Condition: A Report on Knowledge* (Minneapolis: Univeristy of Minnesota Press 1984).
7. Arjun Appadurai, *Modernity at Large: Cultural Dimensions of Globalisation* (Minneapolis: University of Minnesota Press 1996), p.4.
8. R.B.J. Walker, *Inside/Outside: International Relations as Political Theory* (Cambridge: Cambridge University Press 1993).
9. The literature on this topic is vast and growing quickly but for an impressive and comprehensive overview see Manuel Castells, *The Information Age: Economy, Society and Culture* 3 volumes (Oxford: Blackwell 1997, 1998).
10. Michael J. Shapiro and Hayward R. Alker (eds.) *Challenging Boundaries: Global Flows, Territorial Identities* (Minneapolis: University of Minnesota Press 1996).
11. In *Modernity at Large* (note 7), p.31. Arjun Appadurai summarises 'imaginary' in its translation from the French 'imaginaire' to mean a 'constructed landscape of collective aspirations'. It is used in this sense here as a community project of geopolitical imagination, rather than imagination understood as a free floating or individual creation.
12. On geopolitical reasoning see Gearóid Ó Tuathail *Critical Geopolitics: The Politics of Writing Global Space* (Minneapolis: University of Minnesota Press, 1996); Gearóid Ó Tuathail and Simon Dalby (eds.) *Rethinking Geopolitics* (London: Routledge, 1998).
13. John Agnew *Geopolitics: Re-Visioning World Politics* (London: Routledge, 1998); Simon Dalby, 'Continent Adrift?: Dissident Security Discourse and the Australian Geopolitical Imagination' *Australian Journal of International Affairs* 50/2 (1996), pp.59–75.
14. David Newman and Anssi Paasi 'Fences and Neighbours in the Postmodern World: Boundary Narratives in Political Geography' in *Progress in Human Geography* 22/2 (1998), pp.186–207.
15. Martin W. Lewis and Karen E. Wigen *The Myth of Continents: A Critique of Metageography* (Berkeley: University of California Press, 1997).
16. G. Kohler, 'Global Apartheid' *Alternatives: Social Transformation and Humane Governance* 4/2 (1978), pp.263–75.
17. F. Cheru, 'Global Apartheid and the Challenge to Civil Society: Africa and the Transformation of World Order' in R.W. Cox (ed.) *The New Realism: Perspectives on Multilateralism and World Order* (London: Macmillan and United Nations University Press, 1997), pp.205–22.
18. T. Alexander, *Unravelling Global Apartheid: An Overview of World Politics* (Cambridge: Polity 1996).
19. Anthony H. Richmond *Global Apartheid: Refugees, Racism and the New World Order* (Toronto: Oxford University Press 1994).
20. R. Falk *On Humane Governance: Toward a New Global Politics* (Cambridge: Polity Press, 1995).
21. Schelling 'Global Dimension' (note 2), p.200.
22. G. Kohler, 'The Three Meanings of Global Apartheid: Empirical, Normative, Existential' *Alternatives: Social Transformation and Humane Governance* 20/3 (1995), pp.403–13.

23. Kohler, 'Three Meanings' (note 22), p.405.
24. D. Himbara and D. Sultan, 'Reconstructing the Ugandan State and Economy: The Challenge of an International Bantustan' *Review of African Political Economy* 63 (1995); M. Doornbos 'Uganda: A Bantustan?' *Review of African Political Economy* 69 (1996), pp.425–7; R. Love, 'On the Idea of an International Bantustan' *Economy Review of African Political* 71 (1997) pp.129–31.
25. Cynthia Enloe, *The Morning After: Sexual Politics at the End of the Cold War* (Berkeley: University of California Press 1993).
26. Alan During, *Apartheid's Environmental Toll* (Washington: Worldwatch Institute, Worldwatch Paper 95, 1990).
27. P. Dauvergne, *Shadows in the Forest: Japan and the Politics of Timber in South East Asia* Cambridge, MA: MIT Press 1997).
28. On these patterns of resource extraction see Madrav Gadgil and Ramachandra Guha, *Ecology and Equity: The Use and Abuse of Nature in Contemporary India* (London: Routledge, 1995); and in general how this concerns the larger discussions of global environmental security see Simon Dalby 'Ecological Metaphors of Security: World Politics in the Biosphere', *Alternatives: Social Transformation and Humane Governance* 23/3 (1998), pp.291–319.
29. D.N. Nabudere, 'The African Challenge', *Alternatives: Social Transformation and Humane Governance* 19/2 (1994), pp.163–71.
30. Walker, *Inside/Outside* (note 8) and R.B.J. Walker, *One World/Many Worlds: Struggles for a Just World Peace* (Boulder: Lynne Rienner 1988).
31. Alexander (note 18), p.12. See the United Nations Development Program, *Human Development Report 1994* (New York: Oxford University Press 1994).
32. G. Dijkink, *National Identity and Geopolitical Visions* (London: Routledge 1996).
33. Michael Shapiro, *Violent Cartographies: Mapping Cultures of War* (Minneapolis: University of Minnesota Press 1997).
34. S. Strange, 'Territory, State, Authority and Economy: A New Realist Ontology of Global Political Economy' in R.W. Cox (ed.) *The New Realism* (note 17), pp.3–19.
35. As quoted in Valerie Percival and Thomas Homer-Dixon, 'Environmental Scarcity and Violent Conflict: The Case of South Africa, paper of the Project on Environment, Population and Security, The Peace and Conflict Studies Program, University of Toronto and the AAAS, 1995, p.3, quoting Rich Mkhondo, *Reporting South Africa* (London: Heinemann, 1993), p.19.
36. Mitsuo Ogura, 'Urbanisation and Apartheid in South Africa: Influx Controls and their Abolition', *The Developing Economies* 34/4 (1996), pp.402–23.
37. John A. Dixon, Don H. Foster, Kevin Durrheim and Lindy Wilbraham, 'Discourse and the Politics of Space in South Africa: the Squatter Crisis', *Discourse and Society* 5/3 (1994), pp.277–96, at 283.
38. Paul Kennedy, *Preparing for the Twenty-First Century* (New York: HarperCollins 1993).
39. William Wood, 'Forced Migration: Local Conflicts and International Dilemmas', *Annals of the Association of American Geographers* 84/4 (1994), pp.607–34.
40. M. Tesfahuney, 'Mobility, Racism and Geopolitics', *Political Geography* 15/5 (1998), pp.499–515.
41. Nigel Harris, *The New Untouchables: Immigration and the New World Worker* (Harmondsworth: Penguin, 1996.)
42. On the difficulties of such thinking see Eleonore Kofman, 'Citizenship for Some but not for Others: Spaces of Citizenship in Contemporary Europe', *Political Geography* 14/2 (1995), pp.121–37.
43. David McDonald, John Gay, Lovemore Zinyama, Robert Mattes and Fion de Vletter, *Challenging Xenophobia: Myths & Realities about Cross Border Migration in Southern Africa* (Capetown: Southern African Migration Project Migration Policy Series Paper No.7, 1998).
44. Janet Cherry, 'Development, Conflict and the Politics of Ethnicity in South Africa's Transition to Democracy', *Third World Quarterly* 15/4 (1994), pp.613–31.
45. Friedrich Kratochwil, 'Citizenship: On the Border of Order' in Yosef Lapid and Friedrich

Kratochwil (eds.), *The Return of Culture and Identity in IR Theory* (Boulder, CO: Rienner, 1996), pp.181–97.
46. William Wood, 'From Humanitarian Relief to Humanitarian Intervention: Victims, Intervenors and Pillars', *Political Geography* 15/8 (1996), pp.671–95; Médecine Sans Frontièrs *World in Crisis: Populations in Danger at the End of the 20th Century* (London: Routledge 1996).
47. Robert Jackson, *Quasi States: Sovereignty, International Relations and the Third World* (Cambridge: Cambridge University Press 1990).
48. Siba Grovogui, *Sovereigns, Quasi Sovereigns and Africans* (Minneapolis: University of Minnesota Press 1996).
49. See Agnew and Corbridge, *Mastering Space* (note 4).
50. Barber, *Jihad or McWorld* (note 3).
51. Kathryn A. Manzo, *Creating Boundaries: The Politics of Race and Nation* (Boulder, CO: Lynne Rienner, 1996).
52. Manuel Castells, *The Power of Identity* (Oxford: Blackwell, 1997), volume 2 of *The Information Age* (note 9), pp.304–5.
53. Agnew, *Revisioning* (note 13).
54. S. Pile and M. Keith (eds), *Geographies of Resistance* (London: Routledge, 1997).
55. Simon Dalby, 'Critical Geopolitics and the World Order Models Project', paper presented to the Inaugural International Conference in Critical Geography, Vancouver, August, 1997.
56. Andrew Linklater, *The Transformation of Political Community: Ethical Transformations of the Post-Westphalia Era* (Cambridge: Polity, 1998).
57. Appadurai, *Modernity at Large* (note 7), p.166.

Pseudo-States as Harbingers of a New Geopolitics: The Example of the Trans-Dniester Moldovan Republic (TMR)

VLADIMIR KOLOSSOV and JOHN O'LOUGHLIN

In the late twentieth-century, optimistic forecasts of a 'global village' premised on internationalisation[1] are challenged by studies picturing the future in more dramatic colours. Important reports, like those of the Club of Rome, the 'Global 2000' report to President Carter of the United States, the reports of the United Nations-sponsored Brandt Commission on the 'North-South' gap and the Brundtland Commission on the global environment, paid great attention to the gap between the developed countries and the Third World. The reports argued that the global disparities undermine the sustainability of human civilisation but they did not discuss the possibility of an appearance of non-western civilisation models nor did they consider consequences of a global geopolitical restructuring. As documents issued during the Cold War, they took it for granted that geopolitical era would continue and remained silent on the nature of political forms of the twenty-first century, expecting the sovereign nation-state format to remain hegemonic.

Fukuyama's 'end of history' thesis trumpeted the end of large scale conflict in the democratised world but recognised the probability of local wars continuing in the global periphery. Recent works by US commentators challenge this optimistic scenario and cast doubt on such crucial notions as 'progress' and 'democracy'.[2] The limits of the western 'civilisation of consumption' can be defined and recognises a world of disparity and 'a West versus the rest'.[3] A network of islands of 'transitional' or 'incomplete' statehood is emerging and we refer to these states as 'pseudo-states'. These

---

The research reported in this article was supported by a grant from the US National Science Foundation to Professor O'Loughlin and by a Fulbright Visiting Scholar award to Professor Kolossov. The research was completed in the Program on Political and Economic Change of the Institute of Behavioral Science at the University of Colorado after fieldwork in Transniestria in September 1997. We thank Professor A.L. Tschepalyga of the Institute of Geography of the Russian Academy of Sciences for his assistance in arrangements in Tiraspol and to our fieldwork colleagues, Sven Holdar, Andrei Treivish and Alexi Krindatch. Luiza Bialasiewicz assisted with translation of original texts and Bertrall Ross made the map and collected the newspaper accounts of the events in Moldova and Transniestria.

pseudo-states have achieved varying but low levels of recognition by the international community, are highly involved in local wars whilst their unsettled political status makes further conflict possible. They typically constitute part of what Robert Kaplan has called the 'ends of the earth', places where 'scarcity, crime, overpopulation, tribalism and disease are rapidly destroying the social fabric of our planet'.[4]

Another set of 'quasi-states'[5] with fungible territorial control is predicated on criminal or quasi-criminal organisations, frequently specialising in the production and sale of drugs, as well as the illegal traffic of weapons and in the laundering of 'dirty money'. They also maintain an interest in the processing of the flows of transnational speculative capital. This network of 'well organised chaos' is becoming a stable and more and more unavoidable part of the post-modern geopolitical reality, coexisting uneasily with the developed world. Moreover, it has some appendices inside the settled world, for example, in urban enclaves.[6] These quasi-states are "non-institutionalised" and represent a conglomerate of areas under the authority of local chiefs, field commanders, big landowners and/or drug barons. These local leaders can co-operate but cannot conduct wars of 'all against all', and are thus half-institutionalised since they are unlikely to control their territory permanently. Current examples include the Gorno-Badakhshan (Tajikistan), Garm region (Tajikistan), Kurdistan, Northern Afghanistan, 'Golden Triangle', Shan region, Western regions of Cambodia, Western Sahara, southern Sudan, southern Angola, Sierra Leone, and the Medellin part of Columbia. In this paper, we maintain a distinction between pseudo- and quasi-states; this separation allows us to focus on pseudo-states as important, emerging elements of the world political map.

The 'underground' geopolitical world of pseudo-states is relatively neglected by English-speaking social scientists and by political geographers, who traditionally focus their studies on the developed world and on the formal politics of recognised and stable states. Like Peter Taylor,[7] we believe that any political geography worth its name and relevance must confront the whole world, with all its disparities of wealth, comfort, security, ethnic relations and democratic norms. In this article, we turn our attention to those places that have recently experienced civil or interstate wars and where political control and external relations are still under dispute. Most of our 'geopolitical black holes' are barely-visible in the geopolitical codes of Western strategists, who focus on states that have global resources or that have important historical or cultural ties to the core countries

We remain sceptical of descriptions of post-modernist political and social organisations and forms because of the Western biases and blinkered world-views implicit in such accounts.⁸ We find it highly ironic that groups and factions are intent on creating that most modernist of all projects, the nation-state, in these supposedly postmodernist times. At first glance, the profusion of territories that are either self-proclaimed states (Chechnya), recognised by a few neighbours or a single neighbour (Turkish Republic of Northern Cyprus), controlled by an ethnic or political faction (Gorno-Badakhshan) or the object of continuous military skirmishing or serious fighting (Liberia, Somalia, South Sudan or Afghanistan) supports the modernist project of making even more 'nation-states'. Regardless of the reasons for the attempts to carve out smaller and smaller autonomous territories, there seems no end in sight. We believe that the globalisation hype has overstated the imminent demise of the territorial state.⁹

Kaplan exaggerates both his regional descriptions and the global impact of conflicts in the 'ends of the earth'.¹⁰ Only states in the vicinity of the conflicts seem to maintain significant and durable interests in the ebb and flow of political control at the centre and the challenges to central authorities. Russia, above all, is implicated in the pseudo-states because of its pivotal location bordering on many conflict regions and, coincidentally, because of the presence of ethnic Russians in newly-independent titular republics of the former Soviet Union. As both an instigator and a supporter of many armed insurrections, Russia continues to exert significant geopolitical influence on its neighbours in the 'Near Abroad'. Contemporary Russian geopolitical codes intersect with local political and national mobilisations to produce a complex mix of identities, territorialities and state-building projects in places as geographically dispersed as Tajikistan, Abkhazia, and Transniestria.¹¹

Most of pseudo-states are situated along the frontiers of large 'civilisations': between their cores – West Christian (Catholic and Protestant) and the East Christian (Orthodox Russia), between both of them and the Arabic-Turkic-Muslim world, and between Russia and the Chinese world. Dramatic events in the periphery of the core areas of great civilisations and uneasy relations between the core and their peripheries as well as between peripheries, cannot be reduced to the scheme proposed by Samuel Huntington. However, the concept of 'limitrophs' – geopolitically-unstable spaces between civilisational platforms – is very useful in our discussion.¹² Indeed, Huntington understands 'civilisations' as mostly areas of the great world confessions. Obviously, civilisations are based not only on religions (Huntington's reduction) but on a complex of ideas and representations cementing culture, social practice and geopolitics. As one moves from the core area of a civilisation, some of the features that define the civilisation disappear and are replaced with new ones that are more characteristic of neighbouring civilisations. Usually, the areas of limitrophs are in the state of cultural, religious and ideological self-defence from the nearest civilisation that threatens their identity. Geopolitical uncertainty and instability is especially pertinent along the borders of the former Russian Empire-Soviet Union; this zone includes the so-called 'Great Limitroph', abandoned by Russia and identified as the Balto-Pontic belt separating Russia from the core of Europe all the way to Manchuria. Limitroph geopolitics is one of the main reasons for the emergence of pseudo-states. Which feature is considered more important in defining a particular limitroph depends on the geopolitical players and on realities of the geopolitical time-space convergence. The concept of limitroph, unfortunately, continues to be predicated on the traditional geopolitics of force and zones of influence.

In this article, we offer a preliminary classification of pseudo-states. We consider the elements and strategies of state-making in the pseudo-states in the absence of international recognition. We compare four pseudo-states that have emerged from the debris of the Soviet Union and have been the scenes of significant violence in the past decade. Finally, we provide a lengthier case study on one of these pseudo-states, Transniestria.[13]

Classification of Pseudo-States and Quasi-States

The apparently fixed cartography of the world political map yields the false impression that state control extends to the boundaries of neighbouring countries in all cases. It seems probable that states are undergoing functional, rather than spatial changes, with greater permeability and increased sharing of political spaces in some world regions and new, bigger fences in other parts of the world.[14] It seems improbable that pseudo-states emerge only as a result of power relations between major countries, because, as David Knight noted, the international community consisting of mostly multiethnic and multicultural states is clearly motivated to maintain the status quo.[15] Attempts to gain self-determination by indigenous ethno-cultural groups certainly play a role in pseudo-state formation.

Some states maintain a tenuous territorial hold on their territories. By the early 1990s, 27 states were not in full control of their respective territories. Between 1945 and 1990, 14 states chronically did not exercise full control over their territory whilst civil wars occurred between 1945 and 1990 in 41 states. In 15 states between 1945 and 1990, foreign forces occupied at least a part of the territories of other sovereign states.[16] In 1996, 24 states had 27 continuing civil wars; only one conflict (India and Pakistan) was inter-state.[17] There is a downward trend in the number of conflicts during the 1989-96 period. The marginal, usually frontier-like, territories under dispute are frequently the locations for the pseudo-states under consideration in this paper.

It is possible to make a tentative and preliminary classification of pseudo-states. A first category can be labelled 'institutionalised' pseudo-states, those units that have declared sovereignty, have all necessary attributes of a 'normal' state, and are in full control of their territories. However, these pseudo-states are not recognised and have little chance of recognition by the international community or by most neighbouring states. Current examples include the TMR, Chechnya, Abkhazia, Nagorno-Karabakh, Serb republic of Bosnia, Kosovo, Somaliland, and the Turkish Republic of Northern Cyprus. Another method to classify pseudo- and quasi-states is by genesis and functions. Examples include first, self-identification of an area with a specific nationality (Northern Cyprus or Palestinian Autonomous Areas); second, the splintering of an empire or large multi-national state (such as Abkhazia or Chechnya); third, areas of conflict with no permanent control as a result of a civil war and/or a foreign military intervention (such as Afghanistan or Bosnia); and fourth, pirate states based on criminal-terrorist activities (Somaliland, 'the Golden Triangle' or the area of the Medellin cartel in Columbia).

Pseudo-states are typically located in the Shatterbelts of sub-Saharan Africa and Central Eurasia (the Balkans to Afghanistan through the Caucasus).[18] The zones of contact between empires and civilisations, and areas of mixed populations with complicated, hierarchically-organised identities can be considered as geopolitical black-holes. Competing with each other over long historical periods, empires have typically disputed these areas, which frequently shift as a result of war from one side to another, giving rise to blurred and immutable forms of identity, and in turn, often becoming the objects of special manipulation on the part of interested political forces and powers. The Transdniestrian Moldovan Republic (TMR), our case study, provides a good example of such a frontier area. This territory is situated on the border between the Roman cultural realm, the nomads of the Great Steppe and the East Slavic world. It lies in the gateway from the East European plain to the Balkans and southern Europe. Historically, Transniestria was a border area between the Russian and Ottoman empires (like Chechnya and Nagorno-Karabakh).

Uncertainty, Territory and Mobilisation at the Century's End

We live in an age of 'groupism', according to Immanuel Wallerstein.[19] With the weakening of state control in many parts of the world and in the face of economic globalisation that has irrevocably altered the relationship between citizens and their governments, the construction of defensive groups is understandable in regions in which the old certainties have collapsed. Foremost among these regions are the former Communist states where integration into the world-economy after 1989 corresponded to the collapse of the existing political-economic apparatus. Attempts at 'ethnic-based' state construction have already led to war in Georgia and Moldova, created serious problems in Latvia and Estonia, and have provoked a massive exodus of non-titular populations from Kazakhstan, as well as several of the other new republics in Central Asia. Typically, the defensive groups assert identities around which they build solidarity and struggle to survive against other, neighbouring groups. One of the most effective ways to assert this new or re-discovered identity is to assert territorial control that demarcates a region as belonging to the group in question and not to others.[20] The eventual aim of most of these new ethno-territorial groups is international recognition that can be shown by three criteria: membership of the United Nations, political sovereignty and economic autonomy; a distinctive national culture that is both primary and primordial; and political development and separation over time. The conundrum of the principle of self-determination, promulgated most forcibly by US President Woodrow Wilson, is that the people cannot decide on self-determination until it is decided who the people are. The Wilson doctrine has close echoes in the principles of the Leninist national policy of the same era – self-determination, abstract equality and development.[21]

The concept of identity is a thorny one, though it is not usually acknowledged as such by the activists engaged in political struggle. As noted by Brian Graham, it remains an amorphous concept, comprising elements of political allegiance, citizenship, cultural and ethnic nationalism, and constitutional preference.[22] The hegemony of the nationalist identity, persisting for over a century, now extends into the next millenium. Nationalism is recognised by its autonomy, unity and identity trilogy to which we must add territoriality.[23] For Robert Sack, territoriality is always a means to an end, and is used for classification, communication and enforcement of control. Most importantly, territoriality can help engender more territoriality in a space-filling format, whilst Kaiser notes that indigenous national territoriality has produced a reactive national territoriality among non-indigenous groups in the former Soviet Union, especially those living across the border from their former home republic.[24]

In the vast literature on the origins of identity, there seems to be a preponderance of agreement that identity is socially constructed and not primordially ordained. Whilst a nation may be a 'self-aware ethnic group' in Walker Connor's terms, this awareness is generated, manipulated and directed by political, social and economic activists.[25] Our theory of nationalism argues that whereas ethnic/cultural distinctiveness is a necessary condition for nationalist identity, it is not sufficient. The construction of an identity, whether for economic, territorial or cultural control, is needed in order to maintain a nationalist posture. The fact that dozens of ethnic groups do not exhibit the smallest vestiges of nationalism offers powerful evidence for the social construction approach. Many studies of nationalist construction offer clear evidence of the role of the newly-independent state, as well as that of nationalist intellectuals and the educated classes before independence. Other studies have supported the observation that 'if there is any conclusion to be derived from such a study of the *longue duree* of a small nation, it might be that a nation is never fully made'.[26]

Studies of nationalism usually assume that nationalist identity is singular, predominant and unchanging but recent works have challenged these assumptions, especially for the emergent nations of the former Soviet Union. The concept of 'matrioshka nationalism' has special appeal, with layers of identities pocketed inside each other.[27] Rather than trying to identify a singular identity for a group, especially in the new states that correspond to the republics of the former Soviet Union, it is often more appropriate to accept the possibility of many attachments that can be national, local, ideological or super-national. Thus, in the Russian-populated provinces of eastern Ukraine, many residents find it hard to identify with one political territory because of inter-marriage between the ethnic groups and an attachment to some elements of the 'Soviet identity'.[28] For political leaders faced with confusing, multiple or unformed identities, the challenge of constructing an uncontested identity that conforms to the territorial boundaries of the state and that cuts across pre-existing ethnic loyalties is a major task.[29] In pre-independent Ireland in the late nineteenth century, public memorials were especially effective in promoting and defining a revived Irish identity. Fundamentally, identity for both the individual and the community depends on a 'positive and supportive representation of place'.[30]

Writers on nationalism frequently make a neat dichotomy between a west European or North American type of nationalism, based on civic (territorial) attachments, and an east European version that is based on the ethnic majority, is exclusionary and rejects a multi cultural state.[31] The distinction is extended to that between *jus soli* (citizenship based on residency) and *jus sanguinis* (citizenship based on membership of the nation); the US and Germany are considered as the model cases of each type. Some post-Soviet states, such as Ukraine, clearly opted for a civic model, as the new authorities were faced with a high proportion of the population (about 22 per cent) that did not belong to the titular Ukrainian nation. The lack of significant ethnic conflict in the state can be taken as evidence of the success to this point of that strategy.[32] By contrast, other post-Soviet states, especially the two Baltic republics with large ratios of

Russians, Latvia and Estonia, tried initially to implement the ethnic-based definition of citizenship and introduced language rules to make it very difficult for non-titular groups to obtain citizenship despite length of residency. In Moldova, initial post-independence trends seemed to favour movements that would push the ethnic agenda but within a couple of years, the nationalist position had been shunted aside by the electoral strength of cross-ethnic movements that stressed the civic nature of the state.[33]

For our discussion of the state-making efforts in the TMR, we need to provide some background on the pre-independence situation in the territory and in other Soviet republics. The Soviet nationalities policy that emerged in the 1920s was a mixture of concessions to the myriad of ethnic groups in the vast state and centralised control from Moscow. The central elements were recognition of titular groups and allocation of special privileges to these groups in Russia and in the other 14 republics, an attempted construction of a Soviet mentality and identity that would supersede the ethnic loyalties of the regions, a promotion of Russian as a *lingua franca,* and the settlement of Russians and other groups in all territories.[34] The federal structure clearly motivated the various *indigenes* to construct and define a home and, despite national ideology about equality, the Russian population was clearly *primus inter pares,* although not in terms of well-being and incomes. The combination of a strong sense of belonging to a territory and the resentment against Russians as a privileged group was easily translated into national exclusion and an ethnic-based nationalism after 1989, especially in Central Asia and the Baltic republics.

In Soviet times, group identity was (inadvertently) promoted by the disproportionate allocation of skilled, industrial and state jobs to Russians in Kazakhstan, Central Asia and partly in Transcaucasia, whilst in other republics, groupism was maintained by a cultural division of labour between Russians and the titular populations. Russians occupied jobs mainly in industry and construction (especially as engineers and technicians), health care, science, and applied technical research and teaching; titular peoples were concentrated in agriculture, research and teaching in the social sciences and humanities, cultural pursuits and in the state apparatus. The rise of the educational level of titular ethnic groups and their demographic pressures led to increasing competition between Russians and titular peoples for the prestigious jobs, and this competition was easily transferred into an ethnic one. Feelings of relative deprivation came into play and the kind of mobilisation fostered by resentment considered instrumental in rebellion could be seen in many of the republics even before 1989.[35] Russians living outside of Russia perceived a decline in their living standards as the indigenous majority took control of the state apparatus and widespread emigration, especially from the Central Asian republics, resulted. In many newly-independent states, an alliance between Russians as the new minority and 'third-level' national groups, who had become small minorities in the same weak position relative to the new majority (e.g. Jews in Abkhazia), occurred in states such as Georgia, Moldova, Ukraine, Uzbekistan, Kazakhstan and other republics of Central Asia. In their speeches, Russian politicians widely exploited the theme of the civil rights of the Russian minorities in former Soviet republics but did little to aid their co-ethnics in political and cultural fields. Only in recent months have these (conservative) political figures succeeded in drawing international attention to the fate of the Russian minorities in the Baltic states.

In post-1989 conflict near its borders, the Russian state came to the aid of both Russians and the other minorities. In the most violent situations, the main objective of the Russian state was to stop violence in regions that bordered Russia. Despite some controversy both internally and externally in 1992-93, due largely to the dynamics of internal politics in the struggle for power in Moscow, Russia frequently adopted the peacekeeping mantle. In the four pseudo-states on which we focus (Abkhazia, the TMR, Chechnya and Nagorno-Karabahk), Russia was heavily involved, as either a protagonist or as peace-builder, in the wars that helped to make these pseudo-states.

After the ceasefires, the construction of a new or forgotten identity was high on the agenda of the new regimes. As Tom Nairn has remarked, nationalism is Janus-like in looking back to a historical legacy and forward to a programme of continued national construction.[36] For both large groups, like Ukrainians, and small groups, like Latvians, the chequered history of the nation was re-visited and selectively clarified, whilst the separatist identity during the decades of Soviet control was recognised and lauded. For small groups in multi-ethnic territories, such as the Russians in the TMR, the situation was more delicate and required a much more sophisticated and multi-faceted construction of identity. As relative latecomers (only after the incorporation of the Trans-Dniester region in 1792 into the Tsarist empire, did Russians settle in the region in force) and as a 29 per cent minority, the Russian elite perforce had to choose a civic, territorial identity as the only option for construction of the new Transniestrian identity.[37]

The government of TMR declared separation from Moldova late in 1991 shortly after the break-up of the Soviet Union consequent on the failed putsch in Moscow in August of that year. Like any new political regime, the TMR government was faced with the dilemma of creating the state apparatus but, additionally, had the task of promoting its domestic and international legitimacy by maintaining the separate state as well as engaging in state-making. Raising revenues and an armed force, as well as seeking international recognition, became immediate priorities for the TMR. The low-grade war with Moldova, which simmered in late 1991 and exploded in significant violence in June 1992 before the intervention of Russia's 14th Army ended the fighting, occurred at a time when the crisis in Yugoslavia was escalating rapidly and, thus, the conflict along the Dniester did not achieve the kind of prominence in the Western media that such violence might usually have warranted. The complex inter-ethnic security dilemma combined with belligerent leadership and hostile masses on both sides to evolve to war.[38] Despite strenuous attempts by the Yeltsin government in Russia, the intervention of the OSCE (Organisation for Security and Co-operation in Europe), the election of a less nationalist government in Moldova in 1994, and a series of trilateral meetings (Russia, Moldovan and TMR negotiations), the political situation is still at a geopolitical stalemate. The central demand of the TMR government for a special recognition within the Moldovan state has still not been accepted by Chisinau (Kishinev in Russian).

As a 'civic nationalism', the Transniestrian identity that is now being promoted by the government in Tiraspol does not single out one ethnic group for pre-eminence but recalls instances of local, non-ethnic histories and instances of Transniestrian territorial demarcations in its icons. The antecedents of the present state are viewed as pre-existing and the population composition as evolving over a long period of time. 'During the nineteenth century, a polyethnic pattern of population was evolving in the Dniester region and a single socio-political and historical-cultural entity was taking shape – the people of (the) Dniester region.'[39] A recent series of TMR stamps, for example, has scenes of pre-historic humans chasing animals and making fires. The *Atlas of the Dniester Moldavian Republic*, published by the Dniester State Corporative TG Shevchenko University in 1997 in both Russian and English, further declares that 'In 1924, (the) DMR region gained its first ever statehood, earlier than Moldavia, when the Moldavian Autonomous SSR (MASSR) was established within the framework of the Ukrainian SSR with the capital in Tiraspol.... The statehood on (sic) Dniester region was established in 1990 for the second time.'[40] The explanation for the formation of the new state is provided in a brief, but clear, sentence. 'After the adoption by Moldova's parliament of a series of discriminatory laws, especially the laws on languages and the ouster (of) regional deputies from Moldova's parliament, the people of (the) Dniester region had no option but to seek adequate measures to protect their rights and human dignity.'[41] A museum to memorialise the battle of Bendery (the city on the west bank of the Dniester that was the scene of the most intense fighting in June 1992) has now opened in that city, replete with commemorative banners, books, videos and picture albums.

The promotion of a civic kind of Transniestrian identity is, obviously, not uncontroversial. The government in Tiraspol has been assailed for its repression of the Moldovan identity and language[42] and as many 'histories' exist as there are parties to the Transniestrian conflict. It is not our intent to present the dimensions of the many–sided continuing conflict in this article; indeed, this would easily fill volumes. As a pseudo-state and without strong external supporters, the TMR is vulnerable to the internal centrifugal pressures of a poly-ethnic society and, like many post-independence African states, the TMR faces an uncertain future. But as the East German experience has shown, identities can form rather quickly and, in turn, make future political –territorial resolutions more intractable. In a time of conflict, identities can switch and become modified in surprising ways.[43]

Ethno-Cultural Conflicts and the 'Separatist Manifesto' in the Post-Soviet Geopolitical Space

New titular-based states emerging from the ashes of the former Soviet Union discovered that the formal attributes of sovereignty do not guarantee true independence, much less the consolidation of a stable and strong state. State building appears to be a difficult task whose realisation typically requires several generations. Success along this arduous route depends, in large part, upon the identity or the *raison d'etre* chosen by the nascent state. Two choices are predominant. The first is whether to favour the self-determination of a titular (or 'principal') population, thus constructing a nation-state in the best 'exclusionist' image of the European states of the past century. The second alternative is to attempt to construct a 'super-structural' (civic) state that heeds compromise between the common interests of all its population(s), assuring each ethnic group the right and the means to preserve and develop its language, culture and traditions. If the state is not neutral between competing ethnic groups and not equally protective of all identifiable groups, groups may resort to their own devices. As one of the causes of the civil war in Moldova in 1990–92, the actions of the Popular Front in Moldova (promoting restrictive language laws that threatened the hegemonic position of Russian in the newly-independent state) generated a feeling of insecurity by the Russophone minority, though accommodation of Russian minority views might have been possible without the interference of Russia and the machinations of the military-political elites in the TMR.[44]

The formation of a stable country requires that the political regime govern a stable territory and a 'fixed' population, whose majority holds confidence in this regime. It has become a cliché that a regime can only be considered as democratically stable after the passage of at least three consecutive legislative and/or presidential elections with successive (and peaceful) transfers of power accompanying them. None of these conditions has been fully realised in many of the successor states of the Soviet Union: democracy is too 'new', the populations are prone to emigration or frequently involved in nationalist, regionalist and separatist movements directed against the regimes in power. Hirschman's trilogy of exit (out-migration to ethnic homelands by minorities), voice (rebellion by minority groups or by majority titular groups against external influences) and loyalty (a quiet resignation to the new geopolitical realities) can easily be documented in the Caucasian and Central Asian successor states.[45] In addition to these formal political strategies, considerable segments of the territories of the new successor countries have refused to submit themselves to effective control by the central authorities. They have become the domain of local elites and clans but retain the continued appearance of a functioning central state. Within the ex-Soviet republics, all three elements of the state (the regime, the territory and the population) are contested at once, a combination that renders the situation more unstable than other world regions.

The weakness of the new states places in question the system of international relations predicated on stability and affects geopolitical organisation not only in the post-Soviet space proper, but in Europe as a whole. After a territorial transformation generated by a separatist movement is legitimated by the international community, there is the risk of 'infection' in neighbouring countries, harbouring their own disputes and dormant conflicts.[46] The mass exodus of non-titular populations can, similarly, disrupt the national as well as economic equilibria of neighbouring states, thus launching a contagious process of geopolitical transformations, particularly dangerous in the form of refugee influxes and forced migrations.[47]

It is useful to look comparatively at four cases (Chechen Republic in Russia, the Moldavian Republic of Transniestria, Abkhazia in Georgia, and the Republic of Nagorno Karabakh in Azerbaijan), where the governing parties of the new republics have openly proclaimed themselves independent republics, a kind of 'Separatist Internationale' (Table 1).[48] Taking advantage of external support and the prevailing economic and political chaos, as well as the emergent conflicts between the countries of the Commonwealth of Independent States, these actors succeeded in reconfiguring the geopolitical order after the implosion of the USSR. Though there is no single path to conflict, combinations of ethnic competition, external involvement, the security dilemma and elite manipulation can easily result in violence.[49] There is a real (though diminishing) risk that the example of the independence movements cited above will be followed by other minority peoples in the Russian Federation or in other countries emergent from the ex-USSR.[50]

TABLE 1
NUMBER OF VICTIMS AND MATERIAL DAMAGE IN MILLIONS OF U.S. DOLLARS (ITALICS) IN THE SELF-PROCLAIMED REPUBLICS IN THE FORMER USSR.

Region	Nagorno-Karabakh	Transniestria	Abkhazia	Chechnya
1988-89	100	0	0	0
	20	*0*	*0*	*0*
1990	400	0	0	0
	30	*0*	*0*	*0*
1991	500	0	0	0
	40	*0*	*0*	*0*
1992	14,000	800	3,800	0
	130	*380*	*750*	*0*
1993	2000	0	8,000	0
	60	*0*	*1,500*	*0*
1994	0	0	200	4,000
	20	*0*	*50*	*1,200*
1995	0	0	0	25,000
	0	*0*	*0*	*2,500*
1996	0	0	0	6,000
	0	*0*	*0*	*1,800*
Total	24,000	800	12,000	35,000
	300	*380*	*2,300*	*5,500*

Source: Zverev *et al.*, 1997.

The summary figures for the four conflicts shown in Table 1 clearly demonstrate that the Chechen conflict was significantly more violent and destructive than the other three wars. In a shorter time-span, about the same number of people were killed and more damage occurred than in the other three wars combined. The Nagorno-Karabakh war predated the collapse of the Soviet Union whilst the other three wars began after the formal end of the USSR in 1991. Though the estimate for those killed in the TMR war is 800, higher estimates suggest that about 1,000 were killed on both sides.[51]

Nationalist conflicts were certainly the result of the astounding transformation of the power structure tied to the weakening and later disappearance of the USSR, a super-centralised state whose repressive apparatus had successfully 'frozen' all traditional and potential ethnic conflicts. The Cold War arrangement of a hierarchical power dominating a 'geostrategic realm' was thus replaced, bit by bit, by a great number of smaller multi-polar systems embracing not only the previous Soviet republics and their regions, but also neighbouring countries.[52] The "security dilemma", provoked by one group attempting to improve its relative position, thus resulting in a perceived loss for other groups, is critical to understanding conflict escalation and possible peace arrangements.[53]

The profile of the pseudo-states resulting from the four wars varies considerably.[54] Transniestria lies at the juncture of the great macroregions of Europe – Eastern Europe and the Balkans – as well as Central and Southern Europe. In the words of the former commander of the Russian 14th Army in the TMR, General Alexander Lebed, Transniestria is the 'key to the Balkans'.[55] The geographical location of Chechnya has, during recent years, become strategic. The discovery of oil and the start of its exploitation in the Azerbaijanian shelf of the Caspian Sea puts the future transport of oil by pipeline to the Black Sea on the geopolitical agenda. The oil transport issue strongly influences relations between Russia and a number of other CIS states and, in a wider context, between Russia, Iran, Turkey and the West. Russia is extremely interested in using the existing pipelines that cross Chechnya to pump Caspian Sea oil and Chechnya, in turn, would like to obtain as much revenue as possible for the transit rights. These oil-transit revenues are central to the calculation of the chances of the economic viability of the Chechen pseudo-state and the separatists are able to reject Russian entreaties for co-operation because of expectations of a bounty from oil transport.

The ethno-cultural heterogeneity of Transniestria and Abkhazia, or the clear domination of titular peoples in Chechnya and Nagorno-Karabakh would not suffice, in themselves, however, to predict the extremity of the conflicts that exploded after 1989. Rather, we should point to the role played by the wide chasm between the groups involved in the conflicts. Enormous cultural gaps divide the turcophone, Muslim Azeris from Christian Armenians as well as separate Orthodox Georgians from the Abkhazis, who speak an entirely different language and are partly Orthodox. (Azeris are also part Muslim but mostly non-religious). In the case of Moldova, it was the disappearance of the USSR and subsequent machinations of elites in the respective capitals, Chisinau and Tiraspol, that engendered the conflict; in the other three cases, the end of the Soviet Union merely revived pre-existing cultural-ethnic divides. The absence of conflicts with the Moldovan republic prior to 1990 distinguishes the TMR from the other self-proclaimed republics, where the ethnic conflicts date back several centuries or, at a minimum, for several decades.

The crisis phase of the conflicts began, in three of the four cases, by legislative acts implemented by the new parliaments of the republics, elected in 1990 on the wave of democratic (and often nationalist) opposition to the communist regime. It is pointless to ask who took the first step because each successive response amounted to an escalation of the conflict. One view argues that, whilst the Moldovan nationalist fronts made aggressive anti-Russian language moves in 1989 and 1990, it was the response of Moscow and its allies in Tiraspol that allowed the conflict to escalate.[56] Prevailing perceptions of menace, the necessity to mobilise all the forces of the nation to face this impending menace and the lack of time and inclination for a reasoned response all contributed to create the right environment for the explosion of hostilities.

The conflict in Moldova is the most 'internationalised' as the number of internal and external parties involved is much higher than in the Caucasian conflicts which have been largely regional and domestic. Yet in each case, the development of the conflict has tied external and internal factors into a single knot, erasing any clear distinction between domestic and international actors. Political issues are surely at the forefront for most of the metropoles; only Transniestria played a significant role in the economy of its metropole prior to the implosion of the USSR. Mimicking the independent states' quest for a new identity, separatists within the metropoles have structured their struggle around a number of 'threats', to the integrity of their territories, to their national spirit, to the loyalty and confidence of their citizens; the security dilemma is therefore broadened. A final theme centres on the question of the military presence of great powers in the region – a presence that may be real or potential, desired or undesirable. From the separatists' perspective, the key questions revolve around the threat to the very existence of the cultural or national minority, and the associated risk of its assimilation, dispersion, and oppression. Again, it is only in Transniestria that local economic factors have played a role with a separatist strategy to take advantage of the TMR's relative economic power *vis a vis* the rest of Moldova.[57]

Since the cessation of the civil wars, no definitive political solutions have been found. One of the external reasons for the utter failure of all attempts at negotiation and mediation can be found in the instability of the entire system of international relations in the post-Soviet era. It is notable that the division of responsibilities in the space of the ex-USSR between Russia and the Western political community, along with the ambiguity of the internal situation and the foreign policy initiatives of Russia, has helped to both shape and stabilise the geopolitical situations. The Russian Federation was the only external guarantor of the ceasefire in Abkhazia while sharing this role with Ukraine and Romania in the TMR. It was clearly the direct intervention of Russian troops as 'forces of separation' that assured the completion of the Transniestria accords, a situation repeated in Abkhazia and Southern Ossetia. The final balance of military power and the shape of the ceasefire arrangements was imposed by the Russian forces. In the eyes of anti-Russian movements, these arrangements favour the pro-Moscow forces. Open hostilities continued in two conflict zones, Chechnya and Tajikistan, in 1996 but political dialogue has brought ceasefires to Chechnya, the Trans-Dniester region and South Ossetia. The conflicts in Nagorno-Karabakh and Abkhazia remained deadlocked.[58]

The Trans-Dniester Moldovan Republic

The conflict between Transniestria and Moldovan central authorities is a rare example of recent conflict based in cultural (rather than ethnic) divisions involving several states. (See Figure 1 for the location of the TMR in its regional setting). Compared to other post-Soviet conflicts, the genesis of violence in Moldova can be considered quite atypical.[59] A more detailed review of the evolution of this pseudo-state and its external relations with its neighbours will allow consideration of the kinds of choices and constraints facing pseudo-states.[60] Because of its southern European location, the situation in Transniestria affects non-FSU states more directly than the Caucasian wars and the TMR conflict can easily become dragged into current disputes about the boundaries of NATO Europe and relations with the Russian Federation.[61]

More than 50 per cent of the population of the TMR have a mixed ethnic background. Most people simultaneously mix an ethnic identity with one as an inhabitant of the post-Soviet space (i.e. the CIS), or simply label themselves as a 'Soviet citizen'. Residents of the TMR most often identify with Moldova as a whole whilst simultaneously considering themselves as (ethnic) Russians, Ukrainians, or Moldovans, as well as inhabitants of Transniestria. The regional component of identity with the pseudo-state of Transniestria is growing and the state authorities of the TMR purposefully develop the identity by cultivating the representation by political and ideological symbols (iconography). This representation is particularly based on the history of settlement of Transniestria as a part of the Great Steppes, in which Slavic and other peoples played important roles, and the periods of separation of Transniestria from the rest of Moldova. Transniestria was included in the Russian Empire in 1792 as a result of the Iassy treaty with the Ottoman Empire, whilst the Moldovan territory between the Prut and the Dniester was obtained by Moscow only in 1812. The TMR territory experienced two historical expressions of self-identification and a separate

FIGURE 1
THE LOCATION OF THE TMR IN ITS REGIONAL SETTING

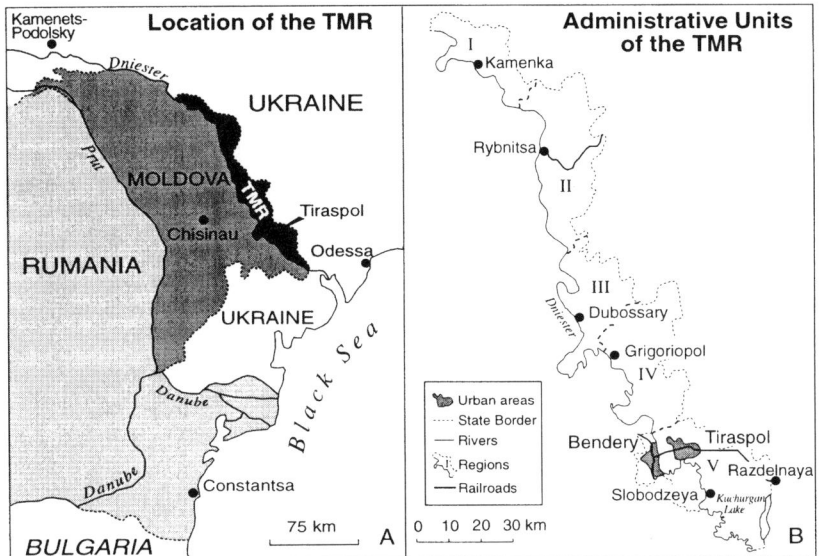

statehood of Transniestria, as the Moldovan Autonomous SSR in Ukraine (1924–40) and in the current pseudo-state since 1990.

More than 90 per cent of participants of the referendum (85 per cent of electors) in January 1990 about the establishment of the TMR voted in favour of it.[62] At the same time, as often happens in such border zones,[63] Transniestrians can manipulate their identities and citizenship. The Transniestrian citizenship is not recognised anywhere and Moldova does not allow a Russian consulate in Tiraspol (capital of the TMR), despite the great number of Russian citizens there. Many Transniestrians, therefore, illegally have two or three passports, typically those of Transniestria, Russia and Moldova.

Eight years after the declaration of sovereignty, TMR has all the attributes of a normal state, except for international recognition. These characteristics include a constitution adopted by referendum, an elected parliament and president, formal government, a system of security (police, an army of 5,000 to 7,000 men, and custom services), a system of elected local administration, and a (weak) currency. In the summer of 1997, the TMR finally succeeded in stabilising its rouble, after years of galloping inflation.[64] The TMR persists, despite blockades and obstacles to foreign economic relations with its main market and raw materials supplier, Russia.

The Geopolitics of the Four Powers – Russia, Moldova, Transniestria and Ukraine

For nearly a half-decade after the severe violence of 1992, Transniestria refused to sign a joint document with Moldova. The TMR argued that, according to its Constitution adopted by referendum, it was an independent country and, therefore, any formula establishing a common basis of the two Moldovan states would be anti-constitutional. The TMR leaders declared also that jumping directly to the solution of the most difficult general political problems was a mistake and they opted instead for step by step confidence-building negotiations. When the Transniestrian leadership, finally in 1997, agreed to participate in the preparation of such a joint document, the position of Moldova had toughened. From the Russian perspective, if the Moscow government fails to succeed to make progress and the abilities of the Russian Federation in peacemaking in the post-Soviet space become seriously undermined, the West would be well placed to replace Russia as the regional peacemaker.[65] In 1997, Russian diplomacy did its best to persuade both Moldova and the TMR to return to the negotiating table and to compromise. A real breakthrough under this Russian pressure brought Petru Luchinschi of Moldova and Igor Smirnov (the TMR president) to a solemn signing in Moscow on 8 April 1997 of a Memorandum on relations between Moldova and the TMR. The document was also signed by Presidents Yeltsin and Kuchma (Ukraine), and the acting Chair of the Organisation of Co-operation and Security in Europe (OCSE), General Petersen. The key article of the Memorandum is its Article 11 stipulating that Moldova and the TMR 'will build their relations in the framework of a common state within the boundaries of the Moldovan SSR by January 1998'. The Memorandum thus confirmed the common future of both sides, as well as autonomy for the TMR, in particular in the field of external economic activity.

Integration of the TMR with Moldova will not follow the example of German reunification, because it is politically impossible to merge 'mechanically' Transniestria and Moldova given the legacy of the conflict and, especially, the 1992 war. The leadership of Moldova hopes that economic collapse and other material realities of day-to-day life will push the TMR toward re-unification. But rational economic reasons rarely work in such situations. Forces of self-identification and the opposition of 'us' to 'them' in critical and transitive historical periods (as is currently the case in Moldova) are often much stronger than the most urgent economic needs.

The 'Triangle': Chisinau–Tiraspol–Moscow

In accepting the compromise formula, President Luchinschi of Moldova in fact accepted the idea that the conflict in Transniestria in principle cannot be solved without Russia. At the same time, Russia let Moldova know that it would continue to consider Chisinau as the sole representative of both Moldovan states, if Chisinau rejected rapprochement with NATO and did not allow any foreign (Western) military presence on its territory. Pre-empting NATO encroachment into the Balkans is a more important geopolitical aim for Russia than the protection of pro-Russian elites in the TMR.

Peacekeeping remains the principal task of the 'Operative Group of Russian Troops in Moldova' (the current name for the remnants of the 14th Russian army). A second task is the protection of the huge warehouses of weapons and of military equipment accumulated over decades near Tiraspol, which had served as the headquarters of the Southern Strategic Direction of the Soviet Army, making it the major springboard of all operations in the Balkans and south-eastern Europe. At the CIS summit in Chisinau in 1997, President Boris Yeltsin clearly stated: 'The politics of Russia towards Transniestria consists of the fact that Moldova is united and indivisible. We shall deal only with it in this way. All remaining questions will be solved only via Chisinau.'

From time to time, Tiraspol likes to demonstrate its economic and political independence from Russia. Since 1996, Tiraspol has patiently awaited an additional company of Ukrainian peacekeepers that were invited to protect the bridges under repair across the Dniester but Kiev has not answered this request. Moreover, the TMR agrees to use the repaired bridges only if they are protected by Ukrainians, arguing that a limited presence of Ukrainian peacekeepers will reduce Ukrainian anxiety about Moscow's intentions in the TMR. Moscow clearly does not like this move and the Russian foreign minister (now prime minister) Yevgeny Primakov responded that 'there was no need for an additional contingent of peace-keepers'. Ukraine, like Russia, officially supports Moldova. The TMR obviously worries that its relations with Ukraine will be complicated by the possible creation of a new political bloc within the CIS (including Ukraine, Georgia, Armenia and Moldova) under the auspices of Kiev aimed at the isolation of Russia. Being very interested in the viability of this bloc and the participation of Moldova in it, Ukraine could easily sacrifice its relative benevolence to Tiraspol. However, this issue largely depends on the outcome of the presidential elections in Ukraine in 1999.

With respect to future geopolitical scenarios for resolution of the crisis, the options remain as they were at the time of the crisis of 1990–92. These scenarios include 1. the Ukrainian option, in which the TMR is included in Ukraine either as a 'normal' oblast, as an autonomous territory within the existing borders, as a part of the recreated Moldovan Autonomous Republic using the 1940 borders or in exchange for the Kiliya territory of the Odessa oblast to Moldova, thus giving access to the Black sea; 2. the Russian option with the TMR included in the Russian Federation as a republic after a referendum; 3. the independence option, in which the TMR remains for a small independent state; and 4. the Moldovan option, in which the TMR is included in the Moldovan state as either a set of administrative units (*Anschluss*), as an integral autonomous territory with special rights for the Russian and the Ukrainian population and languages, or as a constituent part of a confederation accepted by both sides. In the heat of conflict in 1992, the former Moldovan leader, Mircea Snegur, rejected TMR autonomy in Moldova, itself a member of the Commonwealth of Independent States, but he accepted this option in 1994.

Since 1993, public opinion polls in the TMR show consistent percentages of respondents choosing the following options: to join Russia, 26–27 per cent; to enter Ukraine, 16 per cent; to create a federation or a confederation with Moldova, 56–58 per cent (Private communication from Professor Vladimir Grosul, Tiraspol, 24 September, 1997). The government of the People's Front that came to power in Chisinau after the first democratic elections to the Supreme Soviet of the Moldovan SSR in 1990 tried to suppress the Transniestrian multiethnic cultural minority first numerically and then by force.[66] As a reaction, Transniestrian requests rapidly escalated, according to the 'classical' scenario, from a demand of a 'free economic zone', often a hidden form of separatism, to an autonomy within a united Moldovan state, then later to the creation of a federal state and, finally, to a confederation.

In 1998, the official TMR position in building relations with Moldova consists 'in the creation of the common state on a confederal basis and on the issues of partition, of delegation and of integration of competencies by two *equal* subjects'. (Private communication from First Deputy-Chairman of the Supreme Soviet of the TMR, Vladimir Atamaniuk, 25 September 1997; his emphasis). The TMR insists that it should keep its separate constitution. Having its state symbols and the right independently to decide questions of domestic and foreign economic relations, the TMR suggested to Moldova that both sides declare the whole territory of the former Moldovan SSR as a demilitarised zone. Moldova answered that its army was a necessary and an obligatory element of Moldovan statehood.

The probability of a new outburst of violence in Transniestria now seems to be small. But if violence is not used, there are few signs that the *status quo* in the conflict will change despite the obvious continuing economic losses to both the TMR and to Moldova. Over time, the economies of both the pseudo-state, Transniestria, and the rump state of Moldova are adapting to the current situation. Whilst the well-being of the citizens on both sides of the Dniester is more likely to improve with a *rapprochement*, the political elites on both sides have learned to exploit the current situation for their own benefits. Only an economic disaster or significant pressure from below can force the TMR leadership to retreat from its *de facto* sovereignty.[67] In the end, it appears that only patient and continuous efforts by the international intermediaries – Russia and Ukraine – and of the international community as a whole will help to bring about a political, federative solution of the Transniestrian conflict.

Conclusions

Radical geopolitical shifts in the former Soviet Union and in other East-Central European countries in the late 1980s and the early 1990s have generated ongoing issues of transition: How to assist democratisation without supporting the evils of nationalism and separatism? How to defend the civil rights of ethnic minorities without stimulating 'reactive' nationalism? How to develop the principles of federalism to accommodate the claims of ethnic regions for self-determination and for autonomy without promoting the disintegration of the existing state system? Recent events in Kosovo with all the implications for spillover effects into the adjacent states of the Balkans confirm the continuing importance of these issues of ethnic territoriality and the need to resolve traditional political-geographical problems in the context of the *fin-de-siècle*.

In trying to resolve nationalist conflicts, it is essential to avoid a revival of the lines of classical geopolitics, which manufactured a bi-polar world and juxtaposed the West against the East. Both sides were guided by traditional stereotypes of eternal geopolitical interests and by 'natural' friends and foes. Common and unavoidable interests of all states must remain in the foreground; this global interest forms the main basis of what we can call the 'geopolitics of interdependence'. Separatism has typically deep ethnic, religious, economic, historical and political roots. The experience of such protracted conflicts as those in Cyprus, Kosovo, Northern Ireland, Kurdistan and Palestine show how important it is to reveal the reasons for the relative stability of national political and regional identities and/or the rapid changes in these beliefs consequent on recent developments.

Most geopolitical black holes exist in the poorest regions of the world or in areas that are in the throes of difficult transitions. Such regions typically do not cross the televisual gaze of Western viewers except in times of extreme crisis, such as famine or genocide, or in instances when the global interests of the Western states, especially the US, are challenged. Frequently, central governments cannot put an end to separatist movements and take full control of state territory by force because of paucity of resources or because of international constraints on violent suppression; typically, it is in Europe (the former Yugoslavia, for example) that the constraints are most evident. At the same time, it is difficult to imagine that member-states of the UN will allow legalisation of quasi- or pseudo-states, as in the case of the former Yugoslavia. There are often powerful economic and political forces interested in maintaining the *status quo:* some of the new Russian big businesses needed economic chaos in Chechnya for the laundering of dirty money, for illegal imports and exports, and for the expropriation of money that the central government had allocated for the pacification of this region.

A federal solution can be found for some of the current pseudo-states located closer to the world's political and economic core, who abhor the existence of regions of instability with attendant risks of refugees and conflict spill-over near the core's borders. In these areas, including the TMR, internationalisation can triumph. But the semi-permanence of the pseudo-states can also be anticipated as new members of the 'underground internationale' and its veterans remain elements of the world's political map in the absence of a co-ordinated external pressure to settle uneasy and temporary territorial compromises.

NOTES

1. See Daniel Bell, *The Coming of the Post-Industrial Society: A Venture in Social Forecasting* (New York: Basic Book, 1973); Francis Fukuyama, *The End of History and the Last Man* (New York: Free Press, 1992); Kenichi Ohmae, *The End of the Nation-State: The Rise of Regional Economies.* (New York: Free Press, 1995); and Alvin Toffler, *Future Shock* (New York: Bantam Books 1971).
2. See Zbigniew Brzezinski, Z., *Out of Control: Global Turmoil on the Eve of the Twenty First Century* (New York: Charles Scribner and Sons 1993) and Samuel P. Huntington, *The Clash of Civilisations and the Remaking of World Order* (New York: Simon and Schuster, 1996).
3. See Jacques Attali, *Milennium: Winners and Losers in the Coming World Order* (New York: Times Books 1991) and Paul M. Kennedy, *Preparing for the Twenty-First Century* (New York: Random House, 1993).
4. See Robert Kaplan, *To the Ends of the Earth: A Journey at the Dawn of the 21st Century* (New York: Random House, 1996).
5. We distinguish these unrecognised quasi-states from the quasi-states identified for Africa and other parts of the Third World by Robert H. Jackson, *Quasi-States: Sovereignty, International Relations, and the Third World* (Cambridge: Cambridge University Press, 1990). In Jackson's work, quasi-states are legally-independent states, full members of the international community (including the United Nations) but they lack many of the marks and merits of empirical statehood expected after independence from the European colonial powers. Constitutional sovereignty is the only kind that exists in the late twentieth century

and while the quasi-states meet this criterion, they have failed to achieve the economic standards and equal protection of all citizens that are the hallmark of states with 'positive sovereignty'.
6. See Alexi I. Neklessa, 'Perspektivy mirovogo razvitia i mesto Afriki v Novom mire: Sotsialno-ekonomicheskii aspekt' (The perspectives of the global development and the place of Africa in the New World: A socio-economic aspect). *Mirovaya ekonomika i mezhdunarodnye otnoshenia* 8 (1995a); *Krakh istorii, ili kontury Novogo mira? Mirovaya ekonomika i mezhdunarodnye otnoshenia* (The failure of history, or contours of the New World? – World Economy and International Relations) 12 (1995b); 'Postmodernistskii mir v novoi sisteme koordinat' (The post-modern world in a new system of co-ordinates) *Vostok*, (1997).
7. See Peter J. Taylor, *Political Geography: World-Economy, Nation-State and Locality*, 3rd Edition (New York: Longman 1993), p.x.
8. We agree with the view expressed by David Newman that Western academics tend to adhere to the 'boundary disappearance thesis' since they themselves experience no boundaries in their contacts, research communities and identities as international scholars. David Newman, 'Boundaries, territories and postmodernism: Towards shared or separate spaces', Paper presented to the Fifth International Conference on Borderlands under stress, Durham, UK, 15–17 July 1998, pp.4–5.
9. In this perspective, we share the same view as William H. McNeill in his critical review in 'Territorial States Buried too Soon', *Mershon International Studies Review* 41 (1997), pp.269–74. McNeill offers a strong critique of the work of Yale H. Ferguson and Richard W. Mansbach, *Polities: Authority, Identities and Change* (Columbia, SC: University of South Carolina Press, 1996).
10. Kaplan (note 4).
11. For a discussion of the Russian geopolitical views, see A. P. Tsygankov, 'From International Institutionalism to Revolutionary Expansionism: The Foreign Policy Discourse of Contemporary Russia', *Mershon International Studies Review* 41 (1997), pp.247–68.
12. The concept of limitroph is very similar to that of shatterbelt popularized by Saul B. Cohen,. *Geography and Politics in a World Divided* (New York: Random House 1963). For more details on limitrophs, see V. Zimbursky, 'Narody mezhdu zivilizatsiami' (Peoples between civilisations), *Pro et Contra* 2 (1997), pp.154–84.
13. We will use the term 'Transniestria' and 'TMR' throughout this paper to refer to the self-declared autonomous region in eastern Moldova, east of the Dniester river. The official name is the 'Dniester Moldovian Republic' (DMR) or sometimes 'Transdniester Moldovian Republic' (TMR) after the Russian 'Pridnestrovskoi Moldavskoi Respubliki' (PMR).
14. Newman (note 8), p.12.
15. David B. Knight, 'Identity and Territory: Geographical Perspectives on Nationalism and Regionalism',. *Annals, Association of American Geographers* 72 (1982), pp.512–31.
16. For more details, see John MacMillan and Andrew Linklater, *Boundaries in Question : New Directions in International Relations* (London: Pinter Publishers, 1995), p.250.
17. SIPRI, *SIPRI Yearbook 1997: Armaments, Disarmament and International Security* (Oxford: Oxford University Press, 1997).
18. We use the term 'Shatterbelt' following Saul B. Cohen, 'A New Map of Global Geopolitical Equilibrium', *Political Geography Quarterly* 1 (1982), pp.223–42. Though Cohen defined the shatterbelts in the early 1980s as sub-Saharan Africa, the Middle East and South-east Asia, we believe that the definition fits Central Eurasia and sub-Saharan Africa better at the turn of the century, nearly 40 years after Cohen's original use of the term. We find the elements of the definition that stress the cultural complexity and uncertain political control most appealing; we are less persuaded by the relevance of the elements of the importance of resources and external power geopolitical interests. In his most recent work, 'The Geopolitics of the Evolving World System: From Conflict to Accommodation', in Paul F. Diehl (ed.) *A Road Map to War: Territorial Dimensions of International Conflict* (Nashville, TN: Vanderbilt University Press, 1999), Cohen now claims that the shatterbelts are disappearing in the aftermath of the Cold War and in the context of the formation of new geopolitical regions.

19. Immanuel Wallerstein, *After Liberalism* (New York: New Press, 1995), pp.6–8.
20. Alexander B. Murphy, 'Historical Justifications for Territorial Claims', *Annals, Association of American Geographers* 80 (1990), pp.531–48; David Newman, 1998; Anssi Paasi, *Territories, Boundaries and Consciousness: The Changing Geographies of the Finnish-Russian Border* (Chichester: John Wiley and Sons, 1996); and Anssi Passi, 'Geographical Perspectives on Finnish National Identity', *Geojournal* 43 (1997), pp.41–50.
21. Sir Ivor Jennings, *The Approach to Self-Government* (Cambridge: Cambridge University Press, 1956).
22. See Brian Graham, 'Contested Images of Place Among Protestants in Northern Ireland', *Political Geography* 17 (1998), pp.129–44 and Peter Shirlow and Mark McGovern 'Language, Discourse and Dialogue: Sinn Fein and the Irish Peace Process', *Political Geography* 17 (1998), pp.171–86.
23. The authors in the collection of papers on nationalism focus on autonomy, unity and identity at the expense of territory. See John Hutchinson and Anthony D. Smith, *Nationalism: A Reader* (New York: Oxford University Press, 1994).
24. See Robert D. Sack, *Human Territoriality: Its Theory and History*. (London: Cambridge University Press 1986) and Robert J. Kaiser. *The Geography of Nationalism in Russia and the USSR*. (Princeton, NJ: Princeton University Press, 1994).
25. Walker Connor, 'A Nation is a Nation, is a State, is an Ethnic Group, is a...', *Ethnic and Racial Studies* 1 (1978), pp.379–88.
26. Ronald G. Suny, *The Making of the Georgian Nation*. 2nd edn. (Bloomington, IN: Indiana University Press, 1994), p.17. See also Robert Argenbright, 'The Soviet Agitational Vehicle: State Power on the Social Frontier', *Political Geography* 17 (1998), pp.253–72; L. Drobizheva, 'The Role of the Intelligentia in Developing National Conciousness Among the Peoples of the USSR Under Perestroika', *Ethnic and Racial Studies* 14 (1991), pp.87–99; and Paasi,1996.
27. Matrioshka nationalism takes its name from the famous Russian wooden dolls that are layered inside each other. For the original use of the term, see Ray Taras, 'Making Sense of *matrioshka* Nationalism', in Ian Bremmer and Ray Taras (eds.) *Nations and Politics in the Soviet Successor States* (Cambridge: Cambridge University Press, 1993), pp.513–38.
28. Sven Holdar, 'Donbass: On the border of Ukraine and Russia', in Werner Galluser (ed.). *Political Boundaries and Coexistence* (Bern: Peter Lang 1994), pp.43–51 and Paul S. Pirie, 'National Identity and Politics in Southern and Eastern Ukraine', *Europe-Asia Studies* 48, (1996), pp.1079–1104.
29. Benedict Anderson, *Imagined Communities: Reflections on the Origin and Spread of Nationalism*, rev. edn. (New York: Verso, 1991); David Newman and Anssi Paasi 'Fences and Neighbours in the Postmodern World: Boundary Narratives in Political Geography', *Progress in Human Geography* 22 (1998), pp.186–208; and Anssi Paasi, 'Nationalizing the Everyday Life: Individual and Collective Identities as Practice and Discourse', paper presented at the International Geographical Union's Commission on the World Political Map conference on Nationalism and Identities in a Globalized World, Maynooth, Ireland, 16–23 August 1998.
30. See Nuala C. Johnson, 'Sculpting Heroic Histories: Celebrating the Centenary of the 1798 rebellion in Ireland', *Transactions, Institute of British Geographers* NS 19 (1994) pp.78–93 and Graham (note 22).
31. See Hans Kohn, *The Idea of Nationalism*. (New York: MacMillan, 1945) and Clifford Geertz, 'The Integrative Revolution: Primordial Sentiments and Civil Politics in the New States', in C. Geertz (ed.) *Old Societies and New States: The Quest for Modernity in Asia and Africa*. (New York: Free Press, 1963), pp.107–13.
32. One of the key efforts to build a national consensus in post-independence Ukraine was the creation and dissemination of old and new national myths, wrapped especially in the history of heroic and tragic battles for national independence. See Vladimir Kolossov, 'Ethnic and Political Identities and Territorialities in the Post-Soviet Space', paper presented at the International Geographical Union's Commission on the World Political Map conference on Nationalism and Identities in a Globalized World, Maynooth, Ireland, 16–23 August 1998.
33. Jeff Chinn, J., 'Moldovans: Searching for identity', *Problems of Post-Communism* 44 (1997)

pp.43–51 and Jeff Chinn and Robert Kaiser, *Russians as the New Minority: Ethnicity and Nationalism in the Soviet Successor States* (Boulder, CO: Westview Press, 1996).
34. See Chinn; Chinn and Kaiser; and Victor Zaslavsky 'Nationalism and Democratic Transition in Postcommunist Societies', *Daedalus* 121/2 (1992) pp.97–121.
35. For details of the ethnic mobilisation hypothesis, see Ted R. Gurr and Will H. Moore 'Ethnopolitical rebellion: A cross-sectional analysis of the 1980s with risk assessments for the 1990s', *American Journal of Political Science* 41 (1997), pp.1079–103.
36. See Tom Nairn, *The Breakup of Britain: Crisis and Neo-Nationalism* (London: New Left Books, 1977).
37. The proportions of the TMR population as of January 1997 are Moldovan, 33.2 per cent; Russian, 29.1 per cent; Ukrainian, 28.9 per cent; Bulgarians, 6.0 per cent; and Others, 6.7 per cent.
38. There are contrasting views of the causes of the war in the TMR. For a view that largely blames elements in Transniestria, see Stuart J. Kaufman, 'Spiraling to Ethnic War: Elites, Masses, and Moscow in Moldova's Civil War', *International Security* 24 (1996), pp.108–13.
39. *Atlas of the Dniester Moldavian Republic* (Tiraspol: Dniester State Corporative T.G. Shevchenko University, 1997), p.2.
40. Ibid. The use of national texts has been a very important element in building a national consensus on identity, history, boundaries and geopolitical goals of new states. For Finland, see Paasi, (notes 20 and 29), and for Ukraine, see Kolossov (note 32).
41. Ibid., p.2
42. William Crowther, 'The Politics of Mobilisation: Nationalism and Reform in Soviet Moldavia', *Russian Review* 50 (1991), pp.183–202; Charles King, 'Eurasia letter: Moldova with a Russian Face', *Foreign Policy* Winter (1995), pp.106–20 and Kaufman (note 38).
43. Kaufman (note 38).
44. Ibid.
45. Albert O.Hirschman, *Exit, Voice and Loyalty: Responses to Decline in Firms, Organisations, and States* (Cambridge, MA: Harvard University Press, 1970). For details on the central Asia situation, see Chinn and Kaiser (note 33).
46. Paul F. Diehl (ed.), *A Road Map to War: Territorial Dimensions of International Conflict* (Nashville, TN: Vanderbilt University Press, 1998).
47. See Drobizheva *et al.* (note 26); Kaiser (note 24); Alexi Miller (ed.) *Natsionalizm i formirovanie natsii: teorii, modeli, kontseptsi* (Nationalism and the Formation of Nations: Theories, Models, Concepts) (Moscow: Mysl Publisher, 1994) and Vladimir Tishkov, *O natsiakh i natsionalizme: Svobodnaya mysl* (About nations and nationalism. Free Thinking) Moscow, 3 (1996).
48. The data are taken from A. Zverev, B.Koppiters and D.Trenin (eds.), *Etnicheskie i regionalnye konflikty v Evrazii* (Ethnic and regional conflicts in Eurasia) 3 vols. (Moscow: Ves' Mir, 1997).
49. Kaufman (note 38).
50. Roger Brunet, Denis Eckert, and Vladimir A. Kolossov, *Atlas de la Russie et des Pays Proches* (Montpellier: RECLUS – La Documentation Francaise, 1995) and Vladimir Kolossov, Nikolai V.Petrov and Andrei I.Treivish (1996) 'Obiektvnye i subiektivnye faktory dezintegratsionnykh tendentsii v Rossii: opyt kollichestvennoo otsenki'. (Objective and subjective factors of disintegration tendencies in Russia: The experience of quantitative assessment). In: *Geograficheskie problemy strategii ustoichivogo razvitiya okruzhayushchei sredy i obshchestva*. Moskva: Institut geografii (Russian Academy of Sciences 1996), pp.140–8 (in Russian).
51. King (note 42).
52. Cohen (note 18).
53. See Barry R. Posen, 'The security dilemma and ethnic conflict', *Survival* 35 (1993), pp.27–37 and James Anderson and Ian Shuttleworth, 'Sectarian Demography, Territoriality and Political Development in Northern Ireland', *Political Geography* 17 (1998), pp.187–208.
54. It should be noted here, as well, that following the onslaught of hostilities, ethnic purges and the massive exodus of refugees, the population figures for all four republics are only gross estimates.

55. Cited in Kaufman (note 38), p.132.
56. See Chinn (note 33) and Kaufman (note 38).
57. John O'Loughlin and Vladimir Kolossov, 'National construction, territorial separatism, and post-Soviet geopolitics in the Transdniester Moldovan Republic', *Post-Soviet Geography and Economics* 39/6 (1998), pp.332–58. .
58. SIPRI. *SIPRI Yearbook 1997: Armaments, Disarmament and International Security* (Oxford: Oxford University Press, 1997).
59. For this perspective, see Kaufman (note 38).
60. The summary of the events surrounding the Transniestrian conflict is drawn predominantly from the accounts in the Central and Eastern European section of the OMRI (Open Media Research Institute) and Radio Free Europe/Radio Liberty daily reports. The difficulty of obtaining reliable and accurate data and reports from the conflict zones is formidable since reports are heavily coloured by the ideologies and perspectives of the observers.
61. See O'Loughlin and Kolossov (note 57).
62. The honesty and the openness of this referendum have been severely questioned by Western observers and commentators; see King (note 42) and Kaufman (note 38), while the legitimacy of the results remain challenged. See also the International Interim Report 'The conflict in the left bank Dniestr areas of the Republic of Moldova by the personal representative of the chairman-in-office of the CSCE Council', *Political Science Review* 14 (1992), pp.161–201 and Kolstoe, Pal and Andrei Ademsky with Natalya Kalashnikova, 'The Dniestr Conflict: Between Irredentism and Separatism', *Europe-Asia Studies* 45 (1993) pp.973–1000.
63. Peter Sahlins *Boundaries: The Making of France and Spain in the Pyrenees*. (Berkeley, CA: University of California Press, 1989).
64. The weakness of the Transniestrian ruble was evident to us in a visit to Tiraspol in September 1997. An exchange of $300 yielded about 260 million rubles, most in small denominations, and filling a grocery bag. Some bills were *ex post facto* print-marked with three extra zeroes to account for the rapid inflation of the early 1990s.
65. Details of the post-crisis relations between the regional powers and the development of the economic crisis in the TMR can be found in O'Loughlin and Kolossov (note 57).
66. See Chinn (note 33) and Zverev *et al.* (note 48).
67. There is no apparent organised opposition to the TMR leadership, either as an electoral front or as a social movement.

Regional Identity and the Sovereignty Principle: Explaining Israeli–Palestinian Peacemaking

MIRA SUCHAROV

By most accounts, far-reaching changes engendered by the communications and technological revolution, as well as the impact upon territorial hinterlands wrought by the nuclear age, have cast doubt upon the increasing salience of the Westphalian model for understanding contemporary international relations. Drawing inspiration from this debate, while at the same time recognising the violent realities of territorial strife,[1] this paper investigates the function of national sovereignty conceptions in predicting the resolution of territorial conflicts. Focusing on the Israeli-Palestinian case, I argue that the sense that a state has of its own sovereignty confers a 'national role conception' on the state, which in turn helps to determine its orientation toward territorial disputes. To do so, I build upon one strain of foreign policy studies – role theory – to examine the relationship between 'sovereignty conception' and dispute resolution.

Role theory predicts state behavior from a combination of a state's self-conception coupled with external expectations. 'National role conception' – as outlined within role theory – entails two disparate but complementary aspects: the 'role prescription' *conferred upon* the occupier of the role by its environment, and the self-perception of the role occupant.[2] Role theory therefore predicts a state's foreign policy on the basis of its self-perceived function in the international system, combined with the behavior expected from it by others. The relationship between role and foreign policy is thus an interdependent one. As Charles Doran notes, 'international political role reflects the set of foreign policy interests that a state has actually achieved'. These interests, in turn, are fulfilled due to national capabilities and aspirations, and the willingness of other members of the system to allow the state to achieve its interests.[3]

For their helpful comments, I thank Thomas Berger, Jason Davidson, Charles Kupchan, George Shambaugh, Alexander Wendt, Tamara Cofman Wittes; members of the Georgetown Forum on International and Comparative Politics; and two anonymous reviewers at *Geopolitics*. An earlier version of this paper was presented at the 1998 annual meeting of the International Studies Association.

While Doran's emphasis of one aspect of role determination – prior attainment of foreign policy goals – is useful for moving toward an understanding of role, it threatens circularity. If role is determined merely by prior foreign policy behavior, it seems indistinguishable from foreign policy itself. Thus, what role theory – as it currently appears in the field – neglects, is a discussion of the *sources* of a state's role. This paper attempts to fill that gap by adding a central antecedent variable: *state conceptions of sovereignty*. Sovereignty is both a crucial element in territorial conflict (and particularly in cases of contested self-determination) and an illustrative example of role in international politics. Sovereignty 'is a relational identity that exists only by virtue of intersubjective relationships at the systemic level'.[4] Moreover, identifying particular national conceptions of sovereignty helps to unravel the tension between changing Westphalian notions of borders and the increasing prevalence of irredentist and secessionist claims. Identifying aspects of sovereignty conception that are subject to challenge may help us in predicting avenues for conflict resolution.

To construct my model, I draw upon three indicators of sovereignty conception: *symbolic attachment to land*; the tension between *pan-national and state sovereignty*; and the propagation of *exclusionary discourse*. The first two indicators appear most profoundly at the level of *society*, whereas exclusionary discourse refers more directly to the attempt by *elites* to forge ideational cohesion within the polity.[5] In order to test the model, I will examine the decision taken by Israel and the PLO to enter into negotiations surrounding the 1993 Declaration of Principles (DOP). Focusing on the period immediately surrounding the signing of the DOP, I will argue that two of the three indicators – pan-national sovereignty and symbolic attachment to land – are *not sufficient* for determining hawkishness, and that a *lessening* of the degree of exclusionary discourse figures as the more important indicator for predicting the long-term prospects for peacemaking between Israel and the PLO. This conclusion therefore points to the relative importance of elites in initially fomenting change in the state's regional arena.

The article will proceed as follows. First, I will discuss role theory's contribution to international relations theory. Second, I will present an initial testable model for applying role theory to cases of territorial conflict, one which incorporates the antecedent variable of 'sovereignty conception', comprised of three indicators. Third, I will discuss the three sovereignty indicators in each of the Israeli and Palestinian cases, mapping the presence of Israeli-Palestinian co-operation to the varying degrees of each indicator. Finally, I will present a revised role conception model – one which highlights the importance of exclusionary discourse (and the role of elites) in shaping national role conception.

Role Theory and International Relations

Whether one assumes the most useful level of analysis in international relations theory to be the system, the state, or the individual, students of contemporary international politics are revisiting the idea that a state's orientation toward conflict and co-operation is an important determinant of state behavior. That is, the particular goals that a state harbours with regard to the regional or international order – whether it is satisfied with the *status quo*, for instance, or wishes to revise it in line with its national interest, needs to be taken into account in explaining and predicting international behavior. Thus, classical realist Henry Kissinger acknowledged that '[n]o power will submit to a settlement, however well balanced and however "secure", *which seems totally to deny its vision of itself.*'[6] Similarly, in the 1960s, Arnold Wolfers wrote of 'revisionist' and 'status quo' states.[7] It was not until neorealism enjoyed a decade and a half of near intellectual hegemony, however, that a new generation of scholars revisited state 'types'. As Randall Schweller notes, 'neorealism overlooks the importance of revisionist goals (non-security expansion) as the driving force – indeed, the sine qua non – behind most of its theoretical concepts'. Thus, bringing 'the revisionist state back in ... means that ... differences in state goals...have to be accorded an equal consideration along with anarchy and the distribution of capabilities.'[8]

While the attempt to typologise states as 'realist' or 'status quo', as these classical and neoclassical realists suggest, advances our ability to *predict* foreign policy outcomes in particular cases, it fails to *explain* the *sources* of these goals. Role theory, introduced to international relations theory even prior to neorealism, and which has subsequently been largely neglected in contemporary international relations scholarship, can usefully address this lacuna. That is, what role theory contributes to this re-emerging debate is both an added source of recognition that state goals matter, and an initial probe into the sources of state goals. However, even role theory (in its current manifestations) has not gone far enough in outlining the sources of state goals; this article attempts to address this question directly.

Roles can be understood as 'attitudinal and behavioral expectations that those who relate to its occupant have of the occupant and the expectations that the occupant has of himself or herself in the role.'[9] For international relations, what is important is that outcomes are shaped in part by a state's perceived *function* in the international system. This perception is in turn derived from a combination of domestic attributes and environmental constraints.[10] Given the definitional breadth of role theory in international relations, it is evident that each scholar ascribes greater or lesser importance to psychological (individual-level) or sociological (structural-level) variables in determining a state's role. A more psychological approach, for instance, might privilege the individual leader's perceptions of the state's main function in the international system – either derived domestically or internationally, or both. Conversely, a more sociological approach would examine the shared understandings created among states within the system, whereby certain roles are conferred upon the member states through an interactive process of discourse, behavior and institutional interaction. My reliance on sovereignty conception to determine role means that both psychological and sociological factors are accounted for: the extent to which a state conceives of itself as harbouring particular national narratives imbued with land-based symbols, or the degree to which the 'other' is excluded from the political community, have both psychological and sociological components. Psychological – in that (collective) self-perception is important; and sociological given the centrality of communal discourses and shared understandings regarding what it means to reside within particular boundaries.

A Testable Role Conception Model

This paper develops an initial testable role theory model. What I have added to the conventional view of 'national role conception'[11] is the antecedent variable of 'sovereignty conception', which, in turn, makes specific predictions about the propensity for a state to be hawkish or dovish regarding the resolution of territorial disputes. In the Israeli-Palestinian case, hawkishness on the part of Israel would suggest the refusal to enter into negotiations with the Palestinians and/or to relinquish Israeli-owned or occupied territory in order to reach a peace settlement. Conversely, Palestinian hawkishness would refer to the refusal to recognise Israel's existence; in concrete terms, this would mean refusing to begin negotiations toward a peace settlement, as well as to reject co-existence with Israel in the form of two separate states.

Thus, the model is as follows: national role conception leads to foreign policy behavior (in the form of hawkishness or dovishness). 'National role conception' is determined by 'sovereignty conception' which is itself determined by three indicators: state sovereignty versus pan-national sovereignty, symbolic attachment to the land, and exclusionary discourse of political community.

Pan-national sovereignty versus state sovereignty refers to the degree to which a state identifies itself as a member of a multi-state, sovereign collective. The notion of pan-nationalism is especially pertinent in the Middle East, where an historical tension has existed between Arab (single) state sovereignty and Pan-Arabism. In the Israeli case, this tension is embodied (to a lesser degree) in two domains: the tension between the Israeli state and the Jewish Diaspora, and the tension between the Israeli state as ultimate authority over its domestic population versus extremist Jewish nationalist elements that contest the legitimacy of the state to define its geographic boundaries.

The second indicator, symbolic attachment to land, refers to the polity's internal relationship to the territory in question; important is the shared meanings ascribed to the land by members of the given national group. Symbolic attachment to land is particularly salient in cases of inter-state (or inter-ethnic) conflict over a finite territorial resource.[12]

Finally, the process of shaping an exclusionary discourse of political community refers to the sovereign state's tendency to define its own citizenry – within the state's boundaries – as an ideational 'in-group' existing apart from, and in opposition to, an 'out-group' outside of the state's boundaries. Discourse includes not only language, but also actions and symbols that serve as boundary delineators, as well as the degree to which other, competing discourses are permitted. As we will see, the domain from which the 'other' is excluded ultimately shapes state role and hence the propensity for co-operation. That is, an occupying power that effectively excludes the occupied people from the former's own territorial domain, yet entertains the notion that the occupied nation might establish/maintain its own sovereign state alongside it will actually *facilitate* peaceful territorial conflict resolution. Thus, in the Israeli-Palestinian case, as long as Israel 'excludes' the Palestinians from *all of post-1967 Israel* (i.e., including the West Bank and Gaza Strip) prospects for conflict resolution are poor indeed. However, insofar as Israel 'excludes' the Palestinians from pre-1967 Israel, yet allows them to establish a separate state in all or parts of the occupied territories, chances for a peaceful end to the conflict are good. As the ensuing discussion will illustrate, the first two indicators are not sufficient to predict hawkishness, while the third indicator – (a lessening of) exclusionary discourse – is a much more powerful determinant.

Problematising Sovereignty

One of modernity's most important bequests to our understanding of international politics has been the division of the international system into 'territorially defined, fixed, and mutually exclusive enclaves of legitimate dominion'.[13] As the Treaty of Westphalia enshrined the notion of sovereignty within the territorial aesthetic, so too did sovereignty come to be seen as a natural, unproblematic condition of the global order so much so that 'the sovereign territorial ideal became the only imaginable spatial framework for political life'.[14] Historically, the introduction of fixed territoriality was consonant with a broader shift in ontology, neatly encapsulated by the introduction into visual arts of a 'single fixed viewpoint'.[15] While many approaches to international relations theory have re-examined the concept of sovereignty in recent decades to cast doubt on its static quality, only realists have countered that even within a transnational view of international relations, it is still the state which regulates and controls these transnational phenomena, thus underscoring the continued dominance of the sovereign state in international politics.[16]

To reconcile these perspectives, I will present a view of sovereignty which allows for the dominance of the (sovereign) state in shaping political outcomes, but which explores the emergent and intersubjective properties of sovereignty. As Thomas Biersteker and Cynthia Weber argue, 'state, as an identity or agent, and sovereignty, as an institution or discourse' can be understood to be 'mutually constitutive and constantly undergoing change and transformation'.[17] Thus, this paper understands sovereignty as having important *ideational* components which shape national beliefs about the state's *role* in the international system. These ideational components are a combination of the state's 'intrinsic properties' (i.e., territory, degree of population homogeneity, domestic legitimacy accorded the state), and properties that are relationally defined within the international system (i.e., symbolic and legal recognition from surrounding states and the international community).[18] In turn, the interplay between the latter set of properties and the state's internal attributes constitute state identity. Thus, the assertion that 'sovereignty is a social construct, and like all social institutions its location is subject to changing interpretations'[19] can be seen in light of the ability for state-led discourse to shape national and regional conceptions of sovereignty. With reference to the Israeli-Palestinian case, the following discussion will detail the three indicators of sovereignty on which my model is based.

State Sovereignty versus Pan-National Sovereignty

Palestine

The Arab World has historically been wrought by a tension between defining its component states as separate, sovereign entities, versus viewing the entire Arab world as a single nation – the doctrine of Pan-Arabism.[20] As past-Egyptian President Gamal abd-al Nasser sounded the trumpet of Pan-Arabism to rally the Arabs around anti-Israel collective defence arrangements, the Arab states sought to grapple with their own identities. The 1958 Egyptian-Syrian union in the form of the United Arab Republic, which was aborted after only three years, served to underscore this tension.

Nowhere has the tension between state sovereignty and Pan-Arabism been more evident than in the Palestinian case. While the sources of Palestinian nationalism are much contested, and no doubt evolved in part as a response to Zionist settlement in Palestine,[21] Palestinian identity has revolved around a call for self-determination as a legitimating force for furthering Palestinian territorial aspirations over the contested lands that comprise Israel and the occupied territories. Paradoxically, Israeli, and at times American, rhetoric has also served to entrench a Palestinian identity separate from the Arabs: the right-wing Likud party's 'Jordanian option', whereby Israel would annex the West Bank and Gaza Strip while Jordan would effectively become a 'Palestinian state', created resentment within a Palestinian nation committed to establishing a separate Palestinian Arab state in at least part of historic Palestine. Similarly, American proposals such as the Reagan Plan called for establishing a vaguely named 'self-govern[ing]' arrangement in the West Bank 'in association with Jordan'.[22]

In the lead-up to the DOP, a sense of Palestinian single-state sovereignty clearly prevailed over pan-Arabism. The 1978 Camp David accords between Israel and Egypt, while including provisions for Palestinian autonomy, ultimately had revealed the failure of the Arab states to solve the problem of Palestinian statelessness. And Jordan severed its administrative links with the West Bank in July 1988, declaring, 'the independent Palestinian state will be established on the occupied Palestinian land, after it is liberated, God willing.'[23]

Further complicating matters, however, is the Palestinian national movement's complex relationship with its Diaspora. One of the issues, due to its sensitivity, that has been postponed until the final-status phase of Israeli-Palestinian negotiations is the question of the fate of the two million Palestinians living outside of Israel and the occupied territories, including the 800,000 Palestinians and their offspring who fled their homes in pre-1948 Palestine during the 1948 and 1967 Arab-Israeli wars.[24]

Israel

The sources of ambiguity surrounding conceptions of state sovereignty versus pan-national sovereignty in the case of Israel are both less pronounced and more nuanced than those in the Palestinian case. The modern Zionist movement represents the embodiment of Jewish national sovereignty and a departure from Diasporic Jewish identity. Early expressions of Zionism attempted to portray the pioneering movement as embodying a 'new Jew'; a robust 'Jewry of Muscle' divorced from his studious but withered Diaspora counterpart. For this reason, Zionism has even been dubbed 'an erotic revolution',[25] whereby the return to Zion represented a regenerative nationalism.

Not only was Israeli statehood seen to represent a departure from the passivity and weakness of the Diaspora, but the role of the state in achieving legitimacy *vis-à-vis* nationalistic and messianic ideologies has historically been contested. In addition to the ultra-orthodox factions refusing to recognise the Jewish state until the presumed arrival of the Messiah, the right-wing Jewish settler movement has struggled with the state to define the limits of Jewish sovereignty. From Israel's beginnings, Prime Minister David Ben Gurion's declared policy of etatism (*mamlachtiyut*) attempted to recraft a Jewish nation from one that had historically lived on the margins of society (in Exile) to one in which the state has ultimate power over the polity.[26] This orientation jockeyed with self-proclaimed Zionist underground movements (such as the Irgun) to determine the success of Jewish settlement efforts in Palestine. And since 1967, the settler movement in the West Bank and Gaza Strip has occasionally staged vigilante assaults to protest what it sees as the unwillingness of the Israeli government to provide for the settlers' security.[27]

Even two months prior to the announcement of the DOP, extremist nationalist groups in Israel attempted to challenge the legitimacy – and hence the sovereignty – of the Israeli regime. Thus, the Movement for Jewish Autonomy in Judea, Samaria, and Gaza issued a statement on 7 June 1993 declaring that it will resist any IDF orders to evacuate Jewish settlements in the territories in the event of a peace treaty.[28] However, in the aftermath of the DOP, the Israeli government issued stronger statements regarding the jurisdiction of the state to enforce order: Justice Minister David Libai warned Jewish settlers in November 1993 against taking 'the law into [one's] own hands',[29] and the IDF similarly stated that it will apply 'reasonable force' in quelling settler intransigence, if necessary.[30]

Mapping Co-operation: Pan-National Sovereignty

I have hypothesised that high-levels of pan-national sovereignty should result in continued hawkishness, since, in identifying with the broader national community, the state may attempt to acquire more territory either as a 'container' for mass immigration, or as a symbol of nationalist strength. In the Israeli case, it is clear that challenges to state sovereignty have arisen primarily from the right-wing settler movement in the form of vigilantism and threats to disobey military directives to evacuate any part of *Eretz Yisrael*. These challenges indicate that sentiments of pan-nationalism are evident at least at the level of society. Furthermore, Israeli governments from both sides of the spectrum have pushed for mass Jewish immigration, revealing a propensity for the state to ally itself with pan-nationalism as well. Here, the tension between a sovereign state attempting to reign in domestic dissent contrasts with its role as representative of a larger national polity. Implicit in the notion of Israel as being the 'ingatherer of the exiles' is the idea that there is a larger political community beyond its borders.

Thus, the degree of variance between levels of pan-national sovereignty and hawkishness can be measured by examining the degree of co-operation between Israel and the PLO as compared to the degree of pan-national identity. In the Palestinian case, and despite the complexity of the refugee question, it is clear that visions of state-sovereignty ultimately prevailed over Pan-Arabism in the period prior to the DOP. Therefore, the corollary of my original hypothesis that high levels of Pan-Arabism impede conflict – namely, that an identification of state sovereignty over Pan-Arabism may facilitate dovishness – is supported. However, evidence from the Israeli case is more complex: a sense of societal pan-nationalism has been coupled with the state's vision of itself as the pinnacle of a broader pan-national movement (in the form of its role as 'ingatherer of the exiles'). Therefore, Israeli-Palestinian co-operation in the form of the DOP suggests that high degrees of pan-nationalism *in at least one of the parties* is *not sufficient* to preclude co-operation.

Symbolic Attachment to Land

The second indicator of sovereignty conception, symbolic attachment to land, is a more obvious impediment to conflict resolution. Especially in the nuclear age, where hinterland territories have been rendered less important for defence considerations, the national myths that accompany the state's *ideational* relationship to its territory take on added significance as explanatory variables for territorial hawkishness, and as a barrier to territorial compromise. As will be discussed in more detail within the topic of exclusionary discourse, nationalism figures saliently in a state's relationship to land. Students of nationalism and political geography have argued for the importance of naming – attaching a label to a place or thing – in imbuing territories with social meaning.[31] The debate surrounding place names has figured prominently in the Israeli-Palestinian conflict. Some Arab villages in pre-1948 Palestine that were abandoned during the 1948 War were renamed with Hebrew equivalents leading to contestations over municipal rights; the Arab village of Ein Houd, for instance, was re-established in 1953 as the Israeli artists' colony Ein Hod.[32]

Political geographer David Newman notes the centrality of territory in the political socialisation process. Territory is imbued with religious and nationalistic symbols which both strengthen a sense of belonging to, and legitimise national ownership over, the land in question.[33] Historical narratives wherein land figures prominently serve to unify the national group and provide a tangible referent for the expression of nationalism. This phenomenon is even more pronounced in the context of national groups with significant Diaspora populations, as has been the case with both Jews and Palestinians.

Palestine

The degree of symbolic attachment to land is, by all accounts, high in the Palestinian case. Many are the families that retain keys to their original house in pre-1948 Palestine. So too are Arabic names invested with meaning. The Arabic word for Jerusalem, for instance, is *al-Quds*, meaning 'the holy'; from a nationalist perspective, it is clearly difficult to concede sovereignty over an area deemed metaphysical.[34] The issue of Jerusalem therefore serves as a rallying point for Palestinian nationalism, and as a reference point for staking out negotiating stances. As Palestinian delegation head Haydar 'Abd al-Shafi warned one month prior to the announcement of the DOP, unless Israel concedes Palestinian rights in Jerusalem, 'it will kill the peace process'.[35] For this reason, the status of Jerusalem has been left to the final stage of negotiations under the terms of the DOP.

As we will see in the Israeli case, Palestinian nationalism has evolved as a movement defined by dispossession; Palestinian national identity rests largely upon the desire to reclaim the land – both actual and mythologised – from which current Palestinians, and their parents and foreparents, hailed. The call for Palestinian statehood has likewise been an emergent phenomenon, so central was the original goal to reclaim land. Just as the Uganda option – whereby a Jewish state would be established in Africa – was rejected by the Zionist movement at the turn of the century, so too have the Palestinians refused to pursue measures to establish a state anywhere other than within historic Palestine (and now only within a portion of it).

Israel

To nurture their historic claim to Zion throughout the centuries, Jews have had to call up historical narratives and national symbols to strengthen the imagined link between the people and the land.[36] Jews have historically sung folk songs about returning to Zion, and the Jewish liturgy contains references to the sanctity of Jerusalem and the land. Throughout the period of the Yishuv (the Jewish community in Palestine prior to state-formation), the Jewish community rapidly established institutions for renting and allocating the land to Jews, such as the Jewish National Fund (JNF) and the Israel Lands Authority. The blue, tin donation boxes of the JNF, a ubiquitous symbol across Jewish homes in the Western Diaspora, came to symbolise an institutionalised link between the Diaspora and Zion.[37]

The importance of 'naming' as a symbol of national attachment has been present throughout the construction of the Zionist narrative. In addition to renaming Arab locales, natural flowers are given names invoking great battles; one red flower indigenous to the Israeli landscape is called 'Blood of the Maccabees'. And Israeli schoolchildren are taken on regular hikes throughout the varied topography of the country – as if to inculcate them with a sense of intimate ownership over the land. The Hebrew word for Israel itself, *Yisrael*, contains the two-letter appellation for God, (*el*),a subtle invocation of a divine right to the land. Moreover, the name for Israel popular among the more right-wing, nationalist segments of the polity is *Eretz Yisrael* (the Land of Israel). The name *Eretz Yisrael* first appeared with the reign of King Saul and was popularised in modern times during the first wave of *aliya* (immigration) at the end of the nineteenth century. Gideon Biger notes that the boundaries of *Eretz Israel* are unspecified, having fluctuated to varying degrees throughout Biblical history.[38] Thus, those who refer to Israel as *Eretz Yisrael*, instead of the more neutral *Medinat Israel* (State of Israel) are implicitly suggesting that the current borders might be extended.

More recent debate surrounding the historical-symbolic importance of land has revolved around the issue of Jerusalem. Two months prior to the announcement of the DOP, Rabin stated, 'the city is our capital, united under our sovereignty. There will be no compromise of any kind on this issue.'[39] Noteworthy, however, is the fact that the speech was delivered to the Jewish Agency, the political body charged with Diaspora affairs. Despite the importance of domestic (including pan-national) constraints on foreign policy, it is possible that such rhetoric is intended to assuage public criticism of a policy track seen as overly dovish. Just as public opinion was opposed to talks with the PLO prior to the announcement of the secret track (in which Israeli and PLO negotiators met in Oslo),[40] so too might such statements of steadfastness ultimately yield to alternate political arrangements. However, the prospects for a strategic shift are not helped by statements such as one by then-Secretary of State Warren Christopher, who deferred judgment on the status of Jerusalem, characterising it as 'an almost theological discussion'.[41] Nevertheless, there was some indication that Israel had begun to reconsider its relationship to the territories. Thus, then-Israeli Prime Minister Yitzhak Rabin stated during July 1993, 'I am making a clear distinction between Israeli sovereign territory, incorporating unified Jerusalem, and the territories not under our sovereignty.'[42] Despite statements emanating from elite ranks which describe the polity's relationship to particular locales, symbolic attachment to land is ultimately a broadly encompassing phenomenon in which the entire nation participates in creating and reshaping the historical narrative.

Mapping Co-operation: Symbolic Attachment to Land

I have hypothesised that if symbolic attachment to the land is *high*, then national role conception will be akin to 'defender of patrimony', resulting in a *hawkish* stance toward territorial compromise. Measuring the degree of change in Israeli and Palestinian statements and behavior immediately following the DOP may suggest the degree to which symbolic attachment to land may be mitigated. Thus, four months after the signing of the DOP, Israel returned 100 boxes of artifacts discovered in the Sinai peninsula during Israeli rule over the territory (from the end of the 1967 War until Israel's relinquishing of the region in 1982 under the terms of the Camp David accords) to Egypt. The accord which stipulated the returns was reached in 1992 between the Israeli and Egyptian antiquities authorities.[43] Important here is both that the agreement was reached a full year prior to the DOP, suggesting that Israeli attachment to the land (given that the Sinai Desert is believed to be where Moses received the Ten Commandments) might have undergone a shift prior to negotiations with the Palestinians, and the fact that Israel was honouring the agreement so soon after the signing of the DOP, suggesting that as Israel becomes used to relating to its surrounding territories under the terms of bilateral peace arrangements, symbolic attachment to the land may be lessened.

Nevertheless, given the high symbolic attachment which permeated the Israeli and Palestinian polities right up to the DOP, and which has continued, for the most part, since, it is clear that high symbolic attachment to land is *not sufficient* to preclude co-operation. Since a similar conclusion was reached regarding the degree of state sovereignty identity versus pan-nationalism, it seems that if our model is to hold explanatory power, then the final sovereignty indicator – the degree of exclusionary discourse – must emerge as the more important determinant. If this is the case, then we can assume that elite-led processes are the most salient for determining the prospects for initial territorial compromise.

Exclusionary Discourse of Political Community

Consonant with the division of the global map into territorially exclusive domains came the need for the state – as the decision-making apparatus that presides over territory – to maintain and strengthen a sense of political community within the polity as distinct from that outside of the state's borders. As Roxanne Doty observes, 'the inside/outside boundary is a function of a state's discursive authority...its ability, in the face of...uncertainty, to impose fixed and stable meanings about who belongs and who does not belong to the nation, and thereby to distinguish a specific political community – the inside – from all others – the outside.'[44] This view of the function and effects of sovereignty on nation-building is shared by other theorists writing within the tradition of critical international relations theory. Jens Bartelson notes that modernity conceptualised the state as mediating between 'the universal and the particular,[45] and that the threat of 'otherness' is 'spatialized and projected outwards' by modernity 'as a means of securing the identity of the Same. Thus ... what is Other to every particular state is a specific state or a variable pattern of alliances between other particular states.'[46] Finally, defining a national territorial space serves to 'communicat[e] the authority of the controller of territory over people and things' and 'reifies power'.[47]

Moreover, Doty emphasises two additional points regarding the construction of sovereignty that shed light on the Israeli-Palestinian case. First, state discourse is the primary mechanism by which political community is defined and shaped. Second, crises of order provide focal points around which the 'sovereignty effect' is manifested, whereby the instability inherent in crisis situations forces the state to redefine itself in the international order.[48] Drawing upon the notions of discursive sovereignty and crisis points, the following sub-sections will discuss the processes of exclusionary political discourse in the cases of Israel and Palestine.

Israel

Located within a region hostile to its existence as a sovereign state, Israel has been sensitive to the need to propagate an exclusionary discourse to legitimise itself. Doty notes the importance of the terms 'immigrant' and 'refugee' to differentiate normal from abnormal national identity.[49] Israel has historically nurtured an ambivalent relationship to immigration, committed to 'ingathering the exiles', campaigning for the release of oppressed Jewry in the former Soviet Union, Ethiopia and Syria, for instance, while, at the same time, representing a new version of Jewish life – one divorced from the passivity of the Diaspora. Indeed, the Hebrew word for immigration to Israel is *aliya*, literally meaning 'ascent'.

However, as with any nationalist tenet, the practice often lags behind the rhetoric. While Israel pressed fiercely in 1991 for then-US President George Bush not to revoke the American promise to serve as a signatory to $10 billion in loan guarantees primarily to resettle Soviet Jews, domestic protest has since abounded by immigrant groups in Israel claiming a lack of state attention to absorption. The rise of the Russian immigration party led by former Soviet dissident Natan Sharansky in the 1996 elections is evidence of this. In a much more overt expression of revulsion at government policies, the Ethiopian immigrant community held a demonstration outside of the Prime Minister's office two years ago protesting a government policy of secretly discarding donated Ethiopian blood.

The crisis aspect of Doty's analysis relates directly to the Israeli experience resulting in a shifting nationalist discourse – specifically, the five years spanning the Lebanon War and the Intifada which can be seen to have redefined Israel's self-conception as a regional actor. Commonly referred to as 'Israel's Vietnam', the 1982 Lebanon War was the most controversial in Israel's history. Having served under the slogan 'war of no alternative' (*ayn breira*) since the state's inception, the Israeli Defense Forces (IDF) were now forced to confront themselves as the aggressor, which in turn, fueled the cause of the Israeli peace movement and encouraged society at large to re-examine the issue of national security.[50]

If the Lebanon War cast doubt on the IDF's mandate and Israel's role as a defensive state, the outbreak of the Intifada in December 1987 wreaked havoc with the military's identity. No longer was the IDF fighting a war of existential self-defence, but soldiers were relegated to the role of street policemen; or worse, bullies and thugs. Doubts were even raised in Israel as to the future ability for the IDF to maintain its volunteer officer corps.[51] The combination of the Lebanon War and the Intifada can thus be seen to have constituted a crisis of national role, challenging the core assumptions of Israel's national security doctrine, and the identity and image of the military – a crucial nation-building institution in the Israeli context.

What was the result of this crisis period for Israeli conceptions of sovereignty? First, Israel was forced to come to terms with its predominant military power in the face of Palestinian claims to nationhood.[52] Israel mounted the Lebanon offensive initially to counter PLO attacks that were intended to draw international attention to Palestinian statelessness. Second, and more specifically, Israel was forced to confront its role as occupier of the 1.5 million Palestinians residing in the West Bank and Gaza Strip. To settle into this new role, the Israeli state had to create an altered discourse that would distinguish between the West Bank/Gaza Strip and pre-1967 Israel. Thus, there were early signs of a shift toward reconceptualising the occupied territories as non-Israeli space, such as Peres' response to a question regarding Israel's imposed closure over the territories, 'can it be said that the "siege" is a step toward a complete separation from the occupied territories?' To which Peres replied, 'There were reasons for imposing the siege – security reasons. If, however, this has created a new psychological situation, I welcome that.'[53]

The propagation of exclusionary discourse was lessened in other ways, as well. In June 1993, Israel permitted a group of 200 Libyan pilgrims to visit the Muslim holy sites in Jerusalem.[54] The idea of opening one's borders to citizens of such an enemy state as Libya has clear implications for the consideration of inclusion and exclusion. In a similar vein, Foreign Minister

Shimon Peres stated in June 1993 that he would support the establishment of Palestinian radio and television stations in the occupied territories.[55] Organised forms of communication such as radio and television stations are important symbols of national independence, as well as a means to propagate a given discourse. The fact that Israel permitted their introduction indicates a lessening of Israeli attempts to exclude the Palestinian 'other' from developing its own national identity.

Palestine

The discursive formations of inclusion and exclusion are also present in the Palestinian case; and, as in the case of Israel's ambivalent relationship to its own Diaspora, so too is there tension between West Bank/Gaza Palestinians and the 2 million Palestinians constituting the Palestinian Diaspora. The *Intifada* was merely one example of this, whereby the uprising began as a grassroots criticism of the Palestinian leadership in Tunis almost as much as it was a challenge to Israeli occupation. Indeed, the PLO took up the reins of *Intifada* leadership only after the uprising's outbreak. In January 1988, the first *Intifada* leaflet bearing the signature of the Unified National Leadership of the Uprising (UNLU) appeared; soon after, these were accompanied by the signature of the PLO.[56]

Measuring the level of exclusionary discourse, however, is complicated by the fact that Palestine is not yet legally sovereign, and therefore does not yet have its own borders around which to fashion a discourse of exclusion. Furthermore, the primary regional position of the Palestinians – that of being a people under occupation – lends itself to a situation in which identity is *conferred upon* the national group by the regional hegemon. Thus, for the purposes of this study, it is plausible that the level of exclusionary discourse of the occupying power – in this case, Israel – figures more saliently in the prospects for territorial compromise. Therefore, while sovereignty conception is important in broad strokes, it is more crucial definitively to determine sovereignty conception for the currently sovereign state, namely Israel.

Mapping Co-operation: Exclusionary Discourse of Political Community

I have hypothesised that high levels of exclusionary discourse will result in *hawkishness* toward territorial conflict. In the Israeli case, and in line with Doty's predictions, a national crisis served to *alter* the national discourse defining political community; I have argued that this crisis was the ten year period spanning the Lebanon War and the Intifada. Moreover, in the near aftermath of the signing of the DOP, Israel was already lessening its exclusionary discourse. Thus, Deputy Foreign Minister Yossi Beilin, the head of the Israeli negotiating delegation, announced on 12 October 1993 that Israel would increase the number of Palestinians allowed to return annually to the occupied territories under the terms of 'family reunification' from 1,000 to 5,000.[57] Beyond the obvious implications for Palestinian national unity, Israeli compliance with Palestinian family reunification is important for its acceptance of bringing the 'other' into the 'inside'. Conversely, however, as Israel moves toward relinquishing the occupied territories to some form of Palestinian sovereignty, the notion of bringing the 'other' to the 'inside' becomes nullified: the 'other' (the Palestinian refugee) is merely being brought to the 'outside' (in the form of a Palestinian-administered West Bank/Gaza Strip).

Similarly, Israeli Foreign Minister Shimon Peres was quoted one month after the agreement as warning the Jewish settlers that Israeli law in the occupied territories applies to 'whoever is breaking a law, no matter to which nation he belongs'.[58] This statement indicates a lessening of the barriers of political community, whereby everyone is equal under the law. It is noteworthy that a statement of this weight should come in the near aftermath of the DOP, suggesting that interaction under the terms of a given agreement might, in fact, elicit a shift in the identity of the participating parties.

A Revised Role Conception Model

The preceding discussion has suggested that neither high degrees of political attachment to land nor high levels of pan-national identity are sufficient to preclude co-operation. However, the evidence suggests that the state practice of propagating an exclusionary discourse may serve to preclude territorial conflict resolution, and that a *lessening* of exclusionary discourse will, in fact, facilitate territorial compromise. In light of this, a revised role conception model reveals that *change in* exclusionary discourse is the most salient indicator of sovereignty conception, the latter which shapes 'national role conception', which in turn leads to foreign policy behavior (hawkishness/dovishness). These findings suggest that the role of elites may be more salient in initially propelling the state toward territorial compromise. In light of the fact that Israeli-Palestinian co-operation has thus far been extremely limited, we can hypothesise that a societal shift in the other two indicators – toward a lessening of symbolic attachment to land and of pan-nationalism – may be what is required to carry Israel and the Palestinians toward comprehensive peace.

Conclusions

The Israeli-Palestinian conflict has presented a useful testing ground for evaluating the importance of national role conception – as determined by a state's sovereignty conception – in explaining and predicting relative hawkishness regarding territorial conflicts. Examining three indicators of sovereignty, I concluded that the third indicator – the level of *exclusionary discourse* – could be argued to determine *initial* foreign policy dovishness in the form of agreeing to negotiate an interim agreement such as the DOP. This suggests that the role of elites is determinant in setting the stage for early compromise. However, once the initial compromise comes to light, societal attitudes might shift as well, leading to a more comprehensive peace. For the debate over the contemporary relevance of Westphalia in defining the international system, this study suggests that while territory and boundaries are still critical for defining conflict for the actors, the state's relationship to the contested territory is infused with symbolic and ideational significance, and as such, is at least partly malleable. The strength of 'ideas' lies in discursive formations – once these discourses are recast, ideas might shift as well.

This study also carries obvious policy implications, particularly for third parties acting as facilitators to a process of conflict resolution. For instance, the degree to which a state is condoned for creating an aura of political 'otherness', as evidenced by racial laws or inflammatory discourse, may bode ill for territorial compromise. Conversely, mitigating the state's tendency to nation-build through exclusion may facilitate peacemaking. In the Israeli-Palestinian case, paradoxically perhaps, the fact that the territorial conflict is over land inhabited by one national group yet occupied by another, suggests that exclusionary thinking might actually facilitate territorial compromise in the form of Israeli separation from the West Bank and Gaza Strip, and the formation of a Palestinian state/entity therein. Statements by Israeli leaders to the effect that the 'closing' of the territories(whereby Palestinian labourers were denied entry to Israel) had the 'welcome psychological effect' of creating a separation between the two regions suggest the paradoxical importance of exclusionary discourse. Therefore, we can conclude that when exclusionary discourse is used to exclude sub-national groups from *within* the polity, it bodes ill for territorial conflict resolution. If, however, exclusionary discourse is used to bind the community within borders that *exclude* the contested territory in question, it may actually *facilitate* co-operation. Long-term prospects for Israeli-Palestinian peacemaking thus hinge on a delicate balance of discursive inclusion and exclusion, whereby borders can be redrawn to encompass the primary community and allow for the rival national group to assume separate status alongside it.

NOTES

1. David Newman notes the tension between evolving notions of territorial boundaries and ethnic and territorial conflicts that abound in contemporary world politics. See 'Boundaries, Territory and Postmodernism: Towards Shared or Separate Spaces', paper presented to the International Conference on Borderlands Under Stress, The Fifth International Conference of the International Boundaries Research Unit (Durham, England, 15–17 July 1998).
2. K.J. Holsti defines role as 'role prescription' plus 'role performance' (the latter referring to the foreign policy *behavior* of the occupant). I have adapted the second component to avoid circularity: since national role conception *shapes* behavior; it therefore cannot also consist of it. See Holsti, 'National Role Conceptions in the Study of Foreign Policy', *International Studies Quarterly* 14/3 (September 1970), p.239.
3. Charles F. Doran, *Systems in Crisis: New Imperatives of High Politics at Century's End* (Cambridge: Cambridge University Press 1991), p.31.
4. Ronald L. Jepperson, Alexander Wendt, and Peter J. Katzenstein, 'Norms, Identity, and Culture in National Security', in Katzenstein (ed.), *The Culture of National Security: Norms and Identity in World Politics* (New York: Columbia University Press 1996), p.59 n85.
5. The author thanks Tamara Cofman Wittes for this insight.
6. Henry A. Kissinger, *A World Restored – Metternich, Castlereagh and the Problems of Peace 1812–22* (Boston, MA: Houghton Mifflin 1957), p.146; emphasis added; cited in Robert Gilpin, *War & Change in World Politics* (Cambridge: Cambridge University Press 1981), p.52.
7. Arnold Wolfers, 'The Balance of Power in Theory and Practice', in Wolfers, *Discord and Collaboration: Essays on International Politics* (Baltimore, MD: The Johns Hopkins University Press 1962).
8. Randall L. Schweller, 'Neorealism's Status-Quo Bias: What Security Dilemma?' *Security Studies* 5, 3 (Spring 1996), p.92. For a more detailed typology of states, see Schweller, 'Bandwagoning for Profit: Bringing the Revisionist State Back In', *International Security* 19/1 (Summer 1994).
9. James Rosenau, *Turbulence in World Politics* (Princeton: Princeton University Press, 1990), p.212; cited in Michael Barnett, 'Institutions, Roles, and Disorder: The Case of the Arab States System', *International Studies Quarterly* 37 (1993), p.274.
10. In highlighting the component of 'function', I am not advocating a mechanistic approach to studying the international system. Rather, I am emphasizing the *relational* aspect of foreign policy – understood as emerging from the state's perception of itself as defined by its interactions with others.
11. See Holsti (note 2).
12. While some might argue that *all* states exhibit high symbolic attachment to land, it seems more plausible that the level of attachment varies among states. It could be argued that Canadians and Kuwaitis, for instance, imbue their land with less affective, mythical or religious significance than do Israelis and Palestinians.
13. John Ruggie, 'Territoriality and Beyond: Problematizing Modernity in International Relations', *International Organization* 47/1 (Winter 1993), p.151.
14. Alexander B. Murphy, 'The Sovereign State System as Political-Territorial Ideal: Historical and Contemporary Considerations', in Thomas J. Biersteker and Cynthia Weber (eds.), *State Sovereignty as Social Construct* (Cambridge: Cambridge University Press 1996), p.91.
15. Ruggie (note 13), p.159.
16. Noted in Thomas J. Biersteker and Cynthia Weber, 'The Social Construction of State Sovereignty', in Biersteker and Weber (note 14), p.7.
17. Ibid., p.11.
18. The distinction between a state's intrinsic properties and those defined relationally is noted by Jepperson, Wendt and Katzenstein (note 4), p.59 n85.
19. J. Samuel Barkin and Bruce Cronin, 'The State and the Nation: Changing Norms and the Rules of Sovereignty in International Relations', *International Organization* 48/1 (Winter 1994), p.109.
20. For an insightful overview of this dynamic, see Michael N. Barnett, *Dialogues in Arab*

Politics: Negotiations in Regional Order (New York: Columbia University Press 1998), pp.98–103.
21. Though Rashid Khalidi stresses that Palestinian national identity arose independently of Zionism. See Khalidi, *Palestinian Identity: The Construction of Modern National Consciousness* (New York: Columbia University Press 1997), p.20.
22. In Mark Tessler, *A History of the Israeli-Palestinian Conflict* (Bloomington: Indiana University Press 1994), p.603.
23. Ibid., p.715.
24. The two largest groups of Palestinians outside of the occupied territories and Israel reside in Jordan and Lebanon. Edward W. Said, 'Palestinians in the Aftermath of Beirut: A Preliminary Stocktaking', in Said, *The Politics of Dispossession: The Struggle for Palestinian Self-Determination, 1969–1994* (New York: Vintage Books 1994), p.70.
25. David Biale, 'Zionism as an Erotic Revolution', in Howard Eilberg-Schwartz (ed.) *People of the Body: Jews and Judaism from an Embodied Perspective* (Albany: State University of New York Press 1992), p.283. For a more general discussion of the relationship of modern Israelis to the memory of Exile, see Yael Zerubavel, *Recovered Roots: Collective Memory and the Making of Israeli National Tradition* (Chicago, IL: University of Chicago Press 1995).
26. Shlomo Avineri, *The Making of Modern Zionism: The Intellectual Origins of the Jewish State* (New York: BasicBooks 1981), pp.213–16
27. Stewart Reiser, 'Sovereignty, Legitimacy, and Political Action', in Ian S. Lustick and Barry Rubin (eds.), *Critical Essays on Israeli Society, Politics, and Culture: Books on Israel Volume II* (Albany, NY: State University of New York Press 1991), pp.65–6.
28. *Ha'aretz* (7 June 1993), A4 (FBIS).
29. *Mideast Mirror* (16 November 1993); cited in *Journal of Palestine Studies* 23/3 (Spring 1994), p.162.
30. *New York Times* (17 November 1993); cited ibid., p.162.
31. Anssi Paasi, 'Constructing Territories, Boundaries and Regional Identities', in Tuomas Forsberg, ed., *Contested Territory: Border Disputes at the Edge of the Former Soviet Empire* (Hants, UK: Edward Elgar, 1995), p.48.
32. The former residents of Ein Hod subsequently re-established their own village on Mount Carmel which was not granted any state-subsidised services until it gained legal status in 1992. See Susan Slyomovics, 'Discourses on the pre-1948 Palestinian Village: The Case of Ein Hod/Ein Houd,' in Annelies Moors, Toine van Teeffelen, Sharif Kanaana and Ilham Abu Ghazaleh, *Discourse and Palestine: Power, Text and Context* (Amsterdam: Het Spinhuis 1995).
33. David Newman, 'Real-Spaces – Symbolic Spaces: Interrelated Notions of Territory in the Arab-Israeli Conflict,' in Paul F. Diehl (ed.), *A Road Map to War: Territorial Dimensions of International Conflict* (Nashville: Vanderbilt University Press, 1998).
34. For a more detailed discussion of the importance of names given Jerusalem in the Palestinian national narrative, see Khalidi (note 21), p.14.
35. *New York Times* (17 July 1993); cited in *Journal of Palestine Studies* 23/1 (Autumn 1993) p.171.
36. Newman (note 33).
37. Baruch Kimmerling, *Zionism and Territory: The Socio-Territorial Dimensions of Zionist Politics* (Berkeley, CA: Institute of International Studies, 1983), p.90. See also pp.66–90 for a discussion of the role of pre-state Jewish institutions in serving as national symbols. The ubiquity of the 'blue box' in Jewish consciousness is neatly encapsulated in Woody Allen's film *Radio Days*, in which a young, guilt-ridden Allen is chastised by the Rabbi for stealing the box from the teacher's desk.
38. Gideon Biger, 'The Names and Boundaries of Eretz-Israel (Palestine) as Reflections of Stages in itsHistory', in Ruth Kark (ed.), *The Land that Became Israel: Studies in Historical Geography* (New Haven, CN: Yale University Press 1990), p.3.
39. Interview with Israeli Prime Minister Yitzhak Rabin, *Le Monde* (30 June 1993), p.1 (FBIS).
40. A 16 July 1993 poll revealed that 57 per cent of Israelis opposed talks with the PLO (with 42 per cent in approval). Printed in *Yediot Aharonot* (16 July 1993); cited in *Journal of*

Palestine Studies 23/1 (Autumn 1993), p.171.
41. Cited in *Journal of Palestine Studies* 23/1 (Autumn 1993), p.172.
42. Interview with Prime Minister Yitzhak Rabin by *Le Monde* (30 June 1993), p.4 (FBIS).
43. *Washington Times* (5 January 1994); cited in *Journal of Palestine Studies* 23/3 (Spring 1994), p.173.
44. Roxanne Lynn Doty, 'Sovereignty and the Nation: Constructing the Boundaries of National Identity', in Biersteker and Weber (eds.), *State Sovereignty as Social Construct*, p.122. For related discussions, see R.B.J. Walker, *Inside/Outside: International Relations as Political Theory* (Cambridge: Cambridge University Press, 1993); and Paasi, 'Constructing Territories, Boundaries and Regional Identities, pp.46–8.
45. Jens Bartelson, *A Genealogy of Sovereignty* (Cambridge: Cambridge University Press 1995), p.241.
46. Ibid., p.243.
47. Murphy (note 14), p.90.
48. Doty uses the British transformation from empire to nation-state to illustrate this process: the polity engaged in debate over what it meant to be 'British', ultimately resulting in a rejection of the ideal of British Commonwealth to the acceptance of 'little England'. See Doty (note 44), pp.141–2.
49. Ibid., p.128.
50. Mordechai Bar-On, *In Pursuit of Peace: A History of the Israeli Peace Movement* (Washington, DC: United States Institute of Peace 1996), pp.144–5.
51. Ze'ev Schiff and Ehud Ya'ari, *Intifada* (New York: Touchstone 1989), p.159. See also David Newman, 'Citizenship, Identity and Location: The Changing Discourse of Israeli Geopolitics', in K. Dodds and D. Atkinson (eds.), *Geopolitical Traditions? Critical Histories of a Century of Geopolitical Thought* (London: Routledge 1998).
52. For a discussion of the shift in Israeli thinking paralleling its acquired position of military dominance, see Yaron Ezrahi, *Rubber Bullets: Power and Conscience in Modern Israel* (New York: Farrar, Straus and Giroux 1997).
53. Interview with Israeli Foreign Minister Shimon Peres by *Al-Nahar* (in Arabic), 1 July 1993, p.6 (FBIS).
54. *Yedi'ot Aharanot* (30 May 1993), 1, 15 (FBIS).
55. Jerusalem *Kol Yisrael* radio (in Hebrew), 10 June 1993 (FBIS).
56. Baruch Kimmerling and Joel S. Migdal, *Palestinians: The Making of a People* (New York: The Free Press, 1993), p.263.
57. *Washington Post* (13 October 1993); cited in *Journal of Palestine Studies* 23/2 (Winter 1994), p.172.
58. *Mideast Mirror* (17 November 1993); cited in *Journal of Palestine Studies* 23/3 (Spring 1994), p.163.

Abstracts of Articles

De-Territorialised Threats and Global Dangers: Geopolitics and Risk Society
Gearóid Ó Tuathail (Gerard Toal)

The processes of globalisation, informationalisation and the end of the Cold War have wrought many changes in the conceptualisation and practice of geopolitics. During the Cold War, the discourse of threats and risks was predominantly a territorial one and, while this practice persists in 'rogue state' rhetoric, a discourse of 'deterritorial threats' and 'global dangers' has become much more salient in US foreign policy conceptualisations and strategy. This paper interprets this discourse within the terms of Ulrich Beck's theorisation of 'risk society', particularly his notion of reflexive modernisation. It concludes by highlighting some general contradictions in the reflexive modernization of geopolitical threats and risks by Cold War era bureaucracies.

International Boundaries, Geopolitics and the (Post)Modern Territorial Discourse: The Functional Fiction
Fabrizio Eva

With the world no longer 'balanced' between the superpowers, and with the (apparent) instability this caused now behind us, increasingly authoritative voices are calling for supranational rules and bodies and the setting up of a true world government. There is a call to move on from the current 'anarchic' Westphalia System to a world order that is accepted by all and governed for all. The Westphalia System is based on a fiction, but the acceptance of this fiction perpetuates the conditions needed for inequalities in power between states to continue.

In effect, an informal system of world government is already in place founded on the principle of hegemony. But within this system, the establishment of supranational governmental bodies is hampered by contradictions between principles (democracy, the common good, human rights and so on) and the need – created by the state of hegemony – to act hierarchically and 'from above'. It is possible to imagine a balanced and peaceful international system only if one use (or 'rescue' dialectical concepts regarding the centrality of the nation-state.

On Boundaries, Territory and Postmodernity. An International Relations Perspective
Mathias Albert

The article at first introduces the emergence of 'postmodernist' analyses in the discipline of international relations. It then elaborates some central tenets of poststructuralist philosophy. Taking these perspectives together, it shows how 'postmodern' ways of thought can be utilised for the study of borders and boundaries. It argues particularly that seemingly small changes in bordering processes can serve as indicators for far-reaching structural change. It concludes by identifying the merits of 'postmodernism' as not to lie in providing a coherent approach, but as providing an opening of many new routes of inquiry on the subject of borders and boundaries.

Boundaries As Social Processes: Territoriality in The World Of Flows
Anssi Paasi

This paper discusses the changing meanings of territoriality and state boundaries in a situation where the processes of globalisation are said to be increasing all forms of economic, political and cultural links and reducing the role of boundaries and state sovereignty (de-territorialisation), but where nationalism and ethno-regionalism seem concomitantly to be establishing new boundaries and giving rise to conflicts between social groups (re-territorialisation). Instead of perceiving boundaries merely as fixed products of the modernist project, this article aims at conceptualising them as social processes. This means that instead of analysing how boundaries distinguish social entities, we should concentrate on how social action and discourse produce diverging, continually changing meanings for boundaries and how these are then used as instruments or mediums of social distinction. The changing meanings of the Finnish-Russian border are used as empirical illustrations of this approach. The history of this border suggests that instead of understanding the idea of territoriality as one form of control used in strictly bounded territorial units, several forms of territoriality exist concomitantly in diverging social practices and discourses.

Beyond the Borders: Globalisation, Sovereignty and Extra-Territoriality
Alan Hudson

The paper begins by offering a conceptual framework – the idea of 'regulatory landscapes' – for thinking about globalisation, sovereignty and boundaries in the contemporary international political economy. Two moments of geo-regulatory change are described before the paper explains how extra-territorial jurisdictional disputes arise. Processes of globalisation lead to geo-political conflicts as regulatory authorities seek to extend their rules beyond their borders. The paper then turns to consider how such jurisdictional disputes are dealt with, and argues that rather than simply celebrating the dismantling of boundaries and the sharing of spaces in a supposedly postmodern world we ought to pay more attention to the institutional mechanisms through which border disputes and competing jurisdictional claims are managed. It is through the development of such mechanisms that spaces and rule-making authority can be shared. 'With global flows of capital and the internationalisation of production, we live in a world in which the complexity of spatial relations is more obvious than the simple legalistic maps of state sovereignty'. (R.B.J. Walker, *Inside/Outside: International Relations as Political Theory* [Cambridge: Cambridge University Press 1993] p.46).

A Treaty of Silicon for the Treaty of Westphalia? New Territorial Dimensions of Modern Statehood
Stanley D. Brunn

Information and communication technologies are shaping and reshaping the internal policies and external relations of states. The rapid dissemination of faxes, email, listserves, and the World Wide Web call into question the definitions and significance of boundaries, sovereignty, power, representation, and interdependence. There is a need to consider how space-adjusting technologies affect the world's political regions and how the Internet is ushering in a world characterised by rapid speed, the demise of distance, new and powerful state and nonstate actors, and increased flows of transborder information. Features of these evolving contemporary worlds, where nodes become more important than territory, suggest the need for a Treaty of Silicon.

Globalization or Global Apartheid? Boundaries and Knowledge in Postmodern Times
Simon Dalby

Contrasting the models of globalisation and global apartheid as explanations of the global political situation in the postmodern world this paper suggests that boundaries are best understood in relation to the larger geopolitical frameworks within which they function. The global apartheid literature condemns the inequities in the current global economy and analogizes the homelands in South Africa with the poorer states in the underdeveloped world that are both a source of labour, and simultaneously viewed by the beneficiaries of their labour, as a problem and source of politically threatening and destabilising population mobility. The importance of flows across boundaries and the impossibilities of spatially constraining cultures and economies suggests that both globalisation and the model of global apartheid have some explanatory usefulness as heuristic devices to challenge the persistence of unreflective spatial thinking in trying to understand contemporary social processes.

Pseudo-States as Harbingers of a New Geopolitics: The Example of the Trans-Dniester Moldovian Republic (TMR).
Vladimir Kolossov and John O'Loughlin

In addition to economic globalisation, continued attempts to form independent states offer another challenge to the stability of the existing state system. A growing number of self-declared states are now becoming semi-permanent features of the world system as a result of incomplete and contested state-making. Minority groups, dissatisfied with perceived limitations on cultural and economic expression, have been able to carve out pseudo-states, especially in the geopolitical debris of the Soviet Union. A comparison of the causes and courses of conflicts in four pseudo-states (Transniestria, Abkhazia, Chechnya and Nagorno-Karabakh) is presented, followed by a detailed account of the Transdniester Moldovan Republic (TMR). Evolving geopolitical relations between the TMR, Moldova, Ukraine and Russia will determine the course of the conflict and set the terms of the pseudo-statehood of the TMR.

Regional Identity and the Sovereignty Principle: Explaining Israeli–Palestinian Peacemaking
Mira Sucharov

This paper seeks to explain and predict the prospects for territorial conflict resolution. Through an examination of the decision by Israel and the PLO to enter into negotiations surrounding the 1993 Oslo accords, the article argues that 'national role conception', stemming from a state's conception of its own sovereignty, helps to predict relative levels of hawkishness or dovishness regarding territorial disputes. Furthermore, an examination of three 'sovereignty indicators' – pan-national versus state sovereignty, symbolic attachment to land, and degree of exclusionary discourse used to consolidate political community illustrates that the latter indicator is the more important determinant of territorial conflict resolution. This finding draws attention to the relative importance of elites in bringing about initial foreign policy change. However, given that only modest success has been reached in the Israeli-Palestinian peace process, the article suggests that for comprehensive peace to be reached, the entire polity must be mobilised towards such an end. Building upon the current debate regarding the role of boundaries in the contemporary international system, this study suggests that the pursuit of territorial conflict resolution is largely propelled by ideational and discursive factors.

Notes on Contributors

Mathias Albert teaches international relations at Johann Wolfgang Goethe-University in Frankfurt. He has written extensively on the theory of international relations in general and postmodernism in particular. His current research interests focus on modern systems theory and the globalisation of law.

Stanley D. Brunn is Professor of Geography in the Department of Geography at the University of Kentucky, Lexington. Formerly the editor of the *Annals of the Association of American Geographer*, he is an active member of the Commission on the World Political Map (WPM) of the International Geographical Union (IGU).

Simon Dalby is an Associate Professor in the Department of Geography and Environmental Studies at Carleton University in Ottawa. His current research interests are in critical geopolitics and environmental security. Recently he has coedited *The Geopolitics Reader* and *Rethinking Geopolitics*, (both London: Routledge 1998).

Fabrizio Eva was professor at the Institute of Human Geography, State University of Milan from 1995 to 1998. He is a corresponding member of IGU World Political Map Commission. His academic interests include current geopolitical dynamics, international relations, borders and nation-state issues, ethnonationalisms, the geopolitical legacy of Elisée Reclus, and Piotr Kropotkin and anarchic thought.

Alan Hudson is a lecturer in the Department of Geography at the University of Cambridge where he teaches economic and political geography. He has published on sovereignty and financial globalisation in the Review of International Political Economy and Political Geography, and is currently researching the cross-border management of advocacy campaigns by Non-Governmental Organisations.

Vladimir Kolossov is the head of the Centre of Geopolitical Studies of the Institute of Geography of the Russian Academy of Sciences in Moscow and Chair of the International Geographical Union Commission on the World Political Map. His recent publications include articles in *Political Geography, GeoJournal*, '*Post Soviet Geography and Economy* on political-geographic topics. His other publications include (co-edited with R Brunet and D. Eckhart) *Altlas de la Russie ed des pays proches* (Paris: Documentation Française 1995), and with D (Eckhart) *La Russie* [la constuction de l'identité nationale] (Paris: Flammarion 1999).

David Newman is Professor of Political Geography and Chair of the Department of Politics and Government at Ben Gurion University of the Negev, Israel. He is editor of *Geopolitics*. His book, *The Dynamics of Territorial Change: A Political geography of the Israel-Arab Conflict*, is shortly to be published by Westview Press. He has published extensively on territorial aspects of the Israel–Palestine conflict, and on boundary related topics.

Anssi Paasi is Professor of Geography at the University of Oulu, Finland. His research fields are the history of geographical thought, political and regional geography and the problems of territoriality, boundaries and identity at various spatial scales. His recent publications include theoretical and empirical studies on the meanings of boundaries, such as the book *Territories, Boundaries and Consciousness* (Wiley & Sons 1996), 'Fences and Neighbours in the Postmodern World' (with David Newman), in *Progress in Human Geography* 1998) and The political geography of boundaries at the end of the millennium: the challenges of the de-territorializing world (in *Curtains of Iron and Gold*, Ashgate Publishers 1999).

Mira Sucharov is a PhD candidate in Government at Georgetown University. Her dissertation examines the ideational conditions enabling conflict resolution in the Israeli-Palestinian case.

Gearóid Ó Tuathail (Gerard Toal) is Associate Professor of Geography at Virginia Polytechnic Institute and State University. He is the author of *Critical Geopolitics: The Writing of Global Political Space* and an editor of *The Geopolitics Reader, Rethinking Geopolitics* and *An Unruly World? Globalization, Governance and Geography*, all published by Routledge.

Index

Africa 7, 35
Anarchism 48, 49
Apartheid 136, 138, 141, 143, 145
Asia 7, 139
Authority 97–102
Autonomy 156, 184

Beck, Ulrich 19, 22, 24, 29
Ben–Gurion, David 184
Berlin Wall 37, 146
Borderless world 6, 21, 71
Borders 17, 34, 74–76, 79, 81, 94, 96–102
Botha, Pik 141
Boundaries 17, 61, 70, 73, 75–76, 80–85, 91, 112, 134, 144, 147
  international 3, 5, 61, 65

Capital cities 112
Capitalism 48
Carribean 94
Citizenship 133
Clinton, Bill 18–22, 35
Cold War 18–19, 22, 25, 27–29, 32, 35–36, 55, 62, 70, 136, 151
Communism 155
Cross-border 70
Cuba 36, 98–99
Cyprus 152–155

Declaration of Principles (DOP) 178, 186–188, 191
Democracy (Western) 39, 43
Discourse (exclusionary) 191, 193

Economy
  international 90
  political 90
Enlightenment 24
EU 72, 74, 77, 80, 99
Europe 2, 7, 34, 64, 112, 157

Finland 73–74, 77, 80, 82
Foreign Policy 19, 25, 73

GATT 101
Gaza Strip 181, 190
Geography (political) 1–2, 53, 92
Geopolitics 1–7, 91, 133–134, 136, 145, 168
Germany 107
Global danger 18–19, 22, 25, 29

Global security 43
Globalisation 2–7, 20, 25, 70–71, 82, 84, 89, 132–134, 145, 153
Glocalisation 8
Gulf War 58

Hegemony 156
Helms-Burton Act 94, 96, 98

Identity 73, 80, 85, 134–135, 147
Industrial society 24–25
International relations 3, 32, 53, 56, 58, 82, 90, 179
Intifada 190
Iraq 26–27, 37–38
Israel 177–178, 181–194
Israel-Palestinian conflict 179–193

Japan 139
Jurisdiction 96–102

Kissinger, Henry 179
Kjellen 2
Kohler, Gernot 136–137, 139–140

Land 185
Landscapes (regulatory) 91
Law (international) 95
Lebanon War 190–191
Libya 40

Mandela, Nelson 136
Mapping co-operation 4, 40, 186–188, 191
Marxism 32, 48
Metropole 165
Middle East 180
Migration 141, 146
Mobilisation 155
Modernity 24, 27
Moldova 151–173

NAFTA 6, 102
Nasser, Gamal abd–al 182
National identity 69
National Security Council 21
Nationalism 76, 157
  civic 160
Nation-states 6, 69, 72, 77
North America 7, 18, 35, 112, 157

Palestine 177, 180–183, 191
Peres, Shimon 190, 192
PLO 178, 187, 190
Political community 188, 191
Political map
  electronic 114–123
  world 3–4, 8, 107, 111, 152
Postmodern 2, 17, 133, 145
Postmodernism 48–49, 54, 58, 64–65, 147, 152
Postmodernity 56, 62, 70
Poststructuralism 58
Power 79, 82–84, 97

Rabin, Itzhak 187
Ratzel 2, 34, 50
Risk
  geopolitical 26, 28
  residual 24
  society (theory of) 23–25, 28–29
Russia 73–74, 77–78, 153–154, 159–164
Security Council 40, 42
Sharansky, Natan 189
Sociology 90
Somalia 42–43
South Africa 137–138, 141–143
Sovereignty 69, 89, 112, 132, 156, 178, 180–181
  pan–national 180, 182, 184
  state 3, 182
Soviet Union 1, 7, 32, 35, 74, 82, 153–154, 157, 166, 171
Stability 37–38
State (pseudo-, quasi-) 151–155

Technology 108
Territorial
  containment 38
  threat 18–20, 22, 25
trap 70
Territoriality 27, 84
  de- 35, 58, 61, 70
  extra 94, 102
  re- 5, 61, 70
Territorialization 61, 64, 69, 79
Thirty Years War 107
Trans Dniester Moldovan Republic (TMR) 151–173
Transborder problems 110
Transnational threat 21
Transniesta 151–173

Ukraine 151–173
UN 20, 41–45, 140, 143, 156
USA 94, 98, 141

Warsaw Pact 146
West Bank 181–183, 190
Westphalia
  treaty of 106, 108, 114, 119, 181
  system 5–6, 17, 32, 34, 36, 39, 47, 55, 177
  Peace of 33, 57
  state 2, 7, 17
World Trade Organisation 96, 99, 102
World War II 2, 25, 74, 77, 81

Yeltsin, Boris 169

Books of Related Interest

Geopolitics and Strategy

Colin S Gray, *University of Hull* and **Geoffrey Sloan,**
Britannia Royal Naval College, Dartmouth (Eds)

Geopolitical conditions influence all strategic behaviour. Even today, when co-operation among different kinds of military power is expected as the norm, action has to be planned and executed in specific physical environments. The geographical world cannot be avoided – we cannot operate beyond geography – and it happens to be 'organised' into land, sea, air and space (and possibly, the electromagnetic spectrum including 'cyberspace'). Although the meaning of geography for strategy is a perpetual historical theme, explicit theory on the subject is barely more than a hundred years old. Ideas about the implications of geographical, especially spatial, relationships for political power – which is to say 'geopolitics' – flourished early in the twentieth century. However, those ideas fell into neglect, not to say opprobrium even, when geopolitics was found guilty by association with German *Geopolitik*, when the subject seemed to encourage an unhealthy determinism, and when new technologies appeared to place geography at a severe discount.

The authors of *Geopolitics and Strategy* rescue their subject from its unwarranted neglect, demonstrate how geography can be mentally and nationally subjective, as well as physically objective, and generally show what geopoliticians can contribute to the better understanding of strategy and statecraft.

208 pages illus 1999
0 7146 4990 2 cloth
0 7146 8053 2 paper
A special issue of The Journal of Strategic Studies

FRANK CASS PUBLISHERS
Newbury House, 900 Eastern Avenue, Ilford, Essex, IG2 7HH
Tel: +44 (0)181 599 8866 Fax: +44 (0)181 599 0984 E-mail: info@frankcass.com
NORTH AMERICA
5804 NE Hassalo Street, Portland, OR 97213 3644, USA
Tel: 800 944 6190 Fax: 503 280 8832 E-mail: cass@isbs.com
Website: www.frankcass.com

Geoproperty

Foreign Affairs, National Security and Property Rights

Geoff Demarest, United States Army

As James Madison noted, the most common and durable source of factions among men is the various and unequal distribution of property.

Geoproperty rediscovers property as a common denominator in human conflict as well as a useful tool for International Studies. In order to apply property theory as a key to the analysis of human struggle, a broad definition of the term has to be accepted. 'Property' is more than the things people own; it is the mass of rights and duties that associate persons with things especially land. Arrogation of property is usually the precursor to the violation of 'human rights', but Geoff Demarest argues that the crusade for human rights has become a chase after symptoms that ignores the calculus of violated property rights underlying most murder and theft. A better understanding of property dynamics can help us achieve our strategic designs, pacific or not. With *Geoproperty,* Demarest seeks to restart International Studies at the point of property, and in so doing to find a mechanism for interpreting property changes, including those brought about by new technologies.

This work demonstrates that some innovations create new strategic property and new conflicts. Electromagnetic wavelengths, geostatic orbits, genetic code – these kinds of property are difficult to draw on a map, but people are bound to fight over them, and someone's rights will assuredly be violated in the process. But, Demarest argues, we have not reached the end of history, and modern man has not yet thrown off the chains against which he struggles. Indeed, we will continue to fight over property as before, but the property will take on a post-modern character.

288 pages 1998
0 7146 4854 X cloth
0 7146 4475 7 paper

FRANK CASS PUBLISHERS
Newbury House, 900 Eastern Avenue, Ilford, Essex, IG2 7HH
Tel: +44 (0)181 599 8866 Fax: +44 (0)181 599 0984 E-mail: info@frankcass.com
NORTH AMERICA
5804 NE Hassalo Street, Portland, OR 97213 3644, USA
Tel: 800 944 6190 Fax: 503 280 8832 E-mail: cass@isbs.com
Website: 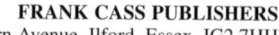 www.frankcass.com

Land-Locked States of Africa and Asia

Dick Hodder, Sarah J Lloyd and Keith McLachlan,
School of Oriental and African Studies, London (Eds)

Since 1991 more than a dozen new land-locked states have emerged to be confronted with the established geostrategic problems of access and communications. For some, establishing transit routes is a crucial question for the exploitation of their energy resources. In many developing countries the condition of land-lockedness has often been an intrinsic factor in their poor economic performance. With the end of the Cold War and subsequent cuts in political and economic support, new alliances are being forged between African and Asian land-locked states and their neighbours.

The authors comprise a balance between regional specialists and those few authorities who have written extensively on the geopolitical implications of land-lockedness. A number of case studies in this book focus on the creation of the state's transportation systems by examining the historical development of trade routes, transportation systems and boundaries.

156 pages maps 1997
0 7146 4829 9 cloth
0 7146 4371 8 paper
A special issue of the journal Geopolitics

FRANK CASS PUBLISHERS
Newbury House, 900 Eastern Avenue, Ilford, Essex, IG2 7HH
Tel: +44 (0)181 599 8866 Fax: +44 (0)181 599 0984 E-mail: info@frankcass.com
NORTH AMERICA
5804 NE Hassalo Street, Portland, OR 97213 3644, USA
Tel: 800 944 6190 Fax: 503 280 8832 E-mail: cass@isbs.com
Website: www.frankcass.com

The State in Western Europe
Retreat or Redefinition?

Wolfgang C Müller, *University of Vienna* and **Vincent Wright,** *Nuffield College, Oxford (Eds)*

Focusing exclusively on the functional rather than the territorial level, this book reveals that the reshaping of the state in Western Europe involves different policies across Europe and conflicting tendencies in the impact of the various reform programmes. Whilst the state may be in retreat in some respects, its activity may be increasing in others. And nowhere, not even in Britain, has its key decision-making role been seriously undermined.

200 pages 1994
0 7146 4594 X cloth
A special issue of the journal West European Politics

FRANK CASS PUBLISHERS
Newbury House, 900 Eastern Avenue, Ilford, Essex, IG2 7HH
Tel: +44 (0)181 599 8866 Fax: +44 (0)181 599 0984 E-mail: info@frankcass.com
NORTH AMERICA
5804 NE Hassalo Street, Portland, OR 97213 3644, USA
Tel: 800 944 6190 Fax: 503 280 8732 E-mail: cass@isbs.com
Website: www.frankcass.com

THE
POETIC TRADITION

Essays on Greek, Latin,
and English Poetry

The Percy Graeme Turnbull
Memorial Lectures on Poetry

*Delivered at The Johns Hopkins University
and published by The Johns Hopkins Press*

THE ENGLISH RENAISSANCE: FACT OR FICTION, by E. M. W. Tillyard (1952)

THE POETRY OF GREEK TRAGEDY, by Richmond Lattimore (1958)

FOUR POETS ON POETRY, edited by Don Cameron Allen (1959)

THE MOMENT OF POETRY, edited by Don Cameron Allen (1962)

THE POETIC TRADITION: ESSAYS ON GREEK, LATIN, AND ENGLISH POETRY, edited by Don Cameron Allen and Henry T. Rowell (1968)

*Don Cameron Allen and
Henry T. Rowell, Editors*

THE
POETIC TRADITION

Essays on Greek, Latin, and English Poetry

THE JOHNS HOPKINS PRESS
BALTIMORE

Copyright © 1968 by the The Johns Hopkins Press, Baltimore, Maryland   21218
All Rights Reserved
Manufactured in the United States of America
Library of Congress Catalog Card Number 68-15448

PREFACE

Since the beginning of written records, men have observed in the flow of human life both a similarity and a difference. Heraclitus of Ephesus, poet and philosopher, put this observation into the metaphor of a river which appeared to be the same but was always something else. Pleased by this figure, the fastidious Ovid phrased and rephrased it, making it part of the literary vocabulary of western culture. The temporal measurements of sunrise and sunset could be expressed in terms of a great torrent, always the same and yet ever new. "What was before is left behind, and what was not is, and all is momently new." The two parts of the comparison present the inevitable third: there is change in permanence, permanence in change. Other Romans were at home with this paradox, and, like Marcus Aurelius with his poignant awareness of being at the center of an immense alteration, employed it again and again. By the fourth century, the metaphor has the Christian authorization of Gregory the Greek and Augustine the Roman, but it is the last of the pagans, Claudian, who discovers, "far from the range of our minds, scarcely approached by the Gods," the great cavern of Time, where the river transformed into a serpent symbolizes the alteration of the permanent.

With the beginning of our own age, the constant river of change becomes a living philosophical pattern. For some men, like Alberti, it is an enigmatic vision of all existence, and it is so accepted by the new poets: Ronsard, DuBellay, Spenser, Shakespeare, Donne.

v

Wandering through the ruins of what once was the *caput mundi*, DuBellay, for example, saw in the Tiber itself the mighty lesson. All that was Rome is here; time destroys what seems firm, only change is permanent. By localizing the Ovidian figure, the author of *Les Regrets* makes the alteration which establishes the tradition. Tradition is always inescapable, but it is, as every artist knows, the innovator who refurnishes it with change, who makes it enduring. This very simple idea is still among us; and when he was near the end of his career, Yeats restated it as the problem of the poet in three well-known lines.

> Shakespearean fish swam the sea, far away from land;
> Romantic fish swam in nets coming to the hand;
> Who are all those fish that lie gasping on the strand?

The conviction that all great poets, Greek, Roman, English, and American, take what their ancestors have given them and change it, perhaps only slightly but enough to make it new, dominates the following seven essays; for all of these critics understand that poets do not dwell in a flat, dry land, but by the river of tradition and are sensitive to the permanence of its changes.

The following seven lectures were delivered during the academic year of 1965–66 at The Johns Hopkins University as the Percy Graeme Turnbull Memorial Lectures on Poetry. The editors wish to acknowledge, in the name of the university community, our gratitude to the Turnbull family of Baltimore for making this a regular feature of our intellectual life.

D. C. A.

H. T. R.

CONTENTS

	Preface	v
John H. Finley, Jr.	Pindar's Beginnings	3
T. B. L. Webster	Euripides: Traditionalist and Innovator	27
Victor Pöschl	Poetry and Philosophy in Horace	47
George E. Duckworth	The "Old" and the "New" in Vergil's *Aeneid*	63
Wolfgang Clemen	The Uniqueness of Spenser's *Epithalamion*	81
Arnold Stein	George Herbert: The Art of Plainness	99
Roy Harvey Pearce	Whitman and Our Hope for Poetry	123
	Index	141

THE POETIC TRADITION

Essays on Greek, Latin, and English Poetry

John H. Finley, Jr.

❧ PINDAR'S BEGINNINGS

Aristotle begins the Fifth Book of *The Metaphysics* with something like a sigh. Every branch of knowledge, he says, deals with causes and principles. But all these branches, he goes on, "mark off some entity or some class and concern themselves with that, not with being absolutely and *qua* being. They fail to give an account of being, but from it as point of departure—either identifying it to sense impression or assuming it by hypothesis—they with more or less rigor demonstrate the essentials of the genus that concerns them." Even Aristotle, it seems, knows the decline of wishing to lay hands on pure being, only to be deflected to some part of it—and, even then, not to the being of that part but to its structure. In spite of his respect for identity, he would no doubt be surprised to have his words applied to Pindar—indeed to anything in history—yet they come to mind because a first motive for studying great figures of the past is the wish to share their outlook and tone of feeling. But the desire to enter into a bygone mind and see the world with its eyes meets obstacles, raised partly by ourselves, partly by the incompleteness of the record, and the attempt to fill in lost details returns us to the secondary kinds of knowledge of which Aristotle complains. The greater the subject, the sharper is the falling away from the original hope to the actual gain, and study of Pindar is no exception. The central fact about him and the source of the exhilaration that he inspires is of course his sweeping and brilliant but at bottom natural and unstrained style. So far as a style may be shared, he shares it with Aeschylus, and it relates in some way to the great events of their lifetimes.

But whence he achieved it, what ideas were its precondition, and from what assumptions it took strength—all this is finally hidden in the state of being that eludes us. Hence the previous quotation from Aristotle. Let us trace some elements of this style in the hope of entering more fully into the mind that fused and united them.

Pindar owed much to two men of the generation just before his own, Theognis and Simonides. Douglas Young's recent edition of Theognis[1] imaginatively, at times ingeniously, presents the elegies as works of one man—a view that corroborates and advances that of E. Harrison's edition of 1902.[2] The conclusion is important; it makes a difference to be able to hear in the collection, not a Babel of voices, but a single voice, broken and interrupted, to be sure, by the tradition, but consistent in its tough self-trust and unblunted definiteness. From Homer through Sophocles we are used to learning of the hard instructions of time and suffering; not so in Theognis, who stays exactly who he is. Young sees in our collection,[3] first, fairly full remnants of an early group of poems reflecting Theognis' involvement at once with Cyrnus and with politics—which poems in pride of authorship and to avoid misquoting he deposited, Young thinks, under seal at the shrine of Apollo Prostaterius at Megara; then, much more fragmentary parts of two longer collections—one of which, says the Suda, extended to twenty-eight hundred verses—from later stages of his long and troubled life; finally, the present Second Book, the so-called Μοῦσα Παιδική (Poems to Boys), contemporaneous with the first group but kept separately. The Suda's notice suggests that all these groups, together with a poem on a Sicilian siege—perhaps, Harrison thinks,[4] that of Megara Hyblaea by Gelon in 483—survived in antiquity; but our tradition perpetuates an anthology, made by unknown hands on unknown principles, which seems to have reached Athens by the end of the fifth century. If the well-known poems near the start of the collection (39–68) on the rise of new classes in Megara are to be connected with the excesses which, according to Aristotle,[5] induced the return of the exiles, his travels

---

[1] *Theognis . . . . post Ernestum Diehl edidit Douglas Young* (Teubner, 1961).
[2] E. Harrison, *Studies in Theognis* (Cambridge, 1902).
[3] Young, *op. cit.*, pp. IX–XIV.
[4] Harrison, *op. cit.*, pp. 295–97.
[5] *Politics* 1300a 14–19, 1302b 25–32, 1304b 31–35. Harrison, *op. cit.*, pp. 301–3.

may date from that disturbed period; he says that he was in Sicily, Sparta, and Euboea (783–85), and the tradition that he was a citizen of Megara Hyblaea would fit those years. In another poem he speaks of spying, apparently from Attica, his own former fields, now tilled by strangers (825–30), and in Thebes he applies to himself, evidently through poverty, the name Aithon which the disguised Odysseus used in Ithaca; he also rebukes a servant girl as Odysseus did Melantho.[6] But he is in Megara when the Persians approach, as Herodotus describes their doing in the spring of 479 when Mardonius retired from the second occupation of Athens.[7] He addresses a Simonides and an Onomacritus, but it is uncertain whether they are the famous bearers of those names and, if so, whether he knew them in the Athens of their joint patron Hipparchus.[8] He inveighs against tyranny but is presumably thinking of the Megarian tyrant; at least, to judge by what seems his abuse of Miltiades and the Athenians for their attack in 506 on Chalcis and their spoliation of the rich proprietors of the Lelantine plain,[9] he is as hostile to the Athenian democracy. Socially and politically, he remains to the end the ἀγαθός (aristocrat) that he was born; in the clarity of his tastes and distastes, in his addiction to poetry, love, and wine, and in his unsinkable confidence he is the talented exemplar of a breed that neither learned nor forgot.

Much connects him with Pindar: parallels of theme and phrase between the elegies and the odes, the two men's overlapping years and the unlikelihood that they failed to meet, their common ties of firm cantonalism. But one reason outweighs the rest: namely, Pindar's quite different sense of his poetic function in the Epinicians and in the sacral poems, such as the Paeans and Parthenia. He personally speaks in the Epinicians, and his "I" and "we" mean Pindar;[10] in the sacral poems "I" and "we" tend to mean

---

[6] Vv. 1209–16. *Od.* XIX, 183; 71–88.

[7] Vv. 773–82. Herod. IX, 14.

[8] Vv. 469, 667, 1349, 503. For possible attribution of the poems to Simonides to a nearly contemporary Euenus or to the better known Euenus, the friend of Socrates, see C. M. Bowra, *Greek Lyric Poetry* (2nd ed.; Oxford, 1961), p. 385, n. 3.

[9] Vv. 891–94, with Young's note.

[10] Mary R. Lefkowitz, "Τῷ καὶ ἐγώ The First Person in Pindar," *H.S.C.P.* 67 (1963): 177–253. Mrs. Lefkowitz dispels such doubts that first persons in the Epinicians always mean Pindar, as those of H. Fränkel, *Dichtung und Philosophie des Frühen Griechentüms* (Philological Monographs, American Philological Assoc., XIII, 1951), p. 541, n. 1.

the chorus. The singer (or perhaps singers) of his Maiden-song[11] is less animated than Alcman's fresh and talkative girls, but she is as feminine. The Abderitan youths of the Second Paean and the Ceotes of the Fourth speak in the person of their cities: "I am a young city," say the former; "I am horseless and inexperienced in cattle-raising," say the latter.[12] This is the voice of the more ancient corporate tradition that descended to the choruses of tragedy; to please a god and woo his favor for a group or city was to speak in its name. Epic poets, by contrast, had sung as lone figures—it is for himself that Homer seeks inspiration in the first lines of the *Iliad* and the *Odyssey*—and this personal role of the singer, restrained in Homer, grew emphatic in Hesiod and the elegists. Their stance as teachers enhanced individuality; Hesiod is the earliest Greek whom we know well as a person; and the weight of self that thus attached to a singer seems with time to have infected the choral tradition. At least Alcman mentions himself,[13] though we do not know in what kind of poem; Ibycus at the Court of Polycrates turned choral toward monodic poetry; and in some fragments of the Paeans and Dithyrambs Pindar's "I" may mean himself.[14] The problem is complicated both by the fragmentary state of these poems and because, as Schadewaldt noted,[15] Pindar's "I" is often formal and bardic, not personal in any strict sense. It signifies his involvement in an occasion and usefully allows him emphasis and transition. This bardic "I" is quite different from

[11] Fr. 84 (Bowra). Cf. Alcman frs. 1, 9, 16, 19, 20, 23, 24, 32, 60 (Diehl).

[12] Frs. 36, 19; 38, 24.

[13] Fr. 94, less certainly 92, 93, 96. Bowra, *Greek Lyric Poetry*, p. 23, thinks the famous lines on the kingfisher and halcyons (fr. 94) from a prelude. If so, the poet may feel free to mention himself, in the manner of the Homeric Hymns, before the formal song begins.

[14] Several Paeans, including those in which the chorus refers to itself in the first person, contain usually near the start or end an "I" or "we" that probably means Pindar: near the end, *Pa.* 2, 65 (fr. 36); *Pa.* 5, 44 (fr. 39); *Pa.* 7b, 6 (fr. 42); *Pa.* 9, 21, 34–40; near the start, *Pa.* 6, 1–15, 58. So also the Dithyramb for the Athenians, fr. 63, 7–10. All these statements fit the chorus, but even if, as seems the case, they mean the poet, he evidently feels no ambiguity because he identifies himself with the chorus. As just noted, this genial license to choral poets to mention themselves (often to adduce inspiration or good intent) may go back as far as Alcman. Choral poets, though vocationally given to speaking in the person of the chorus, may have felt as entitled to self-statement as epic poets.

[15] "Der Aufbau des pindarischen Epinikion" (*Schriften der Königsberger Gelehrten Gesellschaft*, 5 [1928]: 3), 259–343.

the personal "I" characteristic of the monodic and elegiac poets and not uncharacteristic of Pindar in the Epinicians, and the difference returns us to his bond with Theognis. The Epinicians—also the Encomia, Scolia, and Dirges—were not communal or (except for the last) ancient choral forms; they look to men, not to gods, and breathe the new individualism of the sixth century; Simonides seems to have invented the Epinician as a more brilliant and laudatory replacement for the old victory chant, τήνελλα καλλίνικε (hail to the victor).[16] But, if so, Pindar as author of Epinicians—choral poems though they were—is not remote in function from Theognis as elegist. It is his place too to affirm, warn, attest to his powers, and assert his loyalties, hopes, and standards. His role as narrator is something else; that side of his art allies him with Simonides and we shall turn to it. But the brilliance of his choral language should not conceal the curiously hybrid mandate of the Epinician. As choral poem, it carried sacral and communal suggestions and through narrative opened toward gods and heroes; but as sung of a contemporary and in a festive setting, it fell heir also to legacies of the symposium and the elegy, and was intended not only to narrate but to affirm. In a part of his mind Pindar must have conceived himself as only a more resonant Theognis.

Echoes of language need not argue congeniality, and two men more different in native temperament would be hard to imagine: the one hard-minded, outright, invincibly himself, reflective but about actualities, uninterested in what he has not personally known, fierce in his loyalties and angered when they are crossed—the other eager to think well of the world, proud of his powers but pained rather than angered by misunderstanding and prompted by it to self-questioning, entranced by the remote scenes and figures of legend, a seeker of ultimates, inclined to look away from pain and struggle toward fulfillment and harmony. Of the Persian War Theognis characteristically singles out the bickering of the Greeks, Pindar, the flash of victory.[17] Yet their common ground tells something of Pindar. Harrison listed many verbal echoes in the odes,[18] and echoes of theme may be added. Pindar concludes

---

[16] See Bowra, *Greek Lyric Poetry*, pp. 310 f.
[17] Theognis, 780–81; Pindar, *I.* 5, 4–5, 48–50; *P.* 1, 75–78; frs. 64–66.
[18] *Op. cit.*, pp. 314–19.

the early *P.* 7 of 486 to the Alcmaeonid Megacles by regretting the φθόνος (envy) that attends high achievements; then closes

> φαντί γε μάν
> οὕτω κεν ἀνδρὶ παρμονίμαν
> θάλλοισαν εὐδαιμονίαν
> τὰ καὶ τὰ φέρεσθαι

"Indeed, they say, felicity that thus blooms steady for a man endures this and that."

Similarly Theognis holds παρμόνιμον (permanent) only what is just and god-given; he thinks ἀγαθός only the man who is able τά τε καὶ τὰ φέρειν (to endure this and that) (197–98, 398). Harrison shows Pindar repeating the latter phrase with further echoes of Theognis, and plausibly says that φαντί (they say), in *P.* 7, 15, seems to have him in mind. In the Theban ode *I.* 4, 33–35, composed not long after Plataea, Pindar sees the victor's family emerging after long misfortune into success—

> ἔστιν δ' ἀφάνεια τύχας καὶ μαρναμένων
> πρὶν τέλος ἄκρον ἱκέσθαι.
> τῶν τε γὰρ καὶ τῶν διδοῖ

"There exists an inconspicuousness of luck even when men strive, until they reach the steep end. She gives of this and that."

One must bear what the gods give, says Theognis, without excessive dejection or joy, πρὶν τέλος ἄκρον ἰδεῖν (until one sees the steep end) (594). Best not to hoard wealth but to use it for friends, Pindar tells Chromius in *N.* 1, 31–32—

> οὐκ ἔραμαι πολὺν ἐν μεγάρῳ πλοῦτον κατακρύψαις ἔχειν
> ἀλλ' ἐόντων εὖ τε παθεῖν καὶ ἀκοῦσαι φίλοις ἐξαρκέων

"I love not to keep wealth hidden at home, but from what I have, to live well and win a good name, supporting my friends."

Theognis has οὐκ ἔραμαι πλουτεῖν (I love not to be rich) (1155); rather he wants only enough; let the bronze sky fall on him, he elsewhere says,

> εἰ μὴ ἐγὼ τοῖσιν μὲν ἐπαρκέσω οἵ με φιλεῦσιν (871)

"If I do not support those who love me."

These examples of verbal echoes may suffice; in addition are echoes of theme: for instance, the desirability of friendship with the ἀγαθοί,[19] honor toward them but deviousness—even the arts of the cuttlefish—toward the κακοί[20] (the base), the rare friend who shares danger,[21] the virtues of silence,[22] gold tested by the touchstone,[23] καιρός,[24] the impossibility of undoing the past,[25] shipwreck as metaphor for misfortune,[26] the poet's duty to share his σοφία[27] (wisdom), the rare union of looks and virtue,[28] the obligation to praise an enemy when he acts well,[29] the blame that attends even good men but the entire obscurity of common men.[30] A splendid quatrain of Theognis which, standing beside verses of the Persian era, seems to date from those years expresses a mood that Pindar shares in several late odes—[31]

μήποτέ μοι μελέδημα νεώτερον ἄλλο φανείη
ἀντ' ἀρετῆς σοφίης τ', ἀλλὰ τόδ' αἰὲν ἔχων
τερποίμην φόρμιγγι καὶ ὀρχηθμῷ καὶ ἀοιδῇ
καὶ μετὰ τῶν ἀγαθῶν ἐσθλὸν ἔχοιμι νόον (789–92).

"Let no other newer care be mine beyond worth and wisdom, but keeping these let me delight in lyre and dance and song and with the noble keep a worthy mind."

This feeling for poetry and friends expresses the two men's bond beneath all their differences: unspoiled taste for the old-fashioned code of their upbringing. In a changing age Theognis kept throughout his life this provincial clarity, with resulting shock but unwilted crispness. Pindar, no doubt by temperament but also through his early education in Athens and long ties with Delphi, looked more

---

[19] Theognis, 29–38, 69–72; Pindar, P. 10, 72; P. 2, 96.
[20] Theognis, 213–16, 1071–74; Pindar, P. 2, 83–84; I. 4, 51–52; fr. 235.
[21] Theognis, 103–4, 1163–64h; Pindar, N. 9, 37–38; N. 10, 78–79.
[22] Theognis, 359–60, 419–24; Pindar, P. 3, 83–84; N. 5, 16–18; I. 6, 72; fr. 234.
[23] Theognis, 417–18, 450, 499, 1105–6; Pindar, P. 10, 67–68; N. 4, 82.
[24] Theognis, 401; Pindar, P. 4, 286; P. 8, 7; P. 9, 78–79.
[25] Theognis, 583–84; Pindar, O. 2, 15–17.
[26] Theognis, 671–82, 856, 1202, 1361–62, 1375–76; Pindar, O. 12, 11–12; P. 11, 39–40; I. 6, 36–38.
[27] Theognis, 769–72, 1055–58; Pindar, O. 13, 49.
[28] Theognis, 933; Pindar, N. 3, 19; I. 7, 22.
[29] Theognis, 1079; Pindar, P. 9, 95–96.
[30] Theognis, 797–98; Pindar, P. 11, 29–30.
[31] Pindar, N. 8, 35–39; P. 11, 50–51; I. 7, 39–41; P. 8, 67–69.

hopefully on societies and cities other than his own and, as the mighty events of his lifetime unfolded, he grew and opened with them, yet without losing, as the last-quoted parallel makes clear, his native standards. Few gains lack some loss, and the width of Pindar's actual and imaginary worlds sometimes strained his old ties.[32] Passionate addicts of athletics must have been surprised at his Olympian blindness to the details of sport, and rigid ἀγαθοί doubtless better liked and understood Theognis' edge and firmness. Yet for all his sweep Pindar never lost touch with the lucid teachings of his youth; their vehicle was the gnomic element of the Epinician, and their most recent spokesman was Theognis.

On the surface, and perhaps in fact, Simonides was more important to Pindar. As inventor of the Epinician, he created both the form of the song and the public expectation of it to which Pindar in youth fell heir. If, as we saw, the early *P.* 7 of 486 glances to Theognis, the first extant ode, *P.* 10 of 498, composed when he was twenty, draws as clearly on Simonides. Happy and praiseworthy, he says, is the man

> ὃς ἂν χερσὶν ἢ ποδῶν ἀρετᾷ κρατήσαις
> τὰ μέγιστ' ἀέθλων ἕλῃ τόλμᾳ τε καὶ σθένει (23–24).

"Who victorious in hand and merit of foot wins highest prizes by his courage and strength."

This itemization of powers is in the spirit of Simonides' famous ἐγκώμιον:

> "Ἄνδρ' ἀγαθὸν μὲν ἀλαθέως γενέσθαι
> χαλεπὸν χερσίν τε καὶ ποσὶ καὶ νόῳ
> τετράγωνον ἄνευ ψόγου τετυγμένον (fr. 4. 1–3).

"It is hard to be truly a noble man, in hand and foot and mind fashioned four-square, without reproach."

P. 10 was commissioned by the Thessalian dynast Thorax, later notable for joining Hippias in urging Xerxes to his expedition;[33] Simonides' Encomium was composed for the Thessalian Scopas,

[32] Pindar, *N.* 4, 36–43; *N.* 7.
[33] Herod., VII, 6, 130; IX, 1, 58.

and he wrote two other poems for the same family, one perhaps an Epinician, the other the celebrated dirge for the ruin of the clan under a collapsing dining hall.[34] It looks as if Pindar was launched on Epinicians through Simonides' *réclame* in Thessaly and the desire of the Aleuads to emulate the Scopads; even the myth of *P*. 10 treats in Perseus a hero who was venerated in Thessaly[35] and was the subject of a famous poem of Simonides (fr. 13), though whether or not he composed it for a Thessalian audience is unknown. In another early ode, *N*. 2, 10–12, Pindar's reference to the Pleiades matches the older poet's; for the latter Hermes Enagonius is the child of the most beautiful of the seven sisters (fr. 30); for Pindar, who prophesies his patron's mounting success, the rising Pleiades foretell Orion's coming. A number of other echoes connect them[36]—not few considering the scanty fragments of Simonides' choral poetry—and in *O*. 2, 96, the mysterious dual with which the noisy crows vainly chatter at the lordly eagle is taken by the scholiast to mean the uncle and nephew Simonides and Bacchylides. The three men met at Hieron's court as they must have done earlier, but in 476 Simonides was eighty and Pindar forty-two, and the period of formative influence was over.

But, as with Theognis, the formal sides of this influence far outweigh the verbal sides, and it is Pindar's creative adaptation of these—not by one step alone but continuously and mountingly—that shows his mind. The legends of the Mycenaean heroes, initially the province of epic ἀοιδοί, swept into choral poetry during the rise of the Greek city states and with it the flowering of their cults and celebrations. *Epici carminis onera lyra sustinentem*, says Quintilian of Stesichorus,[37] and the titles of his narrative odes—*Funeral Games of Pelias, Tale of Geryon, Boar Hunters, Eriphyle, Sack of Troy, Helen, Oresteia*—show him treating many cycles of legend. The sweeping scope of the Hesiodic Catalogue of Women, which traced through

---

[34] Cic. *de Or.*, II, 352; Quint. XI, 2, 14. Bowra, *Greek Lyric Poetry*, p. 326.

[35] L. R. Farnell, *The Cults of the Greek States*, IV, p. 104.

[36] On κενεαὶ ἐλπίδες fr. 5, 14; *N.* 8, 45. On the pains even of the demigods: fr. 7; *P.* 3, 86–87. On death as a wave awaiting rich and poor: frs. 8–9; *N.* 7, 17–20; 30–31. On Olympia as εὔδενδρον fr. 22; *O.* 8, 9. On silence: fr. 38; *N.* 5, 18. On being checked by the sea: fr. 28; *N.* 4, 36–37. On refined gold: fr. 50; *P.* 10, 67–68; *N.* 4, 82. μόνος ἄλιος ἐν οὐρανῷ fr. 52; *O.* 1, 5–6. On the impossibility of undoing something done: fr. 54; *O.* 2, 15–17. On appearance violating truth: fr. 55; *O.* 1, 28–29; *N.* 8, 34.

[37] XI, 1, 62.

their women the heroic lines of all parts of Greece, attests to the contemporary taste for legends which Pausanias' description of the throne at Amyclae and the so-called chest of Cypselus at Olympia further illustrates.[38] Though he renounces a complete description on the ground that the pictures were well known, he mentions some forty scenes portrayed on the throne and virtually as many in somewhat more detail on the chest. Few of all these are drawn from Homer; they have far closer ties with the Hesiodic Catalogue, and there is notable overlapping of subjects between Stesichorus and the chest of Cypselus. In the generation just before Stesichorus the dithyrambic choruses that, according to Herodotus,[39] Arion taught at Corinth, each with a name—also Alcman's mythological poems—show the same kind of interest. In this era of new prosperity and travel the Greek cities evidently took pleasure in each other's legends, and if, being attached to local cult, choral poetry expressed first of all a new pride of nationalism, the taste of the times seems to have been as catholic as that of Athens in the period of the tragic authors. It was this immense panorama of legend that through invention of the Epinician Simonides opened to Pindar, but with the new emphasis of a poetry directed to living men, not to a god or cult. The intense revelations of monodic poets, the signed vases of potters, the worthy or unworthy self-proclamations of Theognis and Phocylides, the inquiries of Thales and Hecataeus, the politics of Solon, Pittacus, and Cleisthenes, the sayings of wise men, the pomp of tyrants, and the fame of athletes, all fit the temper of Simonides' individualistic invention. But it is just in this tone that Pindar differs from Simonides. Though employed by individuals, he wanted to see himself as not merely a praiser of the successful, much less as a lone and isolated voice, but in the earlier manner as spokesman of communities. A guiding force of his development was his search for means of expressing this belief.

Thin as are the choral fragments of Simonides, their contrast to Pindar is striking. One Epinician fragment (23) humorously or irreverently declares, as Pindar would never have done, that Polydeuces or Heracles could not have opposed a young Euboean boxer; another (22) puns on the name of the Aeginetan Κριός, ram; two others (16, 17) seem to describe actual chariot races in

[38] III, 18, 6–16; V, 17–19.
[39] I, 23.

livelier detail than Pindar's; another (19), quoted to illustrate Simonides' legendary avarice, euphemistically overpraises a mule team. One catches or seems to catch the accent of a quick, amusing, imaginative mind that takes athletics, if not at all in the sardonic spirit of Xenophanes and Euripides yet lightly and informally. Two fragments (20, 21) on the joy of success come nearer Pindar; at least, the charming verses on the two weeks of windless calm in winter when the halcyons breed express a Pindaric sense of peace after struggle, though with characteristic Simonidean lightness. His descriptions of the sea and birds carry the same fresh tone, which in a quite contrasting mood fits the impressionable sorrow of his famous dirges. Pindar does not yield to thoughts of life's changes, swift as a dragon fly (6), or of mortal labor and worry and death's terrible Charybdis (7–9). However genuine may be thought his belief in the so-called Orphic doctrines of O. 2, they extend to another life his bright affirmation of this life. A like contrast appears if one sets beside the limpidity and pathos of Simonides' verses on the infant Perseus the radiance of Pindar's on the birth of Iamus;[40] the one man by temperament saw the quick interplay of lights and shades, the other a firmer brightness. These differences culminate in Simonides' intellectuality; of Greek poets he most nearly repeats Euripides' union of impressionability with speculation. C. M. Bowra well illustrates from Theognis the famous Encomium to Scopas,[41] surely the most tolerant of Greek poems. If an ἀγαθός loses his good fortune, the gift of the gods, Simonides asks, is he any longer ἀγαθός, and Theognis' troubled life exemplifies the problem. Simonides characteristically expects no stability in life but is content if a man is not spineless, knows justice, and of his own will does nothing shameful (4. 19–29). He is much more tentative than Theognis who, in all the changes that he saw and underwent, never doubted that he was an ἀγαθός, hence kept a toughness of conviction that is lacking in Simonides. By the same token, Pindar, who surpasses Theognis in confident affirmation, stands far from Simonides' sympathetic but melancholy impressionability. The Persian Wars, to be sure, brought Simonides in his poem for Leonidas and his celebrated inscriptions a tone

---

[40] Fr. 13. O. 6, 39–57.
[41] *Greek Lyric Poetry*, pp. 329–30.

seemingly of a new age—less individualistic, surer, more lapidary—but it is a paradox that Pindar was then beyond the influence of the man who influenced him most.

Thus his predecessors, if they tell much of his tradition, tell little of his mind, except negatively and by contrast. Bacchylides' use of clearly marked areas of either narrative or gnomic statement shows at once his temperate nature and the two sides of the tradition, but Pindar's interweaving of these sides marks from the first his bolder mood. Something unitary in his outlook evidently guided him, and one way of following his development is to trace this unifying principle as he grew more conscious of it.

Greek myth oscillated between the two poles of history and exemplar—ἔργον (deed) and παράδειγμα (example)—and part of its endless usability was that it rarely invoked the one without implying the other. If Homer first of all conceived himself as transmitting bygone deeds in authentic detail, their illustrativeness as showing the varieties of men and fates was also in his mind. Odysseus saw the cities of many men and knew their minds; Hera in the *Iliad* drops from Olympus as fast as darts the mind of a much-traveled man who says in his shrewd heart, "Would I were here or there."[42] To Homer, Odysseus and this unnamed traveler had seen the panorama of the world, which comparison—for example, as between the Cyclopes and the Phaeacians—made still more instructive. But the deep changes in Greek life from Homer's time to Pindar's tended to force the issue between these two functions of mythology as past event and as prototype, and in the novel present to tell the old stories simply for themselves breathed an antiquarian spirit, like that, for instance, of Pherecydes of Leros. By the same token to find relevance in the old stories was to be more conscious of their force as exemplars—as if, though still historical, they at the same time somehow transcended history in a timeless exhibition of fates and characters. By temperament Pindar intensely felt this commentary of the heroic on the present world; it is the single deepest impulse of his thought and, being apparently in his mind from the first, was to prove through resonance and expansibility his means of echoing the great events of his time. This sense of mighty exemplars is his bond with Aeschylus and the

---

[42] XV, 78–83.

Aeginetan pediments; conversely, it is what sets him apart from Theognis' crispness and Simonides' impressionability as child of a more spacious age.

Yet the early odes show him groping toward what was to become his conscious and characteristic mode of thought. In *P.* 10 of 498 writing, as we have seen, for a Thessalian celebration, he begins somewhat in the mode of Pherecydes—not through influence but simply from historical temper—by likening Thessaly to Lacedaemon because the line of Heracles rules in both. Then after saying, in Theognis' manner, that the victor's success shows both ancestry and, above all, a god's help and after the previously mentioned echo of Simonides in his list of the victor's powers and even a certain Simonidean sadness in the sense of their mortal limits, he suddenly breaks into the bright scene of Perseus among the Hyperboreans. "The Muse is never absent at their haunts. On all sides whirl dances of girls, the cry of lyres, and the ring of flutes. They wreathe their hair with golden laurel and feast in felicity. Disease and hated age touch not that holy breed, but clear of toil and war they dwell escaped from carping Nemesis" (37-44). In his circular mode of composition, already established in this early poem, Athene's guidance of Perseus harks back to the divine help that sped the victor, and the hero's arrival among the Hyperboreans fits the victor's at Delphi, but the tacit likeness of this blissful and magical people to the feasting Thessalians seems an effect of fancy rather than of plan. The Thessalians, he said earlier, possessed "no small share of the pleasant things of Hellas"—τῶν δ'ἐν Ἑλλάδι τερπνῶν λαχόντες οὐκ ὀλίγαν δόσιν (19-20). To his young imagination their northern opulence was nearly Hyperborean; Apollo's people had taken the one further step that released them from age and death. The myth contains Pindar's characteristic analogy of present to heroic actions, but the measure of his youth is not only or chiefly his evident admiration for his rich hosts—it is, rather, that the myth lacks any tone of conscious pronouncement, as if he felt the analogy but was not yet aware of its meaning for his art. Hence the charm and freshness of this ode, but also its relative lack of weight as compared to mature odes in which he illustrates by myth what he pronounces by aphorism. He evidently does not yet consciously see himself as one who judges the present by the past and shows their golden bonds of unity. He is so far chiefly an embellisher of the present, as is evident also from the somewhat hyperbolic *P.* 6 of 490 to the young Agrigentine magnate Thrasybulus, whose success at Delphi with his father's chariot—he apparently did not even drive it—Pindar likens to Antilochus' self-chosen death at Troy to save his father, Nestor. One seems to see in these poems something like Simonides' fancy, if not his lightness, and their moralisms recall Theognis. Though by intuition Pindar already looks to heroic prototypes, he as yet lacks a personally achieved scheme—a poetic stance between past and present—whereby he might make the arts of his predecessors his own.

Three powerful impulses toward self-knowledge—his own maturing, the drastic effect of the Persian War on a Theban, and his visit to Sicily three years after the war—brought his full powers into being. As for the first of these impulses, the opening of *N.* 5, a poem of the middle 480's, declares a new sense of his poetic function, which in turn is subtly illustrated in the myth. This is the first of a series of three odes to the sons of the Aeginetan Lampon, the last of which falls soon after Salamis; they were thus contemporaneous with the pediments of the Temple of Aphaea, which just preceded or spanned the war.[43] As if with reference to these, he begins by contrasting his ode to statues fixed on their bases; rather he says, let his song put out from Aegina on every merchantman and skiff proclaiming the victor and the new honor that he has brought the ancient line of Aeacus. In the following odes *I.* 6 and *I.* 5, he treats the two sacks of Troy which, as greatest feats of the Aeacids, were the subjects of the pediments now built or building, but the myth of *N.* 5, Peleus' marriage in distant Phthia to the sea nymph Thetis (22–37), touches him more closely through its bearing on himself as well as on the victor. If gods had innumerable unions with mortal women and thereby in their offspring brought something of their flash into the world, the opposite is very much rarer, and for a man to achieve a goddess was beyond mortal fortune. Pindar reverts twice again to Peleus' attainment of Thetis;[44] the thought of the serene gods at the wedding, seated on golden chairs, and of the singing of Apollo and the Muses conveyed to

---

[43] G. M. A. Richter, *Greek Art* (New York, 1959), p. 83; T. B. L. Webster, *J.H.S.* 55 (1931): 179–83.

[44] *P.* 3, 88–96; *N.* 4, 62–68.

him a perfection of happiness, like but greater than a victor's. Part of the import of the scene to him was clearly Apollo's lyre and the Muses' voices, and in this ode, just as Peleus journeyed overseas to win his immortal bride and the young pancratiast sailed abroad to his victory, so Pindar like an eagle sweeps across the sea and his ode lifts sail from Aegina (21, 51). Peleus' wedding is far more integral to the poem than was the Hyperborean banquet to *P.* 10; as crown and reward to the hero's virtues, it illuminates the Aeginetan glory now confirmed and adorned by the victor, and Pindar's ode, like Apollo's music, expresses the present, festal realization of justified joy.

Now, needless to say, the dating of fifth-century works is full of problems, and though Aeschylus' Danaid tetralogy is lately most often dated in the 460's by reason of the papyrus connecting it with a contest with Sophocles,[45] the question seems not quite settled. At least, the name Mesatos,[46] which appears in the papyrus, is known of a late fifth-century poet, hence raises the possibility that the Danaid production described by the papyrus was one of those revivals that are specifically attested of Aeschylus.[47] If the *Suppliants* is indeed one of his later plays, evidence should chiefly lie in idea, language, and metre, not in the papyrus. Even so, to accept provisionally a late date for the *Suppliants* is to see Pindar and not least the present ode *N.* 5 with new eyes. The reverberation that the age was to find in the legendary heroes is now clearly expressed and, among works that have come down to us, for the first time. Aeschylus in his huge theme of the transcendence of aboriginal crime and hatred in some form of final harmony was to apply the legendary stories to the present with unrivalled scope, but that was twenty years later. Pindar's judgment of the present by the same standard of legend—and not fancifully or through mere pleasure in the stories, as in his earliest, more Simonidean poems, but rather through achieved method and conscious intellectual stance—seems the authentic accent of a new age. To repeat, the identifying mark of this outlook is to conceive the legends neither as history, glorious but of another time, nor conversely as

---

[45] Printed in Murray's Oxford text (2nd ed.; 1955), 2.
[46] Scholium to Aristoph. *Wasps*, 1502; *Euripidis Epistolae* 5, 2, in R. Hercher, *Epistolographi Graeci* (Paris, 1871), p. 278, 11.
[47] The Laurentian *Vita* 12, in Murray's Oxford text, p. 371, 20–22.

only poignant or lively incidents, but as classic exemplars, fit to clarify the actions of a society.

The two war odes *I*. 5 and *I*. 8, both composed for Aeginetans respectively, in all likelihood soon after Salamis and after Plataea,[48] convey with mounting command the maturing manner of *N*. 5. As already mentioned, *I*. 5 is the last of the three odes to the sons of Lampon; the second poem *I*. 6 had expressed the hope of a crowning victory at Olympia, but if the younger son conceivably tried and failed at Olympia in the late summer of 480, his failure was caught up in the national triumph of two months later. This is not the place to rehearse in detail either the arguments for the date or the brilliance of the poem. The superb opening on the primal goddess Theia, named by Hesiod as daughter of Gaia and Ouranus and mother of the Sun, Moon, and Dawn, mystically exalts a spirit of brightness felt in gold, ships, racing chariots, and victory. Pindar's mood in these lines resembles that of the opening of *O*. 1; in both passages gold conveys the glint of the heroic which, shining in victory, gives it momentary tie with gods and heroes. He goes on to explain his train of thought with exceptional clarity: victors, he says, deserve ungrudging praise. "For among heroes too, brave warriors achieved fame as their reward. They have been celebrated with lyres and the full-toned cry of flutes a myriad time, and worshipped for Zeus's sake have given theme to poets" (26–29). The lines express the ascending scale from man to hero to god that he later states at the start of *O*. 2, but its bearing on himself is clearer here: a victor deserves praise because it has been accorded the great heroes, who in turn have been the theme of poets Διὸς ἕκατι (for the sake of Zeus). The achieved ground of his art could hardly be more clearly stated: it is the example of the heroes who, as seed of the gods, showed the working of divinity among men. The several parts of Greece, he goes on in a passage second to none in showing the bond between nationalism and hero-cult, have their peculiar heroes, as has Aegina in the Aeacids (30–42). Then, after praise of Achilles at Troy and of what he calls the tower of virtues that has remained to Aegina, he rises to the famous lines on Salamis: "And now Ajax's city, Salamis, could testify that it has

---

[48] C. M. Bowra, *Pindar* (Oxford, 1964), pp. 112, 407; J. H. Finley, Jr., "Pindar and the Persian Invasion," *H.S.C.P.*, 63 (1958): 121–32.

been raised upright by sailors in Zeus's ruinous storm hailing with the death of countless men. Nevertheless quench boasting in silence; Zeus accords this and that, Zeus sovereign over all" (48–53). καὶ νῦν carries into the present the bravery and brilliance of the heroic past, but, as Farnell saw, the warning not to boast and the lines on Zeus's uncertain will—both most unusual statements, since Pindar did not think Aeginetans vainglorious—implies something yet to come. The Persians must still be in Greece and Plataea cannot yet have been fought; in sharing the great hour of his island patrons, Pindar had temporarily forgotten the plight of his native Thebes but returns to it in his reverent sense of waiting on Zeus. The bright gold that he sees in victory, the greatness of the heroes through their tie with the divine, the theme that thus descends to poets, and the recent proof that ancient greatness remains in Aegina—this lucid sequence of thought shows Pindar's achieved way of seeing both his times and himself.

The year between Salamis and Plataea must have been very hard for him—together with the years following Tanagra, the hardest period of his life. What Thucydides later called a δυναστεία ὀλίγων ἀνδρῶν (a junta of a few men)[49] drove the old Theban dislike for Athens into Medism, and Pindar's ties of training with Athens and of friendship with Aegina must have pulled against the love of home that he often expresses. The change of mood between *I.* 5 and *I.* 8 is the measure of his pain: while the former ode saw in Salamis the golden flash of victory, the latter sees after Plataea only the ruinousness of discord and the heavy price of its healing. Yet there is no profounder myth in the odes than that of *I.* 8 and its sonority shows him the master of his newly found medium. After the curious and touching oscillation of the opening as between his recent sorrow and new relief, he soon broaches his theme of reconciliation by invoking the legendary ties between the nymphs Thebe and Aegina, twin daughters of Asopus, and thence by familiar steps reaches the island nymph's union with Zeus and the birth of her child, the peerless Aeacus. But whereas the great deeds of the Aeacids formerly prompted only thoughts of glory, now Peleus' attainment of Thetis—the bright subject of *N.* 5—signifies error and loss. This is the myth that Aeschylus was to use in the *Pro-*

---

[49] III, 62, 3.

metheia—he evidently knew the ode and adapts a line from it:[50] how Zeus and Poseidon each passionately pursued Thetis, yet yielded to the warning of the ancient goddess Themis, a divinity of the Titanic generation preceding their own, that the sea nymph was destined to bear a son stronger than his father. She was therefore given to the mortal Peleus, most honorable of men, and in Achilles bore him a still greater son, who saved the Greeks at Troy but died there. Though the Olympians were thus spared overthrow, it is as if discord and passion, even among them, carried an inevitable price of death and loss—the former in the brevity of Achilles' bright life, the latter in Thetis' sorrowful brush with evanescent mankind. Yet the ancient wisdom of Themis—she who, as mother of the Horae, is felt in the benign regularities of nature[51]— declared the deeper bond beneath the transient conflict, and the persistence of the gods testifies to the possibility of accord. Further, since nothing that the gods touch lacks brightness, Achilles' deeds at Troy, though touched also by mortal brevity, showed a saving power, and as in *I.* 5 Pindar declared the divine blood of the heroes to be the theme of poetry, so now he says that the Muses sang at Achilles' pyre and finds in that act the sanction of his lament for a kinsman of the victor (65–67). In *N.* 5 the singing of Apollo and the Muses at Peleus' wedding expressed the scene's relevance to himself as well as to the victor, but in these two later odes he expounds his mandate more consciously and, in the present ode, with deepest feeling. He has fully fused the gnomic and narrative legacies of Theognis and Simonides into his own unity, and the depth of *I.* 8 shows not merely his pain in the year of Plataea but, what is more important, the scope with which he now sees his art. Myth has become for him a kind of other language with which to interpret the greater meaning of events, and his heroic analogues express also what is to his eyes the nobility of the task. If the classic is a mode of vision that endows transience with stability and wins firm forms out of passing incidents, these odes initiate the fifth-century classic.

The occasional nature of the odes—their endless involvement with new people and circumstances—creates, from the point of

---

[50] 37–38. *P.V.*, 922–23.
[51] Fr. 10, 6.

view of any rational discourse about them, both delight and despair. The iridescence of changing scenes causes them to swerve and vary much faster than epic and dramatic poems, with which they nevertheless share much in subject and outlook. As he says in *P.* 9, in one of his rare statements about his method: "Great deeds prompt many tellings, but choose and adorn short incidents from the mass, and the wise will hear. In all things, moreover, the moment is the summit" (76–79). That is to say, he knows that relatively to Homer and even to Stesichorus and other choral poets, he sets forth his heroic incidents tersely, yet he hopes that perceptive people will grasp their meaning, the more easily because relevance, καιρός, chiefly clarifies. The passage, and a few others to like effect,[52] show how carefully he has chosen his heroic incidents and, to his own mind, what illustrative weight they carry. His doctrine of καιρός expresses the unique relevance of the incident to the occasion and its aptness to his poem as embracing both the present and the archetypal past. The reason for citing these words is double: time prevents pursuing much further the anfractuosities of Pindar's ever-changing occasions, even in the Sicilian poems, yet this allusion to his method, composed in 474 just after his return from Sicily, breathes the majestic self-assurance of the odes for Hieron and Theron. To revert again briefly to his beginnings, his gnomic legacy from Theognis on the whole looks to occasions; elegies carried the mood of symposia, bright, immediate, and sententious. By contrast, Simonides' poems, though by reason of his temperament by no means without their sententious sides, as choral poems on the whole look to legend or at least drew on that tradition. By the time of his visit to Sicily in 476, Pindar, as we have seen, had strongly fused these two elements, but they remained recalcitrant, and it is not surprising that the Epinician as a form hardly survived Pindar's generation. For lack of any such stirring impulse as the Persian invasion, he might, one imagines, have relaxed his unifying grip to let his poems sink back again toward the mood of *P.* 10 and 6, bright enhancements of festive occasions. As it was, the novelty—and surely to some degree the shock—of alien Sicily forced him upon himself, and he supplied by coruscation what he lacked in familiarity. His position in Sicily suggests that of Plato

---

[52] *O.* 2, 83–86; *P.* 1, 81–82.

more than a century later. A reason for thinking Plato's Letters genuine—particularly the Seventh and Eighth—is that they show him, though he was older than Pindar and Dionysius II was younger and unsteadier than Hieron and Theron, rallying in the same way to assert the ideas that he brought with him. Coming at the period when they did, *O*. 1 and 2 seem to express Pindar's self-understanding as only novelty forces a man to do.

References in *O*. 1 and *N*. 1 to banquets and to his taking up his lyre may mean, as Wilamowitz thought,[53] that he sang as a lone voice at a dinner party, not through a chorus; *O*. 2 is a personal poem to Theron; only *O*. 3 reflects a traditional occasion like those for which he composed in Greece. Moreover, in these new cities he lacked the sense of local hero-cult of which he spoke feelingly at Aegina in *I*. 5; hence he resorts to more general legends, of Pelops and his cult at Olympia in *O*. 1, of Heracles' founding of the games and planting of the Altis in *O*. 3, of the birth of Heracles in *N*. 1. To clarify the import of these not obviously relevant stories forced him to explain his purpose, and the consolatory *O*. 2 to the old and troubled Theron cast him further on his personal standards. The combined result of these outer and inner circumstances was a new pitch of self-declaration. Now for the first time, and characteristically in later poems,[54] he sees himself as spokesman of the Muses, who guide him to fuller knowledge and confirm its truth. Though poetry, he says, can be dangerous and deceptive, his own is therefore trustworthy; the sanction of his mysterious power is that he has it through nature, not through teaching.[55] Hesiod too had distinguished between true and false poetry,[56] evidently because it was one thing to tell heroic stories in traditional detail, another and harder thing to speak truth about the gods and the origin of the world. Though, unlike Hesiod, Pindar was concerned with legends, the changed Greece of his day forced him, as we have seen, to present his myths not as history but as exemplars, and everything depended on their illustrative scope and traction. He clearly felt the mystery of his insight, which

---

[53] *O*. 1, 7; *N*. 1, 19–22. *Pindaros* (Berlin, 1922), p. 228.
[54] J. H. Finley, Jr., "The Date of *Paean* 6 and *Nemean* 7," *H.S.C.P.*, 60 (1951): 61–80, esp. 70–71.
[55] *O*. 1, 28–35; *O*. 2, 86–88.
[56] Theog. 27–28.

he could explain only as the Muses' gift. If the expression is traditional, his use of it is not. He too of course tells what he thinks actually once took place—hence his way of breaking off a story which, though true, strikes him as unworthy[57]—yet as the previously quoted passage on his method makes clear, he does not tell a story in detail and for itself, rather gives brilliant light to a single crowning incident, because of its illustrative meaning. Hence his purpose, if one may put it so, is more Hesiodic than Homeric; he wants to explain stable truths about the rewards and limits of life and about relationships to the heroes and gods. He is rather a revealer than a narrator, and it is astounding that the narrow base of athletic success should have prompted this visionary flight.

As suggested, formulations of recent odes now recur but with quasi-oracular tone. Thus the mystical brilliance that shone for him in *I.* 5 in the flash of gold, ships, chariots, and victory reappears in the gold, blazing like fire at night, at the start of *O.* 1. The water that just precedes it goes back to the short promissory *O.* 11, composed at Olympia before he left for Sicily; in that poem welcome rain resembles hymns of victory after the strain of effort. The next following lines of *O.* 1 on the stark sun in the empty sky elaborate the Homeric phrase χάλκεος οὐρανός (bronze sky), which in *P.* 10, 27 mortals cannot hope to climb. The sequence—water, gold like fire at night, and the sun in the empty sky—subtly relates to the music of victory, heroic greatness, and Zeus's unattainable transcendence, but the riddling character of the lines shows how deeply they reflect his private understanding. We also saw this mounting triad in a slightly different form in *I.* 5 and *I.* 8: victors are praised because the great heroes became the theme of poetry, themselves the seed of gods. He now almost formulaically states this sequence at the start of *O.* 2: "What man, what hero, what god shall we celebrate?" It is his previously achieved scheme that allows him this terseness. Yet sense of isolation also prompted more careful statement of his scheme than any hitherto; it is his subject in *O.* 1, and he expounds it in two ways, by adage or half by adage and by legend. As for the former, Pelops was not, as evil-minded people said, eaten by the gods; such impious stories are only a commentary

---

[57] *O.* 1, 35; *O.* 9, 35–39; *N.* 5, 14–18.

on those who tell them. On the contrary, the gods, far from being cannibalistic, were only too generous to Pelops' father Tantalus, to whom they offered immortality by sharing with him their nectar and ambrosia (54–55). But in his mortal silliness he could not endure his bliss, and tried to share the gods' gifts with his human boon companions; hence, together with his son Pelops, was expelled from Olympus. This initial contrast, which occupies roughly the first half of the ode, constates an utter gulf between the gods and men, not through the gods' desire but from men's vacuity, which appears the greater through the evil and jealous stories to which they are addicted. But Pelops on reaching maturity sought at Olympia to win Hippodameia from her dangerous father Oenomaus, who had already overtaken and killed thirteen suitors in the chariot race that he set as marriage test. At the shore of the gray sea Pelops prayed to Poseidon, who had loved him in his youth on Olympus: "Great danger," he said, "attracts no supine man. But since we must die, why should one sit in the shadow futilely cosseting a nameless old age? I shall attempt this trial; only give happy outcome" (81–85). Poseidon's magical apparition at the hero's call and his gift to him of winged horses and a golden chariot (87) attest both to the gods' faith and to the possibility of heroism. The gold of Pelops' chariot restates the gold of the first line, and Pelops' emergence into bright heroism from what would otherwise have been the empty shadow of an unremembered life shows the gold again shining out of darkness. Pelops thus illustrates a position bridging the gulf between the serene gods and transient mankind, and mortal life, though utterly distinct, as Pindar later says in *N*. 6, from the divine permanence, yet keeps kinship with it.

There is no time to pursue through later odes either this basic scheme or the poetic attitudes that subtly accompany it. The alienness of his Sicilian visit, by forcing him to fix and declare the ideas that he brought with him, affected him lastingly. He is henceforth more consciously the spokesman of the Muses, and the fervor of his appeals to them shows that, whether he wished or not, he now necessarily stood somewhat apart from any one place or setting, a revealer of the longer and the hidden, not merely an adorner of the visible. Hence in part his future discomfort; for though he doubtless returned with relief to his familiar world of the old Greek cities, his scope got him misunderstanding at both Thebes and

Aegina.[58] This plight is as good a gauge as any of the distance that he had traveled from the clear world of Theognis' ἀγαθοί, and even from that of Simonides' color and impressionability. As was noted earlier, late odes from the years of the Athenian occupation of Boeotia and the ruin of his youthful world express unimpaired the code of fidelity to friends and singing which is his bond with Theognis, but the visionary endings of the latest odes, *P.* 8 and *N.* 11, show his gaze turned never more intently toward a farther light.

What then, more exactly, is the import of the scheme that he sets forth most clearly in *O.* 1 and that thus relates to poems before and after? The difficulty is that he does not, and surely cannot, say that the greatness of the semi-divine heroes is matched by any living man. As noted, Simonides' assertion that Polydeuces or Heracles could not have withstood the Euboean boxer whom he was praising would have been unthinkable to Pindar. Yet the heroes are relevant to the present, seemingly in two main ways: because, as human beings, not gods, they trusted their mortal courage and in so doing found divine support, and because knowledge of such actions, as the theme of poetry, reveals life's openness to strength and purpose and the just joy of their fulfillment. Occupying the middle ground between the changeless gods and transient mankind, the heroes are varyingly represented. Heracles after huge toil became, in the splendid line of *I.* 4, 66, χρυσέων οἴκων ἄναξ καὶ γαμβρὸς "Ηρας, "Lord of golden halls and Hera's son-in-law," and the Dioscuri live alternately on Olympus and beneath Therapne,[59] but Peleus and Cadmus later lost the perfect happiness of their weddings to goddesses,[60] and Ajax's fame was revived only after his death.[61] Similarly among mortals, the so-called Orphic doctrines of *O.* 2 and some fragments of the dirges[62] carry a just man's happiness to fulfilment in another life, but victory also catches momentarily a man's perfect joy. Men tacitly resemble the heroes in this gamut between lasting and momentary completeness, but music is on the side of permanence, and Pindar's pride in his function is

---

[58] *P.* 9, 79–96; *N.* 4, 36–43; *N.* 7.
[59] *P.* 11, 61–64; *N.* 10, 85–88.
[60] *P.* 3, 86–103.
[61] *I.* 4, 41–43; *N.* 7, 24–30; *N.* 8, 21–34.
[62] Frs. 114–17; 127; 131; 83, 8–11.

in his sense of lifting the transitory into the lasting. Unlike Aeschylus, he is uninterested in evolution, and his figures ascend not through historical steps, but through their own achievement into vivid being. The short *I*. 3, which was later added to *I*. 4 after the victor's second success, gives unique comment on this way of thought. It consists of a single triad of strophe, antistrophe, and epode, and lacking time for a myth after his initial description of the victor and his hard-pressed family, Pindar concludes simply: "With rolling days life brings now this, now that. Unwounded yet remain the demi-gods." Space forces him to a kind of ellipsis, and as final commentary on this laborious clan he quite simply gives the heroes. They are for him the exemplars, and the fifth-century classic begins in his vision of them.

T. B. L. Webster

❧ EURIPIDES: TRADITIONALIST AND INNOVATOR

My title, "Euripides, traditionalist and innovator," is a reminder rather than a program. It is a reminder first that the conditions under which the ancient dramatist worked were very different from the conditions under which the modern dramatist works and allowed much less scope for innovation in scenery, costumes, production, language, and subject. It is a reminder secondly how little we know, particularly how little we know about the detailed chronology of Sophocles, who started producing thirteen years before Euripides and survived him by a year, so that what seems to us to be Euripidean innovation may in fact be traditional in the sense that he borrowed it from an earlier play of Sophocles: we cannot say, for instance, who invented the terrible spectacle of a man coming onto the stage again after he has put out his eyes, or had his eyes put out. Euripides' *Oedipus* is late, in his *Hecuba* the blinding of Polymestor may be an innovation in the story, borrowed either from his own earlier *Phoenix* or from Sophocles' *Oedipus;* Euripides' *Phoenix* was certainly produced before 425 B.C. and Sophocles' *Oedipus* may have been produced as early as 429. Probably Euripides' play was the earlier of the two, but, even so, Sophocles may have used this type of spectacle earlier in another play, or Aeschylus may have preceded them both.

Euripides produced all his tragedies, as far as we know, at the city festival of Dionysos, which took place in March. Every year three poets were chosen to produce three tragedies and one satyr play each. They were chosen by the archon, the chief civil magistrate of Athens, who took office late in June. He also appointed to each poet a choregos, who engaged, paid, and dressed the fifteen members of the chorus and the flute-player, and the chief actor, who himself engaged his two assistant actors and any mutes that might be required. The poet provided script and music, and trained both actors and chorus. Euripides produced twenty-two times (i.e., eighty-eight plays) during the fifty years of his working life—on an average nearly every other year—but, in fact, his productions bunched considerably toward the end of his life, and his last five productions covered only seven years. Writing and producing at this rate he naturally used situations, scenes, and concatenations of scenes which had been successful before, whether in his own plays or the plays of others. For instance, scenes in which a girl or youth declares readiness to be killed as a sacrifice for family or country are good theater and show the unselfish heroism of the young: Euripides introduced them six times.[1]

Apart from the need to produce quickly, the conditions of production in Euripides' lifetime made for traditional drama. Scenery remained unchanged throughout the play: circular dancing floor or *orchestra* for the chorus, low stage with altar, central door flanked by panels of scenery representing either buildings (if the scene was a palace, temple, or camp) or rocks (if the scene was in the country). The roof above the door could be used, and a platform or *ekkyklema* could be rolled out of the central door to show a tableau. The crane or *mechane* could present a flying figure and land it on the stage. All these conventions (except perhaps the *mechane*) were established before Euripides began to produce. But sometimes a brilliant use may be called an innovation: Medea with the bodies of her children in her dragon-chariot above the palace while Jason and his attendants hammered vainly on the palace-doors below, or in the *Phoenissae* the shy Antigone led on to the roof of the palace by the old man so that he may point out over the heads of the audience the seven champions attacking Thebes.

Two uses of the *ekkyklema* seem startlingly new. In the *Cresphontes* Euripides wanted to show the awful moment when Merope is about to kill her sleeping son, but is stopped when she has already raised her axe by the old man, who recognizes him. "What a shudder this sent through the theater," says Plutarch, "in their fear that the old man would not stop her in time." This dramatic scene must

---

[1] *Heraclidae, Hecuba, Erechtheus, Phrixus B, Phoenissae, Iphigenia in Aulis.*

have been played on the *ekkyklema*, because nothing except the rolling platform could bring the sleeping boy before the eyes of the audience. In his *Andromeda* Sophocles had a scene in which Andromeda was chained to the rock (like Prometheus in Aeschylus' *Prometheus Vinctus*), but for his *Andromeda* thirty years later Euripides preferred to open the play with the *ekkyklema* rolling out with Andromeda already on the rock, so as to create at once the spectacle of the girl alone in the night, her laments only answered by a concealed Echo, waiting for the monster to come and devour her.

The limitation of actors to three automatically limited the number of speakers in any given scene to one, two, three, or four if the leader of the chorus is included. Any experiment with a larger number of speakers was therefore impossible. But mutes could be used not only for attendants, soldiers, and the like, but for characters: in the *Electra* Pylades is the silent shadow of Orestes all through the play; in the *Orestes* he has an important speaking part in two scenes but is silent in the last scene. This last scene of the *Orestes* shows Euripides at his most daring in the use of mutes and of the different levels in the Greek theater. The speakers are the leader of the excited chorus of women in the *orchestra*, Menelaos on the stage, Orestes on the roof, and Apollo above on the *mechane*. But the spectacle is increased by the mute servants of Menelaos, whom he tells to break in the door, by the mute Hermione, Elektra, and Pylades on the roof (Hermione has a knife held to her throat by Orestes; Elektra and Pylades brandish torches to set fire to the palace), and by the mute Helen, who is being taken to heaven by Apollo.

The metrical and musical shape of tragedy was also well established when Euripides began to write: actor-scenes in spoken iambics separated by odes in lyric meters sung by the chorus (and very occasionally by a subsidiary chorus) and sometimes by dialogues between actor and chorus in lyric or recitative or both. His plays show a steady development, which can be described in technical terms but is not so easy to interpret in terms of the impression which the poet wanted to create. (The following account is based on Zielinski for spoken iambics and A. M. Dale for other meters.)[2]

[2] Th. Zielinski, *Tragodoumenon* (Krakan, 1925); A. M. Dale, *Lyric Metres of Greek Drama* (Cambridge, 1948).

The spoken iambic trimeter of dialogue contains six naturally long syllables; it was permissible to resolve any of the first five of these into two short syllables. Aeschylus uses the permission once every nine lines in the *Persae* of 472 B.C., but only once every twenty lines in the *Oresteia* of 458 B.C. Euripides maintains roughly the same proportion as the *Oresteia*, down to the *Hippolytus* in 428 B.C.; from that time he steadily increases the proportion of resolved syllables so that in the plays of his last three years they average more than one every three lines. For the simple and unemotional phrase "children having been born" he uses at the beginning of the line παίδων γεγώτων in the *Medea* of 431 B.C., but nineteen years later in the *Ion* παῖδες γενόμενοι: the substitution can only be in the interests of rhythm. The actor of the late *Orestes* in 408 B.C. had to be prepared to follow the perfectly stable line 'Ορέστα, γαίας τῆσδ' ὑπερβαλόνθ' ὅρους with the very unstable line Παρράσιον οἰκεῖν δάπεδον ἐνιαυτοῦ κύκλον. In musical terms Euripides, as he progresses, introduces more and more variations on his basic iambic theme.

From 415 B.C. onward in all the surviving plays and four of the lost plays he has actor scenes in recitative trochaic tetrameters, the meter used by Tennyson in *Locksley Hall*. Here my title reminds me to ask "Traditionalist or Innovator"? The figures are interesting: Aeschylus *Persae* 472 B.C., two scenes amounting to 114 lines; none in any later play except the *Agamemnon* in 458 B.C., which has 29 lines; Sophocles, none until the *Oedipus Tyrannus*, which has 9 lines; 7 lines in the *Philoctetes* in 408 B.C.; 5 in the posthumous *Oedipus Coloneus*. For Euripides I give three examples, *Trojan Women*, 415 B.C., 16 lines; *Ion*, 412 B.C. three scenes amounting to 81 lines; *Iphigenia in Aulis*, three scenes amounting to 200 lines. In the *Persae* Aeschylus still liked the recitative trochaic scenes as a kind of middle level between spoken iambics and sung lyrics. But after that classical tragedy practically rejected them as blurring the contrast between spoken and sung, until Euripides revived them in 415 B.C. Once he had revived them, he developed them in the same way as iambics: in the *Persae* Aeschylus has only 16 resolved syllables in 114 lines; Euripides has 41 in the same number of lines in the *Orestes*. Clearly then in his late plays he wanted again to blur the contrast between spoken and sung, and within the trochaic scenes he also wanted the same sort of rhythmical variety that he had achieved in his late iambics.

When an actor uses recitative, and still more when he sings, he is moving out of his own sphere into the sphere of the chorus, to whom music belongs. Aeschylus and Sophocles normally reserved this transference for moments of great emotion (the only likely exception is the ball game in Sophocles' *Nausicaa*). The songs were divided, like choral odes, into metrically corresponding strophes and antistrophes; they were written in simple lyric meters or in recitative anapaests or dochmiacs. Euripides gradually abandoned all these restrictions. As early as 438 B.C. in the *Telephos* Agamemnon quarrels with Menelaos in recitative anapaests; in the prologue of the *Medea* in 431 B.C. Medeia sings of her distress in melic anapaests and the Nurse comments on her behavior in recitative anapaests. Neither of these scenes, nor the anapaestic vaporings of Phaidra early in the *Hippolytus* are moments of great emotion in the old sense; the contemporary Sophoclean Deianeira, who is at least as sorely tried as Medeia or Phaidra, never forsakes spoken iambics. In the plays after 428 B.C. melic anapaests and lyric meters become more common, but both monodies and lyric dialogues are still usually strophic. From 415 B.C. this patterning is often abandoned, and the actor sings freely in lyric meter as the poet chooses.

Many of these later songs would have been accepted even by conservative critics: for instance, the lamentations of Hekabe in the *Trojan Women* and the joyful recognition dialogue in the *Iphigenia in Tauris*—the evidence is their obvious influence on the three last plays of Sophocles. Perhaps even Ion's lovely *aubade*, as he sweeps the temple and drives away the birds, would have been accepted as a brilliant modernization of the ball-dance in Sophocles' *Nausicaa*.

But sometimes Euripides did things which must have made Sophocles shudder and Aeschylus turn in his grave. In the *Orestes* in 408 B.C. he does not use an ordinary iambic messenger speech to describe Orestes' attempt to kill Helen, but instead introduces a frightened Phrygian eunuch, who has escaped from the palace and sings 130 lines of free polymetric lyric divided into six sections by the spoken (or recitative?) iambic questions of the leader of the chorus. He tells of his escape, the miseries of Troy caused by Helen, the entry of Orestes and Pylades, their imprisonment of Helen's Phrygian slaves, their attack on Helen, the rally of the Phrygian slaves followed by the arrival of Hermione and the miraculous disappearance of Helen. This is a brilliant lyric narrative in the most modern musical style; we know that Euripides had comforted Timotheos, the Schönberg of his day, when his first concert failed, and we can justifiably see Timotheos' influence here. In fact a spoken iambic messenger speech, besides awaking too much sympathy with the victim, would have broken the elaborate sequence with which Euripides leads up to the final tableau of the play.

The sequence is worth considering for a moment. Orestes, Pylades, and Elektra have planned to murder Helen and to catch Hermione and use her as a hostage. Orestes and Pylades go in to do their work. Elektra sings an excited lyric dialogue with the chorus, who divide into halves to watch the two ways up to the central door. She goes on singing encouragement in extraordinary pizzicato lyric, as Helen cries out for help inside the house. Then the tone sinks to spoken iambics as Hermione enters and Elektra takes her into the trap. The chorus sing a strophe in dochmiacs rejoicing. Then the Phrygian comes out and sings his long description. This is followed by a brief dialogue in recitative trochaics as Orestes drives him in again. The whole interlude of the Phrygian is rounded off by the antistrophe of the chorus, who sing of the smoke already rising from the roof. The arrival of Menelaos and his order to break down the doors diverts the audience's attention while the tableau is set on the roof. When Orestes speaks again, he is on the roof with his sword at Hermione's throat, and Elektra and Pylades are brandishing torches. Sixty lines later Apollo appears with Helen on the *mechane*. Helen's disappearance had to be told, and the Phrygian's song is the only kind of narrative which fits into the crazy sequence culminating in Apollo's epiphany, which forces the mad mortals to return to sanity—or at any rate to the lines laid down by traditional legend.

This sequence suggests a major question and a minor question. The metrical and musical phenomena which we have been discussing clearly show that Euripides departs further and further from the texture of classical tragedy. The clear contrast between spoken and sung is weakened not only by introducing recitative for actor-dialogue and by giving actors the full range of choral lyric, even in situations which Aeschylus and Sophocles would have cast in spoken iambics, but also by the pizzicato, unstable character of late Euripidean spoken iambics themselves. Spoken and sung are no longer contrasted blocks: spoken itself has a new kind of volatile shimmer; it may give place to recitative, and recitative may fade into song. The major question to which we shall return is whether this change in texture corresponds to a change in Euripides' treatment of the story and the characters.

The minor question arises from the curious ambivalence of Greek lyric meter. Metrically long stretches of Ion's balletic *aubade* as he sweeps the temple are identical with Kreousa's later agonized account of her rape by Apollo. Whether they differed musically we have no means of telling. But Ion's *aubade* suggests that it would be wrong to interpret the Phrygian's polymetric song in the *Orestes* as an expression of his terror. It is rather a piece of musical and poetic phantasy which Euripides needs at this moment. Phantasy can be evoked by lyric meter and sophisticated music as well as agonized grief or exuberant joy. Phantasy is the best single word I can find to generalize the phrase that Gilbert Murray used to translate a line of a chorus in the *Hippolytus:* "The Apple-tree, the singing and the gold." The chorus there has just heard that Phaidra intends suicide, and they wish that they could escape from the horrors. In a lovely poetical lyric they wish that they could take refuge on the top of the mountains and there be changed into birds and fly to the West, where Phaethon's sisters weep for his death in tears of amber, or further still to the golden garden of the singing Hesperides. Earlier their opening song, when they come to inquire about Phaidra's health, begins: "A rock, they say, drips with the water of Ocean, hurling from its crags a flowing stream where pitchers may dip, where was a friend of mine, wetting scarlet cloths in river dew, and she cast them on the back of the warm and sunny rock. From her came the first news of the queen." This is washing day transposed into poetical and musical phantasy to contrast with Phaidra's prostration. Many other choral odes and a few monodies have this quality, and phantasy could be asserted as a world parallel to the world of cruel reality, a world into which the chorus could often and characters sometimes escape.

In every production the poet chose three "historical" legends for his three tragedies. Many of them had been dramatized before and were in this sense traditional, but the audience must have watched for the innovations in each new treatment. Euripides had two different methods of putting his three plays together. Before

415 B.C. he went for variety. In 415 B.C. and in four of the six later productions the three plays have some connection with each other. There is a little evidence that this change corresponded with a change in the order of production at the festival:[3] it is probable that from 450 B.C. to shortly after 420 B.C. each of the three competing poets produced one tragedy on each of the three days, but that after that each poet again produced all his three tragedies on the same day, and this gave the possibility of relating the tragedies to each other.

In 415 B.C. Euripides chose three chapters in the story of the Trojan War: in the first play the lost son of Priam and Hekabe is discovered in the young herdsman Paris, who defeats the sons of Priam in the games and narrowly escapes murder at the hands of Deiphobos. The second play is set in the Greek camp before Troy; Odysseus hoodwinks Agamemnon in compassing the death of the innocent Palamedes, whom he hates. The third play is the surviving *Trojan Women*, dealing with their sufferings after the capture of Troy. The impact of this play is immensely increased by the knowledge gained in the two preceding plays; their sufferings are caused by the selfish cruelty of Odysseus and the weakness of Agamemnon, which have both been demonstrated in the second play. The prophetess Kassandra, who was not believed by the Trojans in the first play when she foretold that the preservation of Paris would cause the disastrous Trojan War, is equally unheeded in the last play when she foresees the wanderings of Odysseus and the murder of Agamemnon. Hekabe, who in the first play weeps for her lost baby Paris and is wildly happy at his discovery, in this play has lost her husband and all her sons and performs the funeral rites for her grandson, Hektor's baby, Astyanax. And finally the unexpected appearance of Helen to have her self-defense torn into shreds by Hekabe is entirely right because the first play ended with the prophecy of her marriage to Paris.

In his next three productions[4] Euripides balances the first play against the second and makes the third an epilogue of a different kind. The *Antigone* and *Iphigenia in Tauris* were both plays about women which ended happily, and the *Hercules* is primarily about

[3] Cf. T. B. L. Webster, *Hermathena* 100 (1965): 21 ff.
[4] On the chronology see T. B. L. Webster, *Wiener Studien*, 79 (1966): 112 ff.

a man and ends unhappily. In 412 B.C. the *Andromeda* and *Helen* are variants on the theme rescue of distressed lady in exotic country, and the third play, *Ion*, has a more bitter flavor. The *Antiope* and *Hypsipyle* are both about the discovery of lost mothers by grown-up twin sons and end happily; the *Phoenissae*, which was probably produced with them, is about the two sons of Oedipus, who kill each other in battle before Thebes. But here, as in the Trojan trilogy, the plays are also linked by subject matter; the *Hypsipyle* is an incident in the expedition which culminates in the *Phoenissae*, and the *Antiope* is an earlier chapter in the history of Thebes. Still later in 407 B.C. the production in Macedonia seems to have comprised the *Temenus*, *Temenidae*, and *Archelaus*. In the first play the two bad elder sons of Temenos expelled Archelaos and murdered their father; in the second play they plotted against their brother-in-law, Deiphontes; and in the third play the good son, Archelaos, after various vicissitudes founded the kingdom of Macedonia—three chapters in the story of a single family.

The two earlier productions for which we have a complete list of plays, 438 and 431 B.C., show an entirely different principle of selection: the three plays are both different in kind and belong to a different cycle of legend. In 438 the *Cretan Women* dealt with Aerope's seduction of Thyestes and the grisly revenge taken by her elderly husband Atreus; in the *Alcmaeon in Psophis* Alkmaion betrayed his wife Arsinoe, who nevertheless remained loyal to him; the *Telephus* is an exciting camp play, which ends with the healing of the wounded Telephos in return for his promise to guide the Greeks to Troy. In 431 Euripides followed the same general pattern—a play about a bad woman, Medeia, who murdered her husband's new wife and then her own children; a play about an unhappy woman, Danae, who had to endure the unwanted attentions of the king, Polydektes; and a play about men, the *Philoktetes*. If, bearing these principles in mind, we inspect the plays which on metrical or other grounds can be allotted to Euripides' first nine productions, 455–428 B.C., it seems very likely that each production contained one play about a bad woman and one play about a suffering woman.

Three of the plays about bad women are about Medeia, (*Peliades*, *Aegeus*, *Medea*). The other six are about wives dissatisfied with their elderly husbands and throwing themselves at a young lover, *Cretan Women, Phoenix, Stheneboea, Peleus, Hippolytus I and II.* The two Hippolytos plays are of great interest because we can see to a certain extent how Euripides remodeled his earlier play, of which we only have fragments, to make the second play, which survives complete. In the first play Theseus is away from Athens, and his wife Phaidra has fallen in love with her stepson Hippolytos. The following seems to me the probable outline. Phaidra sends the Nurse to tempt Hippolytos. He rejects her; he is dedicated to the clean life of the athlete. Phaidra then tempts him herself, and Hippolytos covers his head in shame and throws away his sword, which she has clutched, as a polluted object. Theseus returns to find Phaidra threatening suicide with the sword, which he recognizes as belonging to Hippolytos; she tells him that Hippolytos has tried to seduce her. He uses Poseidon's gift of a magic wish to curse Hippolytos. Hippolytos is brought on dead, and Phaidra commits suicide, probably because Theseus has now extracted the truth from the nurse.

In the revised play Phaidra is quite different. She tries to suppress and conceal her passion; but the story must go on. Hippolytos must be accused, or Theseus cannot curse him. The nurse extracts the truth from Phaidra and approaches Hippolytos. Phaidra overhears Hippolytos storming at the nurse and sees him leave the palace to wait for Theseus' return. Phaidra decides on suicide. It is at this point that the chorus take refuge in "the Apple-tree, the singing, and the gold." Theseus returns to find Phaidra dead with a tablet in her hand which accuses Hippolytos of seducing her. In this way she feels she can help her children by preserving her own reputation. Theseus curses Hippolytos, who arrives at this moment and defends himself; here Euripides has bought our sympathy for Phaidra at the price of Hippolytos; in the first play Hippolytos defends his celibate athleticism to the nurse and possibly to Phaidra herself; here his defense is unsympathetic because it is made to his widowed and desolate father after the much more sympathetic Phaidra has committed suicide. Euripides makes some amends by the later heartbreaking dialogue with Artemis, who tells Theseus the truth. Brilliantly, Euripides hypostatizes Hippolytos' dedication to athletics in Artemis, the goddess of hunting, and Phaidra's disastrous passion in Aphrodite, who speaks the prologue. This is how they themselves feel the forces that drive them, and this justifies a device, which Euripides had probably already used to explain Pasiphae's passion for the bull in the *Cretans* and was to use later devastatingly in the *Bacchae*.

An ancient scholar says that Euripides corrected in the second play what was unseemly and worthy of accusation in the first play. We know that the comic poets called three of the early unsatisfied wives, Aerope, Stheneboia, and the first Phaidra, by the rudest word they could find, "whores"; they must have appeared unseemly and worthy of accusation because Euripides stripped these legendary heroines of their Aeschylean splendor and presented them as fifth-century Athenians, and this is what Sophocles meant by saying that Euripides "presented people as they are." But, as we shall see, Euripides, so far from heeding the criticism and abandoning his formula, extended its application in his later plays. The new Phaidra is not less realistic; she is different, and the question is, Why?

Mr. Barrett[5] thinks of Sophocles' *Phaedra* as an answer to Euripides' *Hippolytus I* and itself answered by *Hippolytus II*. This is very tempting, as the fragments suggest that Sophocles' Phaidra had the excuse that she thought Theseus was dead; she really believed that Aphrodite's power was invincible; she used a go-between to approach Hippolytos instead of throwing herself at his head; and she may have accused Hippolytos to save her own children. Euripides took over the indirect approach to Hippolytos and the motivation of her later accusation, but denied her the excuse that Theseus was in Hades, and transformed Aphrodite from a venerable goddess into a hypostatization of Phaidra's passion. To whitewash Phaidra partly by making her make a pardonable mistake, partly by pseudo-religion, partly by reducing Hippolytos' part (a reasonable deduction from Sophocles' title, *Phaedra*) must have seemed to him too easy a way out. That Sophocles could take such a way out is shown by his treatment of Deianeira in the contemporary *Trachiniae*.

Professor Bruno Snell[6] has supposed a sort of dialogue between Euripides and Socrates. Medeia in 431 B.C. said "I know what evil I am going to do, but passion is stronger than my reasoning." Socrates answered that if you know what is right, then you do it. Phaidra comes back in 428 B.C.: "We know what is right and

---

[5] *Euripides: Hippolytos* (Oxford, 1964), pp. 12 ff.
[6] *Scenes from Greek Drama* (Berkeley, 1964), pp. 59 ff.

recognize it, but we do not work it out, some from laziness, others putting some other pleasure before the good." This is not, I think, a debate between Euripides and Socrates, but Euripides making his characters explain themselves in Socratic terminology. At the end of his life in the *Iphigenia in Aulis* (558ff.) he makes the chorus sing: "men may differ in nature and behavior. But the truly right is always clear. Education greatly contributes to virtue. Modesty is wisdom, and has the exceeding grace of perceiving the right by force of intellect." This is the Socratic position, and they then glance back at Phaidra's problem and judge her: "It is a great thing to pursue virtue—for women in secret love." It is interesting that just about the time when Euripides was writing the *Medea* and *Hippolytus II* the comic poets were saying that Socrates helped him to write his tragedies. They too saw the influence of Socrates on his dramatization of the struggle between passion and reason, evident in Medeia and the second Phaidra but appearing also in a different form in Alkmene in the *Heraclidae* and Hekabe in her name play.

Although the position of Sophocles' *Phaedra* between Euripides' two versions of the story must remain a guess, we have evidence for a later sequence of plays, which will also show how Euripides developed the use of his formula. The way in which Aristophanes quotes Aeschylus' *Choephori* in the second edition of the *Clouds*, which was produced between 421 and 416 B.C., shows both that the *Choephori* had been recently revived and that Euripides had not yet produced his *Electra*, which on metrical grounds must be dated before 416 B.C. Sophocles' *Electra* must be later than Euripides' *Electra* and before Euripides' *Helen* of 412 B.C. Euripides' *Orestes* was produced in 408 B.C. The sequence ran therefore: revival of Aeschylus' *Choephori*, Euripides' *Electra*, Sophocles' *Electra*, Euripides' *Orestes*.

Aeschylus' *Choephori* was sandwiched between his *Agamemnon*—in which Agamemnon returned from Troy to be murdered by his wife Klytemnestra—and his *Eumenides*, in which Orestes was acquitted at Athens of the murder of his mother. The other two dramatists had to write an *Electra* which was complete in itself. In Aeschylus, Orestes arrives back from exile just as Elektra is being sent to pour libations on Agamemnon's grave because Klytemnestra has had an ominous dream. Elektra recognizes him by the hair which he has put on Agamemnon's grave and by his footprint. He tells his sister that Apollo has prophesied terrible tortures if he does not kill his father's murderess. The center of the play is a long lyric dialogue between Orestes, Elektra, and the chorus, in which they invoke the dead Agamemnon to nerve Orestes for his deed. Then Elektra vanishes from the action. Orestes is admitted by Klytemnestra because he says he has brought the news of Orestes' death. Aigisthos is summoned and goes in to be killed. Then, wavering and strengthened at the last moment by Pylades' only utterance in the play, Orestes drives Klytemnestra in to be killed. As he stands over the corpse, he sees the avenging Furies of his mother and rushes from the stage.

Euripides modernizes. The great lyric invocation of the dead King which takes more than 200 lines in Aeschylus is reduced to 13 lines of very effective prayer (*El.* 671 ff.); nor can Apollo be so closely present (he is actually a character in Aeschylus' third play). In one minor point Euripides says clearly what he is doing: the Aeschylean Elektra recognizes Orestes by family hair and family foot; the Euripidean Elektra says "nonsense: a young athlete has his hair cut short, and a woman's hair is soft and long; a man's foot is much bigger than a woman's." We are firmly transferred from heroic legend to contemporary town life. He asks what would Klytemnestra and Aigisthos do with these uncomfortable children who remembered their father; put a price on the boy's head (he remembered his own earlier *Cresphontes* here) and marry off the girl to a poor farmer who will not be dangerous. So here, as in the earlier *Diktys*, the princess is living in a poor man's hut instead of the palace (perhaps he also remembered Mandane in Herodotus).

This change of setting involved a complete remodeling of the two murders. Euripides has, however, gained the moving picture of the poor farmer who respects Elektra and whose friendship she values, however embittered she feels toward her mother and stepfather. Orestes enters with Pylades (who is mute all through this play) and watches Elektra return with her waterpot and the chorus meet her with an invitation to go to a festival of Hera—the married Elektra fetching the household water instead of the Aeschylean Elektra sent by Klytemnestra to pour libations, and the opening chorus transposing an everyday occasion into lyric phantasy, as in the *Hippolytus*. Elektra describes to the unrecognized Orestes her misery, the luxurious life of Klytemnestra, and Aigisthos dancing drunk on Agamemnon's tomb. The farmer returns and invites the strangers in; Orestes is deeply disturbed by the contrast between honest poverty and corrupt wealth. Elektra sends her husband to ask an old servant of Agamemnon to bring food for the guests. He arrives with a lamb, cheeses, and wine; he recognizes Orestes by a scar on his brow. Then the plan is made (and this is entirely new); the old man is first to take Orestes to where Aigisthos is sacrificing (here again Euripides borrows from his own *Cresphontes*) and then to tell Klytemnestra that Elektra had a baby ten days ago and needs her help.

A messenger reports Aigisthos' death, and Orestes comes back carrying his head, over which Elektra vents her hatred: "you killed my father and married my mother. Then you found you had married a tyrant, and you had to amuse yourself by running after girls." (This Aigisthos reminds us of the husbands of later Greek comedy.) Klytemnestra is seen in the distance. Orestes nearly breaks down: "Apollo, your oracle is a great folly," "Was it an evil spirit spoke in the guise of god?" Elektra tells him not to be a coward and sends him in to wait for Klytemnestra. She arrives in a chariot attended by Trojan captives. She defends her murder of Agamemnon, and Elektra tears her defense to pieces. But she has come to help Elektra sacrifice. "Come into my humble home. Take care my sooty house does not dirty your frock. You shall make the sacrifice you ought."

After the murder the two come out bitterly repentant. Elektra accepts the responsibility which the chorus lays on her: "you did a terrible wrong to your brother and forced his will." The Dioskoroi appear on the *mechane* to finish the play. "Apollo is wise but his oracle was not wisdom for you," "the unwise cries of Apollo's tongue." However Pylades will marry Elektra and establish the farmer in Phokis, and Orestes after being pursued by the Furies will be acquitted in Athens.

Euripides has pushed Apollo into the background. Orestes at the crisis has doubts of the oracle, and the Dioskoroi imply at best that it has been misinterpreted. It is Elektra who both plans the murder of Klytemnestra and nerves Orestes to carry it out. Klytemnestra is a snobbish, domineering, vulgar woman; Aigisthos, although we only see his severed head, comes out clearer than in Aeschylus or Sophocles as a vicious young opportunist. Elektra and Orestes are not much better than their mother, but at least they appreciate the loyal friendship provided by Elektra's husband, the old man, and Pylades, and at least they repent.

These are people "as they are." Sophocles was moved to answer. For him the oracle given to Orestes must be the center of the story, and since Apollo cannot command anything that is wrong, Elektra and Orestes cannot repent and Orestes cannot be pursued by Furies. The problem is to present matricide as an act of justice, and to make it tolerable on the stage. The answer is masterly: minimize the matricide and Orestes' part, blacken Klytemnestra, and make the audience identify themselves with Elektra so that they see the matricide with her eyes. This Elektra has lived on in the palace, persecuted by Klytemnestra, who showers favor on the fluffy sister Chrysothemis because she accepts the situation. Elektra is on stage from the end of the prologue, and the climax of the play is her vast upsurge of joy when Orestes reveals himself to her, very late in the play, *after* she has been shattered by the false report of his death. Then the murders are slipped in at the end: after the recognition scene Orestes goes into the house and dispatches Klytemnestra; Aigisthos arrives and is driven in to die where he had killed Agamemnon. Nothing could be more efficient; we have seen Klytemnestra's defense of her past destroyed by Elektra, we have heard her pray to Apollo for the destruction of her own children, we have heard her joy at the report of Orestes' death; but from that moment we are entirely concerned with Elektra's despair at the report, Elektra's desperate appeal to Chrysothemis for help, Elektra's utter desolation when Orestes enters with what purports to be his own funeral urn, Elektra's joy when he reveals himself. We do not see Klytemnestra again: no pathetic appeal to Orestes as in Aeschylus; no commiseration with Elektra's poverty just before the murder and no heartbroken description of her last moments as in Euripides; just a cry off stage.

Gilbert Murray has been criticized for calling the Sophoclean *Electra* a "combination of matricide and high spirits," but that is exactly how Euripides must have seen the play. The Sophoclean Orestes falters for a moment, not because he has to murder his mother but because he cannot bear Elektra's grief; otherwise he is cheerful and efficient, but Sophocles very cleverly allows him to be on stage a little over half as long as the Euripidean Orestes, so that we do not care much about him. Euripides could not accept this and in the *Orestes* of 408 B.C. asks what happened next. In his *Electra* the Dioskoroi see the Furies coming to chase Orestes (κύνας τάσδε); Euripides has accepted for his epilogue the Aeschylean ending to the story since one of the functions of the epilogue is to get the characters back into traditional mythology. In the *Orestes* the scene is the palace five days after the murders. Elektra speaks the prologue. Orestes is in bed starving, but asleep during a respite from his intermittent madness, in which he sees Furies. The city will decide today whether they are to die by stoning. Their only hope is Menelaos, who has already sent Helen secretly into the palace; their daughter, Hermione, has been there for the duration of the Trojan War. Helen is afraid to take offerings to Klytemnestra's tomb; Elektra refuses and tells her to send Hermione. The chorus of Argive women come to ask for news, and Elektra is terrified that they will wake Orestes. Orestes wakes and Elektra tends him, but he has another mad fit and thinks she is a Fury trying to hurl him to hell. He recovers, and in a very moving dialogue doubts whether Agamemnon himself would have approved his action: now brother and sister have only their mutual loyalty and love. Menelaos arrives and Orestes pleads for his help. But he is cut short by Tyndareus, the father of Klytemnestra and Helen, who says that Orestes ought not to have killed his mother but to have prosecuted her; he is going to plead with the Argives to put the murderers to death. Menelaos says that he will wait until the people have calmed down before he tries to put in a word for Orestes (and does not even appear at the trial). The meter changes to recitative trochaics for Pylades, the loyal friend who has been banished from home for his part in the murder and now comes to persuade Orestes to defend himself at the trial. The trial is reported to Elektra: all that Orestes could achieve was permission for himself and Elektra to take their own lives. Orestes and Pylades return, and the three movingly talk of suicide. But Pylades suggests that they should first murder Helen, and Elektra says that they can seize Hermione as a hostage. Then follows the frenzied sequence of scenes which has already been described leading up to the final tableau and the appearance of Apollo.

Sophocles neatly avoided the consequences of matricide. Aeschylus saw the acquittal of Orestes as a step forward in civilization: the solemn establishment of the first murder court by Athena with Apollo as witness and the Furies as prosecutor. Euripides reports what might be a contemporary debate: Talthybios, Agamemnon's herald, sides with the friends of Aigisthos. Diomedes suggests banishment instead of death. A popular orator with doubtful credentials urges stoning in a speech which was inspired by Tyndareus. An honest farmer says that Orestes ought to be crowned for killing a bad woman (did Euripides mean to have us remember the poor farmer who was married to Elektra?) Finally Orestes pleads that if wives are allowed to kill their husbands, men will be either dead or slaves.

Euripides sees not only the trial but the whole story as a contemporary situation. The murder of Klytemnestra has everyday consequences for her whole family: for her son and daughter and his friend Pylades, for her father Tyndareus, for her sister Helen (who is so like her), and for her brother-in-law Menelaos (who is so like the dead Agamemnon). The same family reappears in the posthumous *Iphigeneia in Aulis:* Agamemnon; Menelaos; Klytemnestra; Iphigeneia, Klytemnestra's dower-slave; and Achilles, the supposed fiancé of Iphigeneia. Menelaos, Klytemnestra, and the dower-slave at least are surely additions by Euripides to the story. So too in the *Phoenissae*, which was produced two or three years before the *Orestes*, and perhaps soon after a revival of Aeschylus *Seven against Thebes* in the form in which we now have it, Eteokles' lust for power is shown to affect the whole royal family, his brother Polyneikes, his sister Antigone, his mother Iokaste, his father Oidipous, his uncle Kreon, and his cousin Menoikeus, who all have their parts, as well as the old family seer Teiresias. Even in the posthumous *Bacchae*, where the influence of the traditional resistance story must have been extremely strong, the pragmatical Kadmos, who sees the political advantage of having a god in the family, and the modernist churchman Teiresias, who explains a miracle by philology, are surely Euripidean additions. And who before could have put on the stage either Kadmos the father nursing his daughter back to sanity or Kadmos the grandfather praising after the disaster his errant grandson?

Both the plots and the characters of the late plays seem to me to correspond to the changed metrical texture which I described earlier. The action is no longer dominated and directed by a small number of strong characters but advances falteringly under the influence of family intimacy, family quarrels, family likeness, family diversity, and for this the more complicated metrical texture is admirably adapted. The characters themselves, some of them at least, are less stable in the later plays: the beginning lies in the split personality of Phaidra and the suicidal repentance of the vengeful Hermione in the *Andromache*, but consider later Herakles' confident strength followed by his destructive madness and then by his restoration to sanity by Theseus, the gentle heart-broken Kreousa changing into an inefficient murderess, or the physically starved and mentally crazed Orestes turning into an efficient criminal. They need the shimmer of the late iambics and the full range through recitative to untrammelled lyric to express their instability.

Apollo at the end of the *Orestes* announces the future: Orestes will go to Athens and be acquitted. He will come back and marry Hermione (at whose neck he is at the moment pointing his sword). Elektra will marry Pylades. Menelaos will retire to Sparta. Helen will be honored as a goddess. Pirandello would have left his audience to decide what happened next: Euripides uses Apollo to put the derailed characters back on their mythological tramlines. Why does he think this desirable?

Consistently with his formula of modernization, his people can quote modern interpretations of legend. The chorus in the *Iphigenia in Aulis* wonder whether the story of Leda and the Swan may not be merely a figment of poetry. Iphigeneia in the *Iphigenia in Tauris* does not believe that Artemis likes human sacrifice: the local inhabitants have ascribed their own murderous tendencies to their goddess. When Helen in the *Trojan Women* defends herself by the judgment of Paris and says that Aphrodite came with Paris to abduct her, Hekabe answers: "Nonsense. My son was very handsome, and your mind seeing him became Aphrodite." As in the *Hippolytus,* Aphrodite is a hypostatization of sexual desire, although this interpretation here destroys the whole mythological framework of the trilogy. In the *Hercules* Theseus administers the conventional consolation, that if the gods in spite of their transgressions live in Olympus a mortal should equally be able to endure his sins and misfortunes; Herakles answers: "I do not believe that the gods indulge in rape or imprison one another. These are the figments of singers." Again the whole play is based on Zeus' seduction of Alkmene and Hera's anger thereat, a framework which Herakles' insight shatters. The surprising thing is that Euripides generally puts the pieces together again.

Two possible reasons (apart from tradition) can be suggested. One is that Euripides believed that cult had a value at least for ordinary people, and cult could not be wholly divorced from mythology. The chorus of the *Bacchae* need not necessarily reflect Euripides when he makes it say: "What the ordinary crowd believe, I would accept." But it is remarkable that, even with our insufficient knowledge, we can say that in eighteen plays certainly, and in five others probably, Euripides expressly connected his story, generally at the end of the play but sometimes earlier, with an existing cult, holy grave, or temple. Medeia in her jealous fury has murdered her children, but their tombs will be honored forever in Perachora; Herakles has denied conventional mythology, but after his death the Athenians will honor him with sacrifices and shrines. Euripides, however much he innovates, refuses to cut the traditional link between mythology and cult.

The other reason has been given already. Traditional mythology is a world of beautiful phantasy. Chorus and characters can escape into it; the audience appreciate it as a foil to the realism of modern interpretation. Euripides was too good a poet to abandon completely "the Apple-Tree, the singing, and the gold."

Victor Pöschl

POETRY AND PHILOSOPHY IN HORACE

The poetry of Horace stems from the deep experience of a dreadful catastrophe: the collapse of the order of state and life at the end of the Roman republic. This collapse occurred in a relentless sequence of murderous civil wars. The works of Augustan poetry are real *fleurs du mal*, blossoms that grow out of evil. They are the answer of the Roman mind to this challenge, the result of the meeting of subtle sensibility and fearsome threat.

The most famous testimony of Horace's despair as to the fate of Rome is one of his earliest poems, the Sixteenth Epode. In this poem there is an apocalyptic mood. Wild animals are to take possession of the Roman soil. Barbarians will come to the ruins of Rome and the bones of Romulus will be scattered to the four winds.[1]

In the face of such distress, the poet turns to the "pious" who are ready to sail with him to the islands of the blessed, which he describes in verses of magical beauty. Jupiter preserved the Golden Age for the pious when he introduced the Bronze Age in this world. The land of the blessed in the Western Sea[2] is a symbol of the longing of Horace's time for a guiltless and peaceful existence, a "pious"

---

[1] A similar eschatological tone is sounded in the Sibylline oracles of the same age (*Oracula Sibyllina* III, 464–69, p. 72 Geffcken): "Italy, not from without does Ares, the God of War, come to you. No, native bloodshed, much lamented, will destroy you. You will be laid in ashes and unawares you will tear your own flesh; you will be not mother of good men, but wet nurse of wild animals."

[2] For some aspects of this idea in connection with America, see Harold Jantz, "The Myths about America: Origins and Extensions," *Jahrbuch für Amerikastudien* 5 (1962): 10 ff.

world, separated by an ocean from the impure, contaminated world of contemporary Rome.

From the darkness of his age the poet leads us into a better world. The pastorals of Vergil, written a little before this epode, have the same purpose: they lead us in a realm of peace, philanthropy, love and freedom. Vergil and Horace attempt to fulfill the claim of Greek philosophy: deliverance and redemption of man from his sorrows and pains, from his wrong opinions, from his misconception of what true life is.[3] The center of man's existence is shifting from the political universe to a private life that carries its value and its legitimacy in itself. Thus Horace becomes the creator of a personal culture.

The great Greek name giving this shift its philosophical foundation is Epicurus. He was the Greek philosopher who made legitimate the Roman evolution toward individualism and individual culture. Epicurean philosophy thus plays a very great part in Rome.

The shift from the political to the personal, from flaunting splendor to the simple and unpretentious, is a main theme of Horace's poems, not only in their content, but also in their form and their inner movement. If we let ourselves be guided by the magic power of this movement, which has the effect of music for a sensitive mind, we are introduced spontaneously into this world of peace, of happiness, of quiet detachment. The poet, as it were, conquers this world anew in each poem.

The political realm, the universe of the Roman Empire, with the sublime names of foreign nations and kings, is contrasted with the world of the poet. Though small, it is filled with light and happiness. We have this movement, for instance, in the charming Ode I, 26:

> Dear to the Muses, I will banish gloom and fear to the wild winds to carry o'er the Cretan Sea, all unconcerned what ruler of the frozen borders of the North is object of our fear, or what dangers frighten Tiridates.
> Do thou, sweet Muse, that takest joy in fountains fresh, weave gay blossoms, yea, weave them as a garland for my Lamia! Naught without thee avail my tributes. Him in new measures, him with Lesbian plectrum, 'tis meet that thou and thy sisters should make immortal.[4]

---

[3] V. Pöschl, *Die Hirtendichtung Virgils* (Heidelberg, 1964).
[4] Translation by C. E. Bennett in the Loeb Classical Library.

Or the Ode II, 11:

> What the warlike Cantabrian is plotting, Quinctius Hirpinus, and the Scythian, divided from us by the intervening Adriatic, cease to inquire, and be not anxious for the needs of life, since 'tis little that it asks. Fresh youth and beauty are speeding fast away behind us, while wizened age is banishing sportive love and slumbers soft. Not forever do the flowers of spring retain their glory, nor does blushing Luna shine always with the selfsame face. Why, with planning for the future, weary thy soul unequal to the task? Why not rather quaff the wine, while yet we may, reclining under this lofty plane or pine, in careless ease, our grey locks garlanded with fragrant roses and perfumed with Syrian nard? Bacchus dispels carking cares. What slave will swiftly temper the bowls of fiery Falernian with water from the passing stream? Who will lure from her home Lyde, coy wench? With ivory lyre, come bid her haste, her careless hair fastened in a knot, like some Laconian maid.[5]

We have the same movement, again, in those poems where the splendid, ostentatious way of life is rejected, as in the prayer to the Palatine Apollo in the Ode I, 31. The poet does not pray for the rich harvests of fertile Sardinia, for warm Calabria's pleasant herds, nor gold nor Indian ivory . . . "Olives nourish me and light mallow," the most common food. The Ode closes with these lines:

> Oh, grant me, Phoebus, calm content,
> Strength unimpaired, a mind entire
> Old age without dishonor spent,
> Nor unbefriended by the lyre.[6]

The Ode I, 7, *Laudabunt alii*, one of the most beautiful, belongs to this group also. "Let others praise bright Rhodes and Mytilene and Ephesos and Corinth, Thebes, Delphi. . . . Nothing delights me so much as the grottoes of Albunea that to the Anio re-echo, the Anio which rushes into the depths." To the magnificence of the Greek world is contrasted the simple and beloved countryside of Tivoli. As the song reaches this point, the poet exhorts his friend Munatius Plancus to soften his sorrows with mild wine. It seems as if he should be drawn into the consoling and healing realm of the poet, symbolized by Tivoli. But then it seems, the friend will continue to suffer even when in Tivoli. In the face of this distress and weariness, Horace cites the mythical example of the Greek

---
[5] *Ibid.*
[6] Translation by John Conington in *The Odes and Carmen Saeculare of Horace Translated by John Conington* (3rd ed.; London, 1865), p. 32.

hero Teucer, who when struck by a particularly harsh blow, nevertheless bore his fate with serene composure. After ten years of heavy struggles at Troy, where he had left his brother Ajax, killed in the war, Teucer had gone home to Salamis. There his father Telamon cast him off and expelled him, angry because he had not taken better care of his brother. But Teucer did not lose his spirits. As he exhorted his comrades to come with him on the ship again, to entrust themselves to fate, and not to despair, he says:

> "Now let us drive away sorrows with wine, tomorrow we shall cross again the immense sea."
>
> Nunc vino pellite curas,
> cras ingens iterabimus aequor.

Thus, the Ode closes with the exhortation to look gladly to the present, even when tomorrow we must cross the mighty waters.[7]

The tragic fate of Teucer, who after long years sees again his beloved native country and then is expelled again and forever—a fate to which Sophocles and Pacuvius had given form in famous tragedies—is a fate typical of the age. How many, like Teucer, lost their native country after long years of absence at the very moment when they believed they had found it again. How many of those who fought for Brutus and the cause of the republic came home to find their land expropriated. Horace was one of those who suffered in this way, for his father's lands had been taken away.

In the great poems of the Augustan Age we meet time and again the fate of homelessness, of being expelled, of men finding themselves as if before an abyss. I might recall the first pastoral of Vergil and the *Aeneid*, for both of which the basic theme is the search for a new home.

In the words "Drive away sorrows with wine, tomorrow we will cross the immense sea," something is revealed that is central for the poetry of Horace. His anacreontic serenity stands before a tragic background: the cruel visions of death and all kinds of anxieties, sorrows, and pain that Horace and his friends had experienced in the impressionable years of their youth. It is not an easy composure that is demanded, but one full of tension and effort, one that must be regained time and again.

So the movement of the poem proves to be a gradual concentra-

---

[7] This is a lyrical, epicurean transformation of the famous words, spoken by Odysseus in the sea-storm, imitated by Vergil in the first book of the *Aeneid*.

tion, a gradual narrowing and tightening in the direction of what matters most, of what is most essential. The poem begins serenely and broadly with the splendidly displayed names of Greek towns. Then the splendor gathers, as it were, in one point: in the beloved small town of Tivoli. But then it appears that even this place of seclusion is not necessary for happiness. Even the expelled, the homeless, the man exposed to an unknown fate (brightened, it is true, by the oracle of Apollo), the hero who must leave even Salamis, the poorest of all islands—contrasted purposely with the famous places of the bright beginning—can still enjoy the present hour. From nothing a moment of happiness can grow, and in the face of this moment everything else vanishes. Everything else sinks down before the one thing that remains: the man who knows how to grasp the present with composure.

The same movement toward the essential is to be found in a very famous ode, that has been treated—and mistreated, as I believe—very often in the last years: the Soracte Ode (I,9).[8] It is the first song in the collection of odes written in the Alcaic meter, and this gives the poem a certain prominence: it is an homage to the Greek poet Alcaeus whom Horace chose above all as a model for his lyric poetry.

The poem begins with the picture of winter: the mountain Soracte covered with deep snow, the trees laboring under their burden, the rivers frozen with the sharp cold. This is not the expression of a state of soul and not a symbol of old age.[9] It is the Roman winter and nothing else. I think today one looks too much for symbols. The friend of poetry may enjoy the pleasure of continuing the work of the poet and adding his own poetry. But the philologist has to listen to the poet and to perceive carefully what he says. This is harder than we think, as in life listening accurately is an art mastered only by few.

Against the cold of winter there is help: a good fire and Sabine wine. But there are "other things"—*cetera*—likely to alarm us, things that make our hearts heavy. What can we do against these things? "Leave them to the gods": *Permitte divis cetera.* "Once they

---

[8] For a closer analysis of the poem, see V. Pöschl, "Die Soracteode des Horaz," *Wiener Studien*, 79 (1966): 365–83.

[9] For the opposite view, see L. P. Wilkinson, *Horace and His Lyric Poetry* (Cambridge, 1951), pp. 130 f.; and Steele Commager, *The Odes of Horace* (New Haven–London, 1962), p. 271.

have laid low the winds battling to the end with the seething ocean, then neither the cypresses nor the old ashes are shaken any more."

The storms are a metaphor for the adversities of life we cannot avoid, political and private disturbances, that cause fear, sorrow and suffering. The consolation offered by the poet is: these things will pass as storms pass. Some interpreters believe that here the poet points to the calm of death.[10] They are certainly wrong. Death for Horace is the inescapable necessity[11] that gives every happy moment of this life its value, but never is death in Horace a consolation, as it is in Cicero or Seneca or even in Lucretius.

From the unpleasant things compared with storms the poet quite naturally passes to the central exhortation, that here appears for the first time in the collection of the odes: "Do not ask what tomorrow will bring" (*Quid sit futurum cras, fuge quaerere*) "and set down as gain each day that Chance will give" (*Quem fors dierum cumque dabit, lucro appone*). That does not mean only: each day you live is a gain. The poet points to the Epicurean balance sheet: we must try to gather more happy hours and days in our life than unhappy ones and must not poison them by sad thoughts. We must attempt to make the most out of life, "as long as gloomy grey age is far from green youth" (*Donec virenti canities abest morosa*). "As long as you are young, seek the Campus Martius and the squares" (*Nunc et campus et areae*), not as many interpreters since Giorgio Pasquali[12] believe in order to indulge in love on squares at night— that would be indeed a bit inappropriate to such a season—but to sport: riding, ball games and so on, for which the Campus Martius and the *areae* are the indicated places. Love is mentioned only after that: "Seek soft whispers at the appointed hour of nightfall: now seek the laugh that betrays the girl hiding in a secret corner and the pledge snatched from her arm or finger scarcely resisting":

> lenesque sub nocem susurri
> composita repetantur hora,
>
> nunc et latentis proditor intimo
> gratus puellae risus ab angulo
> pignusque dereptum lacertis
> aut digito male pertinaci.

---

[10] Wilkinson and Commager, *ll.cc.*
[11] *Necessitas. Odes* III, 1, 14: *aequa lege Necessitas sortitur insignes et imos.*
[12] G. Pasquali, *Orazio lirico* (Firenze, 1920), p. 83.

Three antitheses are contained in the poem: the antithesis between the winter and the pleasant banquet with cosy fire and good wine; the antithesis between the storms that bother us, the end of which we must wait for with patience and acquiescence; the antithesis between old age and youth and its joys.

The last stanza belongs entirely to the pleasures of love, wooing and seduction, the gesture of flight and provocative hiding and resisting that are natural feminine expressions of the wish for love.

Thus, we have three steps:

1. the pleasure of a cosy banquet, enhanced as it were by the cold outdoors;
2. the reasonable consideration that every bad thing will pass, followed by the general exhortation of the poet to grasp the moment;
3. the unqualified abandonment to the happy moment of love and expectation of love.

In the last stanzas all things and thoughts evoked by the poet vanish. A cone of light falls on the happy innocent scene of love described in charming details. In the movement of the poem itself, the poet shows us how to put away the gloomy sides of life and how to indulge entirely in the present: the essential reality of life according to Horace and to some modern philosophers. Thus the poem becomes in a way philosophy in action. At its end only the happy moment is present. All threatening matters seem to have disappeared. Have they really? I think old age is present in the person of the poet, in so far as he is supposed to be an elderly man. So the happiness in which the poem culminates is at the same time the poet's recollection of the happy times of youth. This recollection, the awareness of having lived, is happiness too, as the poet states in the great poem that unfolds in a most magnificent manner the main motifs of the Soracte Ode: the Ode to Maecenas (III, 29): *Tyrrhena regum*.[13] In this ode, the poet, with the same conjuring gesture and the same magic of musical movement, turns to Maecenas. He invites his friend to leave Rome and to come to his country house, where vine, roses, and fragrant ointment await

---

[13] For a fuller interpretation, see V. Pöschl, "Die grosse Maecenasode des Horaz (c.3,29)," *Sitzungsberichte der Heidelberger Akademie der Wissenschaften (phil.-hist Klasse)*, 1961, Abhandlung 1.

the noble guest. Maecenas is asked not to hesitate any longer, to get up quickly, and to come: *eripe te morae*. Here sounds a tone that has much significance in this poem. We must not put off living. The invitation becomes an exhortation to change our lives. We are near the Epicurean wisdom: "We are born only once. It is not possible to be born twice. For all eternity I shall not exist. You are not the master of tomorrow's day, yet you put off always what brings joy. Life passes in procrastination and everyone dies without having found leisure."[14]

In the following stanzas Horace confronts the peace of the rural summer with the political sorrows of Maecenas. As in the First Eclogue of Vergil, the bucolic realm of peace is contrasted with the political world of sorrows, a realm where time stands still and only the blissful present rules. The center of the poem contains these lines (III, 29, 29–45):

> "With wise purpose does the god bury in the shades of night the future's outcome, and laughs if mortals be anxious beyond due limits. Remember to settle with tranquil heart the problem of the hour! All else is borne along like some river, now gliding peacefully in midchannel into the Tuscan Sea, now rolling polished stones, uprooted trees, and flocks and homes together, with echoing of the hills and neighboring woods, while the wild deluge stirs up the peaceful streams. Master of himself and joyful will that man live who day be day can say: 'I have lived today; tomorrow let the Father fill the heaven with murky clouds or radiant sunshine. Yet will he not render vain whatever is past, nor will he alter and undo what once the fleeting hour has brought.' "[15]

> prudens futuri temporis exitum
> caliginosa nocte premit deus
>   ridetque, si mortalis ultra
>   fas trepidat . . . quod adest memento
>
> componere aequos: cetera fluminis
> ritu feruntur, nunc medio aequore
>   cum pace delabentis Etruscum
>   in mare, nunc lapides adesos
>
> stirpesque raptas et pecus et domus
> volventis una non sine montium
>   clamore vicinaeque silvae
>   cum fera diluvies quietos

---

[14] *Gnomologium Vaticanum* 14 = C. Diano, *Epicuri Ethica*, 92, p. 58.
[15] Bennett's translation, Loeb Classical Library.

>   irritat amnes. ille potens sui
>   laetusque deget, cui licet in diem
>   dixisse "vixi: cras vel atra
>   nube polum pater occupato,
>
>   vel sole puro: non tamen irritum
>   quodcumque retro est, efficiet neque
>   diffinget infectumque reddet,
>   quod fugiens semel hora vexit."

"Remember to settle the problem of the hour." As in the famous poem *Aequam memento* (*Odes*, II, 3), the well-balanced mind is revealed in living serenely for the present in the face of death. What matters most is to fulfill life. This thought is expressed in the ode *Otium divos* (II, 16) by means of mythological examples. With the fulfilled brief life of Achilles is contrasted the life of the eternal old man Tithonus. It is not sufficient to grasp the moment. Superficial enjoyment is not meant, but the real fulfillment of time, as Lucretius says (III, 596): "Because you ever yearn for what is not present, and despise what is, life has slipped from your grasp unfinished and unsatisfying." Every day, every hour, decides whether life is "*vita perfecta*" or "*imperfecta*," fulfilled or unfulfilled. One of the best formulations of fulfilled life we find in Seneca, in what I believe to be one of the most beautiful exhortations left to us from antiquity: "A great artist shows himself by being able to include the whole in small compass": *magni artificis est totum continuisse in exiguo*.

To the present are opposed "the other things," "all else": the *cetera* as in the Soracte Ode, all that is out of the present and not in the power of man, the realm of politics and fate, where irrational forces rule. "The other things" are seen in the image of the river, symbol of the inexorable coming and going, of that which is exposed to a perpetual change, of mercilessly flowing time, of the perishable—the extreme opposite of the fulfilled present.

But the wild untamed power of the river which whirls to ruin trees and cattle and men's homes recoils, as it were, from the wise man. In the middle of the line its power is broken as by a rock: *ille potens sui laetusque*. To know that the moment really lived is imperishable gives man serene calm and independence from everything to come. Even God cannot destroy what has been. Here the omnipotence of God has its limit. These words have something of a Promethean defiance. At the end of the poem Horace turns to himself:

> Fortune, exulting in her cruel work, and stubborn to pursue her wanton sport, shifts her fickle favours, kind now to me, now to some other. I praise her while she stays; but if she shake her wings for flight, I renounce her gifts, enwrap me in my virtue, and woo honest Poverty, undowered though she be. Not mine, when masts are groaning with the Afric gales, to have recourse to wretched prayers and with vows to strike a compact with the gods that my Cyprian and my Tyrian wares shall not add new riches to the devouring sea. Then the breezes and Pollux with his brother shall bear me through the tempest of the Aegean main, safely protected in my two oared lifeboat.

Poverty is the poet's bride, Virtue his cloak: that is playful and ironical, but none the less serious. It is the expression of the serene smile with which the poet looks on Fortune's raging. And behind Fortune's raging all the bitter experiences of the age are concealed. But the poet sails safely in a small lifeboat after the shipwreck, guided by kindly powers through the tempests of life. The gods protect him. As he says of himself in another poem, "The gods delight in me, my piety, my Muse" (*Odes* I, 17, 13–14).

> Di me tuentur, dis pietas mea
> et Musa cordi est.

Thus the poem ends in a religious realm. Two forms of religious attitude are contrasted: the miserable fear of the gods, which is only a disguised form of greed, the kind of religion condemned by Lucretius, and the personal religion of Horace, the pious faith that the realm of happiness disclosed by him is blessed by the gods. A miracle happens: the waves of the sea do no harm to the small lifeboat of the poet.

In this poem the decision in favor of a personal life full of simplicity and poverty is brought together with the friendship of Maecenas and Horace. This friendship of the minister of the Emperor with the poet is based on the generous recognition which the powerful man seems to give to the poet's decisively proclaimed ideal of an unpolitical personal life. But this does not mean that Horace did not have to struggle for his liberty. Many a poem, especially in the *Satires* and *Epistles*, tells, if rightly understood, about this struggle. In the Epistle to Aristius Fuscus (I, 11) we read the fable of the stag and the horse who lost his liberty in order to eat better. In the Epistle *Quinque dies* (I, 7), Horace interprets his position by another fable. A fox penetrated through a small hole into a woven corn basket. He ate to his heart's content. And behold! The hole had become too narrow and he could not get out. Then the weasel gave him this advice: "If you want to get out, you must become as lean as you were when you went in." And Horace adds: "If that image concerns me, then I am prepared to resign everything. Then I will gladly praise the sleep of the poor not stuffed with fat capons, and I will not give up the leisure of liberty for all the riches of Arabia." These words are followed by the whimsically contemplative story of the great lord Philippus and the poor Volteius, who had been a junk dealer, as Horace's father once was. Once Philippus saw the poor Volteius sitting happily cleaning his fingernails with a knife in a barbershop, and he invited him to come for dinner. At first the poor man refuses. At last, however, he comes, and then comes more and more frequently. The fish swims toward the hook he does not see, says Horace. Philippus gives him an estate in the Sabine Hills, but he soon grows tired of it. Sheep are stolen from him. The goats die off. The fields do not flourish. Then he comes on his horse at night to his patron in the town and implores him: "Turn me back to my former life!" All that recalls, of course, Maecenas and Horace. One must understand that Horace would be ready to give back his Sabine estate to keep his liberty.

But how is this related to Horace as political poet? Were his political poems, his praises of Augustus, insincere flatteries? Were they written to order, propaganda, as Syme suggests in his book on the Roman revolution?[16] Were they something his heart was not in, as Wilkinson suggests?[17] There may be some truth in these statements. The Augustus Odes of the fourth book that praise the bringer of peace are written in the style of other encomia of rulers usual at the time, as we may conclude from inscriptions in Asia Minor. This *is* official poetry.

But first we must not forget that in spite of all the cruelties

---

[16] R. Syme, *The Roman Revolution* (Oxford, 1939), pp. 459 ff.
[17] Wilkinson, *Horace and His Lyric Poetry*, p. 65.

Octavian committed in connection with the civil war and after, struggling against conspiracies, the *Pax Augusta* and the renewal of order, justice, and religion in Rome were an achievement that was decisive for the further development and the stability of the Roman Empire. After endless wars and inexpressible cruelties the *Pax Augusta* seemed like a miracle. The history of the world changed. And then, being a Roman, Horace feels quite spontaneously responsible for the Roman State that was considered as something sacred, something beyond all discussion. Yet he was not blind to the faults of his age. He had the courage to speak with candor. That is proved by the *Roman Odes*, if they are rightly understood. They show a liberty and a depth of historical sense that must be admired.

In the first *Roman Ode* the ideal of poverty is praised. Poverty is considered as the thing to be sought in purposeful contrast to the life of the powerful and rich. The sorrows and fears of the mighty are pitilessly unmasked: You might have much land, you might boast glory and power, yet you must die, and fear and sorrow hang over you like the sword of Damocles and rob you of sleep. Thus the *Roman Odes*, strangely enough, begin with a poem that praises private existence and purposely depreciates political and social power. This ode (III, 1) is closely related to the ode we analyzed before (III, 29) that closes the third book. Thus the book is framed by personal confessions in an Epicurean spirit. Horace here describes his own personal ideal, but this ideal has a firm and necessary place in the system of Roman society. A political order that did not guarantee this private existence would have no value for Horace. For this reason the first *Roman Ode*, which praises this existence, has a firm place in the whole system of *Roman Odes* which are a symbol for the order of the total Roman existence. There is an ideal balance between the personal and the political realm, between individual and state, between Stoicism and Epicureanism. Both philosophies are necessary to give a theoretical basis to Roman life in its whole compass. This balance, which ascribes to both realms an independent and autonomous significance, is the great contribution that the Romans brought to Western civilization. For in Greece these two realms have the tendency to fall asunder. Either the polis or the individual is too mighty. And in the further course of our history this balance has been menaced time and again.

While the first *Roman Ode* remains in the private sphere of the poet, the second praises one of the most important social virtues: courage in military and political matters.

In the third *Roman Ode* too, a courageous and independent attitude is praised: the stoical Roman faithfulness to principle, especially to the central political virtue: justice and the courage to defend it against each menace. The *iustus et tenax propositi vir* who shows courage against the tyrant and the mass, who remains fearless even in the face of the end of the universe, *si fractus illabatur orbis impavidum ferient ruinae*, reminds us more of Cato than of Augustus. But in the next stanza Horace promises Augustus apotheosis on account of this very virtue. Horace seems to have wanted to pay homage to the adversaries of Augustus too, and making him in a way the heir of the Roman republic, commit him to the old Roman values. The legacy of the Republican fighters of Pharsalus and Philippi to whom Horace himself belonged is not to perish in the Augustan State. The ode has its climax in the speech of Juno, in which the condition of Roman greatness and Roman world rule is revealed: Troy has perished, but Rome, her heiress, will attain the empire of the world, if she condemns avarice (*aurum . . . spernere fortior*) and does not rebuild Troy. Otherwise the fate of Troy will be repeated. This is a very serious warning, for Troy is the city of injustice and greed.

The Fourth Ode displays in three ways the concept of *vis temperata*, the tempered power: in the poetry of Horace, in the peace of Augustus, and in the order of the world, that was made possible when the Olympians vanquished the Giants—the forces of destruction. Horace—Augustus—Jupiter: the poet—the Emperor—the god: these are the bearers of right order. The Muses give the advice of clemency. *vos lene consilium et datis et dato gaudetis . . .* , the poet, the "prophet of the Muses" (*Musarum sacerdos:* III, 1) can help the ruler to find the mild way to the right order. Here it becomes clear what Horace aims at: not so much the glorification of the Augustan order as the painting of a picture to which this order must conform.[18] It commits Augustus and the future emperors to the idea of justice and *vis temperata*. Horace becomes the defender

---

[18] The same is true of the speech of Jupiter in the first book of the *Aeneid*. It is much more than a praise of the *gens Julia*. It starts with Aeneas and ends with the Augustan order: the taming and subduing of the *Furor impius*, the self-destroying forces that brought about inexpressible sufferings.

of the order of state, proclaimed by Plato and Cicero. For the central ideas of this order are justice and moderation. Once again Augustan poetry takes over the heritage of Greek thought and Greek philosophy.

After this climax the Fifth and Sixth Odes are a kind of descent. In the Fifth Ode the decay of Roman virtue is described. This line is continued in the Sixth Ode, which paints the sexual demoralization in lurid colors. As a contrast appears the peasant youth of old Rome who worked the earth with a Sabellian mattock. The ode and the whole cycle end with a stanza full of deepest pessimism:

> "What do the ravages of time not injure! Our parents' age, worse than our ancestors', has brought forth us less worthy and destined soon to produce an offspring still more wicked."

> Damnosa quid non imminuit dies?
> aetas parentum, peior avis, tulit
> nos nequiores, mox daturos
> progeniem vitiosiorem.

The feeling of relentless decay intrudes with uncanny force. This dark end of the cycle is so amazing that commentators have passed it over with silence or have tried to explain it by a hypothesis of development in the poet, making the ode belong to a previous stage before the Augustan peace.[19] But I think we must recognize that this consciousness of guilt and sin and decay is one feature of the Augustan Age, too. The awareness that the Roman existence is menaced is not lacking even in the central *Roman Odes*, as is shown by the speech of Juno and the role of the Giants.

The peripheral Odes 1 and 6 treat the different expression of the Roman greed for life: the first *avaritia* and *luxuria* (avarice and luxurious living), the last the sexual demoralization. The Odes 2 and 5 correspond also: there the Homeric bravery of the lionhearted hero, here the betrayal and the cowardice of a depraved generation. The central odes show the rescue, but also the danger: the Third Ode proclaims the Roman rule over the world and its conditions. The Fourth Ode shows the healing force of poetry and the benefit of the *Pax Augusta*. But this benefit can only abide when all are aware of the example the gods gave by the destruction of

---

[19] Cf. R. Heinze, *Vom Geist des Römertums* (Leipzig–Berlin, 1938), pp. 218 ff.

the wicked. So the most important motifs of Horatian poetry are encompassed in the *Roman Odes* as in a cone of light: hope of redemption and awareness of guilt; rescue and decay; the Epicurean salvation of the individual and the Roman virtue that proves itself in many aspects: as heroism in war, as contempt for the seducing goods of this world, as the subduing of the greed for life, and, not least, as the proud faithfulness to convictions that can if necessary defy political rulers. The poet is there, exhorting and helping, showing the way of salvation to the community. But if this way fails, if the forces of self-destruction go their way—and they will, so says the end of the Sixth Ode—then the individual still has a way to withdraw and to find a pleasant and peaceful happiness in the realm of the Muses and the natural joys of life. So Horace encompassed in these odes almost all aspects of his poetic mission, in a marvelously composed structure, written in the meter of the Greek poet Alcaeus. In this way he suggests that like Alcaeus, like the Greek poets of the early times, he unites political exhortation and the appeal to enjoy life wisely and cheerfully. He gathers the best forces of Greek poetry and philosophy and the best forces of Latinity. At the same time these poems grow out of an original and human personality, the poet Horace, who wants to achieve the personal life, this brief life that is given us here, to bring it to achievement through limitation. From such a poet, healing and beneficent forces can flow into our lives, too, if we listen to him.

George E. Duckworth

THE "OLD" AND THE "NEW" IN VERGIL'S *AENEID*

Vergil ranks with Homer, Dante, and Milton as one of the supreme epic poets of Western literature, and, just as Vergil was indebted to Homer, so the achievements of the two later poets would have been impossible without the influence of the Roman poet. Vergil's pre-eminence was realized almost as soon as he began work on the *Aeneid;* the poet Propertius wrote (II, 34, 66): "Something greater than the *Iliad* is being born." A century after his death, as we learn from Martial (XIV, 186), expensive parchment editions of the epic were being produced as *Saturnalia* presents in late December; this was long before the Romans adopted Christianity, but it was a season of good will and a time for exchanging gifts.

Throughout the Roman Empire and the Middle Ages, Vergil was viewed as a source of all knowledge, as a teacher, a prophet, and even a magician.[1] Many of the medieval stories about his magical powers are fascinating and fantastic but, of course, they bear no relation to the true facts of his life. The real Vergil and his work emerge again with Dante, who loved him not only as a poet but as the one who had, in his Messianic Eclogue, bridged the gap between paganism and Christianity; hence it was Vergil whom Dante chose as his guide through Hell and Purgatory.[2] To Tenny-

---

[1] The best treatment of this aspect of Vergil is still D. Comparetti, *Vergil in the Middle Ages*, trans. E. F. M. Benecke (New York, 1929); see also J. W. Spargo, *Virgil the Necromancer* (Cambridge, Mass., 1934).

[2] See G. Highet, *The Classical Tradition* (New York, 1949), pp. 72–80.

son, Vergil was the "wielder of the stateliest measure ever moulded by the lips of man,"[3] and T. S. Eliot calls him "the classic of all Europe."[4] We should, I think, include the Americas and say that he is "the classic of the western world."

The number of editions, books, and articles published each year on Vergil's poetry is amazingly large. In recent years I have had the pleasant, if somewhat laborious, task of preparing for the *Classical World* two rather lengthy surveys of Vergilian bibliography.[5] I chose 1940 as my starting point because in that year an Italian scholar named Mambelli published a two-volume bibliography of Vergil from 1900 on, and he listed almost 4,000 items—an average of 100 a year.[6] This average has continued from 1940 to the present, as I discovered, somewhat unhappily, when I compiled my two bibliographical surveys.

How can we account for this tremendous output of new studies on the poetry of Vergil? One reason, I believe, is that he differed so strikingly from all previous poets and in every aspect of his work created something new. The extent to which this statement is true has been revealed only in recent decades. Earlier scholars were inclined to stress his borrowings from his predecessors, especially Homer,[7] and we cannot deny that he made use of all earlier poetry, both Greek and Roman. We find many deliberate echoes of Ennius, Lucretius, and Catullus. Another great source of the *Aeneid* is Greek tragedy, Euripides in particular,[8] and there seems a strong

---

[3] Highet, *ibid.*, p. 446, says of Tennyson: "He himself was surely the English Vergil; and the address *To Vergil* which he wrote as a mature poet is among the finest tributes ever paid by any artist to his predecessor."

[4] T. S. Eliot, *What Is A Classic?* (London, 1945), p. 31.

[5] G. E. Duckworth, "Recent Work on Vergil (1940–1956)," *C.W.* 51 (1957–58): 89–92, 116–17, 123–28, 151–59, 185–93, 228–35, reprinted in 1958 by the Vergilian Society of America; "Recent Work on Vergil (1957–1963)," *C.W.* 57 (1963–64): 193–228, reprinted in 1964 by the Vergilian Society of America.

[6] G. Mambelli, *Gli studi virgiliani nel secolo XX: Contributo ad una bibliografia generale* (Firenze, 1940).

[7] For the most complete study of Vergil's use of Homeric material, see G. N. Knauer, *Die Aeneis und Homer* (Göttingen, 1964) [= *Hypomnemata*, Heft 7].

[8] See B. C. Fenik, *The Influence of Euripides on Vergil's "Aeneid"* (Ann Arbor, 1960) [= Princeton University dissertation, microfilmed]. E. K. Rand, *The Magical Art of Virgil* (Cambridge, Mass., 1931), p. 381, says: "the poem is not solely epic; in structure it is a fusion of epic and of Attic tragedy, which Virgil enriches by creating a new conception of fate."

probability that the range of his source material extended even to India, to the famous Sanskrit epic, the *Mahābhārata*.[9]

Today, however, thanks to the efforts of many twentieth-century scholars, we have a much clearer conception of Vergil's originality and the magnitude of his poetic achievement; in spite of his use of older material, the *Aeneid* is thoroughly Roman and thoroughly Vergilian, and it is new—new in content, in style, in poetic imagery, in use of language and meter, in its over-all structure. I shall examine briefly these various aspects of the poem.

Vergil is unlike any earlier poet, for he has produced a new kind of epic, with "a new vision of human nature and of heroic virtue";[10] it is a truly national epic, but it includes not only history (past, present, and future) but philosophy and religion as well. The characters are portrayed as individuals but they are also symbols and represent something outside of themselves and larger than themselves. As Pöschl says, "in Vergil the symbolic character of poetry is revealed with a clarity previously unknown in the history of Western poetic art."[11] In his recent and valuable book on Vergil, Otis attempts to explain how it was possible that "Virgil did what no one else had done before him and no one was able to do after him"; he was "the first and only poet truly to recreate the heroic-age epic in an urban civilization"; of all epic poetry "only the *Aeneid* aspired to be both heroic and civilized, both remote and contemporary, both Homeric and Augustan."[12]

Vergil's style is new; Otis calls it "subjective" as opposed to the more narrative, objective style of Homer and Apollonius; by "subjective" he means both the manner in which Vergil shares the emotions of his characters (empathy) and presents his own personal reaction to their emotions (sympathy). Otis writes: "Virgil not only reads the minds of his characters, he constantly communicates to us his own reactions to them and to their behaviour."[13] This "empathetic-sympathetic style" makes possible both a con-

---

[9] See G. E. Duckworth, "Turnus and Duryodhana," *T.A.P.A.*, 92 (1961): 81–127.

[10] C. M. Bowra, *From Virgil to Milton* (London, 1948), p. 35; see also pp. 10–15, 84–85.

[11] V. Pöschl, *The Art of Vergil: Image and Symbol in the "Aeneid,"* trans. G. Seligson (Ann Arbor, 1962), p. 1.

[12] B. Otis, *Virgil. A Study in Civilized Poetry* (Oxford, 1963), pp. 2–3.

[13] *Ibid.*, p. 88.

tinuous psychological narrative and the symbolic structure of the poem.

Vergil's poetic imagery differs from that of his predecessors; he takes over numerous similes from Homer and Apollonius, but he gives them another meaning and a new beauty. The similes are closely related to the inner struggles of the characters and often serve to forecast the fate in store for each. In IV, 441–46, we have the simile of the oak tree shakened by the northern winds; its leaves fall but it remains firm, its roots fast in the rocks; likewise Aeneas is buffeted by the entreaties of Anna, but (449):

> mens immota manet, lacrimae volvuntur inanes.
>
> "His resolve remains fixed, tears fall in vain."

Contrary to the statements in most commentaries on this passage, the tears here are those of Aeneas, for the simile expresses the inner conflict between his determination to depart and his love for Dido.[14] The comparison of Dido to a deer wounded by a shepherd (IV, 68–73) and that of Turnus to a wounded lion (XII, 4–9) not only reveal the state of mind of the two characters but provide a symbolic announcement of their later deaths.[15]

Vergil is painstaking in his use of language; each verse, each phrase, each word is significant, and the full meaning may come only with the second or third reading, and often there may be more than one meaning. The repetitions and echoes of words and phrases from earlier contexts serve to evoke symbolic associations. Alliteration had been a characteristic of Roman poetry from its very beginning, but Vergil is "the great master" of alliteration and expressiveness;[16] cf. I, 55 f. and 124:

> illi indignantes magno cum murmure montis
> circum claustra fremunt;

---

[14] See Pöschl (above, note 11), pp. 46 f.; G. E. Duckworth, *Structural Patterns and Proportions in Vergil's "Aeneid"* (Ann Arbor, 1962), p. 17, note 37. The English versions of the Latin passages given below are from the verse translation by L. R. Lind (Bloomington, 1962); Lind's translation of IV, 449, reproduces the wrong interpretation of *lacrimae inanes* ("his mind was unchanged. Vain tears rolled down Anna's cheeks.").

[15] Cf. Pöschl (above, note 11), pp. 79–81, 109–11.

[16] L. P. Wilkinson, *Golden Latin Artistry* (Cambridge, 1963), p. 85; cf. pp. 74–83 for his analysis of *Georgics* I, 43–392.

> interea magno misceri murmure pontum
>
> "Angry, they loudly protest against their confinement,
> The hill that lies over them.
>
> Meanwhile . . .
> The sea set roaring loudly in wild confusion."

In translation most of the original beauty is lost, and especially the effectiveness of the *m*-sounds. When the two serpents are described as coming from Tenedos to destroy Laocoon and his sons, the words hiss with sibilants, both initial and medial; cf. II, 207 ff.: *sanguineae superant undas, sinuatque immensa, sonitus spumante salo, ardentisque oculos suffecti sanguine.*

Vergil's meter often expresses the meaning of the sentence; the two most famous examples are undoubtedly VIII, 596, in which the horses gallop across the plain:

> quadripedante putrem sonitu quatit ungula campum.
>
> "Horses' hoofs
> with four-footed thud strike the crumbling field."

and VIII, 452, where the many spondees reproduce the sound of the Cyclopes working at their anvils:

> illi inter sese multa vi bracchia tollunt
>
> "Their great power
> Of arm lifted hammers."

The meter varies also in groups of lines and in episodes and speeches of considerable length. Vergil's most frequent combination of dactyls and spondees in the first four feet is *dsss;* this comprises about fourteen per cent of the *Aeneid* as a whole. The pattern occurs much more frequently, twenty to thirty per cent, in narrative episodes, such as battle descriptions, and especially in scenes of the gods and in passages dealing with Roman history and Augustus. In all such scenes a solemn and majestic rhythm is most appropriate. On the other hand, in the more dramatic and emotional episodes, those which best illustrate the new subjective style, the frequency of *dsss* varies usually from three to eight per cent, far below the normal occurrence of this pattern. Meter, style, and subject matter thus go hand in hand.[17] Another metrical innovation which we find in Vergil is a definite striving for variety. The eight most frequent patterns, out of a possible sixteen, had appeared in Lucretius 79.81 per cent of the total verses, and in Catullus LXIV, the Peleus and Thetis poem, the frequency was even higher, 90.98 per cent. Vergil reduced the frequency of his first eight patterns in the *Aeneid* to 72.78 per cent.[18]

The *Aeneid* is one of the most consciously planned and carefully constructed poems of world literature. Its architecture is most unusual; we find not merely one structural pattern but at least three.

First, there is an alternation of the books, those with even numbers being of a more serious and tragic nature than those with odd numbers, which are lighter and serve to relieve tension. The famous books which stand out in the reader's memory are even-numbered: II, the fall of Troy; IV, the tragedy of Dido; VI, the trip to the underworld; VIII, Aeneas' visit to Evander and the site of Rome; X, the great battle, with the deaths of Pallas, Lausus, and Mezentius; and XII, the final conflict and the death of Turnus. Vergil has stressed the significance of these books by means of the alternating rhythm.

The *Aeneid* is divided into two halves, I–VI, often called the "Odyssean" half of wanderings, and VII–XII, the "Iliadic" half of battles after Aeneas and the Trojans arrive in Italy. Vergil himself looks upon the second half as a *maior rerum ordo*, a *maius opus* (VII, 44 f.). The second architectural pattern is the parallelism, by similarity and contrast, between the books in each half, I and VII, II and VIII, III and IX, etc. For instance, in both I and VII the Trojans arrive in a strange land and are welcomed after a speech by the Trojan Ilioneus; in each the goddess Juno laments her lack of power and stirs up trouble for the Trojans with divine

---

[17] See G. E. Duckworth, "Vergil's Subjective Style and Its Relation to Meter," *Vergilius*, 12 (1966): 1–10.

[18] The percentage of the first eight patterns in Vergil's *Eclogues* was 69.09; in the *Georgics* 73.42. Horace surpassed Vergil in his desire for metrical variety: *Satires*, 69.99 per cent; *Epistles*, 66.76 per cent; see G. E. Duckworth, "Horace's Hexameters and the Date of the *Ars Poetica*," *T.A.P.A.*, 96 (1965): 75 f., 92.

or infernal assistance—in I, the storm at sea, and in VII, the war in Latium.[19]

Vergil combines with the alternation of the books and their division into two corresponding halves a third and most important architectonic device—a tripartite division of the epic into three groups of four books each. The *Aeneid* gives not only the story of Trojan Aeneas but also the history of Rome and its destiny under Augustus. This latter provides much of the central core of the poem (V–VIII) and concludes with the victory of Augustus at Actium and his triumphs, described on the shield at the end of VIII. The *Aeneid* is thus a trilogy with the first four books, the tragedy of Dido, and the last four books, the tragedy of Turnus, enclosing and emphasizing the story of Rome and Augustus in the very center of the epic. This division of the poem into three parts is undoubtedly a deliberate attempt on Vergil's part to avoid too sharp a break into an "Odyssey" of wanderings and an "Iliad" of battles.[20]

I have discussed the structure of the *Aeneid* in some detail as it leads directly to my main theme—the "old" and the "new" in the *Aeneid* itself.

Of the even-numbered books the best known and best beloved is undoubtedly IV, which portrays the tragic love and suicide of Queen Dido of Carthage. Book VI is considered "the keystone of the whole poem," the "crowning Book, which Vergil has placed in the centre, to unite all that stand before it and all that stand after";[21] it tells how Aeneas, accompanied by the Sibyl and with

---

[19] For the similarities and contrasts in the corresponding books, see G. E. Duckworth, "The Architecture of the *Aeneid*," *A.J.P.*, 75 (1954): 1–15, expanded in Duckworth (above, note 14), pp. 7–10. Otis (above, note 12), pp. 217 f., 344 f., favors a different parallelism of the halves; he combines I and VII, but arranges the other books in reverse order: II and XII, III and XI, IV and X, V and IX, VI and VIII (see G. E. Duckworth, review of Otis in *A.J.P.*, 86 [1965]: 419 f.). Otis, however (pp. 392, 418), admits the validity of the correspondences in II and VIII, III and IX, etc.

[20] See G. E. Duckworth, "The *Aeneid* as a Trilogy," *T.A.P.A.*, 88 (1957): 1–10; (above, note 14), pp. 11–13.

[21] R. S. Conway, *Harvard Lectures on the Vergilian Age* (Cambridge, Mass., 1928), p. 143. Cf. also H. W. Prescott, *The Development of Virgil's Art* (Chicago, 1927), pp. 360 f.

the aid of the Golden Bough,[22] traverses both a "mythological" and a "philosophical" underworld, gains from his father Anchises an understanding of life and death, and learns of the future destiny of Rome; this book has recently been called "perhaps the most complex and poetically rich book of the poem."[23] On the other hand, Mackail says that Book XII, the final conflict of Aeneas and Turnus, "reaches an even higher point of artistic achievement and marks the utmost of what poetry can do, in its dramatic value, its masterly construction, and its faultless diction and rhythm."[24]

Two other books, likewise even-numbered and therefore of major significance, perhaps best present the basic theme of the *Aeneid;* these are II, the destruction of Troy, the end of the "old" city, and VIII, the rise of the "new" city, containing the description of early Rome and the scenes of Roman history on the shield. Vergil himself summarizes the two halves of the poem and its purpose in the opening verses (I, 1-7):

> arma virumque cano, Troiae qui primus ab oris
> Italiam fato profugus Lavinaque venit
> litora—multum ille et terris iactatus et alto
> vi superum, saevae memorem Iunonis ob iram,
> multa quoque et bello passus, dum conderet urbem
> inferretque deos Latio—genus unde Latinum
> Albanique patres atque altae moenia Romae.

> "I sing of arms and the man who first from Troy's shores,
> Fate's fugitive, came to Italy and Lavinium's
> Coast, a man much tossed on land and sea
> By the gods' force, through Juno's mindful fury;
> He suffered greatly in war until he could found
> A city and bring his gods to Latium, whence
> The Latins would spring, the Alban fathers, and Rome
> With its lofty walls."

The phrase, "to found a city and bring his gods to Latium," stresses both the political and the religious nature of the poem; Vergil adds in line 33:

---

[22] See R. A. Brooks, "*Discolor Aura*. Reflections on the Golden Bough," *A.J.P.*, 74 (1953): 260-80; C. P. Segal, "*Aeternum per saecula nomen*, the Golden Bough and the Tragedy of History," *Arion*, 4 (1965): 617-57; 5 (1966): 34-72.
[23] Segal, *Arion*, 5 (1966): 65.
[24] J. W. Mackail, "The *Aeneid* as a Work of Art," *C.J.*, 26 (1930-31): 17.

tantae molis erat Romanam condere gentem.
"So great
Was the task to found the race and the city of Rome."

Thus it is that Bowra considers the fundamental theme of the epic to be "the destiny of Rome" as "presented in the person of Aeneas who not only struggles and suffers for the Rome that is to be but is already a typical Roman."[25] The miracle of the *Aeneid* is said to be Vergil's ability to treat three different topics simultaneously—the legendary narrative of Aeneas, themes and personages of Roman history, and the praise of Augustus.[26] But, as I wrote some years ago:[27]

> The epic rises far above the patriotic and historical level in the poet's dramatic treatment of character and event and in his introduction of loftier themes of philosophy and religion; it is an epic not only of Rome but of human life as well.

Perhaps nowhere in the *Aeneid* are the basic themes of the poem displayed more clearly than in the two corresponding books, II and VIII. Each, like the other books of the epic, is divided into three main sections. In II we have (1) the stories of Sinon, Laocoon, and the wooden horse; (2) the return of the Greeks, the capture of Troy, and the death of Priam; and (3) the Aeneas-Venus episode, his return to his home, and the departure from Troy, with the loss of Creusa. In VIII (1) Aeneas leaves the camp of the Trojans and goes up the Tiber to Pallanteum, the site of later Rome, where he is welcomed by King Evander and his son Pallas; since a festival to Hercules is being celebrated, Evander describes the victory of Hercules over the monster Cacus; he then leads Aeneas through the town, pointing out spots destined to be famous later in the Roman city, and receives him in his humble abode; (2) that night Venus persuades Vulcan to provide Aeneas with armor, and early in the morning the god goes to his workshop where the Cyclopes make the armor as instructed; (3) after Evan-

---

[25] Bowra (above, note 10), p. 36.
[26] See J. Perret, *Virgile, l'homme et l'oeuvre* (Paris, 1952), p. 89.
[27] G. E. Duckworth, "Mathematical Symmetry in Vergil's *Aeneid*," *T.A.P.A.*, 91 (1960): 185; (above, note 14), p. vii. J. W. Mackail, *Virgil and His Meaning to the World of To-day* (New York, 1927), pp. 74–77, lists twelve aims which Vergil had in mind while composing the *Aeneid*.

der's farewell to Pallas, the Trojans and their Arcadian allies set out for the Etruscan city of Caere and on the way Aeneas receives the armor from Venus; the book concludes with an account of the historical scenes on the shield. Such a brief summary, of course, fails to give an adequate conception of the power and richness of these two books or of Vergil's effective dramatic portrayal of Aeneas and the other characters.

In Books II and VIII, in addition to the fundamental contrast between the fall of the old city, characterized by darkness, despair, and death, and the rise of the new, accompanied by brightness, encouragement, and hope, other contrasts and similarities appear in abundance, as in the other pairs of corresponding books.[28] For example, in II the Greeks destroy Troy and the Trojans suffer at their hands, but in VIII the Greeks help to found Rome and the Trojans benefit from their assistance; the helplessness of the aged Priam in II is contrasted with the helpfulness of the aged Evander in VIII, as is the splendor of Priam's palace with the simplicity of Evander's home on the Palatine. Venus as a goddess appears to Aeneas in each book, in II to convince him that the gods favor the destruction of Troy, in VIII to present to him the armor, and on the shield the gods fight for Augustus and Rome at Actium against the barbarian deities of Antony and Cleopatra. In II Anchises is persuaded to leave Troy by a double prodigy—fire around the head of Ascanius and a comet in the sky; likewise, on the shield in VIII, fire appears around the temples of Augustus and over his head is his father's star, the comet of Julius Caesar. At the end of II Aeneas carries on his shoulders his father—a symbol of the past, and at the end of VIII he raises to his shoulder the shield portraying important scenes of Roman history—symbolic of the future. Aeneas marvels at the beauty of the shield but he is *rerum ignarus* (730); he does not realize the meaning of the scenes, unlike Vergil's contemporaries.

I should like to add two more pairs of passages to the similarities and contrasts already listed; both seem valid and significant.

1. In II the coming of the two serpents from Tenedos and the death of Laocoon and his sons are symbolic announcements of the

---

[28] See Duckworth, above, note 19.

return of the Greeks and the destruction of Troy,[29] and Hercules' victory over Cacus in VIII, wrongly considered by some an episode contributing little to the action of the poem,[30] foreshadows the final victory of Aeneas over Turnus, a necessary step to the birth of Rome, and it also symbolizes the defeat of Antony and Cleopatra by Augustus and the advent of peace in Vergil's own day.[31] Otis looks upon the Hercules-Cacus story as "an example of the conduct by which man can become divine and by which Hercules himself became the true predecessor of Aeneas, Romulus and Augustus."[32]

2. In II Aeneas first receives his commission; Hector appears to him in a dream and urges him to flee with the Penates to a new home across the seas; cf. 289–90, 293–95:

> "heu fuge, nate dea, teque his" ait "eripe flammis.
> hostis habet muros; ruit alto a culmine Troia. . . .
> sacra suosque tibi commendat Troia penatis;
> hos cape fatorum comites, his moenia quaere
> magna, pererrato statues quae denique ponto."

> "Run, goddess-born!" he said, "escape these flames:
> The enemy holds the walls; Troy-towers fall. . . .
>   Now she entrusts
> Her holy rites and statues to your care.

---

[29] See K. Büchner, *P. Vergilius Maro, Der Dichter der Römer* (Stuttgart, 1956) cols. 328 f. [= "Vergilius," *R.E.*, 16 (1958): cols. 1350 f.]; M. C. J. Putnam, *The Poetry of the "Aeneid"* (Cambridge, Mass., 1965), p. 27. B. M. W. Knox, "The Serpent and the Flame," *A.J.P.*, 71 (1950): 380, points out that the image of the serpent suggests not only destruction but rebirth; "the death agonies of Troy are the birth-pangs of Rome."

[30] See W. H. Semple, "The Conclusion of Virgil's *Aeneid*: A Study of the War in Latium, with Special Reference to Books XI and XII," *B.R.L.*, 42 (1959–60): 180. Semple (p. 181) lists the story of Nisus and Euryalus in IX as a similarly detached episode which contributes nothing to the action of the plot or the progress of the war; on this see G. E. Duckworth, "The Significance of Nisus and Euryalus for *Aeneid* IX–XII," *A.J.P.*, 88 (1967): 129–50.

[31] See G. K. Galinsky, "The Hercules-Cacus Episode in *Aeneid* VIII," *A.J.P.*, 87 (1966): 18–51, and bibliography cited therein; cf. Duckworth, *C.W.*, 57 (1963–64): 209. Putnam (above, note 29), p. 35, compares also the forced entrance of Pyrrhus into Priam's palace with Hercules' passage into the cave of Cacus and the revelation of the interior of each (cf. the use of *apparere* in II, 483–84, and VIII, 241–42). The serpent imagery, so prominent in II, is echoed in VIII; see Galinsky, *ibid.*, pp. 42 f.

[32] Otis (above, note 12), p. 335.

> Take them, the comrades of your fate, seek walls
> For them where they may rest, your wanderings over."

Aeneas ignores his duty; overcome by *furor* and *ira*, he rushes into battle in a vain attempt to save the doomed city from the Greeks; cf. 316–17:

> furor iraque mentem
> praecipitat, pulchrumque mori succurrit in armis.
>
> "Furious anger
> Drove me headlong, and all I thought was this:
> To die in battle is the way to glory."

Aeneas receives instructions and information concerning the future on many other occasions, from both gods and mortals: from Venus and Creusa in II; from Apollo, the Penates, Celaeno, and Helenus in III; from Mercury in IV; from Nautes and Anchises in V; and from the Sibyl in VI. Anchises, meeting Aeneas in the underworld, points out the souls to be reborn as Roman kings and heroes, including Augustus who is destined to bring to Rome a new Golden Age, and also describes the war to be waged by Aeneas in Latium and the toils to be undergone; cf. VI, 890–92:

> exim bella viro memorat quae deinde gerenda,
> Laurentisque docet populos urbemque Latini,
> et quo quemque modo fugiatque feratque laborem.
>
> "he told his hero-heir
> The wars which must be waged and described the peoples
> Of Laurentum, Latinus' city, and how he might flee
> From each trial, or bear it."

It is not until VIII 524–29, however, when Aeneas sees and hears the prodigy in the heavens—lightning, thunder, trumpet blasts, gleaming armor—that he realizes most fully that he is the divine man of Roman destiny. "I am summoned by Olympus" (*ego poscor Olympo*, 533),[33] he cries, and he foresees with sorrow the deaths and sufferings in store for the Latins and for Turnus. The *prodigium*, signifying that he will receive divine armor and engage

---

[33] I follow here the punctuation of Sabbadini and most other editors; Hirtzel (Oxford Classical Text) joins *Olympo* to the following sentence.

in war, brings to a close the long series of warnings and instructions which began with the words of Hector in II. This time Aeneas shows no hesitation and accepts willingly the difficult duties which lie ahead. It is thus in VIII that Aeneas becomes a truly religious hero, endowed with the spiritual energy necessary for his destined task.[34]

One important feature of Book II is Vergil's emphasis on the bravery of the Trojans and Aeneas. They were the equal of the Greeks in battle, and it was only by trickery and the will of the gods that they were defeated; cf. 195-98:

> Talibus insidiis periurique arte Sinonis
> credita res, captique dolis lacrimisque coactis
> quos neque Tydides nec Larisaeus Achilles,
> non anni domuere decem, non mille carinae.[35]

> "With such deceits and wicked art of Sinon,
> By tricks and tears, the captive made us believe him,
> We whom no Achilles of Larissa nor Diomedes
> Nor ten years nor a thousand ships had conquered."

and the words of Venus in 601-3:

> "non tibi Tyndaridis facies invisa Lacaenae
> culpatusve Paris, divum inclementia, divum,
> has evertit opes sternitque a culmine Troiam."

> "Do not blame the hated beauty of Helen, nor Paris:
> The merciless gods, the gods, are the ones who have toppled
> The power of Troy and levelled it with the earth."

The Trojans and Aeneas must appear as worthy ancestors of the Romans. Aeneas therefore ignores the instructions of Hector and rushes blindly with his companions to the defense of the city. Father Sullivan says:[36]

---

[34] See F. A. Sullivan, S.J., "The Spiritual Itinerary of Virgil's Aeneas," *A.J.P.*, 80 (1959): 150-61. F. Bömer, "Studien zum VIII. Buche der Aeneis," *R.M.*, 92 (1944): 319-69, discusses the structural importance of the prodigy-episode (520-40) for the unity of VIII and calls it the "Höhepunkt" of the book; cf. pp. 322, 326, 337, 340.

[35] The repetition of the words *dolus* and *insidiae* is especially effective; in addition to 195 and 196, cf. *dolo* (34), *dolis Danaum* (44), *dolos* (62), *dolis et arte Pelasga* (152), *Myrmidonumque dolos* (252), *doli fabricator* (264); *Danaum insidias* (36, 65), *Danaum . . . insidiae* (309 f.).

[36] Sullivan (above, note 34), pp. 152-53.

His *pietas* towards the gods seems eclipsed by *furor;* his *pietas* towards his family is forgotten, and only for his *patria*, now doomed and in flames, does he show any thought. . . . Blind *furor* must give way to a new faith, despair to a new hope before he can become a vessel of election for the great task ahead.

It is in VI and finally in VIII that Aeneas gains the faith and hope which carry him through the difficult days of the fighting in the latter portion of the epic.

I return now to Book VIII, which is perhaps less familiar than II to many lovers of Vergil. After the cruel death of Priam and the destruction of Troy, it comes somewhat as a surprise to find Greeks and Trojans joining in a treaty of friendship. The Sibyl, however, in her pessimistic and enigmatic prophecy, had said (VI, 96–97):

"via prima salutis,
quod minime reris, Graia pandetur ab urbe."

"The first road to safety will open
From a Greek city, where you would least expect it."

There are several reasons for the union of the Arcadian Greeks of Pallanteum and the Trojans, as we learn from the speeches of Aeneas (127–51) and Evander (154–74): the two peoples have a common ancestry from Atlas and they have a common enemy, the Rutulians; they are bound by guest friendship, for Priam and Anchises had once visited Arcadia and Anchises had presented gifts to Evander, then a mere youth. Furthermore, Evander and the Arcadians, like Aeneas and the Trojans, were exiles from their home and had been led to Italy by Fate and Apollo (cf. 333–36).

It was a stroke of genius on the part of Vergil to have Aeneas leave the Trojan camp and visit Evander at the site of Rome. The values of the Evander episode and its effects on the latter part of the *Aeneid* are numerous and far-reaching, and may be enumerated briefly as follows:

1. Structurally, Aeneas' absence from the Trojan camp, like Achilles' refusal to fight in the *Iliad*, gives the enemy an opportunity to play a leading role; this results in the activity of Turnus in Book IX and the fight within the Trojan camp. Aeneas' absence likewise gives Ascanius a chance to display qualities of leadership

and provides motivation for the ill-fated night expedition of Nisus and Euryalus.

2. The numerous leaders and warriors catalogued in VII, 641–817, join the Latins and Rutulians; the Trojans, unless they are to be hopelessly outnumbered, are in desperate need of allies, and Evander not only provides Greek warriors but sends him to the leaderless Etruscans who will add thousands of fighters to the Trojan side. The war now ceases to be a local skirmish and becomes a major conflict involving all of central and northern Italy, even beyond the river Po, as far north as Mantua, Vergil's birthplace (cf. X, 198–206). The fact that Vergil has given Greek ancestry and Greek connections to so many warriors in the catalogue in VII tends to make the ensuing conflict almost a continuation on Italian soil of the Greco-Trojan War.[37]

3. Pallas, Evander's youthful son, who accompanies Aeneas into battle, is a key figure in the later action; Turnus' insolent words and actions when he slays Pallas in X (cf. *iussa superba*, 445; *superbum caede nova*, 514 f.) are directly responsible for his own death at the end of XII;[38] Aeneas was about to spare Turnus when he saw the sword-belt of Pallas and cried out (947–49):

> "tune hinc spoliis indute meorum
> eripiare mihi? Pallas te hoc vulnere, Pallas
> immolat et poenam scelerato ex sanguine sumit."

> "Shall you escape me with spoils you have taken
> From those I have loved? Pallas with this wound shall
> slay you
> In sacrifice, Pallas exacts from your villainous blood
> His penalty!"

4. Aeneas' visit to Evander explains the presence of a Greek cult in Roman religion—the cult of Hercules at the *ara maxima* in

---

[37] Cf. VII, 656 (*satus Hercule*), 672 (*Argiva iuventus*), 679 (*Volcano genitum*), 691 (*Neptunia proles*), 723 (*Agamemnonius, Troiani nominis hostis*), 761 (*Hippolyti proles*), 794 (*Argivaque pubes*). See A. Cartault, *L'art de Virgile dans l'Énéide* (Paris, 1926), pp. 560–62.

[38] See G. E. Duckworth, "Fate and Free Will in Vergil's *Aeneid*," *C.J.*, 51 (1955–56): 362; R. Hornsby, "The Armor of the Slain," *Philol. Quart.*, 45 (1966): 357–59. Putnam (above, note 29), pp. 151–52, 189, 192, presents a picture of Aeneas' force and violence at the end of XII which many will find unacceptable. I do not agree with Putnam (p. 193) that Aeneas, in slaying Turnus, disregards Anchises' words in VI, 853; *debellare superbos* is his duty.

the Forum Boarium; this religious rite goes back to early times, before the foundation of Rome. Evander explains the cult as the result of their gratitude to Hercules for destroying Cacus.[39]

5. The union of Greek and Trojan forces in VIII symbolizes the later incorporation of Greek influences in the Roman State. The culture of Vergil's day was as much Greek as Roman. Likewise, the influence of the Etruscans on Roman architecture, government, and religion had been far from inconsiderable, and this too is symbolized by the union of Trojan and Etruscan forces in the *Aeneid*.

6. Aeneas' visit to the site of Rome provides a strong patriotic and antiquarian interest. One always wishes to know about the early days of one's home town or home city. Less than a hundred years ago the present Lincoln Center in New York City was farmland, from which people moved into the city, as it was too far away for commuting; the Public Library at the corner of Fifth Avenue and Forty-Second Street was a goat pasture. Romans of Vergil's day likewise would be fascinated by the description of the Forum as a cow pasture, and of the Capitoline as merely a grove where the presence of a god, perhaps Jupiter, was felt. The contrast between this early period and the splendor of the city in the time of Augustus would make a strong appeal to the pride of Vergil's readers.

Aeneas visits the very heart of Rome, the Capitoline,[40] Forum, and Palatine—the religious, political, business, and residential centers of the later city. But Vergil not only describes an imaginary primitive settlement of the past; at the same time he recalls the topographical present, certain monuments erected in his own day:

---

[39] The cult was not entirely Greek, however, but contained Italian elements; cf. Galinsky (above, note 31), p. 46.

[40] Cf. 347: *hinc ad Tarpeiam sedem et Capitolia ducit.* W. W. Fowler, *Aeneas at the Site of Rome* (Oxford, 1918), p. 73, suggests that Evander and Aeneas stopped at "the foot of the Capitol"; at this spot it would be impossible to see the *arx* (357); moreover, in order to point out the Lupercal on the right, the asylum on the left, and the Argiletum straight ahead, Evander had already led Aeneas past the Tarpeian rock; why should they retrace their steps? The verb *ducit* (347) is in sharp contrast to *monstrat* (337, 343, 345); it seems more likely, therefore, that Evander, in spite of his age (*obsitus aevo*, 307) took Aeneas up the Capitoline hill (by way of the later *clivus Capitolinus*) from which they could gain a better view of both the Janiculum and the *arx;* cf. Cartault (above, note 37), p. 609; Rand (above, note 8), p. 427, who says: "And now they climb the Capitoline."

porta Carmentalis (338) was adjacent to the later temple of Apollo, and both the temple and the Lupercal (343) had been restored by Augustus; the grove of Argiletum (345) suggests the Basilica Aemilia and the Curia, both completed by Augustus, and perhaps also the Gates of Janus nearby, which the *princeps* had closed after so long a period of civil conflict (cf. I, 293–96); the description of the Capitoline and the presence of Jupiter is probably a reference, not to the great temple of Jupiter, Juno, and Minerva, but to a smaller temple on the Capitoline to *Jupiter Tonans*, dedicated by Augustus in 22 B.C.[41]

However, in spite of these possible allusions to his own day, Vergil actually presents the setting, the "empty stage," for the later history of the city. For the events to take place on this historic site, we turn to the scenes on the shield of Aeneas at the end of the book, beginning with Romulus and Remus and ending with Augustus.[42] The scenes include the rape of the Sabine women and the later union of Sabines and Latins; the punishment of Mettus for his treachery; the fight with the Etruscans and Horatius at the bridge; Manlius defending the Capitoline against the Gauls; Catiline and Cato; and in the center of the shield (*in medio*, 675),[43] Augustus' victory over Antony and Cleopatra at Actium and his triple triumph.

Many have asked why Vergil chose these particular scenes. What is their underlying unity, if any? The poet himself describes the shield in 626, 628–29 as containing:

---

[41] See P. Grimal, "La promenade d'Évandre et d'Énée à la lumière des fouilles récentes," *R.E.A.*, 50 (1948): 348–51; cf. Galinsky (above, note 31), p. 21. On the temple of Jupiter Tonans, cf. also Cartault (above, note 37), p. 609; Bömer (above, note 34), p. 526.

[42] Cf. the juxtaposition of Romulus and Augustus in I, 272–96, and VI, 777–807. Suetonius (*Divus Augustus*, 7) relates that some senators had preferred the title "Romulus" to "Augustus" as more suitable for the second founder of Rome.

[43] Fowler (above, note 40), pp. 100 f., thinks it futile to attempt to locate the scenes on the shield; so Otis (above, note 12), p. 341: the shield "is assuredly *not* to be reduced to any one plan that can be visualized." But Vergil apparently did intend us to think of the arrangement of the scenes; cf. *in summo* (652), *haec inter* (671), *in medio* (675); see Cartault (above, note 37), pp. 622–32, who places the scenes clockwise in a series of outer and inner panels or compartments. Cf. also *The Works of Virgil*, translated by C. Pitt, with Notes by J. Warton (London, 1763), III; the scenes on the reproduction facing p. 321 go counterclockwise; see W. Whitehead, "Observations on the Shield of Aeneas," *ibid.*, pp. 340–52.

> res Italas Romanorumque triumphos . . .
> genus omne futurae
> stirpis ab Ascanio pugnataque in ordine bella.

> "Italian history, triumphs
> Of Romans, the people that were to descend from Ascanius,
> The wars they would fight, each in order."

Fowler suggests that the scenes are all "escapes from terrible perils,"[44] and Otis considers the main theme of the shield to be "the constant opposition of *virtus, consilium* and *pietas* to the forces of violence in all Roman history."[45] I prefer to find the unity of the shield elsewhere. The events described from early Roman history all took place in or near Rome itself, and, after the battle of Actium (675–713), we return to Rome for the triumphs of Augustus and the survey of the conquered nations (714–28). We thus have in VIII a dramatic progression from Evander's primitive settlement, the empty stage, to the shield on which the events to take place at Rome are described, those both of its early history and of Vergil's own day.[46] This completes the rise of the new city in VIII and balances the fall of the old in II. Aeneas lifts to his shoulder a picture of Rome's history and Rome's destiny.

Book II, the destruction of Troy, is one of the great books of the *Aeneid*, but structurally it does not have the significance of VIII, the final book of the central third of the poem.[47] In this respect, VIII is to be compared with IV, the Dido book, and XII, the Turnus book. Each is the conclusion of one section of the trilogy, and the central, more Roman and Augustan portion, reaches a fitting climax in the picture of Rome, its early history, and the battle of Actium which makes possible the Augustan Age—the return of the *aurea saecula*.

[44] Fowler (above, note 40), pp. 103–6; he is troubled by the fact that the greatest escape of all, that from Hannibal and Carthaginian domination, is omitted. However, if we reject Fowler's theory of "great escapes" in favor of "events at Rome," the omission of Hannibal presents no problem; Rome itself was not attacked by Carthaginian forces, as by the Gauls a century and a half earlier. And, in any case, Vergil has stressed the hostility of Rome and Carthage elsewhere in the *Aeneid;* cf. I, 12–22; IV, 622–29; X, 11–14.

[45] Otis (above, note 12), p. 341; cf. Putnam (above, note 29), p. 150: "And this is the story of the shield—violence ultimately leading to peace."

[46] Cf. Cartault (above, note 37), p. 634; Otis (above, note 12), p. 342.

[47] Otis (above, note 12), pp. 273 f., 343–45, 419, adds IX to the four central books; this destroys the climactic effect of the conclusion of VIII and blurs the relation of the Nisus-Euryalus episode to the remainder of the epic; see Duckworth (above, note 30), pp. 141–47.

Wolfgang Clemen

THE UNIQUENESS OF SPENSER'S *EPITHALAMION*

Spenser's *Epithalamion* is one of the great poems of English literature. It has maintained its reputation and rank throughout the centuries in spite of the changes in taste and outlook.[1] In reading it today we can still enjoy it with that immediacy of pleasure which also for a closer scholarly investigation forms the best condition. We can still appreciate the beautiful melody of the stanzas, the imaginative richness of the language, the freshness of the poem and its personal tone, the intensity of emotion, the moving union of the sensuous and the spiritual, the striking fusion of many disparate elements; we can still enjoy the dramatic presentation of scene and action, the wealth of visual and oral impressions, the vividness of concrete details.

There are only a few random impressions which the ordinary, unprepared reader might share with us, but despite their value as an indication of the poem's enduring effect, they are too vague and general for a discriminating evaluation. The scholar is constantly faced with the task of penetrating to the core of impressions such as these, and, by tracing each one back to its component aspects, he may transform a mere impression into demonstrable fact. The effect of artistic perfection and emotional intensity, the impression of what we would call high poetic quality, is usually a product of a number of factors co-operating toward a common goal.[2] In read-

---
[1] For assessments see *The Works of Edmund Spenser. A Variorum Edition, The Minor Poems*, II (Baltimore, 1947).
[2] Cf. René Wellek, *Concepts of Criticism* (New Haven, 1963).

ing a poem only one or twice we cannot become aware of this complicated interplay of various elements. It is only by closer examination that we discover how many different things had to come together to make this achievement possible.

Moreover, a poem of great perfection and great beauty often forms a milestone in the history of English poetry. Its freshness and liveliness derive from the fact that certain structural qualities, certain principles of composition and poetic organization, were achieved here for the first time in a successful manner. The poet who writes a perfect poem that may be regarded as a climax in the poetry of his time has usually succeeded in solving problems for which neither his predecessors nor even he himself in earlier poems had managed to find a satisfactory solution. Poetry, in spite of its claim to inspiration, is an art in which much has to be learned before a masterpiece can be produced. The instruments of versification and diction must be refined to a degree of perfection, devices of composition and organization must have been found, means of poetic expression must have been developed, ways of giving shape to abstract notions must be at the poet's disposal in order that a successful "long poem" of some complexity may be born.

Looking back over the history of English poetry in the sixteenth century, and examining the way in which these arts of poetic composition and expression developed, we would have to admit that the *Epithalamion* could not have been written in the sixties, seventies or eighties of the sixteenth century. A process of gradual development was necessary for English poetry to reach a stage at which a man of genius like Spenser could find at his disposal an instrument sufficiently refined to enable him to write a great poem. This does not mean that the evolution of a style of poetry over a period of several decades would automatically lead to a masterpiece. However, it was not mere chance that Spenser's achievement with his *Epithalamion* appeared at the same time as the crowning achievement of Elizabethan lyric poetry, as a consummation of some of the highest potentialities and poetic endeavors of this important phase in English poetry. It is with a view to this twofold quality of Spenser's *Epithalamion*, as a great representative poem of the English Renaissance and as Spenser's most perfect work of art, that I propose to speak of its "uniqueness."

"Uniqueness" and "perfection," however, are the results of the fortunate co-operation of several basic qualities. I should like therefore to concentrate on the question: What are the distinguishing features which go to constitute the poem's excellence and its uniqueness? It may be appropriate to gauge these qualities first by looking back on works of comparable length and subject matter written before Spenser's poem.

Spenser's *Epithalamion* is one of these "long poems" which in the literature of the sixteenth century form a class of their own. A "long poem" has always set special problems for its author.[3] It has a tendency to become tedious, so variety, change in tone and color, but also growth and development, are essential. But this again might well impair the poem's unity and consistency. Thus the special difficulties attributed to the long poem have often been the problems of organization and of unification. And we can easily see that the long poems before Spenser generally fail in this respect.[4] They could just as well go on for another ten stanzas, they have no climax and often no central theme to which all minor details should be related. They are loosely constructed and their method of composition is rather one of stringing together a series of ideas, conventions, and incidents. The Epithalamies[5] by Bartholomew Young and Sir Philip Sidney are particularly suited for such a comparison as they belong to the same literary genre and employ similar conventions to Spenser's *Epithalamion*. In Young's *Epithalamion*, for instance, the sequence of the stanzas could even be changed without detriment to the intelligibility of the poem; there is no link between the stanzas and little or no connection between the different motifs which are treated separately in the course of the poem. Spenser's poem, on the other hand, displays unity, order, inner cohesion, and clear organization. In fact, it appears to be the first long poem in the history of English poetry to be composed according to a well-calculated plan. It has its own curve and development, its proper preparation at the beginning leading us leisurely and step by step toward the core of the poem and it has

---

[3] On this aspect, in view of Spenser's achievement, see W. H. Stevenson, "The Spaciousness of Spenser's 'Epithalamion,'" *R.E.L.*, 5 (1964): 61–69.

[4] E. G. Daniel's "The Complaint of Rosamond," Ralegh's "Cynthia," Barnfield's "The Affectionate Shepheard."

[5] Reprinted in Robert H. Case, *English Epithalamies* (London, 1896).

its proper ending. We can even detect an elaborate symmetry, so characteristic of Renaissance art, in the construction of this poem.

After the invocation to the Muses ten stanzas out of twenty-three lead up to the great moment when the bride enters the church, so that the actual marriage ceremony takes place in the exact center of the poem. But this marriage ceremony also coincides with the middle of the day, with the sun reaching its zenith. Two structural patterns thus correspond to each other, and the two halves into which we can divide the poem (if we take the middle of the day with the wedding ceremony as the division line) also bear resemblances to each other and disclose correspondences. Thus, as William Nelson has pointed out in his recent book on Spenser[6] "the opening invocation of the Muses, the Nymphs, the Hours and the Graces is matched by concluding prayers to Cynthia, Juno, Genius, Hebe and the 'high heavens.' The bride is roused from sleep at the beginning and is sung to sleep at the end. The rising sun has its balance in the evening star, the moon, and the 'thousand torches flaming bright.' In the morning the Hours are asked to adorn and array the bride; when the sun sets the attendant damsels disarray her." Another critic, Hieatt, has gone even further and has tried to point out, as regards the use of numbers and recurring motifs, subtle correspondences between the stanzas occupying the same position in both parts.[7]

As Spenser describes the progress of his marriage day from early morning until late at night, his poem is given a definite framework of time and experience. But within this running action each stanza depicts a situation, a moment or a phase which is complete in itself and forms a unit within the larger composition of the whole poem. This art of elaborating a situation, presenting it to us as a living picture but integrating this pictorial mode of presentation into a steadily progressing action, is evident in Spenser's *Faerie Queene*. In the *Epithalamion* this art reappears in a more concentrated form combined with a convincing and well-rounded cyclic pattern. For the natural order of a twenty-four-hour cycle binds the happenings of the poem close together and also places the

---

[6] William Nelson, *The Poetry of Edmund Spenser* (New York, 1963), p. 95.

[7] A. Kent Hieatt, *Short Time's Endless Monument. The Symbolism of the Numbers in Edmund Spenser's* Epithalamion (New York, 1960).

reader in a revolving time scheme which he may relate to his own daily experience. The order and ritual of the marriage day in accordance with the custom of the time are carefully observed; the progress of the marriage procession bringing the bride from her home to the church and taking her back to her home constitutes a conspicuous groundplan and allows every minor detail as well as every convention of the epithalamic tradition to fall into its concrete place in time and locality. For when reading the poem we always know where and in which phase of the day we find ourselves. Thus we can say that in Spenser's poem order and organization are closely combined with a constant endeavor to relate all traditional conventions and motifs to the specific happenings of this marriage day; a process which we might call "concretization."

However, order and organization in a perfect poem are inevitably linked with the problem of unity. Unity is not uniformity. For uniformity effected through monotonous versification and diction, the regular recurrence of certain rhetorical figures or conventions was what the poets before Spenser had as a rule produced instead of genuine unity. Spenser's poem, however, is a work of variety, of changing tempo and diction, of surprising transitions between varying levels of style and techniques of description. To give unity to such a poem of many colors and great diversity, Spenser had to use several means. (Whether the poet contrived these means consciously or unconsciously is a problem which we cannot discuss here.) However, we could draw up a long list of features and devices which contribute toward unifying of the poem. I can mention here only a few.

In several respects the bride is the center of the poem, the pervading theme to which everything else is related. To begin with, Spenser succeeds in connecting most of the minor decorative details, almost all the ornament and imagery, with the bride, who is referred to in almost every stanza. The nymphs, the graces, and the village girls are invoked to awaken, to adorn, to dress the bride; to sing her praise, to help in the preparation of the wedding. But the same applies to others appearing in the course of the poem—the "fresh boyes" (112), the minstrels, the damsels in the street, the virgins, and also the non-human beings—the birds, the woods, the moon, the evening-star, the night, the "sonnes of Venus." This unifying effect, if we may put it that way, is enhanced by the fact that it is the poet himself who calls upon all these beings and people to serve the bride in some way or other, to sing her praise, to contribute to her happiness and well-being.

The poet is at the same time the bridegroom, who describes his own marriage day and gives his entire poem as a present to his bride. But his role is also that of a director of a masque or pageant, for, like a master of the revels, he arranges everything and the main initiative always comes from him. He is also the speaker who in his complex role as poet, bridegroom, and master of the revels can address his own bride with the same naturalness as the Muses, Juno, or the "merchants daughters." This continuous presence of the poet himself, acting beside the bride as the second central figure in the poem and to whose voice we listen, not only increases the personal meaning and appeal of this poem but is another important factor in producing its unity. Moreover, the poem in itself appears as a gift from the poet to his bride, as an "ornament" that crowns the activity of adorning and praising referred to in every stanza. The poem's last stanza, the "envoy," reads:

> Song made in lieu of many ornaments,
> With which my love should duly have bene dect,

ending

> Be unto her a goodly ornament,
> And for short time an endlesse moniment.[8]

Now we find that this motif of adorning is one of the recurring leitmotifs. The Muses often helped the poets "others to adorne" (2). The whole third stanza is about the adorning of the bridal chambers, and in the fourth stanza it is the bride herself who is to be adorned. In the sixth stanza the three Graces are called upon to "adorne my beautifullest bride" (105). I quote the third stanza to illustrate the manner in which Spenser interweaves this motif of adorning into the running account of the marriage day:

> Bring with you all the Nymphes that you can heare
> Both of the rivers and the forrests greene:
> And of the sea that neighbours to her neare,
> Al with gay girlands goodly wel beseene.

---

[8] The text used is that of the Variorum Edition of *The Works of Edmund Spenser* (Baltimore, 1947). The letters u-v, and i-j have, however, been modernized.

> And let them also with them bring in hand
> Another gay girland
> For my fayre love of lillyes and of roses,
> Bound truelove wize with a blew silke riband.
> And let them make great store of bridale poses,
> And let them eeke bring store of other flowers
> To deck the bridal bowers.
> And let the ground whereas her foot shall tread,
> For feare the stones her tender foot should wrong
> Be strewed with fragrant flowers all along,
> And diapred lyke the discolored mead.
> Which done, doe at her chamber dore awayt,
> For she will waken strayt,
> The whiles doe ye this song unto her sing,
> The woods shall to you answer and your Eccho ring.

Singing and *rejoicing* are other often recurring motifs which help to convey a certain coloring and mood to this poem. Or note the frequency of words expressing joy: *joyance, pleasure, pleasance, delight, happiness, jollity, cheerful, glad, happy*, or the frequency of other key words like *fair, fresh, sweet, goodly, gentle, seemly*.

Such a use of vocabulary may also be found in other Elizabethan poems. But of a more intricate and subtle effect as a unifying factor is the imagery of light which pervades the whole poem. For it is derived quite organically from the rising and descending sun, followed by the rising moon. These metaphors of light, however, are invariably related to the bride, so that there is a constant fluctuation and correspondence between the real sun and its symbolic significance. The seventh stanza may illustrate this point:

> Now is my love all ready forth to come,
> Let all the virgins therefore well awayt,
> And ye fresh boyes that tend upon her groome
> Prepare your selves; for he is comming strayt.
> Set all your things in seemely good aray
> Fit for so joyful day,
> The joyfulst day that ever sunne did see.
> Faire Sun, shew forth thy favourable ray,
> And let thy lifull heat not fervent be
> For feare of burning her sunshyny face,
> Her beauty to disgrace.

> O fayrest Phœbus, father of the Muse,
> If ever I did honour thee aright,
> Or sing the thing, that mote thy mind delight,
> Doe not thy servants simple boone refuse,
> But let this day let this one day be myne,
> Let all the rest be thine.
> Then I thy soverayne prayses loud wil sing,
> That all the woods shal answer and theyr eccho ring.

Thus we find that the organization of unity is closely bound up with the establishing of correspondences and interrelationships. The course of outward events, the situations visually described, and the stages of this marriage day are at the same time, as a more detailed study might show, expressive of inner moods. The outward form of this poem has become "inner form," for the curve of external happenings on this marriage day coincides with the curve of inner experience. The day's natural cycle governed by the rising and setting sun is a perfect image of what the poet wanted to convey in the sphere of ideas, feelings, and ethical values.

But unity also means integration of heterogeneous elements. Let us begin with the integration of the traditional conventions which belonged to the "epithalamium." The apparatus of epithalamic conventions has been carefully explored by several scholars.[9] Spenser observes most of these conventions but we are scarcely aware of their "conventional origin," for he has enlivened and concretized them by relating them closely to the actual events of the day and by turning them to dramatic account. Even the first invocations to the nymphs and the graces (37, 103) are utilized in this particular manner. The nymphs, for example, are called upon to decorate the bridal bowers with flowers and to wait for the bride at the chamber door, thus resembling the customary bridesmaids who appear at a wedding (45 ff.). But if we read on we notice that the "light foot maids" (67) who are addressed as the "Nymphes of Mulla" are more or less identical with the daughters of the tenants and farmers in the country round the castle of Kilcolman where Spenser's marriage actually took place. In other

---

[9] Thomas M. Greene, "Spenser and the Epithalamic Convention," *Comparative Literature*, 9 (1957): 215–28. Hallett Smith, "The Use of Conventions in Spenser's Minor Poems," *Form and Convention in the Poetry of Edmund Spenser, English Institute Essays* (New York, 1961), pp. 122–45.

stanzas, too, the mythological figures merge into the familiar people of Spenser's own countryside, just as the ideal scenery and the conventional setting of the *Epithalamion* constantly blend with the local Irish scenery and the actual circumstances of Spenser's marriage day.[10] Mythology, on the other hand, is fused with folklore and popular custom, so that there is a constant transition between the literary tradition of the "epithalamium" and the actual wedding customs still in use in Spenser's own time. This point may be illustrated by the stanzas VIII (129 ff.) or XV (260 ff.) where we hear of the festivities connected with St. Barnabas Day, or stanza XIX (334 ff.), where there is mention of "Pouke" and "other evill sprights" and "mischivous witches with theyr charmes." The stanza should be quoted in full:

> Let no lamenting cryes, nor dolefull teares,
> Be heard all night within nor yet without:
> Ne let false whispers breeding hidden feares,
> Breake gentle sleepe with misconceived dout.
> Let no deluding dreames, nor dreadful sights
> Make sudden sad affrights;
> Ne let housefyres, nor lightnings helpelesse harmes,
> Ne let the Pouke, nor other evill sprights,
> Ne let mischivous witches with theyr charmes,
> Ne let hob Goblins, names whose sence we see not,
> Fray us with things that be not.
> Let not the shriech Oule, nor the Storke be heard:
> Nor the night Raven that still deadly yels,
> Nor damned ghosts cald up with mighty spels,
> Nor griesly vultures make us once affeard:
> Ne let th'unpleasant Quyre of Frogs still croking
> Make us to wish theyr choking.
> Let none of these theyr drery accents sing;
> Ne let the woods them answer, nor theyr eccho ring.

If we listen to a reading of Spenser's *Epithalamion* we become particularly aware of the unifying function of the refrain at the end of each stanza. This most musical and perfect refrain not only

---

[10] Thus in the fourth stanza Spenser evokes the scenery round his castle in referring to the "silver scaly trouts" on which Renwick (in his edition of the *Epithalamion*) remarks: "There are good trout in Awbeg still." (*Daphnaïda and other Poems*, ed. by W. L. Renwick [London, 1929], p. 205.)

rounds off each stanza but also evokes the same symbolic background of scenery and echoing music to which the stanza contributes its own particular feature. However, this refrain is more than a recurring leitmotif. For through the slight modification to which each new refrain is submitted we are reminded of the gradual passage of time. Whereas the sixteenth stanza describing the last part of the day ended "That all the woods them answer and their echo ring" the following stanza (the seventeenth) emphasizes the beginning of night with lines like:

> Now day is doen, and night is nighing fast:
> Now bring the Bryde into the brydall boures.
> Now night is come, now soone her disaray . . .

and concludes

> Now it is night, ye damsels may be gon,
> And leave my love alone,
> And leave likewise your former lay to sing:
> The woods no more shal answere, nor your echo ring.

Thus the problem of unity and integration, on which we have so far dwelled, leads us to another important aspect of the poem, its organic growth and its time-consciousness. Looking at comparable longer poems of the period we find that no consistent use is made of the passing of time. Narrative poems of the pastoral kind certainly present an action which moves forward, but we are not really made to feel the lapse of time. Spenser's *Epithalamion* appears to be composed on another principle, which we might call the principle of organic growth alternating between movement and suspense, progress and immobility, for each stanza gives us a new picture and exploits a new situation which gains life before our eyes. But in almost every stanza we are also reminded that the action has moved forward and that time is passing. The natural sequence of the hours of the day serves as a "clock-time scheme." But within this "clock-time scheme" we have the subjective time experience. Time may pass quickly or it may linger on endlessly. The varying tempo produced within each stanza by versification and diction helps to produce this feeling of passing time. There are stanzas with quick movement where several things happen at once in an almost dramatic simultaneity, and there are stanzas of a lingering mood, in which time seems to stand still. The moods of expectancy and impatience, of happiness and fulfilment are invariably expressed by references to the passing of time. Thus we have the subjective experience of slow-moving time in line 280:

> How slowly do the houres their numbers spend?
> How slowly does sad Time his feathers move?

Spenser's subtle use of time contributes to the over-all effect that something is really happening in the poem, happening at this very moment; that we ourselves are taking part in this day and are watching the progress of an actual experience. Indeed we even believe that we are among the bystanders lining the road while the procession moves forward.

But how does the poet achieve this effect of immediacy and of presence? For this is perhaps the most remarkable feature in a poem handling a classical convention, and it is, moreover, an effect we do not find in the "long poems" of the Elizabethan Age. In analyzing this effect we come upon a number of devices which again no other poet of Spenser's time has used in this subtle manner. For all descriptions of events, of situations, of persons grow out of an act of looking, watching, hearing. They are not given "objectively" but are reflected by someone who watches. This may be the poet-bridegroom himself, or the boys and maidens in the street looking at the bride as she passes by, or it may even be ourselves, the audience. For we are constantly called upon to see, to gaze, to hear, to listen (cf. 64, 129, 167, 185, 223, 372, 377).[11] Even the sun and the moon, as well as the angels, are to take part in this process.[12] Thus Spenser, the painter-poet of the eye, has endowed the figures he puts into his poem with his own gift of gazing. This immediacy and directness are further enhanced by the role assumed by the

---

[11] Some of the stanzas actually begin with this request as, e.g.,
  VIII (129) Harke how the Minstrels gin to shrill aloud
  X (167) Tell me ye merchants daughters did ye see
  XIII (223) Behold whiles she before the altar stands.

[12] E.g.
> That even th'Angels which continually,
> About the sacred Altare doe remaine,
> Forget their service and about her fly,
> Ofte peeping in her face that seemes more fayre,
> The more they on it stare (229-33).

poet himself, which we have already compared to the role of a producer or "master of the revels." For it is the poet who directly addresses the nymphs, the bridesmaids, and all other groups which turn up in the course of the day, telling them what to do, what to look at, or what to expect. Thus we find, instead of the objective statement or the detached description, the direct address, the imperative, the question. At one point the poet even addresses his own bride, for in the midst of the ceremony in the church he asks her: "Why blush ye love to give to me your hand?" (238).

Thus a dialogic partnership is established throughout the poem. Of some stanzas we can even say that the dramatic mode is employed, for we are given little scenes with the movements, gestures, and doings of various persons or groups of people. This immediacy and directness of presentation also helps to bridge the gap between the conventions—the learned allusions on the one hand and the familiar contemporary world of Spenser's readers on the other hand. For beside the conventions deriving from the epithalamic tradition, there are spread throughout the poem a great many (in fact hundreds) of references to the Bible, to classical, medieval, and Renaissance authors.[13] Spenser has absorbed and integrated this mass of learned material from myth and legend, from the literary tradition and theology to such extraordinary degree that we scarcely become aware of this background, for it has been transformed into fresh and actual experience, it has been welded and integrated into the organic texture of the poem. As Douglas Bush has shown us, there is in many Elizabethan poems an amalgam of pagan and Christian deities, of legend and mythology together with contemporary allusion,[14] but I would suggest that there is no other longer poem of the sixteenth century in which this fusion of heterogeneous material, of disparate notions and motifs has reached the same degree of perfection, at the same time successfully increasing the poem's complexity, richness, and unity.

However, in Spenser's *Epithalamion* we do not only find the muses, graces and pagan deities like Bacchus, Hymen, Hebe, and Juno side by side with the Christian angels, the "temple gates" by the altar (204, 215), but we also find very different levels of style

---

[13] See the commentary by Cortlandt van Winkle (New York, 1926).

[14] Douglas Bush, *Mythology and the Renaissance Tradition in English Poetry* (New York, 1957).

and of expression. For the scale of Spenser's language reaches from everyday idiom up to the most elaborate diction of Elizabethan poetry. Compare, for example, short monosyllabic phrases like:

>   For they can doo it best (258)
>   And in her bed her lay (301)
>   That no man may us see (320)

with lines like

>   Her long loose yellow locks lyke golden wyre,
>   Sprinckled with perle, and perling flowres a tweene. (154-55)

And compare again these lines with the colloquial simplicity of:

>   Ah my deere love why doe ye sleepe thus long (85)

or

>   Enough is it, that all the day was youres. (297)

But Spenser's vocabulary in the poem also includes archaic words, as had already been used in *The Shepherd's Calender*, though here they are applied with more discretion.

This wide range of his linguistic and stylistic resources allows Spenser to express changes of mood and tempo, to achieve a transition from stylization and formality to a natural and easy manner. Of the many examples which could illustrate this point I should like to draw attention to some contrasting stanzas. Stanza VIII (129 ff.) gives us the bustle and noisy activity in the street with its "confused noyce" and the sound of all the merry music, of pipe and tabor:

>   Harke how the Minstrels gin to shrill aloud
>   Their merry Musick that resounds from far,
>   The pipe, the tabor, and the trembling Croud,
>   That well agree withouten breach or jar.
>   But most of all the Damzels doe delite,
>   When they their tymbrels smyte,
>   And thereunto doe daunce and carrol sweet,
>   That all the sences they doe ravish quite,
>   The whyles the boyes run up and downe the street,
>   Crying aloud with strong confused noyce,
>   As if it were one voyce.

> Hymen io Hymen, Hymen they do shout,
> That even to the heavens theyr shouting shrill
> Doth reach, and all the firmament doth fill,
> To which the people standing all about,
> As in approvance doe thereto applaud
> And loud advaunce her laud,
> And evermore they Hymen Hymen sing,
> That al the woods them answer and theyr eccho ring.

But the following stanza has quite a different pace. It solemnly announces the appearance of the bride; all stir and movement come to a halt and we are arrested by the gorgeous beauty of the poetry:

> Loe where she comes along with portly pace,
> Lyke Phoebe from her chamber of the East,
> Arysing forth to run her mighty race,
> Clad all in white, that seemes a virgin best.
> So well it her beseemes that ye would weene
> Some angell she had beene.
> Her long loose yellow locks lyke golden wyre,
> Sprinckled with perle, and perling flowres a tweene,
> Doe lyke a golden mantle her attyre,
> And being crowned with a girland greene,
> Seeme lyke some mayden Queene.
> Her modest eyes abashed to behold
> So many gazers, as on her do stare,
> Upon the lowly ground affixed are.
> Ne dare lift up her countenance too bold,
> But blush to heare her prayses sung so loud,
> So farre from being proud.
> Nathlesse doe ye still loud her prayses sing,
> That all the woods may answer and your eccho ring.

The mood of solemn gravity and intimate silence finds its place in this poem as well as the mood of jolly merriment, and both are given their appropriate stylistic expression. Thus Spenser gives us in his *Epithalamion*, on different levels, "variety within unity." In emphasizing this aspect, however, we must also consider his versification. For this most elaborate and intricate stanza of eighteen or nineteen lines which Spenser developed out of the Italian *canzone* allows for changes of rhythm and tempo. Short lines alternate with long ones and the meter is often modified and shifted. A special study would be needed to show how this flexible manipulation of meter contributes toward the effect of suspense, of slowing down and speeding up, of heightening tension. And it would also be worth while demonstrating how Spenser makes use of the rhetorical figures of assonance, anaphora, alliteration, of word-echo, of inverted word order or of certain syntactical patterns to underline or intensify the significance of particular passages. It goes without saying that these "arts of language" are given masterly treatment by a poet who had gone through years of intense poetic training. But this refined instrument of poetical expression is not in itself a product of art but merely a servant. It had to find its thematic counterpart, its adequate conception and framework, in order to exert its full power.

I have limited myself to aspects of Spenser's poetic art which combine to make up the poem's high artistic quality. I have omitted Spenser's handling and modification of the genre to which this poem belongs, the marriage poem or "epithalamium" which from antiquity onward up to Spenser undergoes considerable transformation. Such a study, which has already been carried out by other scholars,[15] would confirm the impression which our reading of the poem has so far given us: that Spenser is at the same time traditional and original, typical and personal, private and public, and that the poet has carefully preserved a great many traditional motifs out of which he has built a poem of great originality.

Inquiring into the way by which Spenser includes traditional elements of the classic marriage poem makes us even more aware of Spenser's achievement. For he succeeds in combining his personal concern and his own personal experience with the objective requirements and the "super-personal" validity of the wedding poem.

However, there is one aspect related to the poem's subject matter and purpose which I cannot omit, as it is intimately connected with what I have called the poem's uniqueness. This becomes apparent when we read the last three stanzas of the *Epithalamion*, in which Spenser gives his poem an almost metaphysical or religious

---

[15] See note on p. 81.

turn. Here, too, the poem includes an element that points far beyond the boundaries of the conventional "epithalamium." For the love treated previously in Renaissance poetry had as a rule not been the love between a married couple but mostly love outside marriage. But Spenser, by praising his own bride and dedicating his wedding poem to his own wife, by invoking the blessing of the "high heavens" (409 ff.) for the raising of "a large posterity," gives a new dignity to the institution of marriage. This was a new development in the history of the "epithalamium" in European literature.

The last three or four stanzas may also convey a deeper meaning to all the preceding parts of the poem. For we now realize that the sensuousness and wealth of concrete detail contained in the description of the events of the wedding day and the festivities at night are only a foreground for something else that takes place on the spiritual plane. In fact, sensuality and spirituality are combined in this poem in a unique manner.[16] Spenser gives us a wealth of sensuous impressions to please our ear and eye and to stir our imagination, but he also extends our vision from this worldly level to another plane. We are made to feel that beyond and above this earthly merriment and bustle there is a higher spiritual world. The sequence of stanzas X and XI, where the appraisal of the bride's inward beauty follows on the sensuous description of her physical beauty, is only one case in point. The reference to Spenser's use of neoplatonic concepts[17] is helpful in this connection but cannot fully account for this particular feature in the poem.

Let us sum up: our reading of Spenser's *Epithalamion* has provided us with a number of characteristics which by virtue of their specific combination contribute toward the poem's excellence. Taken individually, however, none of these characteristic features would be sufficient to produce poetry of a high order. Such poetry is born out of a happy coincidence of several factors, at a climax of a poet's artistic career which coincides with a supreme moment in his own inner experience but which also is a consummation of the lyrical potentialities of a whole period.[18] To conclude our lec-

---

[16] This aspect has been particularly stressed by Lawrence W. Hyman, "Structure and Meaning in Spenser's *Epithalamion*," *Tennessee Studies in Literature*, 3 (1958): 37–42.

[17] R. Ellrodt, *Neoplatonism in the Poetry of Spenser* (Geneva, 1960).

[18] Cf. W. L. Renwick in his comments on the poem (*Daphnaïda and other Poems* [London, 1929]).

ture let us look back over the main points we have made in order to decide whether these points may also reveal to us something of a more general significance. We found that Spenser's *Epithalamion* is a "long poem" carefully planned and organized round a significant center; a poem of order and symmetry in which the outward course of events corresponds to the process of inner experience so that the outward form has become inner form. We emphasized the poem's unity and coherence, produced by several means and on several levels, and we stated that it was a unity in spite of its variety. We also noted the establishing of interrelationships and correspondences between the different parts and thematic levels of the poem. We spoke of the "concretization" of all conventions and motifs which helped to relate every detail to a specific, concrete moment and event during the course of the marriage day. We discussed the assimilation and integration of mythology and learned allusions which were enlivened and brought within the reach of the reader's familiar experience. And we mentioned the art by which Spenser takes up many of the traditional conventions attached to the marriage poem but uses them in such a way that they gain actuality and new life. We noticed the sense of time, the observance of time and locality, and we stressed the effect of immediacy, spontaneity, and presence which was in part produced by a dramatic mode of presentation, and we finally hinted at the metaphysical and spiritual level in the poem. But the most striking quality which emerges from most of these points is the poem's inclusiveness, its "triumphant fusion of many different elements" as C. S. Lewis, in discussing the *Epithalamion*, has expressed it.[19] For from whatever angle we look at this poem we are struck by this inclusiveness. Spenser's *Epithalamion* unites the epic and the lyric mode, realism and formalism, high seriousness and jollity, mythology and contemporary custom, objective detachment and personal concern, sensuality and spirituality, and several other such pairs of contrasting qualities.

Thus we may conclude by saying that Spenser's *Epithalamion*, apart from its loveliness and charm, can also disclose to us the co-operation of some basic principles of poetic art. For terms like order, organic structure, unity in variety, amalgamation of traditional material, observance of time and locality, immediacy and

[19] C. S. Lewis, *English Literature in the Sixteenth Century* (Oxford, 1954), p. 373.

directness of presentation, and especially inclusiveness, designate fundamental processes which had to be attained not only in Spenser's age but in all poetry aiming at greater complexity and higher perfection. Some of these principles can be applied with particular aptness to the poetry of the Renaissance, but others are of a universal validity. The taste of a Renaissance audience was different from ours. There are, to be sure, phrases and images in this poem which may be hard to accept for a modern reader, who may also be disturbed by the amount of stylization, by the mythological invocations, by the idealizing glorification of the poet's own bride. But these are features to be appreciated within the context and against the background of English Renaissance poetry, and they do not detract from the poem's inner consistency and its perfection as a work of art. This exemplary nature of our poem may be another justification for speaking of the uniqueness of Spenser's *Epithalamion* today.[20]

NOTE: The author is under obligation for help and advice to W. L. Renwick, Robert Birley, Hans-Jürgen Diller, and Wolfgang Weiss.

[20] For this lecture I have used some of the material contained in my German study of Spenser's poem: *Spensers Epithalamion. Zum Problem der künstlerischen Wertmaßstäbe.* Sitzungsberichte der Bayerischen Akademie der Wissenschaften, Philosophisch-Historische Klasse (München, 1964, Heft 8).

Arnold Stein

⚜ GEORGE HERBERT: THE ART OF PLAINNESS

As a religious poet Herbert addresses God directly or writes with the intention of being overheard by Him. For traditional and for contemporary reasons, both religious and secular in origin, he aspires to an art of plainness that can achieve absolute sincerity. He is impatient with art but must practice patience. He distrusts rhetoric—as who does not?—but in order to speak sincerely he must master the rhetoric of sincerity.

Some of his more severe claims, assertions, and rejections lend themselves, a little too easily, to the purposes of critical definition. But we do not need to take him at his word in poems like the two sonnets which, according to Walton, were addressed to his mother, or in the pair of sonnets entitled "Love" (I and II). In these poems the contest between human and divine love is presented as if it were a moral scandal, to be treated only in terms of extreme contrasts and a single range of emotion. Everything is externalized, as if a safe imaginative distance were the only proper course. If plainness has anything to do with forthrightness and with the manner attributed to plain dealers, then we must acknowledge a kind of plainness in these poems, though they lack something in art. The case against their sincerity would have to point out that the attitude assumed by the author, and eloquently expressed, does not cost him very much. The desire to believe lends energy, vividness, sharpness, but not precision, depth, or fineness to the expression. When we speak of the rhetoric of sincerity, it is not with such poems in mind.

Let us turn to a poem which does not offer a stiff rejection but raises questions, and in a very mild and casual manner seems to present a radical solution. The poem is "A true Hymne," which begins:

> My joy, my life, my crown!
> My heart was meaning all the day,
> Somewhat it fain would say:
> And still it runneth mutt'ring up and down
> With onely this, *My joy, my life, my crown.*

Herbert then goes on to defend these words, which "may take part / Among the best in art" if they are "truly said." We may suspect that the naïvety is in part cultivated; it is plainly meant, however, and comes from a refinement of knowledge rather than a lack of knowledge. These words are symbols; they represent precious wisdom, the soul of living truth which the speaker may pronounce without possessing. It is hard to say them "truly"; the heart was "meaning" them all the day, but even the heart is uncertain—"Somewhat it fain would say," and it runs "mutt'ring up and down." The value of these words, whether in private thought or in art, depends on understanding what they mean and saying them truly.

Herbert ends the second stanza with a firm declaration:

> The finenesse which a hymne or psalme affords,
> Is, when the soul unto the lines accords.

This, though it has an admirable ring and expresses one clear concept of poetic sincerity, does not quite face the problems that have been raised. The accordance of the soul may assume that the heart has understood and that the words have been "truly said," but we are not told how these vital steps are taken, or even that they have been taken. Instead, we have been given a partial definition, which is then extended by a charming example of negative illustration— a whole stanza that shows how not to do it:

> He who craves all the minde,
> And all the soul, and strength, and time,
> If the words onely ryme,
> Justly complains, that somewhat is behinde
> To make his verse, or write a hymne in kinde.

The amused incoherence of the stanza parodies the ambitious poet who starts with high resolution and finds himself hung up, forcing rhyme, splicing syntax, and barely staggering through. After the brave opening, the only words that ring true are "Justly complains." Furthermore, the grounds have been shifted, and we have not followed up the problem of how the words are to be "truly said" or how that accordance of the soul is to be achieved.

The last stanza presents a solution that is indirectly relevant to the problems of literary expression but directly relevant to the heart seeking to address God:

> Whereas if th' heart be moved,
> Although the verse be somewhat scant,
> God doth supplie the want.
> As when th' heart sayes (sighing to be approved)
> *O, could I love!* and stops: God writeth, *Loved*.

We come to see that the writing of poetry has not been at the center of the poem after all. Instead, Herbert has used art as a metaphor to express an experience of religious life. In life, if not in art, the "somewhat scant" expression of the sincere heart may be amended and completed by God. When God writes "Loved," the desire to articulate and the desire to love are at once fulfilled. Their ends are achieved without the ordinary steps of a humanly conducted process. By authoritative acknowledgment virtual expression becomes actual.

If we look at the poem from one point of view, a miracle has taken place; but from another point of view we need recognize only an inspired compression—always possible in dialogue if the correspondent understands the intention, approves it, and fully reciprocates. We may observe, therefore, that Herbert is not simply invoking a miracle, for the ends of expression may often be realized without the full use of normal means. What we cannot do, however, is take the metaphorical analogy of writing poetry as if it were literal. Sincere feelings do not of themselves produce good poems. Herbert surely knew this as well as we do. But he must also have believed that whenever he felt a poem of his to be successful, God's hand had guided his in the composition; and if he felt a poem to be successful that feeling was the sure sense that the expression had realized its end, that God had blessed the end and given him the feeling by reflection. The humility of the man of God and the humility of the artist might both acknowledge that a fumbling, "muttering" intention had by some unexpected swiftness been clarified, and that the awkward wrongness of initial and intermediate stages had somehow been transformed into the triumphantly graceful and right. In retrospect, even the labor of composition—like some fictional by-product of the creative process—might seem to be compressed into a decisive instant of time. (Poets are notoriously inaccurate in reporting on these matters and prefer to believe that their perfect poems were "dictated": which is what we prefer to believe when the evidence to the contrary does not interfere.)

There are at least two ways, then, of looking at the issues raised by this poem. I have been emphasizing the "normal" conditions of the creative process because I am primarily interested in the poet Herbert; and because I am convinced that the religious lyric, though it must fulfill special conditions, must also, and does, answer all the questions we ask of other lyrics. From a literary standpoint the central metaphor of the poem can be interpreted as analogous to the ways in which inspiration figures in the writing of poems. Inspiration is of course the kind of concept that easily crosses a line between the secular and the sacred, and for Herbert so too does the act, or the metaphor, of writing poems. In this poem we are free to interpret the analogy, so long as we recognize that it is a metaphor and is not to be taken literally. But we must also recognize that, for Herbert, though the metaphor may apply to the writing of poetry it has been superseded, as it were, by the higher form of expression to which it refers. The wisdom descending from God crowns, not with understanding but with love, an apparently clumsy human effort to understand and express. We do not expect Herbert to be dissatisfied with the attainment of such an end simply because the means do not seem to justify it. But we do not therefore think Herbert believed that this was the way to write poems, and that the individual details of thought and expression might safely be ignored because they would leap intervening stages if only "th' heart be moved." Herbert knew better, both as poet and as man of God. That he hoped, humbly, for the easier path of inspiration—one does not need to be either poetic or religious to feel the attraction of that course.

But Herbert's metaphors are capable of moving in more than two directions. The central fiction of writing poetry, which may refer to the real writing of poetry and to something real in the experience of religious life, may have still a third reference. In presenting the fictional account Herbert is at the same time confessing his own unworthiness, his own desire, and intimating the authentic joy which he would feel if what he is describing should happen to him. In other words, the narrative is also a concealed prayer, composed by one of the modern masters of that difficult decorum and rhetoric by means of which one may properly address God and suggest to Him certain courses for human affairs.

And so the cultivated clumsiness of the poem, the shifting of grounds, the apparent naïvety, and what may have seemed to be a radical solution to the problems of writing poetry, when taken together are something else, or several things else. But if we are at all right about the poem it cannot be taken as a simple assertion about poetry; what seems to be assertion is ultimately part of a complex and tactful statement. Yet we cannot stop here, at the satisfying literary position. We must remember that, for Herbert, the metaphor of writing is in the poem superseded by the fulfillment of the end of expression—here a confirming act which writes and rhymes as poetry but means as metaphor. If he himself believes in the fiction of his poem, then he will find its conclusion a happier one than most of his poems provide, and toward the slower, labored uncertainties of most composition he will feel some understandable impatience.

At this point, if there were time, I should want to comment on the kind of plain style we find in "The Church-Porch," and to look at some poems in which Herbert accepts, or even flaunts, a division between truth and beauty. But these poems do not finally say anything distinctive or resonant. The gestures of sincerity by which art is used to expose art can at best make but limited points. A better and more characteristic performance is "The Forerunners." Whatever else he is saying in the poem, Herbert is also bidding a fictional farewell to poetry, to the "sweet phrases, lovely metaphors," which he has rescued from the poetic "brothels" in order to bring into the church, repentant and renewed: "My God must have my best, ev'n all I had." The excitement and affection of his address could serve as well for arrival as for departure:

"Lovely enchanting language, sugar-cane,/ Honey of roses," he exclaims, as preface to imagining the unfortunate relapse as poetry returns to its old ways. He argues against what he knows will happen, and in doing so marks both a separateness of truth and beauty and the bridge of normal relations that leads to their unity:

> Let follie speak in her own native tongue.
> True beautie dwells on high: ours is a flame
>   But borrow'd thence to light us thither.
> Beautie and beauteous words should go together.

Here Platonic solution is emphasized, rather than Platonic division. The statement is handsome and, as well as we can judge from the context and from other poems, heartfelt—a major poetic belief, but not therefore the guiding inspiration of every lyrical utterance.

"Yet if you go," he adds, meaning, when you go, as the poet prepares to settle down for a final accounting:

> Yet if you go, I passe not; take your way:
> For, *Thou art still my God*, is all that ye
> Perhaps with more embellishment can say.

And so a significant division appears, if not between truth and beauty, at least between "true beauty" and what can be said in words. That words are treated as no more than a conventionally detachable garment of style may seem a little disappointing, but Herbert does at least say "perhaps." Besides, in the context of the poem "Thou art still my God" *is* an ultimate expression, one that can be and is developed in other poems but cannot be here. Its meaning cannot be improved upon, and the man preparing to give up everything will not need anything else. The expression is complete, syntactically and otherwise, as the plain saying of "My God, my King" and "My joy, my life, my crown" are not. Nor does the poet's own attitude toward poetic language remotely resemble the stiff certitude with which he elsewhere rejects the misguided efforts of misguided poets. He is not rejecting here but parting, and with fine reluctance and such sweet sorrow.

In "The Forerunners" the act of writing poetry stands for the means, made visible and audible, of communing with God; it is a human invention motivated by a borrowed flame "to light us thither," a means of returning to the source of beauty. The house of the church, the house of poetry, and the house of life, the "best room" of which is the heart, are in the poem all reduced to an essential state. As the visible church stands truly, beautifully, but imperfectly for the invisible church, so do the "sweet phrases, lovely metaphors" express imperfectly the "True beautie" on high. In its plainness the essential expression, "Thou art still my God," will fulfill the end of expression, "And if I please him, I write fine and wittie." The essentiality of the expression, when one contemplates its meaning, by itself and in the context of the poem, would seem to be better established than the poet's assurance of writing "fine and wittie." That claim one may perhaps regard as a little assertive, markedly different from the persuasive tact with which art demonstrates the limitations of art in the argument of the poem.

The distinction is a fine one but it needs to be made. I mentioned earlier that if Herbert felt a poem to be successful he would need to believe that the expression had realized its end of pleasing God, and that God had given him his feeling by reflection. But he does not practice the art of silence or the art of discovering only the essential expression, which he can then merely "mutter." He writes poems, even when their aim is to express, or transcend, the inadequacy of poetic expression. We may perhaps regard "Thou art still my God" as a symbolic plainness, an ideal to which his poetic art of plainness may aspire, but it is not itself an expression of that art.

I think we can put matters in the right perspective by drawing a distinction between the symbolic plainness of an ultimate expression and the plainness of a complete poetic action. The latter may (and in Herbert often does) move toward a clarification that resembles the symbolic plainness. But if the poetic action is complete its conclusion will be the result of a process of expression. Though the "true beauty" of "Thou art still my God" may be traced to the compressed inner meaning the expression holds for Herbert, nevertheless that statement does appear three times in the poem, and it works both with and against other statements. In "The Flower" Herbert makes another absolute statement: "Thy word is all, if we could spell." Some of his poems are advanced spelling lessons. If "The Forerunners" were, say, a poem like "Aaron," its process might have included some parsing of the implicit relations between "thou" and "my," or between "art" and "still."

Herbert is acutely aware, as poet and as Christian, of deception, evasiveness, and inadequacy within himself—and, for these, traditional attitudes toward language and art provide useful and established symbols. Besides, many of his more assertive poems take up positions that he does not intend to carry through uncritically. A paradox that furnishes much of his poetic material may help explain why the single attitude is often countered within its own poem and opposed by other poems. The "grosser world," toward the beauty and importance of which the poet feels conflicting emotions, is, in spite of his feelings, a fixed and orderly world regulated by the "word and art" of God. It is the "diviner world of grace" which suddenly alters, and of which God is every day "a new Creatour."[1]

What Herbert writes in "Superliminare" may be applied to all instances when he engages himself to "Copie out onely" this or that. He will admit

> Nothing but holy, pure, and cleare,
> Or that which groneth to be so.

That is a program which leaves room for and grants validity to the hopes of individual effort, without regard to cost and efficiency. Herbert's most important subject is the mystery of God's art with man, a subject he confronts with patience and imagination, both passionately involved and scrupulously detached. That God's art with man reveals God's nature he takes for granted, and he assumes that the mysteries which God has concealed in man encourage the study of things human as an authorized reflection of things divine.

We may put these observations together by saying that Herbert does not give us a single, consistent attitude toward expression, that his art of plainness does not bear a single stamp, and that his arguments with God are conducted with great freedom and inventiveness. Whenever as critics we take a single example as our model to copy, we become aware of statements on the other side

---

[1] "The Temper" (II).

and of stylistic demonstrations that force us to widen our definitions. From one point of view we may be satisfied to locate the essential Herbert in the ringing declarations of "H. Baptisme" (II): "Let me be soft and supple to thy will. . . . My soul bid nothing. . . . Childhood is health." But softness must be "tempered" and suppleness must exert itself in order to be what it is. We do not know enough when we know that the goal expressed so simply is a difficult one to achieve, and that the verbal summation stands for detailed, strenuous efforts by an individual conscious that millions of human beings have in effect said the same thing and have both failed and succeeded. Our general knowledge must also "descend to particulars," for exactness lies not in any general statement but in the clarified order which poetry may achieve when particular expressions work with and against each other. In Herbert's poetry the soul has other lessons to learn, not all of them compatible with what is here presented as the sum of wisdom. For the soul that bids nothing may hear nothing; nor is that spiritual state exempt from posing and artful presumption. Childhood is not health at all in "Mortification," but is only one of several stages in the art of dying. That art would seem to be more valuable than spiritual health itself; for the art of knowing possesses more fully whatever it desires and gains, and Herbert never deviates long from this old principle, which represents the uneasy, but enduring and fruitful, marriage of Athens and Jerusalem. Childhood generally symbolizes the will in his poems, but the education of the will is the patient task of intelligence, and Herbert, to his honor, seldom trusts for long any of the attractive substitutes for intelligence. Even that most famous conversion of "The Collar"—"Me thoughts I heard one calling, *Child!* / And I reply'd, *My Lord*"—rests on the demonstration of an argument that has ruined itself.

As for his plainness, which is not all of one kind, it is above all a rhetoric of sincerity, an art by which he may tell the truth to himself and God. The major devices are not traditional figures but psychological gestures and movements. The excesses of cheerful confidence and the defections of faith decked out as humility are given their full human voice, not as exotic monsters of thought and feeling, but as common faults "whose natures are most stealing, and beginnings uncertaine," faults which are most tenacious when they are not allowed to expose themselves by speaking in their "own native tongue." Belief in the divine desire for human desire grants the human feelings an essential dignity, even in error, and encourages a vigorous freedom of expression. That freedom comes under the general laws of art, and is enlarged, not restricted, by the necessities of religious tact and discipline—as it is enlarged by realizing the complex demands of poetic form.

I propose now to offer more than a token and less than a complete demonstration of his art of plainness by drawing upon three poems: "The Temper" (I), "The Pearl," and "Death."

"The Temper" (I) begins with a declaration:

> How should I praise thee, Lord! how should my rymes
>   Gladly engrave thy love in steel,
> If what my soul doth feel sometimes,
>   My soul might ever feel!

And ends with a declaration:

> Whether I flie with angels, fall with dust,
>   Thy hands made both, and I am there:
> Thy power and love, my love and trust
>   Make one place ev'ry where.

The "plain intention" of the poem is to transform its initial attitude into its concluding one. Our best approach, I think, is from the lines in "Love" (II) where God is asked:

> And kindle in our hearts such true desires,
> As may consume our lusts, and make thee way.

Most of "The Temper" is devoted to the consuming of false love, but the kindling of true desire coincides with the opening lines of the poem, which speak in the high hortatory voice of love convinced that it is sincere and deserves to have its way. The "how should" and the "if" mark the fiction that represents real desire and invokes the conventions of literary and religious praise. Although the power and sweep of the language obscure the personal motive, which is not in the conventions of praise an illegitimate one, Herbert's characteristic exercise of religious propriety never allows personal desire to speak for the whole man without some discriminating process of clarification. "Gladly engrave thy love in steel" rings beautifully, but pretends to forget that the only standard is God's approval of the offering. The poet's desire is not absurd, but he knows that its expression is, and he compensates in the second stanza by acting out his pretentiousness. If there are forty heavens, or more, when things are right with him he can "peere" over them all. At other times "I hardly reach a score." And sometimes there is a general minus, without arithmetic: "to hell I fall." The kindling and consuming are most intense in the next three stanzas, which clarify the issues and stand apart from the first and last two stanzas. In these middle three stanzas the excesses of pride and humility strive against each other in images of expansion and contraction, and in the movements up and down of actual and psychological space:

> O rack me not to such a vast extent;
>   Those distances belong to thee:
> The world's too little for thy tent,
>   A grave too big for me.
>
> Wilt thou meet arms with man, that thou dost stretch
>   A crumme of dust from heav'n to hell?
> Will great God measure with a wretch?
>   Shall he thy stature spell?
>
> O let me, when thy roof my soul hath hid,
>   O let me roost and nestle there:
> Then of a sinner thou art rid,
>   And I of hope and fear.

This last stanza (the fifth) is like the first in advancing personal desire while paying tribute to God. We may note that the eloquence of humility is no less moving, no less an expression of real desire, and no less wrong, than the eloquence of pride. By now the two extremes have exhausted each other, and some *tertium quid* must be called on to make peace. The sixth stanza explains the emblematic title, declares acceptance of the divine will, and advances the metaphor of music as a solution to the problem of praise:

> Yet take thy way; for sure thy way is best:
>   Stretch or contract me, thy poore debter:

> This is but tuning of my breast,
>   To make the musick better.

And so the stanza completes the action of consuming false love by translating the experiences of the poem into terms of acceptance which draw a moral. The metaphor of music discovers a retroactive purpose in the contradictions, a purpose which may also govern present and future action. But Herbert does not stop here, for the kindling and consuming have served "to make thee way," and the seventh stanza is the demonstration of what can happen when way has been made for God:

> Whether I flie with angels, fall with dust,
>   Thy hands made both, and I am there:
>   Thy power and love, my love and trust
>   Make one place ev'ry where.

One may perhaps describe the metaphor of music as a rational discovery which orders in a quiet, reasonable way the passionate contradictions which have been expressed. But the final stanza establishes, without reference to music, a concord that is more comprehensive. In the language of religion the difference resembles that between intellectual acceptance and entire resignation. Herbert himself might well have thought that the old, restrictive terms were consumed in order to make way for the new, and that he was himself, in a minor, personal way, copying the process by which truth had once come to light—in Augustine's summary statement: "the New Testament reveals what was concealed in the Old."[2] In "The Quip" Herbert refuses the arguments of his opponents for he has a single answer ready penned; here the arguments come from his own soul and he must work through them to reach his answer. The simple perfection of that answer cannot be anticipated but comes suddenly, and after a slight pause.

Although the final stanza may be said to express and to demonstrate religious resignation, we may approach it from the traditions of rhetoric. First, we may draw on Aristotle's point that of the three "modes of persuasion furnished by the spoken word" the most important, by and large, is "the personal goodness revealed

---

[2] *City of God*, V, xviii.

by the speaker"; in fact, "his character may almost be called the most effective means of persuasion he possesses."[3] Christian rhetoric accepts the point and advances it; where the unity of eloquence and wisdom occurs we may assume the effective presence of inspiration as a proof of character. The chief goal of eloquence is to move, and Christian high style could be thought of as assimilating all the characteristics of the plain style, deriving its elevation primarily from the personal fervor with which the saving truth was expressed.

The last stanza will not fit into a rhetorical category of style. It is adorned and elevated, but the dominant effect is that of plainness and simplicity. The graces of art are subtle though not inscrutable; and we could point to devices not in the handbooks of rhetoric (as Augustine is pleased to note of a passage from the Book of Amos),[4] and perhaps not even in the annals of microlinguistics. But we may spare that demonstration for now. The issues of the poem are resolved in a final expression that unites beauty and truth, eloquence and wisdom. There is no point of leverage for distinguishing between what is said and the authoritative gift of being able to say it: inspiration is the proof of character. An expression as complete and as final in its way as "Thou art still my God" has emerged from a developing pattern of conflict; and although that expression can stand alone, it was created in the act of completing the poem, and it answers all the immediacies of conflict and form. It can stand alone but does not insist on its privilege, as a few ready-penned expressions make some show of doing. We may perhaps apply Herbert's metaphor of wisdom descending from above, the silk twist let down; though in "The Pearl" inspiration must precede and direct the poem in order to be present for the final confirmation. Or we may say that in "The Temper" when the poet stopped God wrote "loved" and spelled it out in a whole stanza.

Our next example is "The Pearl," a poem with a simpler argument and a basic plot—that of rejecting the ways of the world, the flesh, and the devil, each in a stanza. A final stanza explains why, clarifies the issues, confirms the character of the speaker, and in a simple statement organizes the procedures of the poem into their

---

[3] *Rhetoric*, I, ii (1356a).
[4] *The Christian Doctrine*, IV, vii (15–20).

completed form. We find no acting out of inspiration at the end, but instead a quietly effective definition of the ways of love and understanding. In the penultimate stanza, for the sake of an ultimate plainness the poet unexpectedly elevates the plain style that has been serving him with perfect ease and variety.

The plot is basic and the formula for human temptation is the standard one, but Herbert's conception and performance are markedly fresh and individual. The temptation of the devil, as intellectual pride, he puts first. It is not a temptation at all but little more than an inventory, and not even an explicit rejection. By putting intellectual pride first but not treating it as pride, and by his casual manner and racy diction, he exhibits a surprising and witty indifference to the traditional power of that temptation. Indeed, if we do not recognize the historical issue, the first appearance of the refrain, "Yet I love thee," may seem a little forced and overemphatic. As the poem develops, and as we collect our bearings in motion, we are supposed to recognize that pride is not being located in the intellect alone but is distributed throughout all decisions involving a choice between the love of self and the love of God. In the second stanza the temptations of the world are rejected, without the dignity of a formal recognition but in the course of drawing up an inventory of the ways of honor. The casual raciness becomes intensified, and the tone advances to open mockery:

> I know the wayes of Honour, what maintains
> The quick returns of courtesie and wit:
> In vies of favours whether partie gains,
> When glorie swells the heart, and moldeth it
> To all expressions both of hand and eye,
> Which on the world a true-love-knot may tie,
> And bear the bundle, wheresoe're it goes:
> How many drammes of spirit there must be
> To sell my life unto my friends or foes:
>   Yet I love thee.

Then the third and climactic stanza presents the temptation of the flesh, the ways of pleasure. One does not expect to meet sensitively intelligent Christians who are confident that they are untempted by intellectual pride and the subtle allurements of the world; one expects even less to learn that so rare a person is frankly responsive to the appeals of pleasure:

> I know the wayes of Pleasure, the sweet strains,
> The lullings and the relishes of it;
> The propositions of hot bloud and brains;
> What mirth and musick mean; what love and wit
> Have done these twentie hundred yeares, and more:
> I know the projects of unbridled store:
> My stuffe is flesh, not brasse; my senses live,
> And grumble oft, that they have more in me
> Then he that curbs them, being but one to five:
>   Yet I love thee

These are not, to be sure, the common temptations of the flesh but reflect a refined, more philosophical, concept of pleasure—as if Herbert were revising Socrates' fable in the *Phaedrus* and attributing rebelliousness to the spirited horse of the psychic team. A twentieth-century reader might resent the antique novelty of assigning the products of culture to the ways of pleasure, but he might find some compensation in the formal emphasis on knowledge that echoes through the stanza: "mirth and musick *mean*," and the introductory expression, "I know," is used a second time only in this stanza. What is most distinctive, however, is the passionate immediacy, the full identification of the poet with the feelings expressed. The nonchalance of witty indifference abruptly disappears; and the stanza excludes, for the moment, those quantitative images of profit and loss which partly reflect the amused detachment and superiority of the speaker—the "stock and surplus," "quick returns," "gains," and "drammes of spirit." The controls of knowledge and love are not broken down, but they remain external and neither repress the feelings nor enter into their expression. As for the temptation itself, it is not considered in a formal way, but its presence and force are amply represented by the language of the speaker.

As a measure of Herbert's boldness and candor it is useful to quote an authoritative diagnosis of the symptoms and etiology of imaginative self-temptation. When, according to Augustine, the soul slackens in its powers of determination, the body will try to advance its own interests. Delighted by "corporeal forms and movements," the soul then "becomes entangled with their images which it has fixed in its memory, and is foully defiled by the fornications of the phantasy." When the soul places the end of its own good in the sensuous, it "snatches the deceptive images of corporeal things from within and combines them together by empty thought, so that nothing seems to it to be divine unless it be of such a kind as this."[5] Augustine's diagnosis, with its adaptation of Platonic and Stoic features, may describe the rebellious imagination as we see it, for instance, in "The Collar," and it may help identify an occasional lapse in Herbert's spiritual nerve, but it is remarkably irrelevant to the "corporeal forms and movements" of his third stanza. The feelings expressed there have dignity; they are immediate and real, without defilement and resulting self-hatred, and without confusions of the divine. In fact, only the ways of honor come directly under Augustine's analysis, for they are the artificial products of illusive symbolizing, the "deceptive images" patched together with "empty thought."

The first and second stanzas, we noted, resemble each other in their amused detachment. Their plain style is that of argument, which demonstrates indirectly, by witty analysis, that the major temptations do not tempt at all. The greater intensity of the second stanza by moving toward mockery increases the imaginative distance between the objects discussed and the speaker. The plain style of the last stanza will reverse that direction. It is argument, and intellectual, but not detached. Everything is drawn together, and toward the poet at the center of his experience. But the decisive change is initiated by the third stanza with its personal fervor and elevated style.

Let us compare in their relations these last two stanzas and the last two stanzas of "The Temper" (I). In that poem the penultimate stanza ("Yet take thy way; for sure thy way is best") presents an intellectual acceptance which is rather dry and detached but provides the necessary bridge to the comprehensive solution of the last stanza, which is highly charged with feeling but registers as an inspired clarification. In "The Pearl" the general procedure is the same but the parts are reversed. The conflict does not take shape until the penultimate stanza, where the climax also occurs; that

---

[5] *The Trinity*, XII, 9 (14)–10 (15), trans. Stephen McKenna (The Catholic University of America Press, 1963).

stanza brings about the shift in direction from analytical distance to synthetic immediacy, as the necessary bridge to the comprehensive solution of the last stanza. In "The Pearl" it is the penultimate stanza which is elevated in style and charged with feeling. But its expression is, though intense and candid, consciously limited by the external controls of the context; it cannot speak for the whole man in the poem. Though eloquent and moving, the voice of the stanza cannot possibly bring eloquence and wisdom into the unison of a single speech. The last stanza names inspired wisdom as a presence which has governed the whole action of the poem, but which does not, as in "The Temper" (I), make a personal appearance. The clarification of love and understanding is quietly intellectual, not passionate, and includes the humble disclaimer that whatever has been accomplished by the poem was merely by following instructions:

> Yet through these labyrinths, not my groveling wit,
> But thy silk twist let down from heav'n to me,
> Did both conduct and teach me, how by it
>   To climbe to thee.

In this poem there is no pause inviting God to write the last stanza; an affirming act of the intellect builds on a moment of passion, rather than the reverse. But the proof of character lies in the integration and in the poet's being at one with what he says. There has been no spectacular inspiration, but everything has been drawn together, and the silk twist which has led him through the labyrinths has brought him to the expressive center of what he concludes.

Our final example is the poem "Death," which acknowledges no conflict. The fictional pretext is a slight and transparent one: the difference between the way we used to look at death and the way we look at it now. The plot is not likely to surprise, and since there is no formal conflict the poet's own feelings do not directly participate in the action. Coming to the poem after "The Temper" (I) and "The Pearl," one is at first perhaps more conscious of the differences, but the similarities are more significant.

As in many poems that are relatively straightforward and simple in statement, Herbert invents fine devices on which the materials turn, move, and develop—as if they were proceeding by means of the more visible structures of argument, dramatic conflict, or narrative plot. Each stanza of "Death" is a kind of self-contained scene, into which the last line brings an unexpected effect. The reader is not likely to be aware that an argument is also being produced, until he encounters the open "Therefore" at the beginning of the sixth and last stanza. There are three parts of the argument, arranged in a formal diminution of 3:2:1. The first three stanzas give us the old wrong views of death, the next two corrected present views, and the conclusion is drawn in a single stanza. Let us begin with the first three:

> Death, thou wast once an uncouth hideous thing,
>   Nothing but bones,
>   The sad effect of sadder grones:
> Thy mouth was open, but thou couldst not sing.
>
> For we consider'd thee as at some six
>   Or ten yeares hence,
>   After the losse of life and sense,
> Flesh being turn'd to dust, and bones to sticks.
>
> We lookt on this side of thee, shooting short;
>   Where we did finde
>   The shells of fledge souls left behinde,
> Dry dust, which sheds no tears, but may extort.

The mementos of death are handled with remarkable verve and gaiety. Of "The Temper" (I) we could say that the intention of the poem was to transform its initial declaration into its concluding one. Here we have attitudes rather than declarations; and that strange, bluff greeting to death, though startling, original, and arbitrary, does not register at once as a "wrong" attitude asking for correction. Nevertheless, the tone is the exaggerated one of an extreme which the development of the poem will transform. If we borrow an observation from our study of "The Pearl," we may describe the speaker's opening attitude as detached and superior, as if enjoying his analytical distance from the object of his attention. In the fifth stanza the tone will be countered by an opposite extreme of immediacy and identification. Then the argument, expression, and tone of the last stanza will transform the extremes of psychic distance and immediacy into a final attitude.

The second and third stanzas drop the concentrated focus on skull, bones, and grinning jaws, and drop the harsh, summary definition of life as a music of groans, and death as the arrested image of that music. The reason now given for that hideousness is not concentrated and shocking but leisurely and general, as befits an intellectual speculation prefaced by "For we consider'd." The error in human understanding is caused by our faulty sense of time. We think in spans of six or ten years from now and judge death by its appearances then. The detachment is quietly intellectual but does not therefore eliminate some tension of divided attitude. The reader will not find that the studied casualness of rhythm, tone, and detail prevents him from considering any thought of his own death, "some six / Or ten years hence." Furthermore, the ironic turn in the last line of each stanza reintroduces the opportunity for personal concern and relation: "Flesh being turn'd to dust, and bones to sticks. . . . Dry dust, which sheds no tears, but may extort." And that beautiful euphemism for skeletal remains, "The shells of fledge souls left behinde," is a little too successful; we admire the imaginative act and in so doing are reminded of the natural state of the material thus translated.

In addition to these psychological movements which endue a sense of developing conflict, we may note the presence of significant attitudes toward time. The first stanza greets death as it was, not once upon a time but "once," as it was in time past. But the imaginative time of that stanza is the feeling-present, which the shock of the image produces, in spite of the summary intellectualizing of the cause in the immediate past and the assertion that all of this visible effect is not what it seems to be but is what it was "once." The assertion is left dangling as a challenge that is to be made good, but not in the formal time of the second and third stanzas, which does not go all the way back to the "once." The feeling-present returns, though less emphatically, in the suggestions of personal death and in the reference to the dust "which sheds no tears, but may extort." Still more elusively, the sense of future time enters these stanzas. There is an ambiguity in the "six / Or ten years hence"—depending on whether we were considering the case of stanza one, or were considering some case, perhaps our own, from a point in the past identical with our consideration and extending six to ten years into the future. But since the point in the past is not located firmly, the sense of future time is at best weak. Similarly, the flesh and bones "being turn'd" to dust and sticks presents us with a free composition of past, present, and future; any single dimension of time can dominate in that formula, depending on the formal perspective. Finally, the "fledge souls" do evoke the future in a definite but small way; the transaction itself points ahead, and the habits of metaphorical thought on this familiar subject move naturally from the place "left behinde" to the far future.

Everything we have considered thus far will reappear, with changes, in the next step of the argument, which begins in the fourth stanza:

> But since our Saviours death did put some bloud
> Into thy face;
> Thou art grown fair and full of grace,
> Much in request, much sought for as a good.

The verve and gaiety continue, but now the mementos of death are looked at from the perspective of life after death. Out of the conventions of that perspective Herbert draws details that emphasize the imaginative nature of his presentation. The hideousness of the skull in the first stanza was the product of its appearance, our perspective, and the grotesque associations brought to bear. In the fourth stanza the perspective and associations are changed; a show of appearance is made, but the literal, physical terms are dominated by their symbolic and metaphorical meanings. The language is matter-of-fact, "But since our Saviours death did put some bloud / Into thy face," and more comforting than "Thy mouth was open, but thou couldst not sing"; but both statements are self-consciously imaginative, two opposing ways of looking at death, each an exaggeration based upon a different view of the truth. The stanza continues to emphasize its imaginative play as it moves further from the possibility of literal presentation. Both the face which is now "fair and full of grace" and the beholder's eye are altered, and the newness of the relationship is underlined by the pleasantry of "grace." The last line of the stanza draws back a little, with a kind of wry humor far gentler than the irony in each of the preceding last lines. Death is "Much in request"—as if by a change in fashion. That death is "much sought for as a good" moves the significance further from its physical base and advances the dignity of its attractiveness by the deliberate introduction language that has philosophical associations.

The "But since" which opens the fourth stanza is the sign both of argument and of time. Though the dominant time-sense is present it is derived from the Savior's act in the past and lightly suggests the future in "sought for as a good." The sense of the present, however, is not *felt* as in the first stanza but serves mostly as a kind of intellectual transition to the strong present of the fifth stanza. Finally, to touch again on the point of imaginative distance: the fourth stanza maintains a distinctive kind of detachment, because of its intellectualized emphasis on the metaphorical and the witty.

The fifth stanza completes the corrected view of death, bringing the poem to a sudden climax:

> For we do now behold thee gay and glad,
> > As at dooms-day;
> > When souls shall wear their new aray,
> And all thy bones with beautie shall be clad.

Each of the first three stanzas presents a thesis abruptly at the beginning and then makes additional points to tighten and complicate the scene. In the fourth and fifth stanzas the thought requires the whole four lines for its development, and in the fifth stanza rises to a declarative climax in the last line, reversing the established ironic twist of the first three stanzas and the mildly humorous withdrawal of the fourth. More important, all of the motions of detachment, all of the varieties of analytical distance in the poem are reversed in the sudden rush of imaginative immediacy.

The developing attitudes toward time are also brought to a climax, but the details are more involved and cannot be seen without analysis. Let me summarize briefly. In the first three stanzas the formal time was past, the finished past of "once" in the first stanza and a less definite, recent past in the second and third stanzas. But in the first a sense of the feeling-present dominates; in the second and third present and future both enter, but elusively. In the fourth stanza a similar blend occurs, though the formal time is present. But when we come to the fifth stanza, suddenly there is no sense of the past. The present dominates but draws its intensity from a prophetic vision of the future. That future comes into the poem strongly and positively at this one point, and fully answers the finished past of stanza one. Since that future is imagined as intensely present, the effect is a formal reply to the feeling-present of stanza one.

These answers composed of the oppositions of time and the oppositions of psychic direction are not conclusive. A quiet "Therefore" converts their striking emphasis into mere transition, as if the real answer has been waiting for the commotion to subside:

> Therefore we can go die as sleep, and trust
> Half that we have
> Unto an honest faithfull grave;
> Making our pillows either down, or dust.

Now the time is wholly present: it is the unique product of imagined past and future, but emerging also from the varying stresses on the present which have been drawn like a thread through the labyrinth to this open place. As for either analytical detachment from death or imaginative identification—the final attitude rejects the terms of the contradiction, but draws an essential indifference from detachment and an essential acceptance from identification. The human present of the last stanza copies the calm of eternity, into which no agitations of past or future intrude. Death is not an alien object exciting mixed emotions, nor a lover to be sought and embraced. The imagination of the poem has made death familiar and neutral; it can have no place even in dreams when it has been made subject to a common, everyday idiom which says, "we can go die."

The activity of the mind is less prominent than in the conclusion of "The Pearl," but as in that poem an affirming act of the intellect quietly builds on a moment of passion, and the mind that dismisses itself has demonstrated the power and clarity of its self-possession. There is no pause, as in "The Temper" (I), inviting God to write the last stanza. The spectacular inspiration comes in the prophetic vision of doomsday, which is followed by the rarest kind of personal clarity, casual and laconic, as if inspiration were part of the everyday order and could be taken for granted. The final state of simplicity is not one of reduced but of alert, refined consciousness. One sign is the attitude toward the body, which is no less than

"Half that we have." And even more remarkable than calling the grave "honest" and "faithfull" is doing so with the air of not saying anything unusual. As in "The Pearl," the excited elevation of style in the penultimate stanza is followed by an authoritative descent to the plain style. In "Death" it is an assimilative plain style, confidently challenging comparison with the height of the preceding stanza. The power of that plain style lies in the passion excluded, in the resistance mastered, and in the deliberate grace of saying difficult things with ease. The grandeur and force of the high style are achieved while talking in an off-hand, humble manner in the common imagery of going to bed. An enlightened rhetorician would observe that this plain style does not austerely reject ornament, which may persuade but must first provide esthetic pleasure. He would add, I am sure, that these graces of style are so natural and fine as to seem in the very grain. The last line, "Making our pillows either down, or dust," awakens a delicate echo of the earlier ironies, as a farewell touch of recognition. And the order of "die as sleep" is beautifully reversed and balanced by "down, or dust."

I shall end by introducing another viewpoint for a moment. In reading Donne Coleridge described the delight of "tracing the leading thought thro'out the whole," by means of which "you merge yourself in the author, you *become He*."[6] Herbert he declares to be "a true poet, but a poet *sui generis*, the merits of whose poems will never be felt without a sympathy with the mind and character of the man." A true poet who requires a conscious act of sympathy would seem to have a different and lesser merit than the poet who compels you to "*become He*." Coleridge justly admires Herbert's diction, "than which nothing can be more pure, manly, and unaffected." But some of the thoughts are "quaint," and he does not try to follow a leading thought throughout. Identifying oneself with the author would seem to be a modern extension of the most important mode of rhetorical persuasion, "the personal goodness revealed by the speaker" in ancient rhetoric, or the inspired unity of wisdom and eloquence in Christian rhetoric. The merits of identifying oneself with the poet are debatable. But we can draw

---

[6] These passages are collected in *Coleridge on the Seventeenth Century*, ed. R. F. Brinkley (Duke University Press, 1955), pp. 523, 534.

two firm points from Coleridge's remarks. First, it is clear that Herbert is a master who draws a leading thought through authentic obstacles which both test and refine the ultimate expression of that thought. Secondly, the rhetorical proof of character lies in the poet's convincing demonstrations that *he* becomes what he says, that the flow and shape of his words lead to a unity of eloquence and wisdom, and that he is at the expressive center of what he concludes.

It is tempting to end here, adding only that there are many true poets but few masters of this art of plainness. But it may be well to back up and remember that Herbert's art of plainness is an art and not a summary feature. If we have touched on the essential quality, good; but we can no more do without a full apparatus for understanding his art than he could write poems by plainly saying "Thou art still my God."

Roy Harvey Pearce

WHITMAN AND OUR HOPE FOR POETRY

I take as an initiating text part of the second section of Robert Duncan's "A Poem Beginning with a Line by Pindar." Here Duncan looks back toward an aging Whitman; tries to recover a sense of Whitman's special, if waning, authority as poet in the Gilded Age; imagines how it was to be that Whitman, now—his stroke-affected speech at once a literal and symbolic vehicle—fumbling for the words with which to comprehend his society, its politics, and its failure to find leaders it does not quite deserve. Duncan sees the failure; and, like Whitman, he will not interpret it as a betrayal of the poet. For Duncan sees that Whitman as poet succeeded not as he portrayed failure, but rather as he gave us the means to measure success, thus to know that our forebears' failures, and our leaders', may well be our own. A society does not betray its poets—the argument implicitly goes; rather, it betrays itself. Its poets may indeed betray themselves—when they refuse to, or simply cannot, bear witness to what they see. If, bearing witness, they falter as did the aging Whitman, theirs are not failures but rather "glorious mistake[s]." The line from Pindar with which Duncan's poem begins is "The light foot hears you and the brightness begins." And it is the light-footed poet of our age who listens to Whitman and sees illumined his world—and ours—in its present condition.

This is the passage from Duncan's poem:

> . . . It is toward the old poets
> we go, to their faltering,
> their unaltering wrongness that has style,

        their variable truth,
           the old faces,
words shed like tears from
a plenitude of powers time stores.

A stroke. These little strokes. A chill.
    The old man, feeble, does not recoil.
Recall. A phase so minute.
    Only a part of the word in- jerrd.

    The Thundermakers descend,

    damerging a nuv. A nerb.
        The present dented of the U
    nighted stayd. States. The heavy clod?
        Cloud. Invades his brain. What
        if lilacs last in *this* dooryard bloomd?

Hoover, Roosevelt, Truman, Eisenhower—
where among these did the power reside
that moves the heart? What flower of the nation
bride-sweet broke to the whole rapture?
Hoover, Coolidge, Harding, Wilson
hear the factories of human misery turning out commodities.
For whom are the holy matins of the heart ringing?
Noble men in the quiet of morning hear
Indians singing the continent's violent requiem.
Harding, Wilson, Taft, Roosevelt,
idiots fumbling at the bride's door,
hear the cries of men in meaningless debt and war.
Where among these did the spirit reside
that restores the land to productive order?
McKinley, Cleveland, Harrison, Arthur,
Garfield, Hayes, Grant, Johnson,
dwell in the roots of the heart's rancor.
How sad "amid lanes and through old woods"
    echoes Whitman's love for Lincoln!

There is no continuity then. Only a few
    posts of the good remain. I too
that am a nation sustain the damage
    where smokes of continual ravage
obscure the flame.

> It is across great scars of wrong
> I reach toward the song of kindred men
> and strike again the naked string
> old Whitman sang from. Glorious mistake!
> that cried:
>
> "The theme is creative and has vista."
> "He is the president of regulation."
>
> I see always the under side turning,
> fumes that injure the tender landscape.
> From which up break
> lilac blossoms of courage in daily act
> striving to meet a natural measure.[1]

Duncan's discovery of Whitman is like that of many of his contemporaries. I have chosen to begin with a lengthy passage from his work rather than with a florilegium of bits and pieces from poems of his contemporaries, because bits and pieces, however many of them there could be, simply will not convey the particular import of this, the newest version of our poets' continuing discovery of Whitman.

For the history of American poetry could be written as the continuing discovery and rediscovery of Whitman, an on-going affirmation of his crucial relevance to the mission of the American poet. which is, as it is everywhere, simply to tell us the truth in such a way that it will be a new truth, and in its newness will renew us and our capacity to have faith in ourselves, only then together to try to build the sort of world which will have that faith as its necessary condition. Our great modernist poets—Eliot, Stevens, Pound, Crane, and Williams—of course all registered in their poems their discovery of Whitman, a discovery made sometimes, as it were, in spite of themselves. Their Whitman, however, is not quite the Whitman of Duncan and his contemporaries—our contemporaries—as their hope for poetry is not quite that of Duncan and his, and our, contemporaries. Their Whitman was the lonely Adamic figure—in Emerson's phrase, the self against the world; the poet struggling to define his vocation in a world which seemed to have no place for him; the shape-shifter who at the end

---

[1] *The Opening of the Field* (New York, 1960), pp. 63–64.

tricked himself into believing that it was more important to be a divine than a literatus. Their concern, one with their commitment to define their vocation in their time, was to separate the literatus from the divine and to learn from him all they could. They were little interested in—indeed, were suspicious of—the poet as directly critical of and deeply involved in society, politics, the structure and function of American life and its sheer busyness. They were reacting, of course, against the quasi-deification which was Whitman's boon at the end of his life and immediately after—and also against the politically reductionist understanding of his work in interpretations like those of Parrington and Arvin. They wanted clarity, even if it meant sacrificing charity. And their poems show that they achieved it, and so often precisely at such a cost.

The situation is otherwise now—as Duncan's lines show. Duncan sees those "lilac blossoms of courage in daily act / striving to meet a natural measure." And he will say, with Whitman, that he too is "a nation" which sustains "the damage / where smokes of continual ravage / obscure the flame." And, like Whitman, he is concerned with our leaders, our *political* leaders. In 1860, Whitman had written "To a President":

> All you are doing and saying is to America dangled mirages,
> You have not learn'd of Nature—of the politics of
>   Nature you have not learn'd the great amplitude,
>   rectitude, impartiality,
> You have not seen that only such as they are for
>   these States,
> And that what is less than they must sooner or later lift off
>   from these States.[2]

Duncan, in his address to Presidents, is contemporary by virtue of being Whitmanian. For his peers in our time are—whatever their local affiliations—determined to put political and social criticism back into their poetry. Clarity, yes. And often bitterness of apocalyptic depths; often barbaric howls over the rooftops of our world; often a deliberate and vulgar courting of confusion; often a seeking of shortcuts to poetic insight, which manifest themselves as short-

---

[2] Here and in what follows I quote the poems, except when noted, from *Leaves of Grass*, Comprehensive Reader's Edition, ed. H. W. Blodgett and Sculley Bradley (New York, 1965).

circuits in communication. But still at the end: charity. Such charity demands an unflinching attempt at scope and inclusiveness, and so urges our poets to see the poet involved in the whole of his world, to claim—often tendentiously—that a condition of the whole poet is a commitment to understand the whole world. Duncan of course knows the work of Pound and Williams well; he has gone to school to Charles Olson, and he is immensely learned—a poet-scholar. Still, on behalf of the poets of our age, he evokes Whitman as he would seek the spirit "that restores the land to productive order." This is, in our time, our poets' hope for poetry. And they would make it ours.

My task thus is to be exegete and advocate of that Whitman who sought the spirit "that restores the land to productive order." There are other Whitmans, I remind you, and valid ones. But this is the one whom we appear to need now. I must accordingly turn to an old problem in Whitman criticism: that of the poet as critic of society. And I shall hope to show that the Whitman Duncan has recently discovered is one of the Whitmans American scholar-critics have also recently discovered. At the very least, the one discovery—by the poet—illumines the other—by the scholar-critics—and vice-versa. I should like to think that each entails the other. That is one of my hopes for poetry.

The difficult fact is that we know almost too much about Whitman as critic of American society, pre- and post-Civil War. Inevitably, those who interpret Whitman must write about his "social thought"—inevitably, because it is an integral aspect of his life's work that he should have been a "social critic." In this role he is regularly present in histories of American thought—social, political, and otherwise. This is only proper. For with great and glorious ease and freedom, the newspaperman become poet tells us in the Preface to the 1855 *Leaves of Grass* that as poet he is nothing if not critic of society. He will make his society know all its possibilities and how it may realize them.

Now, the way to that realization is, in the poems of the 1855 *Leaves of Grass*, not so much social as individual, as we all by now surely know. And the tendency of that recent strong line of interpreters of Whitman which prefers the 1855 version of his book to all others is, in fact, to deny him, as poet, much of a role as social critic—or at best to deny him a covert role. Yet even this line of interpreters sees the journalistic work which surrounds the 1855 *Leaves of Grass* as genetically related to it. That is to say, as journalist, Whitman came to know his world in closely examined and expressed detail; and consequently as poet he came to see that what his world needed was a new, or renewed, image of man, whereby it might at long last realize its potentialities. The poet offers himself to his society, offers himself as archetypal for all selves, and thereby rests assured that it will henceforth be whole. The genetic line is from Whitman's journalistic social criticism to his earliest important poems. Out of the world described in the journalism the poet was precipitated. Or rather, out of that world that poet precipitated himself, and in what came be to called "Song of Myself" with loving and daring precision described the act of precipitation, which was in fact an act of self-creation.

But the genesis did not stop there. For now the *poet*, by virtue of being a poet, surely had to continue to be a kind of social critic. True enough, he was no longer particularly a critic of issues and events—except when he wrote something other than poetry, which of course he continued to do. As poet, he had to find a way of speaking about his world and the facts of its life—a way which would let him be a critic by virtue of being a poet. The facts of which he came to speak were not quite those of which he could treat in his journalism, or even in his programmatic prefaces. No longer free soil, abolition, political compromises, forms of manifest destiny, and the like. Indeed, as his recent interpreters have uniformly noted, especially after the Civil War crisis, Whitman, even in his prose writing, was much less interested in specifically sociopolitical issues than he had been before. They have, as a consequence, tended to judge him as a social critic only in contexts outside his poetry, even when they have tried to interpret his post-Civil War poetry as somehow tending to pull (or push) him toward a definite political stance—ranging from that of utopian socialist to anti-ideological conservative. At this point, I must demur. For I think that Whitman, after the Civil War and into the Gilded Age, yet tried, as poet, to be social critic, and succeeded; and that the sort of social criticism he got into his poems was, when, occasionally, it worked as poetry, all the more powerful because it was not so much *pro-* or *anti*-political as *pre*-political.

I want to inquire a little into Whitman's attempt to find a means of dealing in his poetry with the *products* of the sort of world about which he had written at length in his journalistic prose. What— again to echo Robert Duncan— . . . What were the conditions which would have to obtain if the land were to be restored to productive order? For one of Whitman's great insights as poet—an insight which makes him so truly the poet of whom Duncan writes— . . . one of his great insights is that the world of post-Jacksonian democracy, of the common man, of the Gilded Age, was for good and for bad, one in which, through its increasingly rationalized social and political and economic structure, producers were increasingly bowed down under the weight of their products. Whitman not only generalized, as had Emerson, that "Things are in the saddle,/ And ride mankind." He *observed* the "things" as they were at once bound to mankind and also bound it. And in his post-Civil War poetry—or in some of it—he not only declared his insight but gave his readers a means of weighing its significance for them precisely as they would find themselves bowed down under the weight of their products, or their society's. Whitman was only fitfully successful in this vein; and toward the end, so I think the poems show, the burden of his insight was too great for him. He faltered. Yet it is not his failure which I would like to emphasize, but his success, however small: his "glorious failure"—to quote Duncan again It is, I think, a success story which we have not yet read clearly, and one which, so the work of our poets now indicates, has increasingly great significance for us.

Let me begin with the basic facts of the case: The 1855, 1856, and 1860 versions of *Leaves of Grass* are stages in the development of an essentially autobiographical poem. In this poem, or in these versions of it, the poet discovers first himself, then society, then again himself. The 1860 *Leaves of Grass* is Whitman's attempt to write a totally humanistic poem; in it even the cycle of love and death is contained in the magnificently autobiographical humanism which it projects. The Civil War put this humanism into doubt, manifesting to Whitman not only anti-humanism (which he had successfully contained in the 1860 *Leaves of Grass*) but dehumanization. The Civil War poems show the poet's sense of the razor-edge balance between humanism and dehumanization; and he survives, when he does, only by appealing to suprahuman forces, as so memorably in "When Lilacs Last in the Dooryard

Bloomed." The war, then, was for Whitman a new kind of extreme situation—unlike the terrors and torments confronted in the 1855, 1856, and 1860 *Leaves of Grass,* one outside of himself, a product of forces he could in no way imagine himself or any man as containing and controlling. The technique of the pre-Civil War poems had been that of total empathy and total sympathy: give, sympathize, control. And the events of the war, like the social and personal catastrophes it produced, simply were beyond Whitman's, or any man's, powers of poetic empathy and sympathy. One could give and sympathize—as is shown by Whitman's prose memoranda on his hospital journeys and his letters to the soldiers he so lovingly tended. But one could not control. The poet was called upon to enlarge his technique, to amplify his capacities, to examine anew his role as poet. He was faced, crucially, with the discovery that a society, a community, is greater than the sum of its individual parts; that the sum somehow generates actions and events and things which may destroy the parts. The poet, in short, was now called upon to deal with the sum, whereas before he had dealt only with the parts (and with himself as the greatest part, as he had said).

"Long, too long, O land," Whitman wrote in 1865—later changing "O land" to "America"—

> Long, too long, O land,
> Traveling roads all even and peaceful you learn'd
>   from joys and prosperity only,
> But now, ah now, to learn from crises of anguish,
>   advancing, grappling with direst fate and
>   recoiling not.
> And now to conceive and show to the world what your
>   children en-masse really are,
> (For who except myself has yet conceiv'd what your children
>   en-masse really are?)

It was an enlargement of his conception of the poet which Whitman quite carefully announced in the first of the "Inscriptions" which open the 1871 version of *Leaves of Grass:*

> One's-Self I sing, a simple separate person,
> Yet utter the word Democratic, the word En-Masse.
> Of Physiology from top to toe I sing,

> Not physiognomy alone nor brain alone is worthy for the
>   Muse, I say the Form complete is worthier far.
> The Female equally with the Male I sing.
>
> Of Life immense in passion, pulse, and power,
> Cheerful, for freest action form'd under the laws divine,
> The Modern Man I sing.

The poem puts precisely Whitman's attempt to conceive anew of his capacities as poet—here, as if by *fiat*. Note the burden of meaning which is carried by the "Yet" of the second line:

> One's-self I sing, a simple separate person,
> *Yet* utter the word Democratic, the word En-Masse.

Not the co-ordinating "and" nor the subordinating "but." Rather the concessive "yet": which is to say, to claim, that even as the poet celebrates himself as an archetypal ego for us all, he celebrates us (including himself) as we (with him) compose a group. The one celebration is claimed to be precisely the same as the other. So it follows a few lines later that we are to have "freest action form'd under the laws divine." Individual freedom is one with the law which governs the group, the mass, to which the individual belongs. This is but an extrapolation of the heroically confident doctrine of the 1855, 1856, and 1860 versions of *Leaves of Grass*, of course. But at this point in Whitman's career—as in the career of his society—it becomes an issue which must be boldly, bluntly, and at the outset, proclaimed. If he protests too much, we must at least be grateful that he has the courage to protest.

The argument of this little poem is repeated in others of the "Inscriptions" series: in "In Cabin'd Ships at Sea," "Eidolons," and in "For Him I Sing," for example. And the confidence it expresses is manifest in a significant number of poems published in 1871 and beyond—in the Gilded Age. I shall want later to look at one of those poems, and see in somewhat formal terms just how Whitman strives to enlarge his capacity as poet, so to treat of the word democratic, the word En-Masse, by virtue of treating of the simple separate person; how he conceives of freedom under law; how he would celebrate the group's product in such a way as to teach its producers how to relate it to themselves; how, in short, as poet he is critic of society.

But first let me remind you of some of the consequences of this expanded conception of poetry for Whitman's conception of the poet. The major text here is *Democratic Vistas* (1871), which derives in good part from slightly earlier prose writing. A few quotations will serve our purpose:

> View'd, to-day, from a point of view sufficiently overarching, the problem of humanity all over the civilized world is social and religious, and is to be finally met and treated by literature. The priest departs, the divine literatus comes.

> It may be argued that our republic is, in performance, really enacting to-day the grandest arts, poems, &c. by beating up the wilderness into fertile farms, and in her railroads, ships, machinery, &c. And it may be ask'd, Are these not better, indeed, for America, than any utterances even of greatest rapsode, artist, or literatus?

> I say that our New World democracy, however great a success in uplifting the masses out of their sloughs, in materialistic development, products, [note that word: *products*] and in a certain highly developed superficial popular intellectuality, is, so far, an almost complete failure in its social aspects, and in really grand religious, moral, literary, and esthetic results.

> [After detailing the objects and events and excitements of Brooklyn and New York]: But sternly discarding, shutting our eyes to the glow and grandeur of the general superficial effect, coming down to what is of the only real importance, Personalities, and examining minutely, we question, we ask, Are there, indeed, *men* here worthy the name?

> For to democracy, the leveler, the unyielding principle of the average, is surely join'd another principle, equally unyielding, closely tracking the first, indispensable to it, opposite . . . and whose existence, confronting and ever modifying the other, often clashing, paradoxical, yet neither of highest avail without the other, plainly supplies to these grand cosmic politics of ours, and to the launch'd forth mortal dangers of republicanism, to-day or any day, the counterpart and offset whereby Nature restrains the deadly original relentlessness of all her first-class laws. This second principle is individuality, the pride and centripetal isolation of a human being in himself—identity—personalism.

> The word of the modern . . . is the word Culture.
> We find ourselves abruptly in close quarters with the enemy. This word Culture, or what it has come to represent, involves, by contrast, our whole theme, and has been, indeed, the spur, urging us to engage-

ment. Certain questions arise. As now taught, accepted and carried out, are not the processes of culture rapidly creating a class of supercilious infidels, who believe in nothing? Shall a man lose himself in countless masses of adjustments, and be so shaped with reference to this, that, and the other, that the simply good and healthy and brave parts of him are reduced and clipp'd away, like the bordering of box in a garden. You can cultivate corn and roses and orchards—but who shall cultivate the mountain peaks, the ocean, and the tumbling gorgeousness of the clouds? Lastly—is the readily-given reply that culture only seeks to help, systematize, and put in attitude, the elements of fertility and power, a conclusive reply?

I should demand a programme of culture, drawn out, not for a single class alone, or for the parlors of lecture-rooms, but with an eye to practical life, the west, the working-men, the facts of farms and jack-planes and engineers, and of the broad range of the women also of the middle and working strata, and with reference to the perfect equality of women, and of a grand and powerful motherhood. I should demand of this programme or theory a scope generous enough to include the widest human area.

In short, and to sum up, America, betaking herself to formative action (and it is about time for more solid achievement, and less windy promise,) must, for her purposes, cease to recognize a theory of character grown of feudal aristocracies, or form'd by merely literary standards, or from any ultramarine, full-dress formulas of culture, polish, caste, &c., and must sternly promulgate her own new standard, yet old enough, and accepting the old, the perennial elements, and combining them into groups, unities, appropriate to the modern, the democratic, the west, and to the practical occasions and needs of our own cities, and of the agricultural regions.[3]

Thus Whitman in the process of enlarging his sense of himself as critic of society. Central to the enlarging is the introduction of the word "culture" as subsuming and interrelating art, religion, politics, family, trade—all American institutions—as "products": products which, as they are produced, at once make possible the good life in society and yet, because they transcend the individual, threaten that life. If we can trust the standard Whitman concordance, the word—and the concept—"culture" comes first into Whitman's vocabulary in *Democratic Vistas*. Where he got the word we do not know. We do know that it was much on his mind in

---

[3] *Collected Writings: Prose Works*, ed. F. Stovall (New York, 1964), II, 365-403.

the years around 1870. He planned, apparently, to write an essay called "The Theory of Culture." In the Feinberg collection of Whitman manuscripts there are his notes for that essay. With Mr. Feinberg's permission, I quote what I take to be the most important of them:

> The theory of culture fits the specialities of scholars & the literary class; Personalism is for universal use of living men in the practical world, with its qualities, fibre, storms, mixture of good & evil. The latter of the two has heights & flashes to which the former can never attain. The latter is for the Soul, the other for the Intellect. . . .

In short, Whitman was concerned to put "culture" to the test of "personalism," so to distinguish what has in our time been called authentic from inauthentic culture, that which enables and that which disables the American as he seeks to live the life of the simple, separate person, yet democratic, en masse. To discriminate between authentic and inauthentic culture, to write poems which would be the instrument of discrimination—this was the task of the divine literatus. Such discrimination would be a necessary condition of the discovery, or recovery, of that of which Robert Duncan writes: "the spirit . . ./ that restores the land to productive order."

Whitman strove to write poems of this order before the period of *Democratic Vistas*, of course. I think of parts of "A Song of Joys," "Starting from Paumanok," and "As I Walk These Broad Majestic Days"—all of which come into the 1860 version of *Leaves of Grass*, all of which mark Whitman's awareness of the tension between the claims of his radical humanism (that is, his "personalism") and the claims of his burgeoning world (that is, its "culture"). And there is "Years of the Modern," put first into the 1865 *Leaves of Grass*. Still, the tension is somewhat slack in these poems, as the claims and counterclaims seem naturally and easily to resolve themselves.

The tension is as tight as Whitman could allow it to be in a poem first published in the 1871 *Leaves of Grass*, the poem which became "Song of the Exposition." Under its original title, which is its first line as I quote it, Whitman recited it at the opening of the Fortieth Annual Exhibition of the American Institute, in New York, September 7, 1871. Retitled and somewhat changed, it went into the 1876 *Leaves of Grass* in part prefaced thus, the language recalling that of *Democratic Vistas*. The preface enunciates the hope of Institute:

> Struggling steadily to the front, not only in the spirit of Opinion, Government, and the like, but, in due time, in the Artistic also, we see actual operative LABOR and LABORERS, with Machinery, Inventions, Farms, Products, &c., pressing to place our time, over the whole civilized world. Holding these by the hand, we see, or hope to see, THE MUSE (radiating, representing, under its various expressions, as in every age and land, the healthiest, most heroic Humanity, common to all, fusing all) entering the demesnes of the New World, as twin and sister of our Democracy—at any rate we will so invite Her, here and now—to permanently infuse in daily toils, and be infused by them.
>
> . . . .
>
> Ostensibly to inaugurate an Exposition of this kind—still more to outline the establishment of a great *permanent* Cluster-Palace of Industry from an imaginative and Democratic point of view—was the design of the following poem. . . .

"Holding these by the hand. . . .": The phrase, as does so much of Whitman's self-indulgent prose, makes us wince. It is important, nonetheless; for it is yet another attempt of the poet to indicate how, as social critic, he might envisage the things, the products, of his world as at once of the simple, separate person and of the mass. This is his "programme of culture," and it entails no less than the humanization of the actually or potentially dehumanized, the products and institutions of an industrial society moving even in the 1870's precipitously toward over-development.

The poem, in its 1871 version, begins:

After all not to create only, or found only,
But to bring perhaps from afar what is already founded,
To give it our own identity, average, limitless, free,
To fill the gross the torpid bulk with vital religious fire,
Not to repel or destroy so much as to accept, fuse, rehabilitate,
To obey as well as command, to follow more than to lead,
There also are the lessons of our New World.
While how little the New after all, how much the Old, Old World![4]

Then, following immediately upon this call to give identity and freedom to all that which bulks large in the world, there is a small

---

[4] I quote the poem from the pamphlet, *After All, Not to Create Only* (Boston, 1871).

lyric intrusion, a recollection of the primal power celebrated from the beginning in *Leaves of Grass:*

> Long and long has the grass been growing,
> Long and long has the rain been falling,
> Long has the globe been rolling round.

The body of the poem consists of Whitman's attempt to indicate just how that primal power may be discovered in what he had called in *Democratic Vistas* "culture"—culture in its largest, quite modern, extended sense. He asks at length that the Muse come to America from the Old World and find her place here. He sees her

> Making directly for this rendezvous, vigorously clearing
>   a path for herself, striding through the confusion,
> By thud of machinery and shrill steam-whistle undismay'd.
> Bluff'd not a bit by drain-pipe, gasometers, artificial fertilizers,
> Smiling and pleas'd with palpable intent to stay,
> She's here, install'd amid the kitchen ware!

Once in the New World, the Muse finds herself at home in a land where

> We plan even now to raise, . . .
> Thy great cathedral sacred industry, no tomb,
> A keep for life for practical invention.

But how does Whitman conceive that the products of "practical invention" may be those of authentic as opposed to inauthentic culture? The answer is one the reader of earlier versions of *Leaves of Grass* would expect: by seeing precisely, by expressing precisely, the degree to which these are specifically human products; products of the simple, separate person as he is caught up in the communal life of the mass; if not the poet's own creations, nonetheless genuine creations as they are communal creations:

> Here shall you trace in flowing operation,
> In every state of practical, busy movement, the rills of
>   civilization,
> Materials here under your eye shall change their shape
>   as if by magic,

> The cotton shall be pick'd almost in every field,
> Shall be dried, clean'd, ginn'd, baled, spun into thread and cloth before you,
> You shall see hands at work at all the old processes and all the new ones,
> You shall see the various grains and how flour is made and then baked by the bakers,
> You shall see the crude ores of California and Nevada passing on and on till they become bullion,
> You shall watch how the printer sets type, and learn what a composing stick is,
> You shall mark in amazement the Hoe press whirling its cylinders, shedding the printed leaves steady and fast,
> The photograph, model, watch, pin, nail, shall be created before you.

The technique and the form here are familiar to us: the loving catalogue; the careful singling out of the specifically human act involved in industrial production; a dependence upon particularized nouns and verbs of human agency; an essential vitalism. I suggest that in these lines—certainly not among Whitman's greatest, but cumulating toward a certain kind of power—we know again what the poet James Wright has recently called Whitman's "delicacy." It *is* a delicacy, the total delicacy, of the human, of a poet who would (as Whitman says a few lines later) "exalt the present and the real." And he would do so by conceiving of the artisan as artist. The literatus can and must do this. So that, passing in review the very things which, produced en masse, might threaten the simple separate existence of the producers, he can in his art inquire as to the degree that they are and are not integral in the authentic existence of the producers. And at the end he can address the Muse—not God, but the Muse—simply and straightforwardly:

> Our farms, inventions, crops, we own in thee! cities and States in thee!
> Our freedom all in thee! our very lives in thee!

The specific mode of this poem is one with a few others out of Whitman's later career—"Song of the Redwood Tree" (1874) and "To a Locomotive in Winter" (1876), for example. And it has affiliations with the mode of "Passage to India" (1871). Moreover, it is a mode which we know well in Whitman's earlier poetry—particularly in the last segment of "Song of Myself." The difference between the mode in the post- as against the pre-Civil War poems is this: that in the earlier poems (not only "Song of Myself," but poems like "Salut au Monde" and "Crossing Brooklyn Ferry"), the poet reads himself *into* his world, whereas in the later poems he reads an enlarged sense of other men, of humanity, *out* of his world. The aim in the earlier poems was to discover himself; that of the later poems, to discover others. The later task was the more difficult, and was performed with significantly less success, because there the poet had wherever possible to point toward the possibility of the reassociation of that which had been, or was in danger of being, disassociated: producer from product, actor from act, agent from deed. He had to find a source of what he called (in "A Backward Glance O'er Travell'd Roads,") that "ultimate vivification" which would endow "facts," "science," and "common lives," "with the glows and glories and final illustriousness which belong to every real thing, and to real things only." He had, in short, to locate them in social and communal reality, to find in them at once a source and an end of culture.

"The chief trait of any given poet," he wrote in the same essay, "is always the spirit he brings to the observation of humanity and nature—the mood out of which he contemplates his subjects. What kind of temper and what amount of faith report these things?" Whitman's humanist temper and faith—for that is what the aspect of his spirit I have been discussing comes to—only falteringly sustained him after the Civil War. It would not sustain him throughout the history of "Song of the Exposition." For the 1881 version of that poem, he added at the beginning a stanza unhappily out of phase with what adamantly follows it:

> (Ah little recks the laborer,
> How near his work is holding him to God.
> The loving Laborer through space and time.)

The stanza is in parentheses (as an afterthought) and is meant, I suppose, to divinize the all-too-human Muse whom the poet would bring from abroad to dwell among the kitchenware. Only as God could the Muse find safe-conduct in the New World. The literatus would become more divine than literate—as in so much of Whitman's later verse, with its passages to everywhere except home, the only place where the poet could honestly confront the problem of the simple, separate person and its productions en masse. But, with other scholar-critics, I have regretted this change of phase before. I regretted it, I regret it, because it diminishes Whitman's power, and his significance, for us.

And here I would dwell undiminishingly on that power and that significance. I suggest—as a way of thinking about the poet as critic of post-Civil War society—that in his own way, according to his own style, he was discovering what Marx called alienation, the alienation of the laborer from the product of his labor, in that mass-industrial society in which all men willy-nilly become laborers. The "realization of labor," so go Marx's famous words of the 1840's, "appears as *loss of reality* for the workers; objectification as *loss of the object* and *object-bondage;* appropriation as *estrangement, alienation.*"

And with my quotation from Marx I return to our own time, and to the text from Robert Duncan, with which I initiated this inquiry. Let me modify two of Duncan's lines:

> Where among *us does* the spirit reside
> That restores the land to productive order?

"Productive order" is precisely the opposite of Marx's "appropriation as *estrangement, alienation.*" And "alienation" is a word which is perhaps too much with us these days. In any case, it is a word—and a concept—central to that which is most fruitful and promising in radical political thinking in our time. And, in point of fact, poets like Duncan and his peers all over our land share with all of us the discovery of "alienation" and all it implies for the fate of our culture. As I have said, they are putting politics back into our poetry. But it is a politics shot through with their sense of the matter of authentic as against inauthentic culture. They show that in an alienated world, proper politics is impossible, because cut off from the human values and capacities from which derives the very power it must organize. For them, as recent events have shown, free speech and free verse are of a piece. Accordingly, the Whitman to whom they look—although not often with Duncan's superb (and scholarly) awareness of what he is doing—is that Whitman whom I have been discussing.

Let it be freely admitted that this Whitman is, as poet, far from the greatest Whitman. "Song of the Exposition" is, as I have said, not one of the poems which stick with us; nor are the other poems in its vein, including "Passage to India." In all of them a certain religiosity and self-indulgence dull and diffuse, as if Whitman could not bear to carry out the task he set for himself. He faltered. Together, nonetheless, these poems matter deeply to us—if only in falling short of their goal, they help us all the more clearly establish our own. They show, perhaps, that Whitman was successful as prophet inversely as he was successful as poet. Together, perhaps, they amount to that "glorious mistake" over which Duncan exclaims. In all honesty, acknowledging the mistake may well be the price we must pay for apprehending the glory. And it might be possible—if we are lucky—that our poets, apprehending the glory, will not make the mistake. As ever, that must be their—and thus our—hope for poetry.

Whitman knew this well. We should recall that one of the key inscriptive poems to *Leaves of Grass* reads thus:

Poets to come! orators, singers, musicians to come!
Not to-day is to justify me and answer what I am for,
But you, a new brood, native, athletic, continental, greater
    than before known,
Arouse! for you must justify me.

I myself but write one or two indicative words for the future,
I but advance a moment only to wheel and hurry back in the darkness

I am a man who, sauntering along without fully stopping, turns
    a casual look upon you and then averts his face,
Leaving it to you to prove and define it,
Expecting the main things from you.

I add: We yet expect the main things from our poets—our poets to come—as did Whitman. Our hope for poetry now lies precisely in its search for the spirit which will restore the land to productive order.

INDEX OF AUTHORS AND EDITORS

Aeschylus, 3, 14, 17, 19, 26, 27, 29, 30, 31, 32, 37, 38, 39, 41, 42, 43
Alberti, L., v
Alcaeus, 51, 61
Alcman, 6
Apollonius, 65, 66
Aristophanes, 38
Aristotle, 3, 4, 110
Arvin, N., 126
Augustine, v, 110, 111, 113, 114

Bacchylides, 11, 14
Barrett, W. S., 37
Bennett, C. E., 48, 54
Blodgett, H. W., 126
Bömer, F., 75, 79
Bowra, C. M., 5, 6, 7, 11, 13, 18, 65, 71
Bradley, S., 126
Brinkley, R. F., 121, 122
Brooks, R. A., 70
Büchner, K., 73
Bush, D., 92

Cartault, A., 77, 70, 79, 80
Case, R. H., 83
Catullus, 64, 68
Cicero, 52, 60
Coleridge, S. T., 121
Commanger, S., 51, 52
Comparetti, D., 63
Conington, J., 49
Conway, R. S., 69
Crane, H., 125

Dale, A. M., 29
Daniel, R. G., 83
Dante, 63
Diano, C., 54
Donne, J., v
Du Bellay, J., v–vi
Duckworth, G., 64, 65, 66, 68, 69, 71, 72, 73, 77, 80
Duncan, R., 123–25, 127, 129, 134, 139, 140

Eliot, T. S., 64, 125
Ellrodt, R., 96
Emerson, R. W., 125
Epicurus, 48
Euripides, 13, 27–45, 64

Farnell, L. R., 11, 19
Fenik, B. C., 64
Finley, J. H., 18, 22
Fowler, W. W., 78, 80
Fränkel, H., 5

Galinsky, G. K., 73, 78, 79
Gelon, 4
Greene, T. M., 88
Gregory, v
Grimal, P., 79

Harrison, E., 4, 7, 8
Hecataeus, 12
Heraclitus, v
Herbert, G., 99–122
Herodotus, 12, 39

INDEX OF AUTHORS AND EDITORS

Hesiod, 6, 12, 18, 22
Hieatt, A. K., 84
Highet, G., 63, 64
Homer, 6, 12, 14, 21, 64, 65, 66
Horace, 47–61
Hornsby, R., 77
Hyman, L. W., 96

Ibycus, 6

Jantz, H., 47

Knauer, G. N., 64
Knox, B. M. W., 73

Lefkowitz, Mary R., 5
Lewis, C. S., 97
Lind, L. R., 66
Lucretius, 52, 55, 64

Mackail, J. W., 70, 71
Marcus Aurelius, v
Martial, 63
Marx, K., 139
Milton, J., 63
Mombelli, G., 64
Murray, G., 33, 41

Nelson, W., 84

Olson, C., 127
Otis, B., 65, 69, 73, 79, 80
Ovid, v

Pacuvius, 50
Parrington, V., 126
Pasquali, G., 52
Pausanias, 12
Perret, J., 71
Pherecydes, 14, 15
Phocylides, 12
Pindar, 3–26, 123
Pitt, C., 79
Plato, 21–22, 60
Plutarch, 28
Pöschl, V., 48, 51, 53, 65, 66
Pound, E., 125, 127
Prescott, H. W., 69
Propertius, 63
Putnam, M. C. J., 73, 77, 80

Quintilian, 11

Rand, E. K., 64, 78
Renwick, W. L., 89, 96
Richter, G. M. A., 16
Ronsard, P., v

Schadewaldt, W., 6
Segal, C. P., 70
Semple, W. H., 73
Seneca, 52
Sidney, P., 83
Simonides, 4, 7, 10, 11, 12, 13, 15, 16, 21, 25
Smith, H., 88
Snell, B., 37
Sophocles, 17, 27, 29, 30, 31, 32, 37, 38, 41, 42, 43, 50
Spargo, J. W., 63
Spenser, E., v, 81–98
Stesichorus, 11, 12, 21
Stevens, W., 125
Stovall, F., 133
Sullivan, F. A., 75
Syme, R., 57

Tennyson, A., 30, 63–64
Thales, 12
Theogonis, 4, 7, 8, 9, 10, 15, 16, 21, 25

Van Winkle, C., 92
Vergil, 48, 50, 54, 63–80

Warton, J., 79
Webster, T. B. L., 16, 34
Wellek, R., 81
Whitehead, W., 79
Whitman, W., 123–40
Wilamowitz-Moellendorff, E. F. W. U. von, 22
Wilkinson, L. P., 51, 52, 57, 66
Williams, W. C., 125, 127
Wright, J., 137

Xenophanes, 13

Yeats, W. B., vi
Young, B., 83
Young, D., 4

Zielinski, T., 29

Designed by Arlene J. Sheer

*Composed in Baskerville and Baskerville display
types by Monotype Composition Company*

*Printed offset by Universal Lithographers, Inc.
on Perkins and Squier RRR 60 lb.*

Bound by L. H. Jenkins, Inc., in Columbia Bayside Chambray